Person and Community

Catholic Thought from Lublin

Andrew N. Woznicki
General Editor

Vol. 4

PETER LANG
New York • San Francisco • Bern • Baltimore
Frankfurt am Main • Berlin • Wien • Paris

Karol Wojtyla

Person and Community

Selected Essays

Translated by Theresa Sandok, OSM

PETER LANG
New York • San Francisco • Bern • Baltimore
Frankfurt am Main • Berlin • Wien • Paris

Library of Congress Cataloging-in-Publication Data

— — —

Person and community : selected essays / Karol Wojtyla ; translated by
Theresa Sandok.
    p. cm. — (Catholic thought from Lublin ; vol. 4)
    Translated from Polish.
    Includes index.
    1. Ethics.   2. Personalism.   3. Family—Moral and ethical aspects.
4. Christian ethics—Catholic authors.   I. Series.
BJ1136.J64   1993   170—dc20   92-28994
ISBN 0-8204-1446-8   CIP
ISSN 1051-693X

Die Deutsche Bibliothek-CIP-Einheitsaufnahme

— — —

Person and community : selected essays / Karol Wojtyla.
Transl. by Theresa Sandok.—New York; Berlin; Bern; Frankfurt/M.; Paris;
Wien: Lang, 1993
    (Catholic thought from Lublin ; Vol. 4)
    ISBN 0-8204-1446-8
NE: GT
Vw: Wojtyla, Karol [Früherer Name]

The paper in this book meets the guidelines for permanence and
durability of the Committee on Production Guidelines for
Book Longevity of the Council on Library Resources.

Printed in the United States of America.

CONTENTS

PART TWO: Personalism

PART THREE: Marriage and the Family

TRANSLATOR'S NOTE

This volume makes available for the first time in English a collection of scholarly essays by Karol Wojtyla (pronounced Voy-*tih*-wä) that spans his entire academic career, a career that began in the early 1950s with his appointment to teach philosophy at the Catholic University of Lublin and lasted through the late 1970s, up to the time of his election to the papacy in 1978. The essays are for the most part arranged chronologically, allowing the reader to trace both the progression of Wojtyla's thought and the gradual shift in his concerns, which become increasingly more pastoral with the expansion of his leadership responsibilities in the church.

When I first conceived the project of translating a volume of essays by Wojtyla, I intended to restrict the selection to purely philosophical works. It soon became apparent, however, that the nature of his writings did not always lend themselves to classification in one or another "pure" category. Nowhere is this more evident than in the essay "The Problem of the Constitution of Culture Through Human Praxis," an address presented in 1977 by then Cardinal Wojtyla—philosopher-theologian-professor-poet-pastor-Pole—to the academic community at the Catholic University of the Sacred Heart in Milan. This book, then, is not for philosophers only, though the articles in Parts 1 and 2 will be of special interest to philosophers. The articles in Part 3, most of which were written after the Second Vatican Council, tend to be of a more theological and pastoral nature, though Wojtyla's personalistic philosophy permeates his reflections here as well.

Professor Stefan Swiezawski's essay, which serves as the introduction to this volume, is included here to orient readers not only to Wojtyla's thought and the historical context in which it developed, but also to the Lublin School of Philosophy and the other authors represented in Peter Lang's "Catholic Thought From Lublin" series. As a co-founder of this distinctive approach to philosophy that developed at the Catholic University of Lublin in Poland after World War II, Wojtyla focused his attention on the areas of philosophical anthropology and ethics. He became increasingly convinced of the value of a phenomenological analysis of experience for understanding the human person and human action—and this made him something of a maverick among Lublin philosophers. At the same time, he shared the realistic metaphysical orientation of the philosophers of the Lublin School. Consequently, his philosophical contributions often take the form of a critique of the strengths and weaknesses of both the realistic and the phenomenological approach to philosophy and an attempt to enrich the one with the other.

Concerning the translation itself, I have added occasional notes to draw attention to certain nuances in the Polish text that are difficult to convey in English and also to clarify concepts that might not be immediately apparent to the reader. I have also substituted the English versions, when available, of works cited in the original by Wojtyla.

Two people in particular deserve special mention for their contributions to the content and quality of this translation, Rev. Andrzej Szostek, MIC, Assistant Director of the John Paul II Institute, Catholic University of Lublin, and Sister Emilia Ehrlich, OSU, a reviewer for the Commissione per gli Scritti di Karol Wojtyla, Libreria Editrice Vaticana. I relied on Father Szostek's expert advice both for the selection of articles included in this volume and for the basic organization of the book. Once the work was translated, Sister Ehrlich carefully reviewed the text and made many valuable suggestions with regard to style and content. I am especially indebted to her for helping to assure the accuracy of this translation.

Finally, I wish to dedicate this volume to the loving memory of my mother Helen Czyscon Sandok (1920–1992), from whom I first learned the rich and enduring lessons of "person and community."

Theresa H. Sandok, OSM
Bellarmine College
Louisville, Kentucky

INTRODUCTION

Karol Wojtyla at the Catholic University of Lublin

BY STEFAN SWIEZAWSKI

Following World War II, a very distinctive spiritual and intellectual situation existed in Poland. Although the universities and high schools had been closed for many years, intensive intellectual activity of a generally high caliber had continued to flourish in innumerable underground schools. This activity yielded remarkably fine intellectual results, richly developed in circumstances full of tension and danger. Those of us who began teaching at the universities in 1945–1946 know how superbly those schools prepared the young who then came to study. The period of the war and occupation was a time of terrible devastation of life and culture, but it was also a time of great efforts to deepen and enrich our understanding of reality.

This last point explains the remarkable "hunger for philosophy" that spontaneously erupted as soon as the war was over. In 1945 I presented the first series of lectures in metaphysics at the Jagiellonian University in Krakow. The course was held in one of the largest rooms of a new building at the university. It attracted such a massive crowd that students were forced to stand in the aisles, and some even overflowed out into the corridor. The experiences of the war, in their overwhelming realism, were too horrible to allow us still seriously to maintain a subjective or idealistic philosophy. Reality asserted itself so unequivocally that to question its objective character was absurd. On the other hand, the spiritual significance of the immensity of sufferings imposed itself so strongly that

Stefan Swiezawski, "Karol Wojtyla w Katolickim Uniwersytecie Lubelskim," *Obecnosc: Karol Wojtyla w Katolickim Uniwersytecie Lubelskim*, ed. Maria Filipiak and Andrzej Szostek (Lublin: Redakcja Wydawnictw KUL, 1987) 9–18. This essay was abridged and edited by the translator for the present volume.

materialistic realism appeared to us all as too simplistic and paltry a hypothesis to explain the complex structure of the world and the processes taking place in it. And so we rejected idealism, as did the materialists, and we also began an unrelentless battle aimed at preventing materialism from becoming identified with realism, or idealism with spiritualism. Everything, then, favored opting for realism and being open to (if not yet affirming) a spiritual reality. At the same time, metaphysics, as an attempt to penetrate the innermost structure of the whole of existing reality, emerged as the central philosophical discipline.

One other aspect of the spiritual condition of the Polish intelligentsia at that time is worthy of note. We knew with vivid clarity that all the evil that had assailed us in a dreadfully pure form, as well as all the good, which included incredible acts of heroism and sacrifice, had been the work of human beings. What then is the human being? What in the deepest sense constitutes the human person? What causes people at one time to resemble evil incarnate and to engage in acts of satanic brutality, and at another to exhibit superhuman powers of love and devotion? *Quid est homo?* Those of us schooled in philosophical contemplation realized that the theoretical justification of a realistic-objective or idealistic-subjective stance in our philosophy and worldview turned on our philosophical view of the human being. Metaphysics goes hand in hand with philosophical anthropology. This explains the key role played by the philosophy of the human being, a role that goes far beyond any psychological, phenomenological, or existential analysis of human actions and experiences.

Our experiences of the war and occupation and their tragic aftermath became a critical gauge for assessing the philosophical and ideological views we entertained before the war. The great thinker Roman Ingarden, for example, found it impossible to feel at home in the idealistic setting of Husserl's phenomenology. He set the whole force of his acute mind to the task of discovering a road that would lead from the philosophy of possible being to the theory of real being, from ontology to metaphysics. Although this effort was, it would seem, doomed to failure in advance, nevertheless his concrete need for realism impelled him to exert enormous energy in attempting to proceed from an analysis of essences to a reflection on what really exists.

The tension between the awareness of the philosophical poverty of idealistic and materialistic systems, on the one hand, and the need for reflecting on fully authentic reality, on the other, also called into question the value of the whole subjective current of European philosophizing in the modern age and directed keen interest toward classical philosophy, both ancient and medieval. Medieval thought ceased being merely an interesting area for historical research and began to attract various minds precisely because of its decidedly objective character. Many of us joined the pilgrimage to the sources of objectivism, which required deep historical and methodological reflection and painstaking textual studies. This is one of the main reasons for the increased interest in medieval thought in Poland in the post-war years.

At the same time, a very perfidious foe began to rear its head, namely, irrationalism, the enemy of all philosophy. This irrationalism shared common roots with the philosophical idealism of the day. There occurred here a particular *coincidentia oppositorum*: extreme rationalism, which scorned realism, joined forces with irrationalism, which trampled the work of reason. Under the guise of a penetrating analysis of our existential experiences, subjectivism teamed up with irrationalism and ahistoricism. We then heard diatribes alleging the harmfulness of rational analyses, historical studies, and philosophical reasoning for theological reflection. The whole threat posed by Bultmann and his followers—as a prominent French exegete observed—arose as a result of a departure from a realistic and rational philosophy.

In the late 1940s and early 1950s, all of these themes were evolving and were vividly present at the Catholic University of Lublin. The university—both because of the students pouring in from all parts of the country and because of the faculty—became a school that served an area far beyond the Lublin region. But those were also Stalinist times, and scholarly and pedagogical activity at our school became more difficult with each passing year. The newly established Philosophy Department, in which I was privileged to serve from the very beginning, experienced heavy losses in personnel. Several professors were forbidden to engage in teaching activity. Our department turned into a genuine *facultas depopulata*. This tragic circumstance caused a distinctive void in philosophy at the university.

We realized that our most urgent need was to fill the vacant chairs in the department and to bring to the university scholars who would be willing to devote all their talent and energy to the authentic pursuit of knowledge. We all agreed that the most fundamental area in our department was metaphysics, and so we set about searching for someone who shared our conviction concerning the importance of the realistic, classical philosophy of being and who wished to devote his entire life to this area. Providence led us to Dominican Father Mieczyslaw A. Krapiec, who was then just making his philosophical debut. When Krapiec agreed to assume the position of Chair of Metaphysics, I was able to leave the teaching of metaphysics to him and concentrate my energies on the history of philosophy. The next major development in the expansion of our faculty was the successful recruitment of a promising young scholar from the Theology Department at the Jagiellonian University, Father Karol Wojtyla. Wojtyla's ethical, anthropological, and metaphysical interests predisposed him completely to our circle.

Under the energetic and enlightened leadership of our young Dean, Professor Jerzy Kalinowski, we then set about developing the main lines of a new program of philosophical studies at the Catholic University of Lublin. The four of us—Kalinowski, Krapiec, Wojtyla, and I—were all very different in temperament, tastes, and attitudes, and yet we managed to create a very harmonious unit, conferring upon the whole department and on all of its research and teaching activities a special scholarly character. Our collaboration was, I believe, both an extremely rare and exceptionally fruitful phenomenon. What was unusual was not that four individuals who took philosophy seriously joined forces in carrying out a task of great importance, but that, despite our differences in personality and background, we found ourselves in remarkable agreement on several fundamental points.

The most basic point of agreement among us was that we all saw realistic metaphysics, the metaphysics of concretely existing beings, as having primacy among the philosophical disciplines. This tenet was acknowledged by the metaphysician Krapiec, by the logician and philosopher of law Kalinowski, by the ethicist Wojtyla, and by me, the historian of philosophy. And although, upon closer analysis, existence appeared to each of us in a somewhat different light, yet this basic—I would even say radical—realism was the unshakable common denominator of our philosophical convictions.

A second point upon which we concurred was the key significance of philosophical anthropology. Philosophical realism presupposes a certain view of the human being. Extreme spiritualistic dualism tends toward subjectivism, whereas the conception of the human being as a psychophysical unity leads to objectivism. All four of us devoted significant attention to issues in philosophical anthropology, approaching it from various sides.

The third premise that united us, and that gained intensity when the methodologist Father Stanislaw Kaminski and the historian of philosophy Father Marian Kurdzialek joined our circle, was a clear opposition to irrational philosophizing. Although our rationalism assumed various hues, some sharper than others, we all shared an opposition to the irrationalistic style of philosophizing.

Thus, the primacy of realistic metaphysics, the central role of philosophical anthropology, and the affirmation of a rational approach to philosophy were the main canons of our way of doing philosophy, which came to be known as the Lublin School of Philosophy. In addition, we recognized the inseparable link between realistic philosophizing and an historical grasp of philosophical problems. Without basic historical studies there is no way to perceive the enduring value of classical philosophical reflection. Our positive relation to the history of philosophy caused us to cast a critical eye on the ahistoricism of phenomenological and existential philosophies.

In the works and discussions of our group of at first four and then six philosophers at the Catholic University of Lublin, we were deeply convinced that our efforts to "discover" the true St. Thomas and to continue the line of development of European metaphysics and philosophy extending from medieval to contemporary times had crucial significance not just for our university, for Poland, and for Europe, but for the whole world. We had a vision of contributing to that dialog between the West and East that is indispensable for the future of the world and the church—a vision that John Paul II is now so wonderfully bringing into reality.

Karol Wojtyla made a unique contribution to the development of philosophy at the Catholic University of Lublin. For Wojtyla philosophical reflection was a way of exploring the awesome mystery of the human person. He saw the human being as a remarkable psychophysical unity, each one a unique person, never again to be repeated in the entire universe. Wonder at the human being, a being that fulfills itself only by transcending itself, seems to be the point of departure as well as the central focus of all Wojtyla's philosophical reflection.

All of us in the Philosophy Department at that time were fascinated by philosophical anthropology. I wrote my habilitation thesis on the concept of *commensuratio animae ad hoc corpus*, a topic central to Thomistic anthropology. Krapiec also devoted a good deal of attention to anthropological issues, eventually publishing his insights in *Ja—czlowiek* (Lublin 1974). Kalinowski's interest in this area focused chiefly on human reason (logic) and the laws to which humans are subject. In addition, we all shared an interest in natural law, a topic that falls within the realm of practical philosophy.

Our treatment of philosophical anthropology, however, was in danger of becoming overly intellectualistic and rationalistic. Although many of the questions we addressed belonged to the realm of practical philosophy, we had a tendency to succumb to the old Socratic temptation of thinking it is enough to know the good in order to do it. Our philosophy could have become distorted by focusing exclusively on the contemplative side and neglecting the whole sphere of activity. Kalinowski and Wojtyla were the ones in our department who helped us maintain the balance between *theoria* and *praxis*, a balance that might otherwise have been lost.

From the very beginning Wojtyla was keenly aware that the claims of ethical intellectualism were illusory and that by itself even the most perfect and penetrating knowledge of the inner structures and mechanisms of the human being does not guarantee proper human conduct and creativity. His own personal and pastoral experience taught him that even the best sermons and lectures do not automatically lead to real self-improvement. A person must also make a systematic effort to acquire the proper skills and virtues through the constant repetition of rightly performed acts. This explains Wojtyla's great emphasis on action and on the connection of action with the person, a theme he crystalized in *Osoba i czyn* (Krakow 1969). This also explains his sympathy with personalism and his choice of Max Scheler as the subject of his habilitation thesis. Wojtyla did not reject the primacy of *logos* in relation to *ethos*, but he did insist upon giving action its due among the aspects of the human person.

Another important feature of Wojtyla's philosophy is the attempt to establish a relationship between realistic metaphysics and the phenomenological method. The complex interdependence of these two elements in Wojtyla's philosophical synthesis is still a matter of lively debate. Personally, I believe Wojtyla was trying to disclose the basis in concrete lived experience for theoretical—and especially for metaphysical—ethical considerations, and he found the phenomenological method particularly suited to this end. His aim was not to replace metaphysics with phenomenology, but to supplement metaphysical reflection with phenomenological description as a way of gaining access to the processes of knowing and acting. I do not believe Wojtyla ever rejected the primary and fundamental role of the realistic philosophy of being in anthropology and ethics, but he did see phenomenology as a useful tool for describing the experiential base, and he tended to view phenomenological language as more communicative than scholastic terminology.

I would like to conclude by mentioning a few significant personal memories connected with Wojtyla's academic involvement at the Catholic University of Lublin. Right after the war my family and I lived in Krakow for a number of years, and during that time we developed close ties with the young Father Wojtyla. My relationship with him took a scholarly turn when, in August 1953, I was invited by Father Wladyslaw Wicher, Dean of the Theology Department at the Jagiellonian University, to serve as a reviewer of Wojtyla's habilitation thesis entitled "An Attempt to Develop a Christian Ethics Based on Max Scheler's System." Wojtyla also wrote and asked me to be a reviewer of his thesis. Although I was not an expert either in Scheler or in phenomenology, I nevertheless agreed to take on this formidable task. When I accepted the invitation, I had no idea that this would be the last habilitation in the Theology Department at the Jagiellonian University before that department was closed by the government after 550 years of existence and activity.

In my review of Wojtyla's thesis, I wrote: "In addressing the question of Scheler and Christian ethics, the author touches upon...a fundamental issue for every future system of speculative theology, an issue equally essential for theologians and for those philosophers who do not divorce themselves from the religious problematic." I also cited Wojtyla's two main conclusions, which have relevance for all authentic philosophical reflection: "1. Scheler's system...basically does not lend itself to a scientific interpretation of Christian ethics... 2. Nevertheless, it can aid us indirectly in scientific work on Christian ethics." Noting Wojtyla's view that metaphysical reflection has primacy in developing Christian ethics as a science, but that "the phenomenological method gives ethical works the stamp of experience by relating them to the lived experiences of the concrete human being," I pointed out in my review that the author "knew how to perceive...the value that the phenomenological method can bring" to the description of subjective experiences.

Wojtyla's habilitation was an event that deepened our friendship. A small but significant incident that occurred as a result of this friendship bears mentioning. One September day in 1954, Father Wojtyla, my wife, and I decided to go hiking on a mountain trail near Zakopane. During our walk, surrounded by incredibly beautiful scenery, we had a deep discussion about the situation of philosophy and theology in Poland. In the course of our conversation, I strongly encouraged Wojtyla to devote his abilities and his passion for truth to the Catholic University of Lublin and to assume the position of Chair of Ethics in the Philosophy Department. I don't know how heavily that discussion weighed in his ultimate decision to join our faculty. In any case, he accepted my offer, and from then on we met on innumerable occasions, both in Krakow and in Lublin, as well as on the train during our frequent trips between those cities.

When Wojtyla became a bishop, and then an archbishop and cardinal, his ties with philosophy at the Catholic University of Lublin became increasingly looser. We were filled with a special joy and confidence by the fact that a person so devoted to the pursuit of philosophical and theological wisdom was serving the church in leadership roles of ever widening responsibility. Our joy reached its culmination when Wojtyla was elected to the papacy. This joy, however, was mingled in us with a certain human sadness, since with each successive expansion of Wojtyla's ecclesial duties his contact with the university diminished. Nevertheless, given the proper outlook, "this sorrow will turn into joy" (John 16:20), because the small, modest, unassuming kernel of truth so carefully nurtured at one time in the philosophical circle at our university has suddenly found a simply unprecedented opportunity to reach all parts of the world and influence the development of the spiritual face of the coming age in every corner of the globe. We stand before a breath-taking perspective: together with the dawning renaissance of an authentically realistic, metaphysical, classical philosophy there appears, as a counter to the growing evil that assails us like an apocalyptic flood, the first real possibility of a true and deep encounter of all cultures of the East and West.

PART ONE

Ethical and Moral Considerations

1

The Problem of the Will
in the Analysis of the Ethical Act

1. THE CURRENT DIRECTION OF RESEARCH ON THE WILL IN EXPERIMENTAL PSYCHOLOGY

The problem mentioned in the title of this essay is a familiar one in books on ethics; it occupies a place of its own in that science, a place somewhat different but mutually related to the one it occupies in philosophy and psychology. This essay is written from the ethical point of view. In it I wish to present some reflections on the problem of the will that were evoked by my reading of a number of works on the will from the field of contemporary experimental psychology of the will. The works in question are from the school founded by Narziss Ach. For psychologists Ach's scientific activity is of pioneering significance because he was the first to do research on the will along decidedly experimental lines, although certain attempts in this direction had already been made by Wilhelm Wundt. For ethicists, on the other hand, the results of the research carried out by Ach and other psychologists of his school are important because they provide a modern tool for reflecting on ethical experience. The proper interpretation of this lived experience has always been one of the main tasks of ethics, since ethical experience is the experiential fact upon which this science is based. The impossibility of divorcing ethics from experience derives, in turn, from the most general assumptions concerning the nature of all human knowledge, which is always in some way based on experience.

Karol Wojtyla, "Zagadnienie woli w analizie aktu etycznego," *Roczniki Filozoficzne* 5.1 (1955–57): 111–135.

Kant, who pushed the attempt to sever science from experience perhaps farther than anyone else, also contributed in the realm of ethics to a different treatment of the will than the one that characterized the philosophical tradition of Aristotle and Thomas Aquinas. For Kant the will is not merely under the direction of practical reason but is completely identified with it. Kant defines the will as "a faculty either of bringing forth objects corresponding to conceptions or of determining itself, i.e., its causality to effect such objects (whether the physical power is sufficient to this or not)."[1] Such a definition would lead one to assume that Kant recognized the dynamic character of the will. And yet his whole theory of ethical life shows that this dynamic character of the will left no mark on his view of the structure of the ethical act. For Kant motivation plays a primary role, since it allows him to define the set of contents he finds in practical reason. He tries to resolve the entire problematic of the will, and in particular the ethical problematic to which it is so intimately related, in the sphere of practical reason through an analysis of the principles by which practical reason directs the will. Kant goes so far as to literally identify the will with practical reason.[2]

Not only is such an account of the matter one-sided, but—more importantly—it also does not square with experience. Kant inherited his method of investigating the will from Hume. He also exhibited the Cartesian tendency to objectify only what could be known in a clear and distinct way. While the particular contents of practical reason may certainly be one of the clearer aspects of the will, the essence of the will does not lie in them but in the specific dynamism contained in the efficacy of the rational person. Since Kant's philosophy did not provide him with a proper vehicle for apprehending and depicting the dynamism that forms the essence of the will, he reduced this whole spiritual faculty along with its freedom to the noumenal order, asserting that if experience tells us anything at all about the will, it certainly does not tell us anything about freedom of will.

Kant's view of the will naturally has important consequences for his whole theory of ethical life. I shall illustrate these consequences for just one aspect of his theory by analyzing the famous Kantian imperative from the psychological side. Although Kant speaks of the immanent "causality" of the will, he portrays the will as a faculty that is basically submissive. The will is very submissive to the promptings of feelings, which impose their relation to various goods of the "empirical" world on it, and is less submissive to practical reason. When practical reason wants to impose its relation to goods—especially to moral good—on the will, it must resort to a command.[3] This imperative, which has its chief significance in Kant's ethical views, is an expression of his psychological views as well. Reason commands the will with a corresponding power, and the will passively submits its own "causality" to reason's command. In such a treatment, however, all we see are causes operating on the will; we do not see the will itself operating as a cause. And so the cause of the will's activity must lie either in feelings *and* practical reason or in practical reason alone. In the former case the will submits to inclinations; in the latter reason must command it. If there is a "causality" proper to the will, it exists only for the benefit of other psychic agents, and not so that the will itself can act in a causal way.

This problem, which is so important for the ethical life, was viewed by St. Thomas Aquinas in an entirely different fashion. He realized that an act of will can be commanded by reason,[4] but this command always relies on the will. Reason may formulate the command, but the will provides the power inherent in every command.[5] According to St. Thomas, this process occurs as it does because the will's whole natural dynamism has a distinct inclination toward the good (*bonum in communi*). By the power of this inclination that arises from the will's own nature, the will shares in the act of command (*imperium*), for it provides the power upon which reason relies in formulating the content of a command. As far as human activity in general is concerned, the will appears there as a faculty that acts in conjunction with reason—rather than one that merely submits to the causality of motives. In such a view, the immanent power of action proper to the will is no fiction.

As we know, Hume had already challenged the causal-efficient character of the will in psychology prior to Kant. In late 19th- and early 20th-century psychology there were those who regarded the will as a separate element of psychic life. Others attempted to reduce the will to associations of images (Spencer), to sensations of muscular tension (Münsterberg), to emotionally laden representations of goals (Ebbinghaus), and finally to feelings themselves (Wundt).[6] All of these resolutions of the problem of the will have the character of allogeneic conceptions. Against this background, the earlier mentioned position of Narziss Ach and the whole school of psychologists of the will that adopted his experimental method of investigating the will is distinguished by its insistence on the strictly idiogeneic character of both the lived experience of the will and the process of the will in general. For these psychologists, the will is an entirely distinct element in human psychic life and cannot be reduced to any other element of that life. The element of the will comes to the fore in the so-called *actual moment* (*das aktuelle Moment*) of lived experience, which usually takes the form "I do in fact will," although it can also assume a somewhat different form, e.g., "I can," "I must," "I ought."[7] The term *moment* here is used in the sense given it by Husserl and means a "non-independent part of a certain whole."

Along with the actual moment, Ach also distinguished in the simple act of will the *objective moment* (*das gegenständliche Moment*), which consists in the presentation of an end in an intuitive or nonintuitive way and in the presentation of a relation to future action, which is given "intentionally" as a means of achieving the intended end. An act of will also contains an *intuitive moment* (*das anschauliche Moment*), which is characterized by intense bodily tension, and a *dynamic moment* (*das zuständliche Moment*), which involves a sense of effort.

Ach himself concentrated mainly on the simple act of will—the actual moment. Worthy of note here is the distinct connection of this moment, which is a simple and irreducible element of psychic life, both with the subjective self in the lived experience "I do in fact will" and with the object or end at which this self aims in a corresponding action. The lived experience of willing includes an anticipation of the action that leads to the realization of the content of that simple act of will. Both in simple willing and in the will's subsequent activity aimed at realizing the content of that willing, the self exerts a determinate influence. The determinate tendency arising from this self must overcome various resisting forces that take the form of associational-representational tendencies, perseverational tendencies, and other determinate tendencies. But this is also what brings into clear relief the dynamic character of the act of will, the tendency that originates in the self as a result of the actual moment and develops into a broadly diversified process, whose various aspects provide psychologists with material for experimental research.

Such research was pursued with great intensity and insight. First A. Michotte and N. Prüm[8] studied the problem of motivation, taking into consideration not just the simple act of willing but the whole process of the will from the moment of the onset of stimuli and the appearance of motives to the moment of decision. Earlier investigations of the will are mentioned by Johannes Lindworsky in *Der Wille*,[9] and later developments in this area are discussed by Mieczyslaw Dybowski in *Dzialanie woli*.[10] In Poland this experimental direction of research on the will also found adherents and yielded results. At the same time as Narziss Ach was conducting his investigations, Edward Abramowski was working on the problem of the control of the emotions, which he saw as an expression of will power. Dybowski studied performance as the factor that brings to completion the process of the will begun in the lived experience of willing; he also focused on the typology of the will.[11] Other Polish exponents of the psychology of the will directed their experimental efforts toward a number of different problems, some focusing more on issues related to the dynamic aspect of the will's activity and others more on issues related to its objective aspect. Thus, for example, Wladyslawa Mielczarska[12] concentrated her research on problems such as effort and defiance, and Józef Reutt[13] on the presentation of goals and the problem of indecisiveness.

It would be difficult to list all the individual studies that contemporary psychologists—or even just Polish psychologists—have generated on the topic of the will. Moreover, moral philosophers reading these works will quite naturally attach greater importance to certain things than do empirical psychologists. For example, the method of investigation is of only incidental interest to moral philosophers, whereas they are extremely interested in what psychologists are studying and the conclusions they reach. Psychologists in their investigations often approach the boundaries of ethics. Ach, for example, in his work *Über den Willensakt und das Temperament*, discusses the topic of the psychological basis of conscience,[14] and others (e.g., Lindworsky[15]) touch upon the problems of upbringing that are so prominent in connection with the will. But regardless of how much light these discussions may shed on ethical experience, the most important thing they do for moral philosophers is establish the psychological problematic that allows them to arrive at a proper interpretation of ethical experience.

2. THE RELATION OF EXPERIMENTAL PSYCHOLOGY OF THE WILL TO ETHICAL EXPERIENCE

In what does this "establishing" consist? In other words, what do these psychologists of the will bring to ethics through their investigations? First of all, the science of the will that they developed is based on the premise that an act of will is any lived experience in which the personal self appears as a real efficient cause of its actions. Ach expresses this when he writes: "In activities of the will, the individual has, upon the appearance of a determinate presentation, a distinct awareness that he or she is the cause of its realization (*Verwirklichung*). The self appears as the cause of action."[16] Lindworsky expresses the same view in the following words: "An act of will is that particular lived experience in which the self appears as the cause of activity."[17] This assertion is treated as a fact of phenomenological experience. The most evident feature in an act of will is the efficacy of the personal self. This efficacy is immediately given: it is reflected in the awareness of the acting person as an act of will. Ach treats this fact of phenomenological experience as the basis for all experimental research on the will. All such research focuses on the different individual moments of that lived experience in which the will appears as a causal expression of the personal self.

The fact that the will reveals itself in the lived experience of the efficacy of the person directs us to the specific dynamism that constitutes its proper essence. Kant abandoned this dynamic essence of the will in his interpretation of ethical life, confining himself to an analysis of the contents of practical reason as the determining factors in the direction of the will. And yet the first and most fundamental aspect of ethical experience is the very efficacy of the personal self, which Ach, Lindworsky, and other representatives of the same school of psychology describe as essential for the will. The awareness that I am the efficient cause of all my individual actions is a necessary psychological basis for the ethical experience that I am responsible for those actions. Consequently, when psychologists point to efficacy as the primary element of the lived experience of will, they take the same position that ethicists must take in apprehending ethical experience. The will reveals itself here as the true core of such experience. Ethical experience is contained immanently in every human activity in which the personal self is conscious of its efficacy. This means that ethical experience is contained immanently in the act of will itself, and not in something outside of it, e.g., in feeling, as Max Scheler suggested.[18]

Consequently, the phenomenology of the will upon which Ach and his school of psychology base their experimental research threatens not only Kant's position; it also strikes no less forcefully at the position on ethical experience that Scheler was led to adopt as a result of his aprioristic emotionalism. Although Scheler is a phenomenologist in his assumptions, he derives his view of the ethical life of the human being primarily from the set of emotional factors he sees as comprising that life. He realizes that ethical experience is connected with the willing of value.[19] For Scheler, however, this willing of value is only a tendency connected with the presentation of a desirable object.[20] Because Scheler believes values cannot be adequately presented in any image or concept but can only be felt, he connects willing with the feeling of value and not with the efficacy of the person. For this reason, too, ethical experience is not contained immanently in willing, in the act of will, but has its source, according to Scheler, in emotion. The very core of ethical experience, in Scheler's view, is not the efficacy of the person but the emotional experience of value.

Scheler's emotionalism—a full analysis of which must be left for another occasion—is expanded into a rich system of an ethics of values. From the point of view of experience, however, I cannot agree with his system, precisely because he completely disregards the efficacy of the person. If persons are not the efficient cause of their actions, then there is no explanation for where ethical values come from. The experience upon which ethics is based reveals that persons who experience themselves as the efficient cause of their actions simultaneously experience themselves as subjects of ethical values—moral good and evil.

The distinct immanence of ethical experience appears, therefore, in the lived experience of the efficacy of the person, that is, in the phenomenologically apprehended act of will. This is also suggested by the sense of responsibility that accompanies action and is related to ethical value. If the efficacy of the person is the basic element of the experiential whole we call ethical experience, and if the experience of responsibility is connected with it, then ethical value originates, so to speak, between these two elements. Ethical value originates in the lived experience of efficacy, that is, in the act of will apprehended phenomenologically—and this is what gives us the experiential basis for connecting ethical value with the person as its proper subject. When Scheler speaks of the purely emotional experiences of happiness and despair, these experiences already presuppose an action involving the efficacy of the person. These experiences are elicited by the awareness that the ethical value arising from an action remains in the person as a subject, and its presence is for this person a source of happiness if it is a positive value and of despair if a negative one.

The lived experience of responsibility is a confirmation of the relation that exists between an action's moral value and the person's efficacy, both when this experience occurs after the deed is done and when it occurs before it. The lived experience of responsibility points to the will as the psychological factor that constitutes the very core of ethical experience.

By bringing to light the efficacy of the person as the phenomenological fact in which the will is revealed, the contemporary experimental psychology founded by Ach, which is also pursued in Poland, enables us to overcome some of the consequences of Kant's critical philosophy for ethics. In the experience of the efficacy of the personal self, the dynamic essence of the will is once again given its due. The discovery of the actual phenomenological moment forms a common point of departure for both psychologists and ethicists. Empirical psychologists will proceed from this moment to their own investigations, employing the experimental-inductive method; ethicists will find in this moment the key for apprehending ethical experience, and from there they will proceed using a method proper to their own science. Nevertheless, the point of departure is the same.

But there must be a convergence at a later stage as well. As we know, in Kant's ethics, as a result of his failure to perceive the efficient and dynamic moment of the will, there appeared an excess of the objective moment. Kant's whole view of the will and its significance in ethical life, as he developed it particularly in the *Critique of Practical Reason*, is partially reducible to an analysis of the influence of feelings on the will; basically, however, it is reducible to an analysis of practical reason and its imperatives. A similar situation, but in a different form and based on different assumptions, occurs in Scheler's ethics. In place of the rational-practical apriorism we encounter in Kant's ethics, Scheler adopted a different apriorism, an emotional one.[21] Both forms of apriorism lead to a disproportionate excess of the objective moment at the expense of the efficient moment of the will, an excess of motivation at the expense of dynamism. The will in both of these views remains completely enmeshed in the apriorism of either practical reason or emotion. There can be no doubt, however, that the will itself contributes a dynamic element to human psychic life, an element that appears in a tendency determined by the very self. Scheler does, in fact, say that willing has the character of a tendency, but unfortunately this tendency remains for him somehow completely submerged in the emotional elements that he regards as an *a priori* factor in the life of the person.

Consequently, both Kantian and Schelerian apriorism in ethics lead to an essential analysis of static forms, which for Kant are imperatives or maxims and for Scheler values, but neither of these apriorisms allows us to objectify the dynamic factor of action, which is fundamental for ethics. Action, after all, is the locus of authentic ethical experience. And so apriorism becomes the enemy of experience. Ethics must be free of apriorism if it is to remain properly related to experience.

When, on the other hand, we take as the point of departure in our investigation of the will the familiar inner experience of efficacy, which has its source in the personal self and manifests itself in the whole act of will, we cannot help but grasp correctly the balance that occurs between motivation and action in the process of the will. The excess of motivation at the expense of action that characterizes Kant's and Scheler's view of ethical matters then disappears. After all, a motive has meaning only in relation to the act of will it motivates. An analysis of the contents that are motives and operate as such (whether they be Kantian maxims and imperatives or Schelerian values) that does not take into account the activity of the will must necessarily distort the very essence of those contents, for such an analysis is inconsistent with the demands of the actual facts known from experience.

What is at stake here is an accurate apprehension of the whole practical order. In the practical order, an act of will (which is often most clearly revealed in self-control) is always an essential factor, and the practical function of reason arises under the influence of impulses of the will. Consequently, all motivation belongs to the process of the will and must be considered within the context of the will. We cannot, therefore, conceive the matter by examining the activity of practical reason in isolation, and then later adding the "activity" of the will to it from without—which is precisely what Kant did. The actual structure of practical reason is different. The activity of the will is a primary factor here, and it shapes and permeates the entire practical activity of reason. Reason becomes practical by acting in conjunction with the will. Hence, there are no *a priori* practical principles of reason, which would subsequently be presented to or imposed upon the will.

Scheler takes a different position. For Scheler it is not principles of reason—maxims and imperatives—that have an *a priori* practical character, but rather emotionally experienced values. These values can only be felt; they cannot be grasped by reason. Neither reason nor the will plays any role in the apprehension of values, which, as Scheler maintains, are later to become objects of the will's striving, or goals to be realized. Schelerian values are not the same as principles of practical reason. They do not direct or command the will but only draw it to themselves. Scheler replaces Kantian *a priori* imperative motivation with *a priori* emotional motivation, and so instead of an ethics of pure duty we have in Scheler an ethics of pure value. Nevertheless, this emotional motivation does not occur within the framework of the process of the will. Values are something ready-made and *a priori* practical when they appear before the will in order to draw it in the direction they want it to go.

Motivation is what inwardly links the whole act of will, and so if we do not connect it organically with the act of will a proper and adequate interpretation of ethical experience becomes impossible. Here again the school of psychologists of the will that I referred to above assists us in interpreting ethical experiences because, in keeping with experience and reality, it treats motivation in the context of the process of the will. The process of the will is not the same as the simple act of will. The lived experience "I will" (or other analogous experiences) is the simplest experiential fact in which the efficacy of the personal self is revealed. This simple experience, however, develops into a specific process thanks to the appearance of motives. The appearance of motives should lead to a decision. Frequently, however, in the course of the process of the will, a weighing or even a conflict of motives must take place. The result of such a weighing or conflict of motives is the victory of some one motive, followed by a choice made by the will. Decision leads to performance. Performance is an extension of the actual process of the will and remains closely dependent upon it. In experimental psychology, we find discussions of the *causal*[22] problem of the will, a name that embraces the various ways performance manifests its dependence on forms of the process of the will. The very name of this problem points to the causal-efficient character of this dependence. This character qualifies the activity of the will in all of its dimensions.

This causal character, however, which qualifies all the will's activity that has its efficient source in the self, takes on distinctive features thanks to motivation. As a result of motivation, simple willing develops into the process of the will, until finally, depending on the motivation, it leads to performance. Motivation is an immanent part of the whole lived experience that goes by the name *an act of will*. This is how the matter looks in the light of experimental research. As we know, the problem of motivation was studied by Michotte and Prüm.[23] Lindworsky stressed the importance of motives in the task of training the will.[24] Ach accentuated the so-called formal development of the will as consisting in the exercise of effort, whereas Lindworsky took the position that motivation is of fundamental importance for the development of the will. A motive of the will is always some value or other, and values create stronger stimuli for the will when they are connected with feelings. Nevertheless, the immediate power of feelings is not directly proportionate to the duration of their influence on the will. Although higher feelings operate more weakly, their influence on the will lasts longer than that of lower feelings. Reutt,[25] who approached this problem from a somewhat different angle, also arrived at the conclusion that higher aims, those that involve values beyond ourselves, are for the will a source of greater strength and permanence than aims that involve only values pertaining to ourselves.

These and other psychological works based on the experimental method show time and again that there is a strict connection between motivation and the will's activity. This connection can be verified experientially: it can be investigated by empirical, statistical, and inductive methods. The results psychology achieves by these methods can even function as empirical laws for the formation of the will. If experimental psychology of the will is in keeping with experience in its stance that motivation is contained within the precincts of the process of the will, then ethicists must also adopt this stance when they attempt to interpret ethical experience in keeping with experience. Ethical experience, as I said earlier, is contained immanently in the efficacy of the person, in the whole act of will, which has its efficient source in the personal self. The immanence of ethical experience in the act of will appears with particular intensity, however, in the process of motivation, in the weighing or outright conflict of motives and the ultimate choice the will makes.

It should be noted that the psychology of Ach's school, to the extent that its method of experimentation and field of empirical-inductive science permit, presents the psychological problematic in such a way that it interprets ethical experience in the context of its approach to the lived experience of the will. The will appears there in lived experience as a determinate experiential structure in which the efficacy of the personal self is organically connected with motivation. This is the type of experiential phenomenological structure that the psychologists of this school took as the basis of their research, which, by means of experimentation combined with introspection and statistically based induction, are meant to lead them to particular knowledge of the will as a lived experience. This same phenomenological structure must also be adopted by ethicists as the basis of their interpretation of ethical experience. This empirically ascertained experience is contained within the framework of the phenomenological structure that empirical psychologists, using their own methods, investigate as the act of will.

The most important thing in this structure is the strict organic connection of motivation with the efficacy of the person and the activity of the will. This connection prevents what I earlier referred to as the "excess of motivation at the expense of action" that we see in Kant's ethical system and, in a different way, also in Scheler's. Strictly speaking, however, we cannot call what happens in their systems an excess of motivation at the expense of action. They simply present a method of apprehending the problematic of the will in ethics by analyzing *a priori* practical forms (which for Kant are maxims or imperatives and for Scheler are values) in separation from the activity of the will and the efficacy of the person. The reason why this method cannot be called an excess of motivation at the expense of action in the strict sense is that these forms, insofar as they are divorced from action, are not *de facto* motives, even though Kant and Scheler regard them as *a priori* practical forms. Hence, the definition in this case was more of a working definition. In reality, an excess of motivation at the expense of action can only occur in persons in whom the number of rational reasons for and against a certain action, or else the intensity of emotional experiences connected with the decision to act, clearly surpasses the intensity of the act of will.

In the phenomenology of the will, therefore, moral philosophers and experimental psychologists converge with respect to the structure of the lived experience that presents itself as the will in immediate experience. After that their paths diverge. Nevertheless, this convergence in their point of departure is important in that it establishes moral philosophers in their relation to experience. Once we become acquainted with the phenomenological structure that empirical psychologists investigate as the experiential act of will in all its dimensions, and especially when we explore the essential connection between efficacy and motivation, we can see a definite relation to the teaching on the will contained in Thomas Aquinas' *Summa*.

St. Thomas arrived at his conception of the will by a different route, namely, through a metaphysical analysis of human reality, and especially of the substantial soul, whose essence (*essentia*) does not operate by itself but through the medium of faculties (*potentia*). The will, like reason, is a faculty for which the spiritual substance of the soul itself is the subject, whereas the other faculties of the human soul are subjectified in the *compositum humanum* as a whole.[26] The activity of the will is understood by St. Thomas as having two basic sources of actualization. One is the nature of the will itself, for the will is by nature an appetite (*appetitus*), and so it exhibits an inclination toward everything that is in any way good (*bonum in communi*).[27] Because this appetitive inclination constitutes the very nature of the will, the will does not need any external causal-efficient impulses in order to operate. The only such causal-efficient impulse is the act of the Creator, who endowed the will with such a nature.[28] By virtue of this nature, the will is itself already a causal-efficient source of impulses in the human being, impulses that have various goods as their object. That which St. Thomas calls *motio quoad exercitium* comes from the will itself and is the will's natural motion.

But since the will is a rational faculty, rationality permeates the inclination toward the good that the will has by nature as an appetitive faculty. The rationality of desire constitutes the essence of the will, which is why St. Thomas always defines the will as a rational appetite (*appetitus rationalis*). The will's natural rationality of desire is actualized when the will conforms its motion to reason and to reason's judgments concerning objects of desire. These judgments have a practical import: they specify the goodness of particular objects of desire. The proper object of reason is being and truth. Reason's task, in cooperating with the desire for good that naturally resides in the will, is to objectify for the will the true goodness of those goods and thereby direct the inclination of the will. This objectification is the other source of the will's actualization. St. Thomas calls it *motio quoad specificationem*,[29] and says that this motion, which comes from practical reason, consists in directing the appetitive efficacy that constitutes the essence of the will toward appropriate objects. These objects are the various goods objectified by reason. The will with its whole natural dynamism is in potency with respect to these goods, and this potency of the will is actualized by reason. That is why St. Thomas defines *specificatio* also as *motio*.

St. Thomas is well aware, however, that the will's activity as we know it from experience is not based merely on the peaceful, sedate objectification of reason. Feelings arising from the senses and from sensory desire—*passiones appetitus sensitivi*—are always trying to affect this activity. According to St. Thomas, these feelings do not directly influence *motio quoad exercitium*. The will's appetitive motion remains distinct from the motion of sensory desire (if this were not the case, it would be difficult to understand the rationality of the appetitive motion of the will). Rather, the feelings attempt to influence reason's objectification of the objects of desire and to conform these objects to the feelings themselves and their own relation to the objects.[30]

The above observations are not intended to be an exhaustive analysis of St. Thomas' teaching on the will. Nevertheless, even in such cursory form, we must be struck by the similarity between it and the relation to the will we find in Ach and his school of experimental psychology, despite the totally different methods employed. St. Thomas constructed his view of the will by analyzing the fundamental reality of the human being, and that is why he speaks of the faculties through whose medium the soul operates.

If, however, we consider the internal efficacy of the faculty that expresses itself in the desire for all that is in any way good and in the inclination toward the good of the whole human being, then it is not hard to agree that philosophers must find just such a faculty in their metaphysical analysis of the lived experience of the efficacy of the personal self, which is the basic moment of the phenomenology of the will. As to the strict connection of this experience with motivation in the process of the will, we must again acknowledge that the Thomistic view of the process of the will, in its notion of the will's dual motion (*quoad exercitium* and *quoad specificationem*), faithfully reflects what is presented in immediate experience as the unity comprised of the actual-dynamic moment and the objective moment.

Even in the case of feelings, we find that they play the same role in the experimental view as in the Thomistic view, for they are said to give a particular intensity to the lived experience of value and thereby influence motivation in the process of the will. The so-called determinate feelings that arise below the activity of the will are a separate issue. They are discussed by Ach,[31] who focused mainly on the actual-dynamic aspect of the will. It would not be difficult to show that they constitute a new point of similarity with St. Thomas' view.

If these various elements of similarity suggest themselves despite the totally different methods and terminology employed by St. Thomas and Ach's school of experimental psychology in their science of the will, it is because both of these views are united in basically the same relation to the will as an empirical whole known from lived experience. One could say that the same phenomenology of the will that the psychologists of this school adopted as a basis for their experimental research in a certain sense also accompanied St. Thomas in his metaphysical analysis of the will. It turns out that the phenomenological image of the will must be basically one, namely, that presented by experience.

Consequently, the first condition of the truth of a view is a proper relation to experience. Obviously, the kind of results we reach will differ depending on whether we use such a proper relation to experience as a basis for experimental research or as a point of departure for constructing a metaphysical view. In the end, however, both endeavors will yield true results, though each in a different realm. Their truth will depend in each case primarily on a proper relation to the empirical facts, whereas their different realms will depend on the selected method. Experimentation produces different true assertions about the will than those arrived at by metaphysical analysis. Both types of assertions about the will are true, even though they render the truth about the will in different realms.

3. THE PROBLEM OF AN ADEQUATE INTERPRETATION OF ETHICAL EXPERIENCE

Moral philosophers realize, of course, that experimental psychology, by adopting a proper relation to experience, can arrive at many true particular assertions concerning the will. At the same time, however, they believe that by means of these assertions alone they cannot formulate an interpretation of ethical experience that would serve as a basis for ethics, which is, after all, a normative science. To conclude these reflections, therefore, I wish to indicate the principal reasons for this belief.

Experimental psychology of the will is based on the lived experience of the efficacy of the personal self, which presents itself in immediate experience as a phenomenological fact. Ethics, in interpreting ethical experience, proceeds from the affirmation of this same fact, because this fact forms the psychological core of that experience. Characteristic for the efficacy of the person is the whole process of the will, a process that depends on motivation and initiates the realization of a chosen end. This is the sort of structure of the will that psychologists observe and investigate experimentally. Ethicists, on the other hand, are interested in ethical experience. Using contemporary phenomenological terminology, one could say that ethical experience is that lived experience in which a new value appears, namely, ethical value. Scheler, who regarded the phenomenological method as sufficient for interpreting ethical experience (and even for interpreting ethics in general), maintains that this value appears in the person as its proper subject. According to Scheler, the person experiences himself or herself not only as the subject of ethical value but also as its very source.[32]

The manner in which the person is the source of ethical value is a point in which I definitely cannot agree with Scheler. He maintains that the person is the source of ethical value merely by reason of a certain emotional exuberance of the person's nature, which distinguishes the person from, say, an animal, and which causes the person's willing of various objective values to be accompanied by this new "additional" value—ethical value. In the light of the correct assumptions of the phenomenology of the will upon which Ach, Lindworsky, and the earlier mentioned Polish exponents of the psychology of the will based their research, I must firmly insist that the source of ethical values is the efficacy of the person. The person experiences himself or herself as the efficient cause of his or her actions, and ethical value is connected with this experience. Scheler did not perceive this efficacy; in his assumptions, he was not only an emotionalist but above all an essentialistic phenomenologist. Consequently, he lacked the tools to reveal and objectify such a dynamic factor as the will. Nevertheless, the will definitely presents itself in this manner, and the service rendered by Ach and his school of psychologists is precisely the discovery of a complete phenomenology of the will.

But the disclosure of the immanence of ethical experience in the efficacy of the person still does not completely resolve the problem of an adequate interpretation of this experience. Scheler maintains that ethical value manifests itself experientially primarily in the person and only secondarily in the person's acts. Thus, according to Scheler, the person is the proper phenomenological subject of ethical value. This position is correct. Even though I cannot agree with Scheler that the person's acts are only a secondary subject of ethical values[33] (Scheler held this view because he did not regard the efficacy of the person as a phenomenological fact of experience and did not perceive the immanence of ethical experience in this efficacy), I cannot deny that ethical values are essentially connected with the person as their proper subject. I hold, then, on the one hand, in contrast to Scheler, the immanence of ethical experience in the efficacy of the person, and, on the other, in keeping with Scheler, the immanence of ethical values in the person.

These are two phenomenological poles of a single whole. These two poles, which are very clearly interrelated in lived experience, do not reveal phenomenologically the full structure of that whole, but they do provide an adequate basis for apprehending, by another method, the structure of the whole to which they organically belong. If the person's lived experience, which has a distinct, experientially ascertainable, efficient-causal character, brings with it the subjective experience of ethical value, then we must acknowledge that this ethical value, which the person experiences internally as its proper subject, was causally engendered by that person's lived experience. I also find support for this conviction in the experiential fact that the person who experiences himself or herself as a subject of ethical value simultaneously feels that he or she is the source of that value. The person cannot be the source of ethical value, however, except through his or her own efficacy. This is, after all, substantiated experientially by the perceived immanence of ethical experience in the lived experience of efficacy. Thus the efficacy of a person in some way gives rise to ethical value, which this same person then perceives experientially as its subject.

This is how a complete account of ethical experience looks when apprehended phenomenologically. The account Scheler left us in his ethics is incomplete because it fails to consider the efficacy of the person. Even after including the efficacy of the person, however, Scheler's phenomenological explanation does not present an adequate interpretation of ethical experience because it still does not conceptually apprehend the essential core of this lived experience. The *psychological* core of ethical experience is the efficacy of the person together with motivation, whereas the *essential* core of ethical experience is ethical value itself. Phenomenologists maintain that this value manifests itself in the person as a subject; they even say that it is a consequence of the efficacy of the person. These assertions, however relevant they may be to ethical value, do not conceptually apprehend the very essence of this value, for it must be conceded that ethical value resides essentially in the trans-phenomenological order. If ethical value were only to "reside" in the person as its phenomenological subject, even as its uniquely proper subject, then despite all else it would not be found in the place where we *de facto* discover it experientially.

By *ethical value* I mean that through which the human being as a human being, as a concrete person, is simply good or bad. Ethical value is a qualification of the very person as a rational and free concrete being. And this is why the phenomenological "place" of ethical value is not its real place. From experience, we know that ethical value is not just that which we experience "in a person" as his or her "goodness" or "badness," but consists in the fact that this person as a person is simply good or bad. If, in turn, we wish to emphasize the nevertheless accidental character of ethical value in relation to the very being of the person, then we will say that ethical value is that through which a given person as a person is good or bad.

The person, then, is not just the uniquely proper phenomenological subject of ethical values but is their ontic subject as well. This fact indubitably belongs to experience, which in turn belongs to the general human experience upon which ethics is primarily based. This experience is more fundamental than so-called phenomenological experience. It deals with concrete beings themselves as genuine wholes, and not just with the "moments" of them that in some way or other "manifest themselves."

For ethicists, the acting human being is just such a genuine whole. The human being is a person, a being that is conscious of itself. When the human being acts as such a person then each of his or her conscious acts is an ethical experience. In apprehending and investigating this lived experience as a phenomenological fact, we focus only on what happens in the person while performing an action. Although we then perceive the lived experience of efficacy and ethical value, these phenomenological elements do not present us with the actual whole so long as we do not apprehend what happens to the person through the act that person consciously performs. What happens to the person is that the person himself or herself *becomes* good or bad depending on the act performed. And this becoming good or bad of the person through the performance of a conscious action is what constitutes the essential core of ethical experience. This becoming of the person also belongs to the totality of experience: the person *experiences* his or her ethical becoming.

Scheler himself expressed this in a sense when he wrote that the person experiences himself or herself as the source of "good" or "evil." And yet this ethical becoming of the person did not fall within the orbit of what Scheler took to be the content of phenomenological experience, even though its experiential character is not subject to doubt. Ethical experience does not just occur in the person, but it is the lived experience of the person because it involves the person's very being.

If ethical experience essentially consists in this specific becoming of the person, then the only interpretation of it that can be considered adequate is one that apprehends and expresses this ethical becoming. This is what also leads me to believe that we should consider the view of the human act developed by Thomas Aquinas[34] an adequate interpretation of ethical experience. I do not intend here to analyze his view or its adequacy in relation to the complete structure of ethical experience. I only want to draw attention to its origin. St. Thomas based his view of the human act on Aristotle's theory of potency and act, a theory by which the philosophy of being explains all changes that take place in beings. Every change, whether it is of a material or spiritual nature, whether it takes place in an organism or in the psyche, can be said—in an analogical sense, of course—to be a form of passage from potency to act. A conscious human act is for St. Thomas not merely a stage upon which ethical experience is enacted. It is itself an ethical experience because it is an act of will. An act of will is for St. Thomas a passage from potency, since the will is a faculty (*potentia*) of the soul. A separate study would be needed to show how the ethical becoming of the person is reflected in this view as a whole.

Nevertheless, the reasons presented in this last part of the essay clearly show that phenomenology of the will alone does not suffice for interpreting ethical experience, even if this phenomenology happens to be as much in harmony with experience as that upon which Ach and his whole experimental school are based. Phenomenology can indirectly assist us in overcoming certain errors in views of the will that arise from an improper relation to the empirical facts, but it cannot serve as a tool for the sort of interpretation of ethical experience upon which ethics as a normative science is based.

NOTES

1. Immanuel Kant, *Critique of Practical Reason*, trans. Lewis White Beck (Indianapolis: Bobbs, 1956) 15.

2. See, for example, Kant, *Critique of Practical Reason* 23–24: "Reason [is] a truly higher faculty of desire, but still only in so far as it determines the will by itself and not in the service of the inclinations."

3. Kant, *Critique of Practical Reason* 18.

4. "*Actus voluntatis potest esse imperatus*" (Thomas Aquinas, *Summa theologiae* I–II, 17, 5).

5. "*Relinquitur, quod imperare sit actus rationis, praesupposito actu voluntatis, in cuius virtute ratio movet per imperium ad exercitium actus*" (Thomas Aquinas, *Summa theol.* I–II, 17, 1).

6. Johannes Lindworsky, *Der Wille: Seine Erscheinung und seine Beherrschung* (Leipzig: Barth, 1923) 1–4.

7. Narziss Ach, *Über den Willensakt und das Temperament* (Leipzig: Quelle, 1910) 237 ff.

8. A. Michotte and N. Prüm, "Étude expérimentale sur le choix volontaire et ses antécédents immédiats," *Archives de Psychologie* (1910).

9. Lindworsky, *Der Wille.*

10. Mieczyslaw Dybowski, *Dzialanie woli na tle badan eksperymentalnych* [*The Activity of the Will in the Light of Experimental Investigations*] (Poznan, 1946).

11. Mieczyslaw Dybowski, *O typach woli: Badania eksperymentalne* [*On Types of Will: Experimental Investigations*] (Poznan: Ksieg. Akademicka, 1947).

12. Wladyslawa Mielczarska, *Przezycie oporu i jego stosunek do woli* [*The Experience of Defiance and Its Relation to the Will*] (Poznan: Poznanskiego Tow. Przyjaciol Nauk, 1948); *O wplywie wysilku na wynik pracy* [*The Influence of Effort on the Results of Work*] (Poznan, 1947).

13. Józef Reutt, *Przedstawienie celu a postepowanie* [*The Presentation of Goals in Relation to Behavior*] (Poznan, 1947); *Badania psychologiczne nad wahaniem* [*Psychological Investigations of Vacillation*] (Poznan, 1949).

14. Ach, *Über den Willensakt* 273.

15. Johannes Lindworsky, *The Training of the Will*, trans. Arpad Steiner and Edward A. Fitzpatrick, 4th ed. (Milwaukee: Bruce, 1955).

16. Ach, *Über den Willensakt* 265.

17. Lindworsky, *Der Wille* 21.

18. Max Scheler, *Formalism in Ethics and Non-Formal Ethics of Values: A New Attempt Toward the Foundation of an Ethical Personalism*, trans. Manfred S. Frings and Roger L. Funk (Evanston: Northwestern UP, 1973).

19. Scheler, "The Relation of the Values 'Good' and 'Evil' to the Other Values and Goods," *Formalism* 23–30.

20. Scheler, "Conation, Values, and Goals," *Formalism* 30–38.

21. Scheler, "The Non-Formal A Priori in Ethics," *Formalism* 81–110.

22. Dybowski, *Dzialanie woli* 195 ff.
23. Michotte and Prüm, "Étude expérimentale."
24. Lindworsky, *Der Wille.*
25. Reutt, *Przedstawienie celu a postepowanie* 95.
26. Thomas Aquinas, *Summa theol.* I, 77, 5–6.
27. Thomas Aquinas, *Summa theol.* I–II, 9, 1.
28. Thomas Aquinas, *Summa theol.* I–II, 9, 6.
29. Thomas Aquinas, *Summa theol.* I–II, 9, 1; I–II, 9, 3, ad 3.
30. Thomas Aquinas, *Summa theol.* I–II, 9, 2.
31. Ach, *Über den Willensakt* 307 ff.
32. Scheler, "The Stratification of the Emotional Life," *Formalism* 328–344; "The Idea of Sanction and Reprisal in Relation to the Connection between Happiness and Moral Values," *Formalism* 354–369.
33. Scheler, *Formalism* 27.
34. Thomas Aquinas, *Summa theol.* I–II, 18–20.

2

The Problem of the Separation of Experience from the Act in Ethics

In the Philosophy of Immanuel Kant and Max Scheler

1. THE STATE OF THE PROBLEM

In this essay I wish to draw attention to certain basic aspects of a problem that has great significance for understanding the difference between the ancient and modern ways of approaching ethics.[1] Ethics, as we know, is the science of human actions from the point of view of their moral value—the good or evil contained in them. Every human action involves a particular lived experience that goes by the name *ethical experience*. The awareness that I am performing a certain action, that I am its author, brings with it a sense of responsibility for the moral value of that action. I then experience myself, my own person, as the efficient cause of the moral good or evil in the action, and through this I experience the moral good or evil of my own person. Ethical value intensifies the sense of the bond that exists between the action and the person. This whole lived experience has a thoroughly empirical character, and it is upon this empirical fact that ethics as a science is based. The fact that ethics is a normative science can in no way obscure the fact that it is deeply rooted in experience. And so ethics, a normative science, is also an empirical science, because it is based on authentic ethical experience.

Karol Wojtyla, "Problem oderwania przezycia od aktu w etyce na tle pogladow Kanta i Schelera," *Roczniki Filozoficzne* 5.3 (1955–57): 113–140.

The manner in which the empirical and normative aspects come together in the structure of ethics is a separate issue, and certainly a fundamental one. I shall not, however, be analyzing that problem here. In this essay, I am interested only in ethical experience, which serves as the empirical point of departure for ethics as a whole. This experience was well known to Aristotle and St. Thomas Aquinas, as can be seen from reading their works.[2] In order to apprehend the whole of ethical experience scientifically, they formulated a view of human action based on the theory of potency and act. The theory of potency and act belongs to the Aristotelian and Thomistic philosophy of being and is used to explain every change that occurs in being. Every such change consists in a "passage" from potency to act, from potency to a certain actualization. The scope of this theory is as universal as that of the concept of contingent being itself. Every change, regardless of the concrete character of the being in which it occurs, can be expressed in the categories of this theory. In this way, by means of the theory of potency and act, the dynamic character of reality can be reflected in the philosophy of being.

Aristotle and St. Thomas pursued ethics within the context of their philosophy as a whole, using concepts developed in that philosophy. There can be no doubt that the concepts of potency and act are an expression of a broadly conceived relation to experience, for they reflect what in various ways is contained in that experience. Since Aristotle and St. Thomas employed these concepts in their philosophical interpretation of ethical experience, we may safely say that they perceived the dynamic character of this experience. Ethical experience appears in such an interpretation as a particular change brought about by a personal acting subject, as a certain actualization of that subject. In every human action we can observe a whole series of external and psychosomatic changes, or passages from potency to act, but the very essence of human action consists in the actualization of the will acting under the direction of reason. The actual ethical act takes place in the will. And so St. Thomas, adopting Aristotle's view, tends to ignore all the other empirical cofactors of ethical experience and concentrate primarily on its essential element, namely, the actualization of the will connected with both the activity of practical reason and emotional factors, along with all the other factors that, by belonging to the *compositum humanum*, take part in the ethical act.

As we can see, the concept of the ethical act in its proper sense is an expression of the kind of relation to experience that guides the philosophy of being as a whole. Only with such a relation to experience does the concept of the ethical act achieve its full value. If this relation is altered, then "ethical act" remains merely a name. We know that this relation to experience, which served as the basis for the philosophy of being and ethics, including the concept of the human act in ethics, was in fact altered with the coming of modern empirical-inductive science. But so long as this science did not extend to the interpretation of ethical experience, this change had no significance for the ethical act. Nevertheless, the development of the particular sciences contributed to a rise in the critical approach to the traditional philosophy of being. At the same time, there was also a rise in tendencies to pursue ethics as an empirical science similar to other empirical sciences and in separation from the philosophy of being. Such tendencies were prevalent especially in British ethics in the period just prior to Kant's appearance.

Kant's appearance first of all affected the scientific character of metaphysics. As a result of his critical views, Kant fundamentally challenged not only the possibility of constructing the philosophy of being as the basic philosophical science, but also the possibility of constructing moral philosophy according to the assumptions that Aristotle and St. Thomas used in the construction of their ethics. Kant's critical stance had immediate repercussions for the concept of the ethical act. All attempts to pursue ethics on the model of the particular sciences by means of the empirical-inductive method were incapable of dissolving the ethical act as long as the basis of the theory of potency and act upon which this concept rests was not attacked, as long as the relation to experience that served as the basis for the Aristotelian-Thomistic concept of the ethical act and philosophy of being was not called into question. And that is just how ethical experience, the empirical whole that forms the point of departure for ethics, was definitively severed from the concept of the ethical act. For Kant and for any thinker who rejects along with the philosophy of being the theory of potency and act, "ethical act" has no real meaning. And yet for Kant, as well as for every thinker in some way influenced by him, there remains ethical experience, which calls for a proper interpretation.

I do not intend here to explore the problem of the separation of experience from the act in ethics in all of its historical dimensions. I will be focusing instead on just two points neuralgic to this problem. One of them is Kant's system itself, and the other is the system of the ethics of values developed by the contemporary phenomenologist Max Scheler. Using these two systems as examples, I will attempt to establish certain basic elements in the problem of the separation of ethical experience from the act in ethics. This issue, in turn, has great significance for understanding the different positions from which ethical questions were approached in ancient and medieval times and from which they are approached today.

2. THE EXPERIENCE OF DUTY IN KANT'S THOUGHT

Kant takes the position that it is not the actualization of the will as a whole that has ethical meaning but only one element of it, namely, *duty*. This view is the result of a whole series of assumptions in his system. Above all, however, it is a consequence of the relation he takes to experience. Kant believes that empirical knowledge provides us with only a chaos of impressions, whereas it gives us no basis for such concepts as substance or cause. These are, in Kant's opinion, categories that derive solely from reason, and so they are completely *a priori*. Reason, or, more precisely, understanding (*Verstand*), makes use of such categories so as to introduce the order it needs into the chaos of the impressions derived from experience. Consequently, science—certain knowledge—is not based on experience but only on sensory or rational *a priori* forms. We cannot, however, base metaphysics on these forms because metaphysics does not refer to experience, and so metaphysics is not a science. According to Kant, metaphysics is a product of reason (*Vernunft*), which is not directed toward an understanding apprehension of empirical data by means of *a priori* categories, but produces—beyond experience—the ideas of God, the world, and the soul. These ideas, however, have no scientific foundation, because in formulating them reason uses categories such as substance and accident, which apply only to objects of experience. That is why metaphysics has no scientific value for Kant.

Kant used this same assumption as a basis for constructing a scientific ethics. To construct such an ethics, he needed the concept of free will. When, however, we apprehend the human being and human activity in an empirical and phenomenological way (*homo phaenomenon*), we find no trace of this free will in the human being. Everything about human action that we find in the field of empirical observation is subject to the same causality that governs the surrounding material world. *Homo phaenomenon* lives in the realm of necessity. This does not, however, lead Kant to reject free will, but only to seek it in the transphenomenal realm of *homo noumenon*. If anything gives us the right to accept this noumenal free will, it is a properly analyzed ethical order. The basis for this order is the moral law,[3] which Kant defines as an *a priori* form of practical reason. Just as theoretical reason has its *a priori* categories by which it organizes all empirical data, so, too, practical reason has its *a priori* form. This form has the character of law, and so it can *a priori* introduce ethical order into human life. That is the point that interests me in this inquiry. In my treatment of Kant, I shall be focusing on law—the form of practical reason—not as the basis for constructing a scientific ethics, but as the basis for the ethical life and activity of the human being.

Ethical life arises out of practical reason itself and is connected with free will, which Kant does not see manifested in the empirical order. In the noumenal sphere, however, he associates free will with law as an *a priori* form of practical reason. For theoretical reason, free will is an idea that does not lend itself to scientific objectification. Practical reason, on the other hand, enjoys a certain kind of immanence of freedom insofar as the moral law as such, which is an *a priori* legislative form of practical reason, becomes an object of the will and a motive of its activity. This takes place, of course, in the ethical life of the human being. The subordination of the will to law as a pure *a priori* form of practical reason constitutes the actual ethical life of the human person. The immanence of the will in the moral law, however, resides in the noumenal sphere in such a way that theoretical reason cannot by reflection extract it from that sphere and objectify it in a scientific way. Hence, ethical life directs our attention to the transphenomenal sphere of the human being, to the person's noumenal depths, but it does not allow us to form an image of the essence of the human person that would have scientific certitude.

Nevertheless, Kant takes it as an *a priori* certitude that the ethical life of the human being is based on the will and on law. He calls the will a faculty,[4] but his analysis in the *Critique of Practical Reason* and in the *Foundations of the Metaphysics of Morals*[5] shows that all we have here is a term borrowed from the Scholastics, and not the reality that this term signified in their philosophy. The will, in Kant's view, is devoid of any innate dynamism of its own. This is because the will has no proper object to which it would naturally turn in its activity, but is in each case subject to the motives that practical reason gives it. Kant so completely failed to perceive the real separateness of the will as a faculty that he sometimes even simply identified it with practical reason. This, of course, has consequences for Kant's view of the human being in general and for his view of ethical life in particular. Even though Kant maintains that the qualities of ethical good and evil are connected with the will, the source of ethical life still lies in reason alone. Reason is somehow *a priori* ethical, just as it is *a priori* practical. And so in ethical life it is not a matter of molding one's actions to conform to the requirements of an objective good crystalized in the moral law, but only of allowing one's practical reason to live by the moral law. To the extent that this is done, the immanence of freedom is somehow revealed in the moral law, and as a result all humanity in its transcendence of the sensory and natural order receives a deep affirmation. Such an affirmation of humanity is, according to Kant, the very essence of ethical life. Ethical life, as Kant perceives it, is turned inward toward the revelation and affirmation of that which for him became cognitively inaccessible as a result of his critical assumptions. In this sense, ethical life supplements our limited knowledge of the human being. It is not, however, turned outward toward objective reality—upon which, after all, the human being impresses not just the stamp of productive reason but also the stamp of the good born of the will.

In order for this inward direction—this affirmation of trans-empirical humanity—to take place effectively, the will must be liberated from all the motives that entangle its activity in the natural world of empirical goods. These goods operate on the will through the mediation of various feelings of pleasure and pain. Some of them produce pleasure, inclining practical reason to make them the "determinants" of the will's activity. Others, through the mediation of the feeling of pain, influence practical reason in the opposite direction. Whenever practical reason formulates principles of the will's activity (or motives, which Kant calls *maxims*) on the basis of feelings, the will falls within the orbit of natural causality. Its activity is then not free but subject to the same necessity as the world of nature. Kant calls such activity of the will *pathological* or *empirical*.[6] It really has nothing in common with ethical life, because ethical life is based on free will. Consequently, as far as Kant is concerned, we have no right to use the term *ethical* experience for the empirical whole that every external or internal human act forms by virtue of arising consciously from the will and thereby having the person as its efficient cause. What served as an empirical basis for the founders of the concept of the ethical act ceased to do so for Kant.

Thus, the experience in which the activity of the will exhibits a dependence on feelings ceases to be an ethical act. But that is not all. Even the activity of the will that originates in practical reason but turns toward some good in the external or even internal world has no ethical significance. In addition to maxims, Kant also distinguishes so-called *imperatives*. This term derives from the fact that reason, in aiming at some good, commands the will to do what is needed to attain that good. Imperatives of this kind show that the will is built into the structure of the human being in such a way that it tends to submit to feelings of pleasure and pain, and so reason must somehow impose its relation to the good upon the will—hence, the imperative. The imperatives discussed above are so-called *hypothetical imperatives*. This term derives from the fact that the respective command of reason for the will states: "If you want to achieve this or that good, which I regard as necessary, then you must do such and such." Hypothetical imperatives also have no ethical significance in Kant's eyes, and for basically the same reason as maxims. They in no way change the fact that the relation to goods originates in practical reason. Practical reason itself is still not the basis of ethical facts; their sole basis is the law alone, as the *a priori* form of practical reason. Consequently, even the sort of experience in which a person consciously chooses a certain good for which to strive in action is not an ethical experience. And those human actions that bear a distinct mark of personal efficacy by virtue of the fact that in them reason consciously directs the will toward a chosen good cannot be called ethical acts. One wonders, then, whether any human activity has the value of an ethical act. In any event, none of the experiences upon which Aristotle and St. Thomas based their view of the ethical act achieved such status in Kant's eyes.

For Kant, the ethical act—if we can still speak of it here, given such a drastic change of position—is connected solely and exclusively with the so-called *categorical imperative*. To understand this concept, which is so fundamental to Kant's ethical doctrine, we need to consider his doctrine on law. Law is an *a priori* product of reason, and so it is not based on knowledge of the order that governs nature. Rather, law derives from reason itself the order that should govern human beings in their striving for various goods. Law also, therefore, always has to do with goods of the empirical world, because the human will turns toward that world when directed by practical reason through maxims and hypothetical imperatives. But this function of law, which is connected with the whole internal and external empirical sphere, is only its matter. The matter of law must be distinguished from its form.[7] This is the form of universal legislation or law-giving, which contains no material content but arises from practical reason itself. It constitutes the inner content of practical reason and its sole inner content. And it alone provides, in Kant's opinion, a basis for ethical life. Hence, if the will is to achieve a genuinely ethical act, it must realize the form of the moral law, and not its matter.[8] As long as the will realizes only the matter of the law, it is turned toward goods. Because it turns toward them in keeping with what the law commands, its activity is legal, but we cannot yet speak of a genuinely moral act. Only when the will turns entirely and exclusively toward the form of the law, when the law as such becomes its motive as well as its object, when the law is fulfilled because it is the law—only then does the will act morally.

Given such assumptions, the moral activity of the will requires a complete turning away from all goods. As long as the will in its activity strives for any good whatsoever, even a good of the objectively highest order, we are not dealing with morality. Such a position, however, which results from an unconditional break with experience, does not embrace any concrete human action within its scope. A concrete action by its very nature aims at some good, and so in every real human action arising from the will we must encounter an inclination toward some good. Such human action, therefore, is still without moral worth, even though the inclination toward an objective good constitutes the matter of an ethical act. For Kant, the fact that an act of will aims at some good is ethically irrelevant. The act derives its whole ethical quality solely from its form, and not at all from its matter. The will must, therefore, focus only on the form and ignore the matter—and then it takes on ethical worth. Through his formalism, Kant ended up maintaining that what Aristotle, St. Thomas, and all their followers called an ethical act ceased to have an empirical counterpart. The ethical act—given Kant's assumptions—disappeared from the empirical order and remained only in the noumenal sphere. There, beyond all experience, is the place where the will turns completely toward the form of universal legislation, which is expressed in a categorical imperative with the following content: "Act in such a way that your action could become a principle of universal legislation." (Kant regards this content as completely *a priori*, arising from practical reason without any relation to experience.) There, too, in the noumenal sphere of humanity, the immanence of freedom in practical reason, by virtue of the categorical imperative itself, is realized in a positive sense as the autonomy of practical reason. In the imperative, practical reason is legislative through its own form and is thus completely independent of the "matter" of any good in the empirical order. But can the categorical imperative, thus understood, be found in any concrete human action known from experience?

This distancing of the genuinely ethical from the concrete content of human experience escapes being unconditional and complete only to the extent that Kant acknowledges a feeling of respect for the law. It is rather significant that a feeling should have met with such distinction in Kant's eyes, for he regarded all other feelings as a hotbed of eudaimonism and hedonism in the ethical life of the human being. This singular feeling, on the other hand, became in his system an expression of the whole ethical life in the subjective sense.[9] Objective ethical life is contained in the noumenal sphere. It is impossible, however, to deny that every person also experiences ethical content. Since for Kant the law is what constitutes true ethical content, the experience of that content can only take the form of respect for the law. Kant emphasizes that this respect has an emotional nature. The feeling of respect for the law is the only feeling that has no contact with any goods of the empirical world but is aroused solely by reason and its *a priori* form of the moral law. Hence, the more one nourishes such a feeling, the more deeply one experiences duty, which is nothing but a total subordination of the will to the law just because it is the law. We have no other way of verifying in the empirical order that the will is truly subordinated to the law alone—that the will is truly "living" ethically. A mere analysis of human acts tells us nothing in this regard, whereas a feeling of respect for the law is an infallible sign of what is happening in the noumenal sphere of the will.

Now that we have before us an outline of the Kantian view of ethical life we may ask: Wherein lies that "separation of experience from the act in ethics" referred to in the title of this article? It lies in the fact that 1) Kant removed the very essence of ethical life from the realm of personal experience and transferred it to the noumenal, trans-empirical sphere, and 2) he crystalized the whole ethical experience of the personal subject into a single psychological element: the feeling of respect for the law. There can be no doubt that the experience of duty, which may be accompanied by a feeling of respect for the law, is contained in the empirical structural whole we define as ethical experience and upon which the concept of the ethical act is based. On the other hand, the Kantian experience of duty as crystalized only in the feeling of respect for the law is not identical to the feeling of duty that is contained in the empirical structural whole of ethical experience. The experience of duty is one of the elements of this whole. It cannot be said, however, that within the structural whole of ethical experience Kant only emphasized the element of duty. For Kant, duty is not just the dominant feature of ethical life: it constitutes the *whole* ethical life of the human person. Kant does not merely emphasize the feeling of respect for the law *within* the total empirical ethical experience, *within* the total act, but he truly detaches this feeling from it, because for him human acts viewed empirically as structural wholes do not contain genuine ethical experience. Consequently, the feeling of respect for the law is not contained in human acts as an internal cofactor of their concrete structure. It appears only alongside various human acts as an external sign of the ethical quality that the will possesses in the noumenal order beyond experience. Thus, the "act" as a concept reflecting the empirical structural whole of ethical experience disappears from ethics. Ethical life lies concealed beyond the boundaries of experience. And yet, because it is impossible to deny that ethical life nevertheless has an empirical character and is expressed in some sort of experience, the whole of that life becomes "empirically" subjectified in this one psychological act, the feeling of respect for the law.

3. THE EXPERIENCE OF VALUES IN SCHELER'S THOUGHT

We know what an influence Kant had on the philosophy of the 19th century and what an influence his critique still has on philosophy today. This influence was felt by individual thinkers as well as by whole schools, such as the Marburg School and the Baden School. Kant's criticism also paved the way for positivism in philosophy, and certainly for positivism in ethics and the theory of law. In the latter part of the 19th century, however, a reaction against Kantianism arose in various circles of philosophical thought. Neo-Thomism, on the one hand, and Marxism, on the other, rejected Kantian idealism and subjectivism. Here, however, I wish to draw particular attention to the philosophy of Franz Brentano and his student Edmund Husserl. Husserl is the founder of the contemporary phenomenological school, to which Max Scheler also belongs. Scheler, in turn, deserves consideration because he formulated an ethical system in the context of phenomenology that contrasts sharply with Kant's system. After nearly one hundred and fifty years, the Kantian ethics of law and duty finally met with a vocal critique from the direction of a contemporary phenomenologist. Scheler's main work, *Der Formalismus in der Ethik und die materiale Wertethik*,[10] already even in its title sets itself against Kant's ethical views. Scheler's opposition to Kant stemmed from his different relation to experience and was crystalized in his notion that value, not duty, is the essential element of ethical experience.

As far as its relation to experience is concerned, phenomenology—despite the similarity of its name—differs decisively from Kantian phenomenalism. Phenomenalism assumes that the essence of a thing is unknowable; phenomenology, on the other hand, accepts the essence of a thing just as it appears to us in immediate experience. Phenomenology is therefore intuitionistic. It does not make a clear distinction between sensory and rational elements in human knowledge, and it attaches no weight to abstraction. It treats knowledge as a certain whole known from experience; experience, in turn, reveals the phenomenological essence of objects and the relations and connections occurring between them. As to the manifestation of this essence, not only does the so-called cognitive faculty have a role to play here, but emotional factors are also especially important in bringing to our consciousness certain spheres of objective reality. Some phenomenologists even assign the greater role here to emotional factors: reality manifests itself primarily through them, and not through the factors traditionally qualified as cognitive (the senses and reason). This is precisely Scheler's position. He is an emotionalist in his theory of cognition; he is likewise an emotionalist in his ethical views.

When it is said that the essence of a thing is manifested in immediate experience, this should not be understood to mean the essence in the metaphysical sense. What interests phenomenologists is not what a thing is in itself, but how something manifests itself to us in immediate experience. Phenomenologists do not have the kind of cognitive ambitions that Aristotelians and Thomists have—they do not give priority to the philosophy of being; but then, on the other hand, they also differ from Kantians, who sever experience from the noumenal essence of a thing.

In the present inquiry, I am interested in the problem of the ethical act and ethical experience. In the light of phenomenology's epistemological assumptions presented above, it is obvious that phenomenology contributed, by virtue of those assumptions, to a partial rebuilding of the relation to the experience of ethical life that had been completely demolished by Kant. Scheler's ethics is indubitable proof of this. He treats the ethical life in the context of the assumptions of his system. Every lived event, including the ethical event, directly imposes itself on experience and in this experience reveals its phenomenological essence. The phenomenological method adopted by Scheler allows him to approach ethical life as an empirical whole and to arrive at a certain interpretation of it. And so right in the point of departure we already seem to be far removed from Kant's position. Scheler's assumptions guarantee that he will investigate the ethical experience of the human person as a lived experience, for he is a phenomenologist; he passed from a position of apriorism and subjectivism to a position of objectivism. He also does not try to reduce the entire scientific-investigative enterprise to the single empirical-inductive method used by the particular sciences.

When Scheler stands before the empirical whole constituted by human ethical experience, he immediately affirms that this experience has the character of a personal act.[11] This diagnosis might make him look like an Aristotelian in our eyes, but on closer examination we must reject that notion. Scheler is not an Aristotelian, although his view of the structures of ethical experience contains certain reminiscences of Aristotle. These reminiscences come by way of Brentano, whose philosophy took shape in contact with the views of the Stagirite. Nevertheless, the act of which Scheler speaks is not act in the Aristotelian sense; it does not signify the actualization of a potency. It is only the so-called intentional act. This concept was introduced by Brentano,[12] who studied the structure of human psychic acts. Brentano maintained, in opposition to Kant, that to the extent that these acts are subjective, they remain in the realm of consciousness; the objects toward which they are turned, however, do not come from the subject, but are transcendent in relation to it. Because psychic acts turn toward such transcendent objects on account of consciousness, they are called *intentional* acts (from the term *intendere*). The objects of intentional acts can be either ideal or real, abstract or concrete. In each case, we are dealing with an intentional act. It would be hard not to admit that such a view, born of reliable psychological research, constitutes a basic step in the direction of empirical reality and, in particular, in the direction of the reconstruction of the very contours of the ethical act.

Scheler perceives in ethical experience an intentional element, and along with it the structure of an intentional act. The intentional element that resides in every ethical experience is value. On behalf of value, Scheler declares war on the ethics of Kant, who detached the whole ethical life of the human being from values, from goods, and confined it to the noumenal sphere, relegating it entirely to duty. Scheler goes so far as to reject duty in ethics completely, seeing it as a basically negative and destructive factor.[13] Only value as an objective content of experience has ethical significance. The possibility that duty might be an objective content of experience is something Scheler does not even consider, and the notion that duty could arise in this objective content from value itself is something he refuses to admit into his system at all. Value and duty oppose one another and are mutually exclusive. It would be difficult to deny that Scheler here set himself in extreme opposition to Kant; on the other hand, he lost touch with the real, organic, empirical whole of ethical experience. There can be no doubt that this experience includes the element of duty. I do not, of course, mean duty as merely a feeling of respect for the law, as a psychological factor detached from the lived structural whole of ethical experience. I mean the element of duty within the structural whole of the ethical experience of the human person. Scheler rejects this element and presents value as the sole content of this experience.

And so all we can find in the structure of authentic ethical experience are intentional acts directed toward values. These intentional acts are primarily acts of an emotional nature, because the experience of value is based exclusively on emotional acts. According to Scheler, reason only apprehends being; it does not apprehend the good. Only the "thing-like" structure of objects manifests itself to reason. This structure, however, is neither the most important nor the most fundamental. The primordial element of objective reality is value, and we grasp value in a proper and adequate way only in emotional experience. Consequently, Scheler maintains the primacy of emotion, which entails in a certain sense the primacy of practice over theory and the primacy of ethics over knowledge. The emotional experience of values is still a cognitive experience, but it is not one in the first place. Fundamentally, emotional experience is simply either love or hate, which, says Scheler, does not arise from knowledge but just the opposite: knowledge arises from it. This knowledge born of purely emotional love or hate takes the form of intentional feelings in which the respective objective values manifest themselves. Scheler in this regard adopts a position of emotional intuitionism, which underlies his ethical system as a whole.[14] The emotional intuition of values not only allows us to feel values but also allows us to arrange them in a hierarchy, since specific values manifest themselves in feeling as either higher or lower, as well as highest or lowest. Consequently, the whole difficulty connected with the rational hierarchization of values disappears; in fact, reason should be excluded from the experience of values as much as possible. We each have our own world of values (*Ethos*), which arises on the basis of our emotional life and is the expression of the love or hate by which we live. This should not, however, be understood to mean that values are purely subjective or that they are exclusively a function of experience. Values are objective; they inhere in objective reality. Emotional experience allows each of us to make personal contact with them and in this contact to live by them, by their specific content, which does not manifest itself in its true essence outside of emotional experience.

Scheler acknowledges that, in the structural whole that we know from experience as the ethical life of the person, we are dealing not only with feeling but also with the realization of value. And yet he never really fully explains to us what this realization of value means. He tells us only that it takes place in intentional acts of a nature different from feeling, in acts of striving and willing.[15] Acts of willing turn toward values—this much we know of the structure of that realization the phenomenologist perceived in ethical experience. When acts of willing turn toward values, the person remains in some felt relation to the feeling itself of those values. Scheler tells us that in this feeling some values are higher, others lower. The person who turns toward them in willing is aware of the kind of values toward which he or she turns. The respective values naturally draw the person toward themselves—hence, Scheler speaks of the phenomenon of emotional motivation. When the values felt to be higher draw the person toward themselves insofar as the person's willing is directed toward them, then in such a realization of values the person feels "good."[16] "Good" is a positive ethical value that, like every other value, manifests itself in emotional intuition. The person, in realizing higher objective values, feels this "good" directly within, and as a result of this feeling an experience takes place. This experience culminates in ethical value and, strictly speaking, consists once again in feeling, and not in realization, not in willing. In relation to the feeling of "good," the willing of value plays the role of something material.

Scheler describes his system as an ethics of material values. Material values play the leading role in ethical experience, and true ethical values are also merely a variety of material values. Most importantly, ethical values are not an object of willing. The person's willing not only does not turn toward ethical values but simply cannot. If a person were to will the "good," then, in the light of what we know of Scheler's assumptions, that person would want to feel inwardly "good," would want to feel that he or she *is* good—and such an attitude would bespeak something pharisaical. That is how Scheler views the matter. Nevertheless, this view of his proves that "good," in the very same way as "evil," is inseparably connected with emotional experience and somehow enmeshed in emotion, such that the acting person cannot separate the good from emotion and realize it with a full sense of objectivity and disinterestedness.

The situation with respect to the experience of negative ethical value is similar to that of the experience of positive value. When the person allows himself or herself to be drawn to a value intuitively felt as lower and makes this value an object of willing, then this willing is associated in feeling with the experience of "evil." Clearly, however, such a cognitive feeling of "good" or "evil" is based within the whole structure of the person's emotional life on the purely emotional experience of love or hate. Love, as a purely emotional act, tends to expand the human being's whole *a priori* relation to values; it makes the person's world of values richer. Scheler, therefore, speaks of a certain kind of emotional *a priori* in the life of the human being.[17] Hate, again as a purely emotional act, reduces and narrows the human being's *a priori* relation to values; it makes the person's world of values poorer. That is what happens in the case of the different objective values that form the "material" object of willing. In the case of "good" and "evil," however, the emotional core of the person reacts with particular force. These values produce not just a feeling that has an intentional character, but an experience of happiness or despair that encompasses the whole human being, an experience that, from the point of view of intensity, has no equal in the whole emotional life. The happiness evoked by the experience "good" and the despair evoked by the experience "evil" are so great that Scheler sees absolutely no sense in allowing any external sanctions into ethical life. After all, no "good" evokes such happiness and no "evil" such despair as positive and negative ethical values. Once again, however, we see how deeply Schelerian values are inextricably enmeshed in emotional experience. I should add that in ethical life thus conceived Scheler also distinguishes a relative degree from an unconditional degree. Ethical life takes on an unconditional degree when the object of willing is the value that the acting person feels as the highest value. The person then also experiences unconditional "good." When, on the other hand, the person in willing realizes the value felt as the lowest, he or she then experiences unconditional "evil." If we grant that a person's love is susceptible to such a highest value and the person's hate to such a lowest value, we can fathom the whole depth of happiness associated with the turning of willing toward the former and the whole depth of despair when willing turns toward the latter.

I must admit that the picture of ethical life that Scheler has painted using only his phenomenological method is very suggestive and in many points agrees beautifully with what we know from inner experience. The suggestiveness of the picture, however, does not make it immune criticism. Scheler based his interpretation of ethical experience on a concept of intentional act that he inherited from Brentano. The content of this experience is simply value, and if the element of duty should happen to get mixed in one should try to expunge it. Value is only experienced emotionally, and so ethical experience is an emotional experience from beginning to end. Emotion determines the inner unity, the cohesion and continuity, of ethical experience. Ethical experience arises from emotion and returns to it. Emotion is the authentic ground of personal life, since through it the person comes in contact with what is most important and most fundamental in objective reality—value. It is precisely this notion of Scheler's regarding the essence—and even the phenomenological essence—of ethical experience with which I take issue. The structure of ethical experience, that whole that we all know from our own inner experience, does not consist primarily in emotion, even though I am willing to concede that an emotional cofactor plays a significant role in it. The central structural element of ethical experience is the element of willing. Scheler is aware of this element, but he proceeds true to his emotionalistic views, probably with the aim of distancing himself as far as possible from Kant's ethics, whose main error Scheler took to be the supremacy of duty taken to the point of the total rejection of value and the feelings through which we come in living contact with value.

According to Scheler, willing—or the act of will, if one prefers to use nonphenomenological terminology—is not the structural backbone of ethical experience. Willing as such does not have ethical value. Although ethical value emerges only "on the occasion" (*auf dem Rücken*) of willing, it does not emerge from willing but—as always—from emotion. In that case, however, the person does not realize ethical values, good and evil, the values that belong most intimately to the person. We are standing here in the presence of the phenomenologist's fatal mistake. Scheler fails to perceive a most elementary and basic truth, namely, that the only value that can be called ethical value is a value that has the acting person as its efficient cause. The kind of emotional atmosphere in which such a value arises and in which it becomes a property or real quality of a given person is already something secondary. What is primary is the fact that this value comes from the person as its efficient cause. And this is also where the very core of ethical experience lies. Because Scheler did not manage to objectify this basic fact in his phenomenological interpretation of ethical experience, his whole interpretation deals only with secondary elements, which he tries—at times rather artificially—to elevate to the primary level. This is the error of Schelerian emotionalism, and both the will and reason, along with its theoretical and practical cognitive powers, fell victim to it.

Scheler speaks of willings that have the character of intentional acts but that are different from feelings. Still, the dependence of these willings on feelings is so great that we can assume that they, too, in their inner essence are acts of an emotional nature. They do not exhibit, in Scheler's interpretation, any innate activity of their own; they merely submit to emotional motivation. This submission is already somehow determined *a priori* in the emotional organization of the person. As far as the will's relation to reason is concerned, Scheler retains only a meager vestige of a relation, speaking of presentations that always accompany willings but do not accompany other appetitive experiences of the person. These presentations, however, play no role in directing willings toward a particular value. This role belongs exclusively to the emotions. The will is one of the functions of the emotional life. We should, however, consider the consequences this has for the whole concept of the person and, in particular, for the concept of the ethical life of the person. According to Scheler, the person is deprived of will to the extent that each of the person's willings remains in the power of an *a priori* emotional element, which for Scheler is the most profound and decisive factor in ethical life. Consequently, the person cannot attain acts of an efficient character, acts that have the person as their efficient cause. And yet the experience of this efficacy of the person stands at the basis of our every ethical act. We experience "good" or "evil" because we experience ourselves as the efficient cause of our own acts.

Scheler, then, based the entire ethical experience on secondary elements, because he stripped it of the backbone of the will. And here we must reproach Scheler from the standpoint of phenomenology itself. There is no doubt that the initial discovery of the will takes place in the context of phenomenological experience. A whole contemporary school of the psychology of the will, using the empirical-inductive method, bases its cognitive investigations on this discovery. This school takes its origin from Narziss Ach and Albert Michotte; it also finds representatives in Poland in the persons of Edward Abramowski, Mieczyslaw Dybowski, Wladyslawa Mielczarska, Józef Reutt, and others.[18] The representatives of this school have pointed out repeatedly that we encounter the will immediately (phenomenologically) precisely in that experience in which we experience ourselves as the efficient cause of our acts.[19] I am convinced that a deeper awareness of the nature of the will can be achieved only by a thorough analysis of ethical experience. Such an analysis gives us all the more reason not to doubt that ethical experience implies a lived experience of the efficacy of the person, an experience in which the will manifests itself phenomenologically as a basic structural element of the whole empirical fact. Because Scheler did not emphasize this element to the same degree in which it appears in ethical experience, his whole phenomenological interpretation of the ethical fact significantly departs from experience.

4. THE NEED FOR A PROPER RELATION TO EXPERIENCE IN ETHICS

Kant's approach to the ethical fact resulted in a division between two elements of ethical life. One of them is an *a priori* rational element, which is expressed in normative judgments arising from the content of the categorical imperative; this element is to be investigated separately by logical methods. The other is an experience that takes the form of the feeling of respect for the law; this element, like any other psychological phenomenon, is to be investigated by psychological methods. Thus Kant's critical approach to ethics split the unified content of ethics, reducing it to logic and psychology respectively. Such a split, however, is at flagrant odds with experience. The facts of ethical life cannot be reduced to logic and psychology because ethical experience is a personal whole whose specific properties cease to be themselves apart from this whole. One element that is not itself is the so-called real element of the ethical experience of duty, crystalized by Kant merely in the feeling of respect for the law. In real ethical experience, duty is something more than just this feeling of respect for the law. But another element that is not itself is the so-called real element of the ethical experience of value, conceived as proposed by Scheler in the light of his concept of ethical experience. In the empirical structural whole that we know as ethical experience, value (and I am speaking here mainly of ethical value) is something else. It is by nature primarily a work of the person, brought about causally in the individual's personal essence, and not just an objective content felt in this essence. We see, then, in both of these views so important for the history of ethics, Kant's and Scheler's alike, that the abandonment of the ancient concept of the ethical act led in their respective interpretations to a certain distortion of ethical experience itself.

As far as Scheler's view is concerned, there can be no doubt that in many respects it not only opposes the Kantian ethics of pure duty, but it also attempts to overcome Kant's assumptions. This is especially apparent in the case of the relation to psychological experience. The view of the ethical act that Scheler borrowed from Brentano freed him considerably from the legacy of subjectivism and apriorism that Kant left behind. But Scheler still retained a certain degree of apriorism. He replaced the noumenal depth of the person with a poorly defined emotional depth, which determines the course of the person's ethical life in an *a priori* way. Dynamism, however, is completely absent from this view. The person does not act—or at least the activity of the person does not bear any visible signs of the person's own efficacy—because the autonomy of the will is reduced to practically zero. Scheler's entire philosophy lacks a concept of motion, change, actualization. If he speaks of modifications in the emotional life, he does not have in mind any dynamic changes, but only the expansion or contraction of the field of feeling with respect to content, and mainly with respect to the hierarchical scale of experienced values. This adynamic character of the assumptions of Schelerian philosophy, which reflects the essentialism of phenomenology as a whole, does not provide a proper context for interpreting ethical experience. Ethical experience is by its very nature something dynamic; its whole psychological structure involves motion: a passage from potency to act. And ethical experience found just such a dynamic structure in the Aristotelian theory of potency and act, which also served as the basis for constructing an authentic conception of the ethical act.

The concept of intentional act is a kind of timid reference to the structure of Aristotelian philosophy. In Scheler's case, however, we see that this concept does not suffice to interpret the empirical whole constituted by ethical experience. This experience appears in his view not so much as a single intentional act but more as an aggregate or bundle of such acts, some of which have the character of the feeling of value and others the character of willing or realizing the felt values. Scheler, as we have seen, believes that true ethical experience should be sought in the latter rather than in the former. Within the structural whole, however, the ethical act appears as composed of a whole series of intuitive psychological elements, because each intentional act within the whole forms an empirical whole of its own. While it is true that each of these intentional elements is in some way turned toward value, this circumstance alone does not determine the ethical character of either any one of these elements taken individually or the structural whole they together compose. What Scheler gives us, then, is a very penetrating study in the area of the psychology of values, but not an interpretation of ethical experience. Scheler is convinced that he does provide an interpretation of such experience, but in point of fact this is not the case. The structural whole of ethical experience contains not only values as its objective content, but also a normative element in which these values are organized and presented as a task to be fulfilled. This task, which arises from the normal character of ethical experience, entails duty. We can be certain, then, that values alone do not exhaust the content of ethical life—if we take experience as our guide for knowledge of this life.

As we know, Kant in his view divorced the norm from experience. Experience then remains in an external relation to the norm: it is the feeling of respect for the law, but it does not manifest any immanence of the normative element. And yet authentic ethical experience *does* manifest such an immanence. Ethical experience is not just an experience of value but also an experience of the realization of the good. When Scheler rejected the experience of duty, he thought he had set himself in complete opposition to Kantianism in ethics. In fact, however, he rejected only the whole normative side of Kant's ethics and the logical problematic of ethical judgments and confined himself to the other side of it—the one Kant in his theory assigned to those who investigate ethics empirically. Scheler remained in the psychological sphere of experience, and here he set himself in opposition to duty while accentuating value. This is precisely why he did not manage effectively to extricate himself from Kant's assumptions, which entail the divorce of experience from the norm and the reduction of the whole of ethics to logic and psychology. And so Scheler, too, despite all the changes he introduced with his system, treats the experience of value—and there can be no doubt that this also includes ethical value—in separation from the ethical act. Ethical value manifests itself in the background (*auf dem Rücken*), and the very act, the very realization, in which (if we go by experience) this value actually arises remains outside this experience of ethical value; it remains, as in Kant's view, something merely material. Scheler in his view does not capture the full immanence of the ethical in the object of experience. Are these not, then, despite all Scheler says, remnants of Kantian noumenalism in his ethics?

Scheler in his phenomenology partially rebuilt the relation to experience. What we need, however, is a complete restoration of this relation. Ethical experience forms a certain structural whole, which cannot be split up into logical and psychological elements, the investigation of which is then reduced to the methods of logic and psychology. Ethics has a distinctive method because it is based on a distinctive experience. The method of a given science must always respect the experience upon which that science is based, since all our knowledge is built on experience. Hence, the first condition for pursuing ethics as a science is a proper relation to experience. As a result of such a relation to experience, one in which ethical life is grasped as an organic unity and a structural whole, ethics ceases to be an allogeneic conglomerate of logic when dealing with the normative character of ethics and psychology when considering the experiential side. At this point I am convinced that the ethics of Aristotle and St. Thomas Aquinas is based on a proper relation to experience and, moreover, that their view of the ethical act is the only proper and adequate description of ethical experience. I shall, however, have to put off presenting the justification for this conviction to another occasion.

NOTES

1. The terms *ethical* and *moral*, though different in meaning, are used interchangeably in this essay.

2. See, for example, Aristotle, *Moralium Eudemiorum* I, 6, 9–11, and Thomas Aquinas, *Summa theologiae* I–II, 1, 1–2.

3. "The moral law is the only condition under which freedom can be known" (Immanuel Kant, *Critique of Practical Reason*, trans. Lewis White Beck [Indianapolis: Bobbs, 1956] 4n).

4. "The will...is a faculty either of bringing forth objects corresponding to conceptions or of determining itself, i.e., its causality to effect such objects (whether the physical power is sufficient to this or not)" (Kant, *Critique of Practical Reason* 15).

5. Immanuel Kant, *Foundations of the Metaphysics of Morals*, trans. Lewis White Beck (Indianapolis: Bobbs, 1959).

6. "Reason [is] a truly higher faculty of desire, but still only in so far as it determines the will by itself and not in the service of the inclinations. Subordinate to reason as the higher faculty of desire is the pathologically determinable faculty of desire, the latter being really and in kind different from the former, so that even the slightest admixture of its impulses impairs the strength and superiority of reason" (Kant, *Critique of Practical Reason* 23–24).

7. "If all material of a law, i.e., every object of the will considered as a ground of its determination, is abstracted from it, nothing remains except the mere form of giving universal law" (Kant, *Critique of Practical Reason* 26).

8. "A free will must find its ground of determination in the law, but independently of the material of the law. But besides the latter there is nothing in a law except the legislative form. Therefore, the legislative form, in so far as it is contained in the maxim, is the only thing which can constitute a determining ground of the [free] will" (Kant, *Critique of Practical Reason* 28–29).

9. "Thus respect for the law is not the incentive to morality; it is morality itself, regarded subjectively as an incentive" (Kant, *Critique of Practical Reason* 78).

10. Max Scheler, *Der Formalismus in der Ethik und die materiale Wertethik: Neuer Versuch der Grundlegung eines ethischen Personalismum* (Halle, 1916). [For the English edition see Max Scheler, *Formalism in Ethics and Non-Formal Ethics of Values: A New Attempt Toward the Foundation of an Ethical Personalism*, trans. Manfred S. Frings and Roger L. Funk (Evanston: Northwestern UP, 1973).]

11. See Scheler, "Person and Act," *Formalism* 382–476.

12. Franz Brentano's main work is his book *Psychology from an Empirical Standpoint*, trans. Antos C. Rancurello, D. B. Terrell, and Linda L. McAlister (New York: Humanities, 1973). See also *Vom Ursprung der sittlichen Erkenntnis* (Hamburg: Meiner, 1969) and his works on Aristotle: *Aristotle and His World*

View, trans. Rolf George and Roderick M. Chisholm (Berkeley: U of California P, 1978); *Aristoteles Lehre vom Ursprung des menschlichen Geistes* (Leipzig: Veit, 1911); *The Psychology of Aristotle*, trans. Rolf George (Berkeley: U of California P, 1977); *On the Several Senses of Being in Aristotle*, trans. Rolf George (Berkeley: U of California P, 1975).

13. See Scheler, "Value and the Ought," *Formalism* 203–238.

14. See Scheler, "'Higher' and 'Lower' Values," *Formalism* 86–100.

15. See Scheler, "Conation, Values, and Goals," *Formalism* 30–38.

16. See Scheler, "The Relation of the Values 'Good' and 'Evil' to the Other Values and Goods," *Formalism* 23–30.

17. See Scheler, "The Non-Formal A Priori in Ethics," *Formalism* 81–110.

18. See Narziss Ach, *Über den Willensakt und das Temperament* (Leipzig: Quelle, 1910); Mieczyslaw Dybowski, *Dzialanie woli na tle badan eksperymentalnych* [*The Activity of the Will in the Light of Experimental Investigations*] (Poznan, 1946); and Józef Reutt, *Przedstawienie celu a postepowanie* [*The Presentation of Goals in Relation to Behavior*] (Poznan, 1947).

19. See, for example, Johannes Lindworsky, *Der Wille: Seine Erscheinung und seine Beherrschung* (Leipzig: Barth, 1923) 21.

3

In Search of the Basis
of Perfectionism in Ethics

1. THE PROBLEM

The aim of this article is to present a sketch of a problem that, to develop in full, would require an extensive monographic study. Ethics attempts to define what is good and evil in human actions, not being content with a compilation of what in various circumstances may seem or have seemed to be good or evil. Its task is directive—and in this character it is a practical science. Because, however, the direction in question is the direction of actions in keeping with what is objectively good and evil, ethics has a normative character—and in this character it is a practical science. When in ethics we emphasize that a good action essentially perfects the person performing that action, we are then speaking of perfectionism in ethics. We also sometimes speak of perfectionism in another sense,[1] although the difference in meaning probably does not deserve too much attention. Perfectionism in the first sense involves more than perfectionism in the second sense to the extent that it places the emphasis on the person becoming better through each good action, whereas perfectionism in the second sense speaks of the moral improvement of the person in general. In this essay, I will be using the term *perfectionism* in the first sense.

Perfectionism is not identical with the normativism of ethics. We can, after all, define what is good or evil—the kind of action that is objectively good or evil—while abstracting from the fact that the action either perfects the person performing it or devalues that person's humanity. In any case,

Karol Wojtyla, "W poszukiwaniu podstaw perfekcjoryzmu w etyce," *Roczniki Filozoficzne* 5.4 (1955–57): 303–317.

it is generally agreed that a person is perfected morally by good actions and devalued by bad ones. Perfectionism is an important aspect of the moral life. This aspect must find a reflection in ethics, if ethics claims to have a comprehensive view of the facts of moral life. As I said above, this perfectionistic aspect, which consists in emphasizing that the person who acts well is perfected morally and vice versa, is not identical in ethics with the normative aspect, which concerns only the definition of what is morally good and evil. Even so, it should be noted that a norm in ethics in a sense stands out more fully against the background of perfectionism and in connection with it. Ethics is always in some way about the human being; the human being is—in the broadest sense of the term—the material object of ethics. Norms, therefore, do not have full meaning apart from the human being, who, by living according to them, simply lives in a good way and is perfected as a human being, or, in the opposite case, deteriorates and loses value. In the present article, which is only a sketch of this important problem, I will attempt to show that the perfectionistic aspect in ethics appears in an adequate way only if we adopt the assumptions of the philosophy of being. The ethics of Aristotle and St. Thomas can serve as proof of this. When, on the other hand, the philosophical system proceeds from an analysis of consciousness alone, the perfectionistic aspect disappears from the ethics based on such a system. We see this in Kant and in the contemporary phenomenologist Max Scheler. I have selected these two thinkers here in order to show, by contrasting them with the two mentioned earlier, that only the assumptions of the philosophy of being allow us to construct a consistent perfectionistic ethics.

2. ARISTOTLE AND ST. THOMAS AQUINAS

Aristotle considers the good in the context of being. Wherever we encounter a purposive tendency, we find both a being and an end toward which that being tends. This end is a good. If to be a good is to be an object of a tendency or desire, this means that the good in some way and in some sphere corresponds to the nature of the being that tends toward or desires it. This correspondence, in turn, is highlighted in the fact that the good perfects the being. As we can see, Aristotle, in keeping with his style of philosophizing, bases himself first and foremost solidly on experience. In experience we everywhere encounter the fact of tendencies toward ends. This fact testifies that the good is a constitutive element of reality. The good is an end: that at which a thing aims. In order to explain why the thing aims at the good as an end, we must turn our attention to the being that does the aiming and consider its nature. We find that the good is always that which in some way corresponds to this nature, that which contains what is needed to perfect this nature in some respect. And so, at the close of this philosophical reflection on the relations that occur in empirical reality between being and the good as an end, we find perfectionism. The good is that which contitutes the object of an aim, i.e., an end—the good is that which perfects a being: the essence of Aristotle's philosophy of the good can be summed up in these two statements.

This philosophy formed the basis for his ethics.[2] Aristotle's ethics is a science about human beings, who, in striving for various goods, must seek above all the good most suited to their rational nature. Such a good is the proper end of human life and activity; all other goods should serve as means to this end. Aristotle teaches that such a good makes us profoundly happy; it is also a befitting good [*bonum honestum*], one that makes us perfect and objectively worthy of esteem. The perfection in question here is moral perfection, which finds expression in the possession of virtues that lead us to strive for various goods beyond ourselves, while constantly realizing the basic good that resides within our very own person. This inner good is the ultimate end of human activity; for it, we should do all that we do as rational, conscious beings. As can be seen, Aristotle's ethics is deeply humanistic, and his humanism is ethical to the core: human fulfillment is brought about by moral perfection. To avoid any suspicion that there might be a possible individualism lurking in the Aristotelian notion of perfectionism, we need only recall that for Aristotle ethics is a part of politics, the science of the morally good life of society. A person characterized by moral perfection is not an egoist seeking only his or her own good, but a mature personality who constantly takes into account the real requirements of the common good.

There was much about the concept of perfectionism in Aristotle's ethics that lent itself to being transplanted onto the soil of Christian philosophy and moral theology, once his view was amended to reflect the new truth about human beings and human perfection presented by revelation.[3] The acceptance of the Aristotelian concept of perfectionism in ethics, as was true of many other philosophical concepts, was the work of St. Thomas Aquinas. And so we should now turn to a consideration of the relation that exists between the concept of perfectionism in St. Thomas' ethics and his philosophical concept of the good.

Aquinas proceeds, like Aristotle, from an affirmation of the strict connection that occurs between the good and being. This assertion took on new force in the light of numerous remarks in Genesis and other books of the Bible—and it had already been enunciated frequently by St. Augustine.[4] Aquinas, in his philosophy of the good, appeals to the traditions of both Aristotle and St. Augustine. The good is the end of a being, since it makes the being perfect. And so the good is always the perfection of a being. St. Thomas paid particular attention to this aspect of the good. His philosophy of being takes fully into account the whole dynamism of reality. Reality is dynamic, for we observe that beings undergo change. A change is always an actualization of some potency. The actualization of potency consists in the real coming-into-existence of something that previously existed only in potency—in other words, really did not exist. Once a being has already begun to exist and continues to exist, actualization is the perfection of that being. Thus the actualization of potency in a being is linked to the perfection of that being. Actualization, then, always refers to some passage from nonexistence to existence, and act always implies existence; consequently, every perfection or good consists in existence. St. Thomas believes that this thesis is supported by a perceptive observation of reality. After all, the thing that every being defends most of all is its existence.

Existence is, therefore, the most basic good. Furthermore, we call a being good only to the extent that we find in it the fullness of the existence proper to it: not just when its substance exists (*ens simpliciter*), but when all the accidents needed in it exist as well (*entia secundum quid*). Only then do we say that the being is completely good in its kind (*bonum simpliciter*). Substance alone is only a *bonum secundum quid*, and the absence or nonexistence of any needed accident is an imperfection of that being—an evil. Thus existence is decisive for the good. A being that is self-subsistent existence, namely, God, is also the unconditional fullness of good and, as such, is self-subsistent good. Every being other than God, even if it has the fullness of existence proper to its nature (which is relative, of course), has only a certain participation (*participatio*) in the unconditional fullness of good that is God.

The fullness of existence suitable for a given being by reason of its nature is nothing other than perfection. St. Thomas,[5] proceeding from Aristotelian tenets, adopted a position of realism in his view of the good, and he also incorporated into his philosophy of the good the Platonic doctrine of participation, reformulated in a realistic spirit by St. Augustine. Realism consists in connecting the good with being. All beings are good.

One being is a good with respect to another if the other being tends toward it for its own perfection. The good is that which perfects a being in some respect, that which actualizes a being, that which somehow enhances a being's existence in keeping with its nature.

In this existential view of the good—which is how we may refer to St. Thomas' view—the identification of the good with being is understood precisely in terms of perfectionism as the principle of advancing toward perfection, a law that applies to every being. His philosophy of the good is thoroughly immersed in the philosophy of being, understood existentially and dynamically. St. Thomas' ethics is also thoroughly situated in the philosophy of being. Our every conscious activity is an actualization of our rational essence and thus perfects some aspect of our being. If this activity corresponds to a good we perceive as true (*bonum sub ratione veri*), it contributes to the moral perfection of our being, whereas if it does not so correspond, it results in moral evil, and then our whole rational being is devalued and corrupted.

As can be seen, perfectionism, which permeates St. Thomas' view of the good to the core, has very significant consequences in his ethics. Ethics is for St. Thomas, as it was for the Stagirite, a science about human beings, who are perfected in keeping with their rational and social nature in both the natural and the supernatural order. Every element of St. Thomas' ethics flows from these perfectionistic assumptions derived from his philosophy of the good.

3. KANT AND SCHELER

Kant set about his critique of theoretical and practical reason in order to find an answer to the question: Is metaphysics as a science possible? His answer to this question turned out to be negative. Together with a rejection of the philosophy of being, Kant ushered in a crystalization of the philosophy of consciousness, for he conceived reason in his *Critiques* as an autonomous subject of activity. For Aristotle and St. Thomas, reason was a faculty of the soul, an attribute of the human being. Separated from this being and conceived as an autonomous subject of acts, reason became pure consciousness. The road to idealism was thus left wide open. The philosophy of consciousness replaced the philosophy of being.

Consciousness, according to Kant, has no access to objective transcendent being; consciousness is primarily a consciousness of its own special, *a priori*, cognitive forms, by means of which it organizes the whole multiplicity of phenomenal content. Ethics as a science can be based only on a form supplied by practical reason.[6] This is the form of universal legislation, which appears *a priori* in consciousness in the guise of an imperative. Because this form commands unconditionally, the ethical content of consciousness centered around the imperative is reducible to an active command and an experience of duty in response to the command. Such imperativism, however, does not exhaust the entire ethical content of consciousness. The experience of an imperative is linked, in Kant's view, with the experience of freedom. All determination is an actual exclusion of free will. We find such determination throughout the phenomenal world in the phenomena of nature. We also find determination in the human being when apprehended from the empirical side—in *homo phaenomenon*. When stimuli from the phenomenal world give rise to feelings of pleasure or pain, sensory consciousness undergoes determinations. Morality, however, excludes determination and is connected only with freedom. Consequently, we must seek morality, or the so-called ethical content of consciousness, in the transphenomenal *homo noumenon*. To it alone belongs autonomy, or freedom.

This autonomy, in turn, is intimately connected with an imperative, because the *a priori* form of practical reason is expressed in an imperative. When practical reason is directed solely and exclusively by this form, the experience of pure duty arises in practical consciousness, and in this pure duty "supersensible" humanity (*homo noumenon*) simultaneously experiences its total freedom. Duty, thus understood, is free of all determination from without, from the side of the phenomenal world; it is subject to determination only from within, from the side of consciousness. Consequently, pure duty involves the experience of self-determination, the experience of freedom—an experience that gives consciousness a certain nonsensory satisfaction. Such satisfaction places consciousness somehow above all things human. And, at the same time, in this satisfaction derived from the experience of autonomy connected with the fulfillment of duty for its own sake, consciousness finds the most fundamental affirmation of humanity.

Nowhere in this view is there mention of moral good properly speaking. One might easily conclude, however, that if this good were to be found anywhere, it would be in that act of consciousness that is pure duty. Kant does not respond to the question of what kinds of human acts are good and evil, as earlier moral philosophers attempted to do. He only tries to show what it is that gives rise to the experience of freedom or self-determination in human consciousness, for it is within this experience that morality is contained. The fact that the experience of freedom provides human beings with a complete affirmation of their "supersensible" humanity (supersensible = trans-sensory, noumenal) would suggest that moral perfection is itself in some way reducible to the self-determination or autonomy that is directly manifested in the experience of pure duty. Perhaps we have here a distant echo of perfectionistic views in ethics: the perfection proper to the human being is found in the consciousness of self-determination. The constitutive factor of ethical perfectionism transferred to the plane of the philosophy of consciousness would not be an objective moral good or a good amenable to objectification, but merely freedom as a purely immanent content of consciousness. Thus morality is explained by Kant without appealing to any objective factors—through an analysis of consciousness alone.

Max Scheler proceeded in a manner seemingly quite different from Kant.[7] Kant's subjectivistic apriorism had already been criticized by Franz Brentano in the light of psychological experience. This experience showed the structure of the psychic acts upon which moral life is based to be different from Kant's conception of it. Such acts have a distinct intentional character, a distinct direction from the subject toward an object. Consequently, Kant's subjectivistic apriorism is untenable. In its place, Scheler introduces an objectivistic apriorism: the source of the contents by which consciousness lives are not in the subject, not in consciousness, but outside of it. Scheler reconstructed the philosophy of consciousness in the light of this objectivistic assumption. I should also note at the outset that, whereas for Kant consciousness had a primarily intellectual character (consciousness = reason), for Scheler it has a primarily emotional character. Scheler is not concerned with the theoretical side of the activity of consciousness, but with its practical side. He constructs an ethics that is related to the practical sphere of consciousness. Kant's ethics of the imperative and duty met with vigorous opposition on the part of Scheler. Consciousness does not have a basically subjectivistic orientation toward some *a priori* form, from which it would then derive the whole content of its moral experiences, but has a basically objectivistic orientation toward various kinds of values.

Values, then, are an objective content of consciousness, and this content arises in consciousness when it comes in contact with the objective world of goods. What these goods are in themselves is something Scheler cannot fully explain. All he can say is that the values immediately experienced by the emotional consciousness of the person qualify as such goods. Because values are contents that always have a strictly qualitative character, and never have the nonqualitative characters of things (the term *Ding*, which Scheler uses here, bears a distinct Kantian stamp), goods must also have such a character. The original experience in which we encounter objects (*Sachen*) directly, without yet differentiating their qualitative content (values) from their nonqualitative content (things), requires us to accept goods as having a certain thing-like structure: values appear in them as a certain objective quality on the model of the unity that things possess. The good, understood as a valuable thing (*Wertding*), stands beyond consciousness. Scheler, however, does not concern himself with it, but throughout his philosophy and ethics deals only with values. In effect, then, just as in Kant, we again find ourselves exclusively in the realm of consciousness.

The moral life of this consciousness arises from experiences of an intentional character that have values as their object. These experiences are primarily feelings, and also the willings based on such feelings of values. According to Scheler, we feel that values have a hierarchy, for we experience some values as higher and others as lower. In our emotional experience, values spontaneously assume different ranks around some value felt as highest and some other value felt as lowest. Such a hierarchical feeling of values gives our experience of them a certain ethical flavor, because when we will values felt according to a certain hierarchy our whole consciousness feels new values. These are values that can be defined in no other way except as "good" (*gut*) and "evil" (*böse*)—moral values. These equally objective contents of emotional consciousness that accompany the willing of any other value are distinctive in that they only appear upon the willing of other values. They themselves, however, cannot be sought; they cannot be willed. The willing of moral value always evokes a negative reaction in emotional consciousness. Consciousness feels a certain pharisaism in such willing: to will to experience moral value (in the sense of the good, i.e., positive moral value) has something immoral about it—and consciousness feels this immediately.

Consciousness always feels positive and negative moral values in an extremely vibrant way. This feeling is accompanied by a happiness that embraces the whole person in the case of a positive value—and emotional despondency, in the case of a negative. These experiences are hard to compare with anything else; emotionally speaking, they are the most profound and intense experiences. They allow consciousness to stand face to face with the very being (*Sein*) and value (*Wertsein*) of the person.

At this point, however, we must ask a basic question: Do these values really perfect the person? This question is fundamental to our inquiry, for we are concerned here with the possibility of constructing a perfectionistic ethics. It should be noted that the Schelerian concept of value does arouse perfectionistic associations, whereas the Kantian concepts of the imperative and duty do not. In Scheler's ethical system, we find ourselves in a realm close to the ethics of Aristotle. Scheler speaks of ethical value as a typical personal value, which is always connected with the realization of a certain personal ideal. That ideal, in turn, is always realized through the imitation of personal models. This is, therefore, again the realm of the person, and the person is the proper subject of moral improvement.

A closer analysis of Scheler's system, however, shows that such perfectionistic associations are not fully warranted. The person, in Scheler's view, is in no sense a being, but is merely a unity of experiences. In every experience, e.g., in the feeling of value or in willing, we simultaneously co-experience the unity formed by all experiences. The person is merely this conscious unity of experiences, this conscious unity of acts. And so in Scheler's view the person is not a being, but solely and exclusively a consciousness. This is a consciousness of being a person, but this is not the objective being of the person. This consciousness experiences certain emotional shocks (for it is, as we know, a primarily emotional consciousness) in moral experience. Moral experience opens up this consciousness in an especially profound respect—precisely as a personal consciousness.

Be that as it may, with such assumptions one definitely cannot maintain that any values perfect the person. One also, therefore, cannot maintain that moral values perfect the person. In this view, values are merely contents of consciousness, and as such they do not perfect the being of the person. This also applies to moral values (I am speaking here of positive ones, of course). They do not perfect the person's being; they merely impress the personal consciousness in an especially deep way. It also makes no sense to speak of the perfection of consciousness itself. In St. Thomas' philosophy, the content of the cognitive act does in a certain sense perfect reason, and indirectly the person as well, to the extent that this content is true—for truth is a good, a perfection proper to reason. But in Scheler's philosophy this notion is abandoned. Every value, including moral value, is merely an intentional object of feeling. The person's intentional feelings of moral value, however, cannot be equated with the real perfection of the person's being through moral value.

Thus Scheler's system allows us to witness the perfectionistic tendencies that pervade consciousness, but it does not allow us to construct a truly perfectionistic ethics. This is, as in Kant, a consequence of an idealistic understanding of consciousness. Consciousness is understood realistically when it is connected with the person's being as its subject, when it is an act of this being. Consciousness divorced from the being of the person and treated as an autonomous subject of activity is consciousness understood idealistically. This is how Kant understood consciousness, and this is also how Scheler—despite all his differences from Kant—understood it. Such a consciousness can only be a subject of values as intentional contents, but it cannot be a subject of values as qualities that really perfect the being. The objectivism of acts of consciousness upon which Scheler based his system in contrast to Kant is still in no sense an objectification of the conscious being. But without the objectification of the conscious being, we cannot speak in any meaningful way of perfectionism in ethics.

4. CONCLUSIONS

In the discussion above, which as I said at the beginning is only a sketch, a clear opposition has emerged between the philosophy of being and the philosophy of consciousness as a basis for constructing an ethics. The philosophy of being is a realistic and objectivistic system, in which the good is identical with being, and moral life is consequently seen as the activity of perfecting the conscious being. The philosophy of consciousness, as a result of Kant's critique of the cognitive abilities of reason, can no longer produce a consistent perfectionism in ethics—even if an analysis of Scheler's system reveals rather distinct tendencies in this direction and even if we overlook the impressions made by certain passages in Kant's *Critique of Practical Reason.*

A perfectionistic ethics cannot be constructed upon the assumptions of the philosophy of consciousness, whereas an ethics constructed upon the assumptions of a realistic philosophy of being cannot help but be perfectionistic in some sense. I am not sure which part of this conclusion is more important. In any event, this dual conclusion supports the thesis I advanced at the beginning of this essay. That is why I introduced Kant and Scheler in juxtaposition to Aristotle and St. Thomas in the above discussion.

One could easily succumb to the illusion that for the construction of ethics it is best to proceed from an analysis of consciousness: if whatever is moral is also conscious, an analysis of consciousness alone should allow us to discover all that is moral, all that forms the content of ethics. In the light of the above discussion, however, this turns out not to be the case. An analysis of consciousness alone allows us to discover only the contents of consciousness. Moral good, however, is not just a content of consciousness; it is also a perfection of the conscious being—and it is this first and foremost. The perfection of a being can be apprehended only through an analysis of that being.

The ethical systems constructed by Kant and Scheler lost the perfectionistic aspect discussed at the outset because they divorced human consciousness from the objective human *being*. Consequently, the connection was severed with ethics' material object broadly understood, namely, with the human being as that object. This occurred despite both Kant's and Scheler's otherwise extremely humanistic and personalistic orientations. As a result, both the Kantian norm and the Schelerian value ended up being suspended in a vacuum, so to speak, because the complete human being is a being and not just a consciousness. The perfectionism that arises from the realistic assumptions of the philosophy of being allows us to perceive the very roots of both the norms and the values of the integral human being. And therein lies its inviolable position in ethics.

NOTES

1. Wojtyla uses two slightly different Polish terms here—*perfekcjoryzm* and *perfekcjonizm*—to refer to what I am rendering as the "first sense" and the "second sense" of perfectionism. So far as I know, there are no separate English terms that capture this subtle distinction. I have also amended the text accordingly wherever Wojtyla speaks of this distinction. —Trans.

2. My remarks in this section are based on Aristotle's ethical works. In addition to the *Nichomachean Ethics*, the other works consulted are the *Eudemian Ethics*, the authenticity of which is defended by Werner Jaeger in the monograph *Aristotle: Fundamentals of the History of His Development*, trans. Richard Robinson, 2nd ed. (Oxford: Clarendon, 1948), and the *Magna Moralia*, the authenticity of which is defended by Hans von Arnim, *Die drei aristotelischen Ethiken* (Vienna: Hölder, 1924)—cf. Tadeusz Sinko, *Historia literatury greckiej* [*The History of Greek Literature*] 780. The references below are from the Greek-Latin edition of Aristotle, *Opera omnia* (Paris: Firmin-Didot, 1883). The passages upon which my remarks are based include the following: *Nichomachean Ethics* I, 1–4, 7–8, 12; II, 6 (3); IX, 4 (3), 9 (7); X, 5 (10), 9 (6); *Eudemian Ethics*, I, 3 (5); VII, 15; *Magna Moralia* II, 9 (2–5).

3. See, for example, Matt. 5:48.

4. I am appealing here to such passages as the following from Aurelius Augustinus, *Opera omnia* (Paris: Migne, 1965): I, col. 811; II, col. 658, 1347; III, col. 31; IV, col. 203, 1686, 1740; V, col. 185, 853; VI, col. 17, 701; X, col. 308.

5. Among the many texts in St. Thomas' works to which I could refer here, I wish to cite the following: *Scriptum in IV Libros Sententiarum* I, 5, 1; I, 5, 3, 1; I, 8, 1, 3; I, 17, 4; I, 19, 5, 1, 3; I, 19, 5, 2, 3; II, 1, 2; 2; *Quaestiones*

disputatae de veritate I, 1; I, 5, 1, 1; I, 5, 4, 2; I, 6, 3; XXI, 1; XXI, 2; XXI, 5; XXI, 5, 6; XXI, 6; XXIV, 4; *Summa contra Gentiles* I, 19, 4, 1; I, 23, 4, 1; I, 37; I, 62, 8; II, 41; *Quaestiones disputatae de potentia Dei* I, 48, 1; III, 6; *Quaestiones disputatae de malo* II, 5, 2; *Summa theologiae* I–II, 18, 1; I–II, 18, 3 ad 3; I–II, 18, 4 ad 3; I–II, 19, 6 ad 1; I–II, 19, 7 ad 3; I–II, 20.

6. Immanuel Kant, *Critique of Practical Reason*, trans. Lewis White Beck (Indianapolis: Bobbs, 1956).

7. Max Scheler, *Formalism in Ethics and Non-Formal Ethics of Values: A New Attempt Toward the Foundation of an Ethical Personalism*, trans. Manfred S. Frings and Roger L. Funk (Evanston: Northwestern UP, 1973); see especially 9–30, 81–110, 253–264, and 572–595.

4

On the Directive or Subservient Role of Reason in Ethics

In the Philosophy of Thomas Aquinas, David Hume, and Immanuel Kant

The question of norms is certainly a central question in ethics. As a philosophical discipline, ethics is not only concerned with norms, i.e., propositions universally acknowledged to have the character of general rules or guidelines that refer to matters of great import.[1] Before considering particular norms, ethics first attends to what a norm is as such: it tries to define the essence of a norm. This task is accomplished quite differently depending on the general epistemological assumptions that lie at the basis of a given system of practical philosophy. The concept of a norm is always a reflection of those assumptions and, to some extent, of the whole structure of the system in which the philosopher constructs his or her moral philosophy. Since the present discussion will focus on the views of three thinkers whose systems differ considerably, we will have occasion to see for ourselves the effect of these differences on the notion of a norm.

This will be possible, however, only to a certain degree, since the main topic of this inquiry is a comparison of the role that these three philosophers assign to reason in ethics (and in morality). That role is either directive or subservient. Since the whole notion of a norm is crystalized around reason, whether the role of reason is viewed as directive

Karol Wojtyla, "O kierowniczej lub sluzebnej roli rozumu w etyce na tle pogladow Tomasza z Akwinu, Hume'a i Kanta," *Roczniki Filozoficzne* 6.2 (1958): 13–31.

or as subservient will have repercussions for the character of norms. It will determine the perfectionistic, utilitarian, or formalistic character of the whole ethical system.

This inquiry has comparative and systematic significance; it is not a work in the history of philosophy, even though the comparison of views takes place in a historical context.

1. THOMAS AQUINAS ON THE RELATION OF REASON TO THE GOOD

The good is the object of the will, for the aim of a tendency or desire is always some good. The cognitive apprehension, or objectification, of the good is, according to Thomas, a task and work of reason. Reason and the will work closely together (*utraque ad actum alterius operatur*): the will wills so that reason may know; reason, in turn, knows that the will wills and what the will wills. A result of this close interaction of reason and the will is that the true and the good in some sense mutually permeate and contain one another: when reason apprehends that the will wills a good, and, even more so, when reason affirms that something is good, then the good as an object of reason becomes a kind of truth. On the other hand, truth is the good of reason, and so truth is also an end of the will, which, so to speak, urges reason on to truth. The truth concerning the good can be of both theoretical and practical significance. Reason apprehends the good in a speculative way when it defines the good's essence and reflects upon the principles governing it. Above all, however, the good is an object of action. Practical reason apprehends the good precisely from this point of view (*bonum ordinabile ad opus sub ratione veri*).[2]

The general concept of the good, by which reason encompasses all that in any way is or can be an object of desire, an object of the will, applies in an analogical way to different goods. Reason, therefore, not only apprehends how different objects of the will are alike, but it also perceives how they differ from one another. Of the many distinctions we find in the Thomistic doctrine of the good, the most significant is the distinction between *bonum honestum*, *bonum utile*, and *bonum delectabile*.

This distinction is dictated by the very structure of human activity. It was introduced already by Aristotle,[3] who employed it only in the realm of human activity. Thomas extended this distinction to the activity of all beings and regarded it as characteristic of the good as such. Every acting being tends toward some good, and this good (*bonum secundum quod bonum est*) can be either an end of an action or a means to that end. In the former case, we are dealing with a good that the being or one of its powers tends toward for its own sake (*honestum dicitur, quod per se desideratur*). In the latter, on the other hand, the being desires one good for the sake of another. Thomas uses the term *bonum honestum* for the good that is an end, and the term *bonum utile* for the good that is a means. The Polish counterparts of these terms (*dobro godziwe*—befitting good, and *dobro uzyteczne*—useful good) completely obscure the true meaning of the distinction. This is especially true of the term *dobro godziwe*, which to us would already imply a positive relation of the good to a norm. This is not what Thomas had in mind. *Bonum honestum* precedes the normative functions, although it serves as their immediate basis. In itself, however, *bonum honestum* refers to a good that conforms to the nature of a rational being because it is in keeping with what that being desires for itself. *Bonum utile* is a good that is a means to an end—in this case, the Polish term *dobro uzyteczne* comes a little closer to the meaning of the Latin term.

Both of these types of good should be distinguished from the subjective good of satisfaction or pleasure—*bonum delectabile*. This good flows from the repose of the will or other appetitive faculties in the good attained by them.[4]

The difference Thomas sees between *bonum honestum* and *bonum utile* deserves special attention here. He speaks of this, for example, in *Summa theol.* II–II, 145, 3,[5] where he emphasizes the special excellence a befitting good has by reason of its conformity to reason and, through reason, to our whole rational nature. This is also why a befitting good is a natural source of human satisfaction. We know, however, that in addition to this satisfaction there are sensory pleasures, which do not directly serve to perfect our being. The only satisfaction that qualifies in this regard is one that derives from a good in keeping with our rational nature, a *bonum honestum*, whose nobility and spiritual beauty are worthy of deep esteem. For this reason, too, if something is incompatible with a *bonum honestum* it cannot be regarded as a true *bonum utile*, for it is incompatible with our true and ultimate end, even though it may serve as a means to certain partial ends.[6]

A *bonum utile*, which is always only a means to an end, can be directed either to a *bonum honestum* or to a *bonum delectabile*, for each of these may be an end attained by suitable means.[7] When pleasure is opposed to befittingness, however, the pleasure in question must obviously be sensory pleasure. A *bonum honestum*, as we heard earlier, is also connected with its own special kind of satisfaction, and so simply by realizing the befitting we also get satisfaction. In this instance there is no need for befittingness and pleasure to be mutually opposed.

A *bonum utile*, which is always a means to an end, may be directed merely to sensory pleasure.[8] Reason is then put at the service of the senses and pleasure, for usefulness is always related to reason. Reason's task, after all, is to subordinate some goods to others as means to ends. What determines the value of a *bonum utile* is not the useful good itself, but the good it is used to achieve. If the *bonum utile* is used to achieve a good compatible with our rational nature, then it indirectly takes on the value of that good. If, on the other hand, it is used to achieve a merely sensory pleasure, then a basic inversion occurs from the point of view of the concept of the human being that was developed and justified in a fundamental way by Thomas, an inversion from the point of view of the order of values operative in this concept.

What makes this inversion so harmful is that it deprives reason of its proper role. Reason's proper role in human life is superior, not subservient. Reason performs its superior role when it defines what is good in itself and, therefore, also compatible with the will when it presents us with this good as an end. Reason then directs our whole being and sets the course for our objective development and perfection. This directive character of reason is connected strictly with a *bonum honestum*. A shift in reason toward a *bonum utile* diverts reason from this superior and directive position and reduces it to a secondary, subservient position. The search for means to an end takes place on a level compatible with our human dignity only when that end conforms to our rational nature. When, on the other hand, the end conforms only to our senses, then the subservient role of reason appears as *sui generis* an enslavement of this most excellent human power. When reason is oriented toward the search for means to a *bonum delectabile*, to satisfaction or pleasure, it easily runs the risk of serving only the senses, whereas when reason is oriented toward a good in keeping with its nature such disorder is precluded.

One could say that Thomas, by presenting the matter in this way, basically set himself in opposition to all utilitarianism in ethics. Utilitarianism, as we shall see, does not consist merely in placing utility or expediency before befittingness. This transposition in the sphere of the good presupposes a fundamental conversion of the directive function of reason to a subservient function. This will become more apparent when we analyze Hume's views in this regard. Thomas, by focusing reason's activity on the good that conforms to the dignity of human nature, is speaking from perfectionistic assumptions: the perfection of our being, and not mere expediency, determines the course of our behavior.

We can see here that Thomas' position is in no way directed against pleasure or satisfaction. In fact, a good that is in conformity with our rational human nature brings with it genuine satisfaction. But because we are composite spiritual-corporeal beings, not all of the satisfactions or pleasures we experience go hand in hand with what conforms to our rational nature. Often they may only conform to the senses, to the lower part of human nature, without also conforming to reason. Moreover, sensory pleasures, despite being objectively and intrinsically (*secundum se*) lower than spiritual ones (St. Thomas explains in some detail why this is so), are nevertheless immediately more attractive to us, especially if we have developed an irresistible craving for such pleasures, and they are also always more insistent and violent.[9]

2. HUME'S VIEW OF THE ROLE OF REASON IN MORAL ACTIVITY

David Hume, in the second and third book of his *Treatise of Human Nature*,[10] assigns a subservient role to reason in the moral life and activity of the human being. Thomas Aquinas had already alluded to this role, although he did not refer to it in this manner. From Thomas' remarks, however, it is not hard to see that the role of reason would have to be precisely such were it oriented exclusively to *bonum utile*, renouncing the task of defining the end corresponding to our rational nature, the end in keeping with this nature. Reason's role would then be subservient, especially because, when we do not seek the good compatible with our spiritual nature, we submit without choice to the inclination toward pleasurable good. This process can be treated as a consequence of the natural tendency toward happiness—but that is already a separate issue.

Hume comes out clearly on the side of the subservient position of reason in human activity. He does this first in the third section of Book II of his *Treatise*, where he is basically discussing the will. Hume understands the will as one of the original impressions we feel and are aware of *"when we knowingly give rise to any new motion of our body, or new perception of our mind."*[11] He is speaking here from an empirical standpoint, which leads him to distinguish the body as an object of external experience from the "mind," which lies in the realm of inner experience. In the realm of inner experience, Hume sees two kinds of mental perceptions, or, speaking generally, two kinds of contents that appear in the mind. These are impressions and ideas. Original impressions or sensory impressions are those that without any antecedent perception arise in the soul "from the constitution of the body, from the animal spirits, or from the application of objects to the external organs." Secondary impressions or reflective impressions arise from original impressions either immediately or through the mediation of the ideas of those original impressions. To the first group, original impressions, belong the impressions of pleasure and pain, as well as all sensory impressions. The second group, reflective impressions, are further divided by Hume into the calm, which he calls emotions, and the violent, which he calls passions. In keeping with what was said earlier, pleasure and pain are the source of many emotions and passions, "both when felt and consider'd by the mind." Pleasure and pain, which "arise originally in the soul, or in the body," are also the elementary and basic forms of good and evil.[12]

It is also worth remembering that the subject of all the perceptions that appear in the mind, namely, the human self, is understood by Hume as "that succession of related ideas and impressions, of which we have an intimate memory and consciousness."[13] This is, as can be seen, a purely ephemeral concept of the human being. The self, thus conceived, is the natural focal point mainly of our passions and emotions. The idea of this self is for each of us our closest idea, the one most intimately given in experience, and it also most easily turns into an impression. In this tenet lies the seed of the Humean notion of egoism and individualism—which, however, I will not go into here.

Ideas can turn into impressions and vice versa, because these two forms of perception, according to Hume, differ not in content and essence, but only in the degree of intensity in which we experience them: "These two kinds of perception [are] in a great measure the same, and [differ] only in their degrees of force and vivacity."[14] An idea is merely a feeble impression. The most original impressions—pleasure and pain— also have far greater significance as motives of the will than any idea.

In expressing this belief, Hume is fully aware that he is touching upon a problem of age-old concern to moral philosophers. Setting himself in opposition to those who maintained that to be virtuous we must be guided by reason in our actions, Hume goes so far as to say *"first,* that reason alone can never be a motive to any action of the will; and *secondly,* that it can never oppose passion in the direction of the will."[15]

Hume reduces the activity of reason to the formulation of judgments based on strict demonstration or on probability, in the process of which reason reflects upon either the abstract relations among our ideas or the relations among things known from experience. Knowledge of the relations among ideas can in no way be the cause of action, because the will, which leads us into the world of real things, is far removed from that world of ideas with which reason deals. There remains only one possible way for reason to influence action: by directing our judgment regarding causes and effects.

And this is just where the basically subservient role of reason comes to light. Reason informs us of what can produce pleasure or pain, and in this way it inclines us to pursue some objects and avoid others. Reason's role here, however, is in no way directive, but only instrumental. The impulse comes from the passions—and, in the final analysis, from pleasure or pain. They initiate the movement of the will (the will, of course, as conceived by Hume). It makes no sense, therefore, to speak of a conflict between reason and passion in directing the will: "We speak not strictly and philosophically when we talk of the combat of passion and of reason. Reason is, and ought only to be the slave of the passions, and can never pretend to any other office than to serve and obey them."[16]

We see that Hume emphasized decisively even as a principle what from Thomas' point of view appeared merely as a perversion of the role of reason—one we must guard against if we are to remain true to our nature. Thomas realized, of course, that such a perversion can easily occur, considering the great force and intensity of sensory feelings and the pleasure connected with them. He saw this, however, as a debasement of human dignity, as activity beneath the level of our rational nature and its abilities. For Thomas, reason is a power—an energy—of human nature that stands close to action because it unites with the will; the will is, after all, a rational appetite (*appetitus rationalis*).

Consequently, what in Thomas' eyes appeared as activity beneath the nature of reason and its abilities, Hume regarded as reason's natural activity. It should be emphasized that this view of Hume's is a consequence of his empirical assumptions. Hume proceeds from an analysis of perceptions of the mind—the contents of pure inner experience—divorced from the living totality of the person's being, which, however, is the proper subject of all activities, including activities of the mind. Thus perceptions of the mind become somehow independent, and the observation of them in separation from the totality of the person's being suggests a completely different view of the human being from that which we find in Thomas.

In order to determine whose position is correct—Hume's or Thomas'—we must go all the way back to their points of departure.

Hume's view is a consequence of his empirical assumptions. In the realm of inner experience, impressions essentially have more intensity and vivacity than ideas. This, however, is no basis for concluding either that ideas and impressions are identical or that impressions alone influence the will. The will in this view is also just an impression, one that accompanies motions of the body or "movements" of the mind. Perhaps here more than anywhere else it becomes apparent that Hume's empiricism stands outside the actual object of experience. The will as an object of experience manifests itself precisely in the experience of one's self as a cause of activity—so says Ach and other like psychologists.[17] In any case, the will cannot be identified with an impression accompanying the appearance of activities. To speak of motives of the will must then be pointless, in which case to deny reason an influence on the will's activity in favor of the passions must also arouse all sorts of reservations.

Hume's reduction of reason to a subservient role, or simply to the role of a slave of the passions, is, then, at least partially a consequence of his epistemological assumptions. In the kind of view of the human being that Hume adopts, the significance of pleasure and pain increases inordinately and determines the whole inner life of the human person. Reason performs only an ancillary function in that life. Because passions are accompanied by judgments, a passion may sometimes be called unreasonable. This occurs when we assume the existence of certain objects that do not exist in reality, as well as when the means we choose to realize a certain passion are inadequate. Since, however, it is reason's task to select appropriate means, we should really speak in such cases of a false judgment rather than an unreasonable passion. "The moment we perceive the falsehood of any supposition, or the insufficiency of any means, our passions yield to our reason without any opposition."[18] Hume is convinced that the passions will readily comply with reason so long as reason takes a subservient role in relation to them.

It is quite understandable that reason in a subservient position cannot perform a normative role in action and morality. Because "reason [is] inactive in itself" and because its role in action is merely secondary and subordinate to the passions, it makes no sense to seek "measures of right and wrong" in reason and to claim, moreover, that these measures impose an obligation not only on humans but even on God. There is no connection between the ideas with which reason deals, on the one hand, and passions, volitions, and actions, on the other. "Actions may be laudable or blame-able; but they cannot be reasonable or unreasonable: Laudable or blame-able, therefore, are not the same with reasonable or unreasonable... Reason is wholly inactive, and can never be the source of so active a principle as conscience, or a sense of morals."[19] Just as reason cannot evoke actions by its approval or disapproval, it also cannot be the source of the moral good and evil contained in them.

If reason's judgment cooperates with the passions and also indirectly influences them in the manner described earlier, then mistakes can happen. But these mistakes are of merely logical significance and have no ethical significance at all: they are simply errors of reasoning, not moral faults. Hence, we can only sympathize with a person who happens to make such a mistake, but we should not blame or punish the person. If reason does pass judgment on the rightness or wrongness of an action, it is then just an echo of the moral sense and not an autonomous judge.

Hume reduces all moral distinctions to responses of this moral sense. "Morality, therefore, is more properly felt than judg'd of; tho' this feeling or sentiment is commonly so soft and gentle, that we are apt to confound it with an idea."[20] The feeling of pleasure that virtue arouses in the moral sense and the feeling of pain that moral failing arouses in it contain their own approval and disapproval—these, in turn, are our real basis for regard-ing something as morally good or evil respectively. A characteristic feature of this approval or disapproval is its disinterestedness: the moral sense responds to good and evil without seeking therein any interest of its own.

By reducing normative functions to a response of the moral sense, Hume was acting on behalf of morality as he understood it. He was con-cerned that morality have an influence on human passions and actions. If such an influence is to occur, then morality must "go beyond the calm and indolent judgments of the understanding."[21] The operations of passion and the will take place beyond reason; reason has no real influence on them or they on it.

Making a judgment of reason, whether it be true or false, does not by any means imply the intention to act on it. In his opposition to intellec-tualism in ethics and to the intellectualization of morality, Hume appealed to an argument already advanced long ago against Socrates' views and to some extent Plato's as well: it is one thing to know what virtue is and another to conform our will to it.

From his empirical standpoint, Hume distinguished impressions from ideas as perceptions of the mind that differ from one another in intensity. Ideas are less intense than impressions. They are as though too feeble, too faint, and too dull to grasp the actual content of moral life. Reason itself, which deals mainly with ideas, is, so to speak, not a sensitive enough instrument to have an influence on morality or to grasp the lively difference between good and evil, between virtue and vice. Reason's activity consists in grasping the relations between ideas and between things, and in drawing inferences from facts. None of these functions, however, are precise enough to connect reason with the positing of practical norms.

Each of the four types of logical relations—resemblance, contrariety, degrees in quality, and quantitative relations—is just as applicable to our actions, passions, and volitions as it is to external objects. And so [if morality were to consist in such relations] we could easily associate virtue and vice either with what is contained solely in our consciousness, independent of a relation to the external world, or, conversely, with objects of the external world, and even with inanimate objects.[22]

Hume, too, basically went in this direction, explaining in one place that from the point of view of reason there would be no difference between, say, the crime of murdering one's parents and the "fault" of a sapling that grew up from the seed of an old tree and eventually cast its shadow over, or even destroyed, the parent tree. To take another example, if incest is not a moral fault between animals but is between humans, this, according to Hume, is merely because animals lack a moral sense—not because they lack reason, which would bring nothing to this realm. Within the field of vision of reason alone, we will never discover a "matter of fact" called—for example—vice. We will only find certain passions, motives, volitions, and thoughts, but vice will totally elude us so long as we apprehend an action merely with reason. Not until we turn our reflection inward and find a response of the moral sense in the form of a disapproval of the action in question will vice appear in its true form.[23]

In Hume's view, then, reason completely loses its directive and normative role. Reason can perform only a subservient function in relation to human passions and actions, and the content of reason's activity is totally removed from the living content of human activity. As a result, normative propositions containing the term *ought* or *ought not* are devoid of all meaning. There is no basis, in Hume's eyes, for deriving such propositions from predicative propositions joined by the term *is* or *is not*.[24] Reason, which was dismissed from its superior and directive position in human life, was also consequently divested of its normative role as well.[25] Henceforth, all it can really do is describe the responses of the moral sense. In Hume's view, ethics really ceases to exist, but the door to a positivistic science of morality is left wide open.

Moreover, in this view perfectionism in ethics and morality loses its justification, and only utilitarianism retains one. This consequence of the subservient role of reason could already have been foreseen from a thoughtful reading of the previously mentioned texts of Thomas. Utilitarianism means *using* reason in such a way that it results in the maximum happiness, or greatest possible sum of pleasure, for all involved. For this very reason, Bentham will question the value of the moral sense, while at the same time expressing the deepest regard for a purely utilitarian prudence that allows us to skillfully employ the hedonistic calculus and thereby efficiently administer the "proceeds" of happiness.[26]

3. THE DIRECTIVE ROLE OF REASON IN ACTION AND THE CATEGORICAL IMPERATIVE

In the light of the foregoing analysis, the opposition between Thomas Aquinas and Hume becomes sufficiently clear. Hume, as we have seen, defines the role of reason in action as subservient, and, as a result, he denies normative functions to reason—a position that flows in large measure from purely epistemological assumptions. In Thomas Aquinas' practical philosophy, the directive role of reason in action is determined in large measure by a wholistic view of the human being as a being for whom reason is a property and faculty and thus a kind of "part." This "part" exists in the whole and also performs its practical functions within this whole. The superior and directive character of these functions is determined in a fundamental way by the fact that reason defines the good that is the end of the human being—the end of human existence and action— the *bonum honestum*. This is precisely what guarantees reason a directive role in human life. The positing of norms of action is a concrete expression of this role. We can speak meaningfully of the normative role of reason only if we have established that reason directs action and, indirectly, the person's whole being as well. In Thomas' ethics, reason performs this role through the mediation of the *bonum honestum* as a result of the significance the *bonum honestum* has in his practical philosophy and ethics. In Hume, on the other hand, both the directive and the normative role of reason disappear because of the disappearance of the *bonum honestum*. The only form of good for Hume is pleasure, the *bonum delectabile*. Since reason is "used" to determine the means leading to pleasure, utilitarianism becomes closely linked to eudaimonism. Kant attacked utilitarianism from precisely this angle.

I will now present a brief analysis of Kant's position in order to show that reason's directive role in action is not identical simply with the mere independence of reason from feelings.

Kant opposed both utilitarianism in morality and the notion of a moral sense.[27] He described the latter as a "more refined, but equally untrue...pretense," thereby aptly exposing the crux of the eudaimonistic utilitarian view of morality.[28] Kant's opposition to utilitarianism went parallel with an overcoming of empiricism in favor of rationalism. We can easily detect the stages of this process in the *Critique of Practical Reason.*

Proceeding from the assumption that practical reason "deals with the grounds determining the will," Kant then asks: "Is pure reason sufficient of itself to determine the will, or is it only as empirically conditioned that it can do so?"[29] Because the reason in question here is practical reason, "empirically conditioned" is reducible to "conditioned by the sensory feelings of pleasure and pain." When these feelings determine the direction of the will, the respective maxims of reason are permeated with the principle of utilitarianism conceived eudaimonistically, a principle that, according to Kant, is identical with the principle of egoism and comes in conflict with morality.

Such a state would be identical with that enslavement of reason by the passions proclaimed by Hume. Kant, on the other hand, sees the possibilities of practical reason differently. Practical reason is capable of producing its own practical principles, which, in contrast to maxims, are called *imperatives*. The principles of action produced by practical reason have an *a priori*, imperative character. This character alone should suffice to establish reason's sovereign and superior role in action. But this does not suffice for Kant. When imperatives determine the direction of the will with regard to some desired outcome, they still do not fully reveal the independence of reason from the natural, deterministic causality that reigns outside the human being. They also do not reveal the complete independence of practical reason from feelings, through which the determination that reigns in the phenomenal, natural world is, so to speak, transferred within the human being.

Consequently, Kant sees a need to distinguish from hypothetical imperatives a so-called categorical imperative, an imperative that determines the direction of the will apart from any desired or expected outcome, one that determines the direction of the will as such, the "pure" will. Only such an imperative has the objective meaning of law. The categorical imperative is an expression of "pure" practical reason, unconditioned by any desire and unattached to any "matter," i.e., to those objects of human action upon which all material laws are normally focused. The categorical imperative is identical simply with the *a priori* "form" of all possible laws—with "the mere form of universal legislation." This "form" can be objectified; we then get the familiar form of the categorical imperative: "So act that the maxim of your will could always hold at the same time as a principle establishing universal law."[30] Subjectively, however, the pure form of all possible laws is reducible simply to "pure duty," which is also, according to Kant, the essence of true morality, whereas abiding by laws is merely lawfulness.

The attempt to free reason from all possible dependence—from dependence both on feelings and on the whole sensory, phenomenal world that evokes these feelings by means of natural determination—led Kant to an aprioristic formalism in ethics. This formalism is a consequence of his epistemological assumptions. Kant conducted his critical analysis of the activity of practical reason—which was meant to show, among other things, that reason does not perform a subservient role (in relation to feelings)—from the point of view of "pure" reason.

"Pure" reason seems to be an artificial construct specially designed for philosophical analysis. From the standpoint of experience as the first and fundamental source of our knowledge, we have to say that we know reason only as a property or power of the human being, as a distinct "part" of this being. The notion of "pure" reason as a kind of autonomous subject of *a priori* cognitive forms evokes reservations not unlike those raised by the Humean "mind"—an autonomous subject of perceptions. In fact, the subject of activities, including intellectual activities, is basically the human being as a being. This is especially important when dealing with the practical sphere. Can an analysis of practical reason be divorced from the drives and activities of the human being as a whole?

Such a question suggests a need to move to the position of Thomas Aquinas for metaphysical reasons.[31] First, however, we should note—since this is the main focus of our discussion—that Kant's position on eudaimonistic utilitarianism did not manage to establish the directive role of reason in the moral life of the human being. Kant managed only to assert the inner independence of practical reason from sensory feelings and, indirectly, from all natural causality. This independence of "pure" practical reason, which from another perspective is really identical with the autonomy of the will, is, in Kant's eyes, also a kind of synonym for all human morality.

Independence, however, is by no means equivalent to the directive role of reason in moral life and action; in fact, it is not equipped for that role. If reason is totally oriented solely toward freeing itself from the deterministic influences of feelings and "nature," this means that it is not oriented toward directing those spheres of our activity with which we are constantly involved externally and internally. In the final analysis, then, Kant basically succumbs to Hume's suggestions concerning the relation of reason to the passions. The position assigned to reason in the concept of the categorical imperative is defensive rather than superior. Formalism means an escape from teleology. Hume managed to convince Kant that the search for means to an end is always nothing but a pursuit of pleasure. No other end apart from pleasure can be seen—and so morality also cannot be seen: teleology could only be connected with utilitarian eudaimonism.

By comparison, we are now able to grasp the role that the *bonum honestum* performs in Thomas' practical philosophy and ethics. His thesis that reason is capable of defining what the objective good is and what as good should constitute an end for the will forms the basis for accepting the directive role of reason in action. This alone provides a foundation for the positing of norms, which consists in directing the human being's actions toward the realization of a good that is a proper end for the human being's rational nature. In order, however, for reason to posit norms, it must first of all possess the ability to direct both activity and the being. This, in turn, is possible only if reason defines the end-good that ought to be an end for the human being. Thomas Aquinas is convinced that human reason is capable of attaining a view of objective good, although this must be combined with the effort needed to overcome the resistance offered by pleasure (subjective good). There is, however, no basis for maintaining that reason's whole energy should be expended merely in overcoming this resistance. This also would not suffice to construct morality. Morality is constructed only upon the foundation of befittingness [*bonum honestum*]. On this basis, too, all the dubious "usefulness" of actions finally becomes genuinely beneficial.

NOTES

1. See Maria Ossowska, *Podstawy nauki i moralnosci* [*The Foundations of Science and Morality*] (Warsaw: Czytelnik, 1947) 103–104.

2. Thomas Aquinas, *Summa theologiae* I, 16, 4 ad 1; I, 59, 2 ad 3; I, 79, 11 ad 2; I, 82, 3 ad 1; I, 82, 4 ad 1; I, 87, 4 ad 2; I–II, 9 ad 1; II–II, 109, 2 ad 1; *Quaestiones disputatae de veritate* III, 3, 3 ad 9; *Quaestiones disputatae de malo* IX, 6; etc.

3. See, for example, Aristotle, *Nichomachean Ethics* II, 3, 1104b 30 ff.

4. Thomas Aquinas, *Summa theol.* I, 5, 6 ad 3; I–II, 8, 2 ad 2; *Scriptum in IV Libros Sententiarum* III, 5, 1, 4, ad 1.

5. *"Dicitur enim aliquid honestum...inquantum habet quemdam decorem ex ordinatione rationis. Hoc autem, quod est secundum rationem ordinatum, est naturaliter conveniens homini. Unumquodque autem naturaliter declaratur in suo convenienti. Et ideo honestum est naturaliter homini delectabile; sicut operatione virtutis Philosophus probat (Ethic. c. 8). Non tamen omne delectabile est honestum, quia potest etiam aliquid conveniens esse secundum sensum et non secundum rationem. Sed hoc delectabile est praeter hominis rationem, quae perficit naturam ipsius... Honestum dicitur, secundum quod aliquid habet quandam excellentiam dignam honore propter spiritualem pulchritudinem; delectabile autem, inquantum quietat appetitum; utile autem, inquantum refertur ad aliud"* (Thomas Aquinas, *Summa theol.* II–II, 145, 3).

6. *"Nihil potest esse simpliciter et vere utile, quod repugnat honestati. Quia oportet, quod repugnet ultimo fini hominis, quod est bonum secundum rationem, quamvis possit forte esse utile secundum quid respectu alicuius finis particularis"* (Thomas Aquinas, *Summa theol.* II–II, 145, 3 ad 3).

7. *"Bonum in tria dividitur: in utile, delectabile et honestum. Quorum duo, scilicet delectabile et honestum, habent rationem finis, quia utrumque est appetibile propter seipsum. Honestum autem dicitur, quod est bonum secundum rationem, quod quidem habet delectationem annexam. Unde delectabile, quod contra honestum dividitur, est delectabile secundum sensum"* (Thomas Aquinas, *In X Libros Ethicorum* I, 5, 3). See also Thomas Aquinas, *Quaestiones disputatae de malo* 1, 4, 12.

8. *"Delectatio enim invenitur in omnibus animalibus, quia non solum est secundum partem intellectivam, sed etiam secundum partem sensitivam. Sed utile et honestum pertinet ad solam partem intellectivam. Nam honestum est, quod fiet secundum rationem—utile autem importat ordinem alicuius in alterum, ordinare autem proprium est rationis... Honestum est delectabile homini secundum quod est conveniens rationi; utile autem est delectabile propter spem finis"* (Thomas Aquinas, *Ethic.* II, 3).

9. On this topic, see, for example, Thomas Aquinas, *Summa theol.* I–II, 31, 5; I–II, 33, 2; I–II, 34, 2 ad 1; II–II, 145, 3; II–II, 20, 4; *Sent.* IV, 49, 3, 1, ad 2; IV, 49, 3, 5, ad 1; *Ethic.* I, 5; *De malo* XI, 2; *Expositio in Job* VI, 4.

10. David Hume, *A Treatise of Human Nature* (Oxford: Clarendon, 1968).

11. Hume, *Treatise* 399.

12. Hume, *Treatise* 275–276.

13. Hume, *Treatise* 277.

14. Hume, *Treatise* 354.

15. Hume, *Treatise* 413.

16. Hume, *Treatise* 415.

17. Narziss Ach, *Über den Willensakt und das Temperament* (Leipzig: Quelle, 1910); A. Michotte and N. Prüm, "Étude expérimentale sur le choix volontaire et ses antécédents immédiats," *Archives de Psychologie* (1910); Johannes Lindworsky, *Der Wille: Seine Erscheinung und seine Beherrschung* (Leipzig: Barth, 1923); Mieczyslaw Dybowski, *Dzialanie woli na tle badan eksperymentalnych* [*The Activity of the Will in the Light of Experimental Investigations*] (Poznan, 1946).

18. Hume, *Treatise* 416.

19. Hume, *Treatise* 458.

20. Hume, *Treatise* 470.
21. Hume, *Treatise* 457.
22. Hume, *Treatise* 463–464.
23. Hume, *Treatise* 466–469.
24. Hume, *Treatise* 469.
25. Be that as it may, Georges Lechartier, in his book *David Hume moraliste et sociologue* (Paris: Alcan, 1900), noted in this regard a certain inconsistency in Hume, especially in relation to subsequent sections of Book III ("Of Morals"). Lechartier writes: *"Ayant reconnu que la morale ne pouvait se passer de certains éléments dont la raison seule pouvait rendre compte, il a dû, à tout instant, les postuler... Il n'a répudié de la Raison que le nom."* A somewhat similar suggestion can also be found in a Polish work by B. Güntzberg, "David Hume a teoria umowy spolecznej" ["David Hume and the Social Contract Theory"], *Kwartalnik Filozoficzny* (1927).
26. Jeremy Bentham, *Déontologie*, 47–49, vol. 4 of *Oeuvres de Jérémie Bentham*, trans. Étienne Dumont (Brussels: Société belge de librairie, 1834) 47–49.
27. Immanuel Kant, *Critique of Practical Reason*, trans. Lewis White Beck (Indianapolis: Bobbs, 1956).
28. Kant, *Critique of Practical Reason* 40.
29. Kant, *Critique of Practical Reason* 15.
30. Kant, *Critique of Practical Reason* 30.
31. I am drawing here on two comparative works: Francisco Ibrányi, *Ethica secundum S. Thomam et Kant* (Rome: Collegio Angelico, 1931), and Edgar Schorer, *Die Zweckethik des hl. Thomas von Aquin als Ausgleich der formalistischen Ethik Kants und der materialen Werethik Schelers* (Vechta in Oldberg: Albertus Magnus, 1937).

5

On the Metaphysical and Phenomenological Basis of the Moral Norm

In the Philosophy of Thomas Aquinas and Max Scheler

This comparative study ought to justify its right to be included in a collection of articles dedicated to the memory of Father Jacek Woroniecki, one of the greatest Polish moralists in recent times. We know that he was a Thomist and that he imbued Polish thought and wide circles of Polish scholars with the ethical doctrine of St. Thomas Aquinas, while also insightfully developing and bringing up-to-date certain elements of that doctrine (e.g., the topic of justice). At the same time, he frequently expressed an interest in the contemporary "ethics of values," referring especially to certain ideas of its most vocal exponent, Max Scheler. This reference had a sporadic character—nowhere in Father Jacek's scholarly output do we find a very extensive treatment either of Scheler or of the ethics of values in general. It would be fair to say, then, that he merely sensed in an intuitive way certain points of contact or similarities with St. Thomas' ethics. Perhaps, therefore, this present, more in-depth study will allow us not only to find ourselves in the world of thought so near and dear to Father Jacek Woroniecki, but also even to deepen and expand that thought. This, in turn, presupposes above all a continuity of human knowledge and a genuine respect for its leading figures.

Karol Wojtyla, "O metafizycznej i fenomenologicznej podstawie normy moralnej (w oparciu o koncepcje sw. Tomasza z Akwinu oraz Maksa Schelera)," *Roczniki Teologiczno-Kanoniczne* 6.1–2 (1959): 99–124.

1. ST. THOMAS AQUINAS

AN EXISTENTIAL VIEW OF THE GOOD

St. Thomas adopted a basically Aristotelian position. He accepted realism and pluralism in his philosophy of the good, while rejecting Plato's aprioristic idealism, crystalized above all in the Platonic doctrine of the Idea of the Good. At the same time, however, Thomas accepted Augustine's works, and through them certain Platonic views, after being modified by Augustine in a realistic spirit, found their way into Thomas' philosophy. Augustine's writings showed conclusively that revelation, upon which he constantly relied when adopting Platonic views, has a thoroughly realistic orientation. Consequently, once those views had been modified in a spirit of realism, Thomas was able to incorporate them into his system, which, in keeping with the Aristotelian orientation of his philosophy as a whole, had decidedly realistic assumptions. Most important among these genetically Platonic views was the concept of participation. With it, Thomas, like Augustine, was able to grasp the relation of created goods to God as the supreme good. Because the good is really identical with being, this relation goes hand in hand with the relation that occurs between contingent beings, which exist by participation (*esse per participationem*), and necessary being, which is subsistent existence (*esse subsistens*). The Aristotelian concept of the good, which placed the primary emphasis on teleology, underwent a reconstruction in Thomas' view, which gave priority to the aspect of existence, such that Thomas' concept of the good may properly be called existential.

Existence is a good, and it is impossible to think that a being might not have existence (*esse*). Consequently, every being is a good precisely because it has existence. And so every really existing being is a good: *bonum et ens conventuntur*.[1] What determines a good in the first place is sheer existence. Existence is primarily that through which a being is a being, and this itself is a fundamental perfection.[2] That is why every being loves its existence and strives to preserve it.[3] Existence is also the principal basis for predicating goodness of things: everything is a good insofar as it exists. Because God has an unconditional fullness of existence, God is the highest good. Other beings each have their own respective fullness of existence. Because they are each composed of substance and accidents, the existence of these substances and their corresponding accidents determines the fullness of existence that each of them should possess.[4] Potential beings, which have no actual existence, are good to the extent that they contain an ordination toward existence (*ordo ad esse*). This is the way in which prime matter is a good—not by being the object of an aim, but by "aiming" toward act, by striving to exist under a determinate form.[5]

Form divorced from the existence of the essence of a thing is not a real good in any sense, whereas form combined with existence as a factor co-constituting every being not only determines a being's real goodness but is also the basis—or at least one of the bases—of the metaphysical "measure of being" upon which the entire normative order is ultimately based.

THE MEASURE OF BEING

Thomas adopted from Augustine the tenet that all beings are constituted according to the measure of mode, species, and order (*secundum speciem, modum, et ordinem*) proper to each. Every being is perfect to the extent that it lacks nothing in keeping with the mode of perfection proper to it (*secundum modum suae perfectionis*).[6] On the other hand, a being is what it is because of its form; form, then, basically determines the perfection of a given being. Form, however, must be suited to matter; it must, so to speak, be "measured" to matter. This suiting of form to matter goes hand in hand with the operation of the efficient cause to which a given being owes its constitution. Since this constitution takes place in a particular way because of the union of form with matter, because of the "measuring" of one to the other, Thomas says *mensura modum praefigit*: measure defines the mode of existence—the respective kind of existence— a given being has. This mode or kind is basically determined by the form to which that being owes its membership in a particular species. Hence, in the adage under discussion, right after *modus*, which implies a certain "measurement" within a given being, Thomas mentions *species*, which in a sense defines the being's position among other beings, a position that is a real consequence of the being's internal "measurement." The element of measure is also highlighted here by the fact that St. Thomas sees in species—in species membership—a certain similarity with the mathematical order: just as the addition or subtraction of a unit changes a number, which Thomas regards as a counterpart of species, so the addition or subtraction of any differentiating factor changes the species membership of a being.

The being's internal "measurement" entails an external "measurement" of it in relation to other beings, which is expressed in the adage above by the word *ordo*. The formed being brings with it a certain inclination to action, and action is oriented toward other beings as ends, to those that correspond to it by reason of their own form. Augustine regarded this as a sort of indication of a reciprocal weight (*pondus*) among beings, which gives rise to a certain natural order (*ordo*) among them. The inner nature and perfection of a being entails a relation (*comparatio*) of it to other beings.[7] The following formulation is very typical of St. Thomas: *Unumquodque bonum, inquantum est perfectivum secundum rationem speciei et esse simul, habet modum, speciem et ordinem. Speciem quidem quantum ad ipsam rationem, modum quantum ad esse, ordinem quantum ad ipsam habitudinem perfectivi.*[8] From this we can see that the good is identical with the whole being: with its essence and its existence. The basis of a being's real perfection in the mode proper to it should be sought in the order of existence, whereas the good becomes an object of knowledge only from the point of view of essence—only essence is conceptualized. Order, however, is based on the real perfection itself, for a good in the existential order displays a tendency toward other beings either as ends for it or vice versa.

In beings we find different degrees of perfection, which are connected with the different degrees in which the three cofactors of the good—mode, species, and order—occur with respect to different beings. Not only substantial beings but also accidental beings have their measure according to this principle. Thus, for example, one type of good that exists in us is the good of our nature, which is defined according to the mode, species, and order proper to it; another type of good that exists in us is moral good (*bonum virtutis*), and this again is measured according to the mode, species, and order proper to it.[9] The good of our nature is not destroyed by sin, but moral good is. Elsewhere[10] St. Thomas analyzes this problem in still greater detail: the good connected with the very substance of our nature is not even diminished by sin, but the good connected with our natural inclination is reduced by sin, although not wholly destroyed, unlike the goods of virtue (moral good) and grace (supernatural good). Thomas observes in this regard that sin is the direct destruction of the mode, species, and order in which the good of human action consists.

Thus the perfection of every created being is in this sense "measurable." Only Divine Being is beyond the scope of mode, species, and order. As a good in every respect, God excludes all measures of good, while at the same time constituting their basis: every mode, species, and order has its cause in God.[11] God's knowledge is the supreme model (*exemplar*) of beings, and in this sense God knows their measure (*mensura*). If a given being lacks an appropriate form—substantial or accidental—this implies a privation of mode, species, and order (*privatio modi, speciei, et ordinis*).[12]

Such a lack has significance not only in the immanent sphere. The perfection of created beings is essentially related to God: God is the fullness of existence, and creatures participate in this fullness because they owe their existence to God. The more perfect they are, the more they participate in the unconditional fullness of existence that is God. Hence, they may be said to be more like God. Participation in existence always entails resemblance. A greater degree of participation in the unconditional fullness of existence that is God expresses itself in the form of a more perfect nature of a given created being.

The inner measure of a being's perfection necessarily moves outward, so to speak, transcending the being itself: the perfection of a created being always causes that being to tend toward the ultimate end that is God, by virtue of the being's own resemblance to God. The higher this perfection, the more the being tends toward God, for the better it represents God's perfection in the world. In this view, perfection itself is already a tendency: perfection is "charged" with purposiveness. Less perfect creatures exist for more perfect ones, and the whole universe exists, in turn, for God, whose unconditional perfection is most fully expressed in the universe as a whole.[13]

In St. Thomas' thought, Aristotelian teleology is essentially combined with Platonic-Augustinian participation. At the basis of this union stands the idea of exemplarism, which has its ground in divine reason. God is the supreme, transcendent measure of all beings through the unconditional perfection of God's own being, through the unconditional fullness of existence that God is. This entails the resemblance of all creatures to God in being—and this resemblance has its degrees. Both the resemblance and its degrees are cognitively encompassed in the divine mind as their exemplar: the Creator sees in itself the supreme model of created beings and knows these beings in their exemplification, that is, insofar as they exemplify its essence, which is what the Creator knows in the primary sense. Herein lies the very heart of the normative order. Purposiveness alone does not yet entail it. Even the resemblance of creatures to the Creator in being does not determine it, for this resemblance says nothing about the normativeness of the world of goods as a whole.

Only exemplariness speaks of such normativeness, for the exemplar is the transcendent measure for what is modeled after it. Consequently, every being has its own immanent and transcendent measure. The immanent measure results from the internal relations that prevail in a given being, such as, for example, the relation between its form and matter. The transcendent measure results from the being's exemplification of the supreme perfection of Divine Being. And this exemplification can occur to a greater or lesser degree.

It is very significant that the metaphysical "measure of being" is primarily connected with the order of exemplar cause (*causae exemplaris*) and is based on exemplariness. Created beings are more or less good depending on the measure in which they exemplify in themselves the unconditional perfection of the First Exemplar Cause. Human beings are more or less good depending on the measure in which they exemplify in themselves the perfection of God. Exemplariness, in turn, is the basis of purposiveness: the more perfectly a created being exemplifies the perfection of the Creator, the more fully it attains its end. The same applies to human beings, taking on for them the significance of a moral norm—articulated in the familiar words of Matthew 5:48.

The question of the relation of purposiveness to exemplariness in Thomas' view of the good as a whole, and especially in connection with his view of norms, would require a separate study, including a comparison of Thomas' view of the good with Aristotle's. Here it will suffice to observe that Thomas in his ethics and in his teaching on norms does not proceed merely from the assumption of a "world of goods and ends," an assumption that Scheler so strongly repudiated in our own day—following the suggestion of Kant, who attempted thereby to rescue ethics and the normative system from utilitarianism. St. Thomas proceeds instead from the assumption of a "world of goods (beings) and models," in the context of which purposiveness ultimately arises. This is precisely what accounts for the possibility of norms, which must always stand beyond the totality of actual goods and ends.

THE HIERARCHY OF GOODS

A consequence of exemplariness in the sphere of beings is an objective hierarchy of goods. Aristotle acknowledged this hierarchy, and St. Thomas provided it with a basis in exemplariness: in the doctrine of participation. Goods of the soul are higher than goods of the body, for the body is related to the soul as matter to form. External goods are still lower than bodily goods. They are goods for us insofar as they remain subordinate to reason; consequently, they must be subjected to a proper measure, and only in this rational measure will they also be human goods. The principle of the subordination of all temporal goods to spiritual goods and of the subordination of action to contemplation is based on a belief in the objective superiority of the spiritual, rational soul over the body. This belief in Thomas' philosophy has its roots in his concept of being and being's connection with the good.[14] The spiritual is more perfect than the material because spirit is a greater perfection of being than matter. And so the more spiritual or independent of matter something in us is, the more perfect it is. The hierarchy of goods is basically objective; when, in turn, it finds its way into human action, it endows this action with a mark of genuine objectivity as well.

It should be noted here that the objective hierarchy of goods, a hierarchy that for Thomas was warranted by the order of beings and based on an exemplariness that has its origin in God, must have particular significance for the positing of norms in the ethical sense. Goods are primarily ends of action, but they may also be means to ends. An end is in some sense a measure for the means. The ends themselves, however, must also have a measure. The measure for the ends is determined by the hierarchy of goods. The hierarchization of goods allows us to aim toward ends in an objectively ordered way; it allows us in our aiming toward ends to rely on the objective measure of the perfection of beings. This is not, of course, a measure in the mathematical sense. The basis for the transcendent "measure" of the perfection of beings—the basis for measuring objective goods—is metaphysical analogy: the analogy of proportionality (*proportionalitatis*). We know that created beings are more or less perfect and that they all stand in a certain relation of resemblance and exemplification with respect to Divine Being. Human reason grasps these resemblances and differences in the beings that become ends of human action or means to such ends. Reason indirectly thereby also grasps the different degrees in which these beings exemplify Divine Being.

This movement of reason amid the hierarchy of beings and goods certainly enters into the positing of norms in the moral sense. According to St. Thomas, this process is thoroughly rational and objectively justified. Whether in each concrete instance we justify it for ourselves, and even whether we experience it in a primarily rational way, is still another matter. I mention this because of Scheler, who will be discussed later, and who holds that the hierarchization of values, and indirectly of goods, is a function of pure feeling, a function of a unique kind of reflex of the emotional sphere in us, whereas rational reasons for the practical hierarchization of values—even if such reasons could be given—do not play any role. Here I merely wish to emphasize once again that, since the rational measure (the kind St. Thomas accepts) of goods as objects of our action does not exhibit a mathematical precision, we cannot demand such precision in the positing of ethical norms, which, as we have seen, is a process that always in some way moves within a hierarchy of goods. In any case, St. Thomas maintains that we grasp this hierarchy sufficiently to be able to assume a proper attitude toward the objective order of goods.

THE FUNCTION OF REASON AND THE WILL

The good is the object of the will, whereas the cognitive apprehension of the good—its objectification—is, according to St. Thomas, an object of reason. Both of these faculties work closely together with one another (*utraque ad actum alterius operatur*): the will wills so that reason may know; reason, in turn, knows that the will wills and what the will wills. A result of this cooperation of reason and the will is that the good and the true somehow mutually include one another: when reason sees that the will wills a good, and still more when reason sees that something is good, then the good becomes an object of reason and *eo ipso* a particular truth. Truth, in turn, is the good of reason, and so truth is also an end of the will, which, so to speak, urges reason on to truth.[15] The truth of the good may have a speculative meaning. Reason apprehends the good in a speculative way when it defines the good and thereby reveals its essence; this is a purely theoretical knowledge of the good. In addition, however, reason knows the good in a practical way when the good is an object of action (*bonum ordinabile ad opus sub ratione veri*).[16]

It is the second kind of knowledge of the good, practical knowledge, that basically interests us in this essay, since the topic under discussion is the norm in ethics, and ethics is a practical science because it deals with human action. At this point, however, what I wish to emphasize most of all is that our ability as human beings to posit norms is fundamentally linked to our ability to apprehend by means of reason the very essence of the good in a general way. Other creatures turn toward particular goods, and often toward the same goods toward which we ourselves turn in action, but only we humans know the essence of the good in a general way (*communem rationem boni*), and our will turns toward the good known always in this way.[17] Only because of such knowledge is our orientation toward various goods in action permeated with norms. The positing of norms arises in the form of judgments, but these judgments always presuppose a general concept of the good. This concept encompasses the whole world of goods in their analogousness: it includes the good in every respect—that good in which the essence of the good is fully realized—and it also includes all those goods in which the essence of the good is not realized in full, but only in a certain measure. In our field of intellectual vision, along with the general concept of the good, there can be found a whole hierarchy of goods, which appear as higher or lower depending on the measure in which they exemplify in themselves the supreme good. Reason is able to apprehend their measure ultimately because reason is able to conceive the very essence of the good. This, in turn, occurs without some sort of vision of the "good in itself," without a contemplation of the "Idea of the Good" conceived in a Platonic way. Reason abstracts the general concept of the good from the concrete, particular goods we encounter in our actions. St. Thomas freed his doctrine of knowledge of the good from every remnant of Platonic idealism.[18]

At the same time, however, Thomas strongly emphasized the connection between goodness and truth. Truth is the essential object of reason; it is what reason properly seeks in all that it knows. The good, on the other hand, is the object of the will. Because the will is a rational appetite (*appetitus rationalis*), reason, which is so naturally connected with the will, must also seek the truth in whatever the will aims at, in every action of the will. Action, in turn, is an act (*actus secundus*) of existence— *operari sequitur esse*. Thus our whole existence is continually being actualized in conjunction with truth. And this is inevitable and necessary because it flows from our nature as human beings. The function of truth in human action and existence constitutes the very essence of the moral norm, which St. Thomas conceives existentially and not merely formally, just as he also conceives the good existentially.

2. MAX SCHELER

VALUE AND ETHOS

Scheler was also a strong opponent of formalism in ethics. He took the position that the proper object of ethics is solely and exclusively value, or rather the different values that make up the "matter" of human lived experiences, of human feelings and willings, and that all such values in human beings are connected with moral value. In Scheler's view, values form a distinctive *a priori*, but one that differs radically from the Kantian *a priori*.[19] Kant's *a priori* excluded all objective, nonrational elements, whereas Scheler's is based precisely on such elements. Values belong to objective reality, but they remain concealed in it as long as they are not disclosed by a corresponding experience of a human subject or some other subject capable of experiencing them. Scheler does not deal with these other subjects, but the possibility of them nevertheless remains. Only in a particular subject's experience do values produce that distinctive *a priori*. Scheler maintains that the lived experience of values has a primarily emotional character, because values are an object of either love, which enriches and expands the world of values, or hate, which impoverishes and narrows this world. In the view espoused by Scheler, the cognitive experience of values is merely something secondary, and it, too, has an emotional character because it arises through an intentional feeling. Any possibility of knowing values in an intellectual way is excluded by Scheler.

Thus, for Scheler, the *a priori* referred to above is in no way subjective, although the emotional disposition of the respective subject conditions the form this *a priori* takes in the lived experience of values. Emotional acts, however, do not create values; they only disclose or reveal objective values. It cannot be said that Kant's intellectual apriorism was replaced in Scheler's system by an emotional apriorism. There is, however, a certain feature of Scheler's theory that gives rise to some difficulty in this regard, especially because it has ramifications for the development of the problematic of the ethical norm. Values are immediately disclosed or revealed in emotional experience according to a certain hierarchical order—as higher or lower. The intentional "highness" or "lowness" of values involves some sort of immanent relation to the value that a given subject experiences as highest and the one that he or she experiences as lowest, although this is not a relation grasped by reason or directly understood and justified, but an immediately felt relation.

The emotional cognition of value is accompanied by a certain sense of duty. This, however, is only an ideal duty (equivalent to "value *x* ought to be realized"). Scheler stresses in this regard that no duty belongs to the essence of value, because value as such is indifferent to existence and, therefore, also to the realization of value on the part of a given subject. Consequently, the lived experience of "ideal" duty can only arise from that subject: duty is a kind of invitation for the subject to realize a certain value. This invitation, however, should not be brutally destroyed by a command, an imperative, or a norm (by *norm* here Scheler understands a rule within a general radius). The value, since it has announced itself to the subject by means of a feeling that was combined with a lived experience of ideal duty, ought to become an object of realization for the subject solely on the basis of its emotional appeal, which a value always evokes in the subject.

Scheler, therefore, accepts an *ideales Sollen* of value, but he is opposed to every form of *normatives Sollen*, for the latter destroys the whole independence of the lived experience of value and subjects the agent "blindly" to the will of another. Every command entails such subjection. Both suggestive commands ("you shall do such and such"), in which there is no mention at all of the existence of the will of the person to whom the command is addressed, and even pedagogical commands ("you will be better off if you do what I want you to do") make it impossible to independently experience the value that is supposed to be the object of realization. For this same reason, Scheler is even opposed to all advice in ethics, including that of the so-called evangelical counsels, for advising involves influencing the will of another person. Only in what Scheler calls "moral counsel" is there no suggestion associated with pointing out a value, but merely straightforward information about the value, which makes it easier for another person to know for himself or herself what to do.[20]

This systematic dismissal from ethics of every form of real duty and obligation, of every form of rule and even advice, is, in Scheler's eyes, synonymous with overcoming the negativism in ethics that has prevailed in it since the time of Kant and the categorical imperative. We each have our own personal world of values with some specific hierarchy—our own *a priori*. There are also, however, systems of values peculiar to certain epochs or social groups, systems distinguished by a hierarchization proper to those epochs or social groups, by relations of "highness" and "lowness" intrinsic to what Scheler calls the *ethos*.[21] This ethos is subject to change and development. Scheler does not accept the notion of a permanent, "finished" world of objective goods, but tells us to consider the particular perspective in which values are gradually unveiled before us as the "matter" of moral life. He stresses that the full richness of these values cannot be encompassed within the lived experience of any one person or even any one historical epoch.

We can see, though, that Scheler is concerned not so much with encompassing all values as with grasping as correctly as possible the hierarchical relations that occur among them. This is what forms the basis for Scheler's affirmation of the Christian ethos, an affirmation that is hard to miss in his works. Jesus Christ, whom Scheler regards as the greatest moral and religious genius of humankind, grasped the hierarchical relations among values in the most correct way; one could say that he achieved the most perfect organization of ethical "matter" as a whole. This was, according to Scheler, a work of the "heart" and not of reason, for all progress in the realm of morality is a work of the heart and is reducible

to the kind of regularity with which emotional acts of love and feelings
are involved in fashioning the ethical *a priori.*

THE REGULARITY OF THE LIVED EXPERIENCE OF VALUES AND NORMS?

The "ethical *a priori,*" which in practice is always identical with some
form of ethos, is directly linked to the lived experience of moral values.[22]
These values appear upon the occasion of the realization of certain "matter," that is, certain objective values having a specific *a priori* hierarchical
position. When I realize a value that I experience as higher (and this
realization always takes place through willing), then along with this
realization I feel morally good: a positive moral value appears in my
emotional world. The lived experience of this "good" contains a certain
relativity, which is easily explained by the fact that the height of the
value that is the object of realization implies a relation to a highest value.
Were I to make this highest value itself the object of my willing, its
realization would have to be accompanied by the lived experience of
"good" in the absolute sense.

My moral experience develops in the opposite direction when I take
as an object of my willing a value I feel to be lower in my emotional
field of vision. Such realization is accompanied by the feeling of "evil":
a negative moral value appears in my emotional world. This "evil," too,
has a relative hue, which is easily explained by the fact that every "lower"
value essentially implies a relation to some lowest value. Were I to make
this lowest value the object of my willing, I would then feel evil in the
absolute sense. Thus both "good" and "evil"—both positive and negative
moral values—take rank in my experience depending on the "matter" of
my moral action.

This is how Scheler grasped the basic regularity that strikes the
phenomenologist in connection with the lived experience of moral "good"
and "evil." Could it be said, though, that in grasping this regularity Scheler
posited a normative principle or defined an ethical norm? Even setting
aside the fact that Scheler himself would not have wanted to establish a
normative principle because of the supposedly negative character that accompanies every norm (anything intended to define and especially to en-
gender duty), I would insist that this regularity of the lived experience
of moral good and evil basically does not have the character of a norm.
It says nothing about what is good and what is evil, but merely asserts
that, upon the occasion of a certain thing (some value), "good" or "evil"

is experienced. This, however, is a fundamental difference. The regularity in question has a primarily descriptive character, not a normative one. Still, it cannot be said to be purely descriptive, since values do come into play. Furthermore, a certain hierarchy of values—their highness or lowness—always comes into play. All of this implies in a rather remote way a certain element of positing norms, of situating action (willing) in a world of values. I already drew attention to this in a different philosophical context in my analysis of St. Thomas' views on the topic of norms.

The highness and lowness of values undoubtedly provides certain *a priori* normative directives, but these are only, so to speak, more remote directives. Scheler did not present more proximate directives, more proximate grounds for positing norms, but he probably also could not do so, given the view of reality he had at his disposal in his philosophical system. On the other hand, the more remote directives, upon closer contact with life, prove to be inadequate. They simply do not satisfy the need for the concrete positing of norms, for the concrete predication of good or evil with respect to human action. Thus, for example, the feeling itself of the highness of certain values, such as the religious values connected with the concrete action of prayer, still does not provide me with a more proximate and adequate basis for saying that this concrete prayer is a morally good act. Similarly, it would be hard to say that the kind of experience of sensory values that is unquestionably associated with eating, for example, is morally evil because I feel sensory values as "lower."

A host of other examples could be advanced to show that the mere feeling of a hierarchy of values does not provide us with a sufficient basis for the immediate positing of norms, even though it cannot be denied that values have a certain remote influence on this process. Thus, for example, it cannot be denied that prayer as such is regarded as a more perfect action than eating as such—precisely because of the main value that forms the object of experience in the one case and the other. The positing of norms, however, does not deal merely with actions as such, but must deal with concrete actions in their natural and practical forms. Otherwise the world of moral good and evil would take shape in a way rather incompatible with our nature. If "good" were systematically and *a priori* associated only with what is higher (spiritual—holy—divine) and "evil" with what is lower (vital—sensory), we would inevitably lapse into a kind of Manichaeism. More importantly, however, moral good would then be too unequivocally enmeshed in "matter," in the objects of human action (this much would also hold true for moral evil), and would not be a sufficiently distinct and characteristic perfection of the subject—the acting person.

I have even more serious reservations about another form of regularity according to which, in Scheler's view, moral good and evil appear in the lived experience of the acting person. The person would experience good when a positive value in some higher class of values was made an object of willing, and evil when a negative value in that same class was made an object of willing. This rule seems to be a complement of the previous one and is wholly consistent with it. It presupposes the existence of certain classes of values—which again are higher or lower. The good would accompany a positive value in a higher class realized by willing, as opposed to a negative value in that class. If, then, we take, for example, the class of aesthetic values, the experience of moral good would always have to be connected with the willing of beauty, and the experience of evil with the willing of ugliness. It would be hard to deny that some sort of good and evil is connected with these forms of willing—but is it moral good and evil? This gives us all the more reason to ask whether Scheler does not obliterate the essential distinction that moral values have, in favor of the "matter" alone of human action, and whether he does not in some sense transfer moral values *in aliud genus*.

All of this is very intimately connected with the question of norms. I call a norm that which in some way generates moral values and is found to some extent directly with the birth of values, or at any rate makes the emergence of values possible in the human being as a person. As we have seen, objective values essentially make this emergence of moral good or evil possible in the human being, but only in a kind of remote sense. The most proximate factor was not indicated by Scheler—at least that is what this analysis leads me to conclude.

For Thomas, if we recall, the most proximate source from which moral "values" (moral good and evil) "spring," so to speak, is reason's natural ability to know the truth in everything that the will wills, in every good that happens to be a "material" object or end of the will. According to Scheler, on the other hand, moral values somehow erupt spontaneously within our emotional experience upon the occasion of our experiencing any other values, although according to a certain characteristic regularity—which I have just discussed. Scheler's analysis does not reveal here the presence of any subjective normative factor whatsoever: values simply arise beyond subjective norms and independently of them—and even counter to anything that could perform a normative role and contribute to the lived experience of duty. It seems that Scheler was so exclusively and single-mindedly intent on overcoming Kant's formalism in ethics that he completely failed to see the whole positive and constructive side of norms. I would even go so far as to say that he could not properly objectify them given the assumptions of his system—but this, again, is a separate issue and calls for a more extensive and detailed analysis. On the other hand, an important matter that deserves at least a cursory treatment here is the emphasis that Scheler placed on the significance of exemplariness in his ethical system.

THE PROBLEM OF THE MORAL IDEAL AND IMITATION

The "materiality" of moral values, which causes these values not to differ sharply enough from all the other values we experience, is reflected very clearly in Scheler's presentation of one of the main theses of his ethical system, the thesis concerning exemplariness and the moral ideal. I see this thesis as the culmination of the personalistic character of Scheler's system in contrast to Kant's system, where the basis of human morality is thought to be an impersonal norm—an *a priori* form of pure practical reason. According to Scheler, no such abstract and general norm can be effective in real moral values. Only a human being—a personal model or ideal—can be morally effective. Such a model embodies a value that could be called typical, and this value must be embraced as the main content of the model's emotional life, of his or her loves and feelings. To the extent that this value becomes an object of love and feeling for another person or persons, the model is effective, because those other persons become like the person they regard as the ideal, that is, they realize the willing of the same values in themselves. It should be noted, however, that the value in question is always some "material" value: saint-ly value, spiritual value, vital value, or sensory value.[23] Around such a value is crystalized the whole exemplary personality of the teacher, and, in turn, the personality of the disciple. In this way, we are presented in life with the characteristic types of human perfection crystalized in the personalities of the saint, the genius, the hero, and the epicure (*Künstler des Genusses*).[24]

It would be hard not to notice that Scheler, who in this point essentially overcame Kantianism, appeals to the healthy humanistic traditions of Aristotle's ethics. For Aristotle, an essentially good person was a moral "model and measure" for others. Such an individual, however, was a *good human being*, someone who realized inwardly the perfection proper to a rational human being—moral perfection. According to Scheler, on the other hand, this perfection, moral value itself, is neither the center of exemplariness and imitation nor itself an end of willing. It is experienced only upon the occasion of the process of imitation, which, therefore, in Scheler's view, is not essentially but only indirectly productive of moral value. The significance of the model and ideal is primarily psychological and only indirectly ethical.

To complete this picture, I should add that in addition to positive models Scheler also distinguishes negative models, the imitation of which is associated with the "production" of negative moral value, the development of "evil" in us. And, finally, God is not really an object of imitation. God accompanies the process of imitation and the acceptance of personal values to the extent that, in the light of the idea of God as the highest personal Spirit, there develops in us all that determines our personality, and thus a kind of resemblance to God, a kind of "theomorphism." Obviously, Scheler would not agree with St. Thomas' view of exemplariness.

3. FINAL OBSERVATIONS AND CONCLUSIONS

This essay is both expository and comparative in character. An analysis of two philosophical sources (Thomas Aquinas and Max Scheler) so far removed from one another in their epistemological and methodological assumptions should end with some conclusions of a comparative nature. But drawing such conclusions must be done with extreme caution. It would be easy to take a certain similarity or convergence in tendency for an identity in point of view, when, in fact, there can be no talk of identity precisely because of the divergence of the very assumptions. These differences at the ground level do not merely remain there but permeate every concept and theory of the two thinkers, giving their concepts and theories an essentially disparate character despite their external resemblance. With these reservations in mind, I will now attempt to draw a few conclusions.

EXEMPLARINESS IN ETHICS AND MORALITY

In both thinkers, we find the tendency to emphasize exemplariness as an important element for morality and as a constitutive element for ethics. According to St. Thomas, the normative order presupposes an *ordo causae exemplaris*. God as subsistent existence is the fullness of good and thus the supreme model for all beings as goods, and in a particular sense for human beings as beings and goods. The whole exemplary order branches out, so to speak, and differentiates according to the various species of beings. We humans are the only beings to whom moral "goodness" (*bonitas moralis*)—one could even say moral "value," setting aside all phenomenological implications of the word—essentially belongs. As beings of a rational nature, in order for us to be goods in keeping with this nature, it is not enough for us to be physically good, but we must also and above all be morally good. Morality as a specific actualization of rationality and freedom and as a specifically human ontic potentiality is also a specific "terrain" of exemplariness, a terrain in which the exemplary order, extending all the way to the supreme Model, is particularly applicable.

Of course, the "terrain" of morality remains in a particular exposition, so to speak, in relation to God as the Supreme Good and Model. This truth was clearly accentuated in the Gospel. St. Thomas as a philosopher-theologian is certainly influenced by this suggestion that has its source in revelation. Scheler, however, in appealing to the notion of exemplariness in his system, weakens the theological exposition of exemplariness and obliterates the truth upon which such a clear accent was placed in the Gospel. He narrows the exemplary order in morality to relations between one human being and another, between the model human being (teacher) and the imitator human being (disciple). Still, we find in his view a striking convergence with the Gospel in the Model Human Being of Christ and Christ's imitator disciples. This also explains why certain contemporary Catholic moralists (e.g., Tillmann) were so attracted to Scheler.

Although the analogies between the role of exemplariness in St. Thomas and Scheler may seem striking at first glance, upon closer examination they turn out to be far less so. Because of Scheler's different assumptions, which are phenomenological assumptions, one cannot speak of the person-disciple being a good like the person-teacher, and one cannot even maintain that the person-disciple is good (in the moral sense) like his or her model. The person-disciple only experiences moral values upon the occasion of adopting values like those embraced by his or her teacher and model, and especially upon the occasion of "realizing" them. Exemplariness is transferred from the ontological to the psychological order and also from the real to the intentional order. We obviously, therefore, cannot speak of resembling and becoming like God; and resembling and becoming like Christ also occurs in a purely human manner—in a psychological and merely intentional manner.

THE PROBLEM OF THE HIERARCHY OF GOODS

Here again analogies with the Schelerian hierarchy of values may suggest themselves. Scheler, however, says only that values, which we experience according to a certain hierarchy as higher or lower, are also hierarchically ordered in themselves. But St. Thomas deals with a hierar-

chy of goods, that is, with beings that are goods of higher or lower perfection. On this topic, Scheler has really nothing to say—because of the
very assumptions of his system: phenomenology is not metaphysics. What
is a "good" for Scheler? Roughly speaking, one could say that it is an
object that in some way contains a source of value. Phenomenology, however, allows us to speak only of a hierarchy of values and not of a hierarchy of goods.

Scheler also appears to assign greater importance to the hierarchy
of values in his ethical system than St. Thomas does to the hierarchy
of goods in his ethics. According to Scheler, the moral value experienced by a given person depends directly and exclusively on the
position the value that is an object of experience (willing) occupies in
the hierarchy of values. I have already attempted to show why this
view seems wrong.

According to St. Thomas, the hierarchy of goods is intimately connected with the exemplary order: the more perfectly a good exemplifies
the supreme Good, the higher it stands in the hierarchy. This view contains
a general basis for all norms and all positing of norms. As far as the role
of the hierarchy of goods in the concrete, particular positing of norms is
concerned, St. Thomas is rather silent on this issue. At most, it could be
said that our moral life—and thus also the positing of concrete norms—
takes shape and takes place in some sense against the background of the
objective hierarchy of goods outlined by St. Thomas, which places supernatural goods above natural goods, goods of the soul above goods of the
body, and internal goods (of the human being) above external goods
(things). This hierarchization contains a kind of general directive for every
choice made by the human will, but this directive can be regarded as the
highest norm in a further sense, namely, insofar as the hierarchical order
of goods determines the order that should prevail in human action. This
order alone, however, still does not entirely resolve the matter of the
moral value of a concrete human act.

THE ESSENCE OF THE MORAL LIFE

As I examine all these differences, I become more and more convinced
that St. Thomas and Scheler have completely different and separate views
of morality, especially when it comes to the "moral life." For St. Thomas,
the moral life consists in attaining the truth in all our action and behavior,
and activity by nature always aims at some good. Consequently, the essence of the moral life is the "lived experience" of the truth of the good

realized in action and the realization in that action of the good subjected to the criterion of reason and thus placed in the light of that truth. This is not ethical intellectualism in the Platonic sense. Rather, it is the belief that the positing of norms enters into the essence and structure of all conscious and free human acts, which always have objective moral value. We, of course, "experience" this positing of norms as an essential and constitutive element of our moral actions. This experience can be understood as a reflex of consciousness, one that accompanies those actions and mirrors what is going on in our being—in our reason and will.

This view of positing norms and view of human action as essentially involving the "lived experience" of positing norms—and thus also of norms—an experience with which the moral value of an action is directly linked, is strictly connected with the Thomistic view of spiritual life in general and of the spiritual life of the human being in particular. The essence of the spiritual life based on reason is truth, especially truth in all that is an object of the will. We know that whatever is an object of the will is in some sense a good, and so the essence of the spiritual life is the truth of the good.

Scheler, on the other hand, has a different view of the moral life. For him, the moral life consists in the emotional experience of moral value. Moral value, in turn, arises spontaneously upon the occasion of our emotional involvement in some world of values or other and becomes the object and content of a separate experience precisely because this emotional involvement in our world of values is connected with the experience of a certain hierarchy of those values—this was already discussed above. In this view, the essence of the moral life—or, taken singly, the essence of a particular moral "experience"—is not the positing of norms, that is, the "lived experience" of the truth of the good of our action, but the "lived experience" of value alone. And herein lies the basic difference between the two views. The "lived experience" of value has—one could say—eliminated the "lived experience" of the truth of the good. Thus a real element has disappeared from the Schelerian view of the moral life—the element of positing norms, understood as the lived experience of the truth of the good. And this seems incompatible with experience and incompatible with reality: the essence of the moral life is not just the "lived experience" of value (or even of the good), but precisely the "lived experience" of the truth of the good that is an object of action and that is realized in this action.

THE LIVED EXPERIENCE OF VALUE

Scheler's position amounts to placing the whole ethical problematic somehow beyond norms. Could it be that the phenomenological method, at least as it appears in Scheler, is incapable of apprehending and objectifying norms—even in the subjective sense as the function of positing norms? Leaving aside the extent to which this may be a consequence of Scheler's emotionalism in his view of the human being and in his view of the spiritual life of the person, I believe that it is also a consequence of his view of values. A value, as Scheler himself says, is not the same as an objective good. Rather, a value is the content given in our lived experience when we come in contact with a good—with a thing we experience as a good. Scheler calls such a thing a *Sache* and sharply distinguishes it from a *Ding*. A *Sache* is an object in which cognition has not yet differentiated the thing-content (*Ding*) from the value-content (*Wert*).

Such an object would simply be a being in the ordinary sense of the term (*res = ens*), and, as St. Thomas says, every being is a good from an existential point of view—a point I discussed at the beginning. The consciousness of value, on the other hand, arises in us when that existential good (something that exists in a determinate degree and becomes an object of action) is evaluated in a certain way, namely, is placed, so to speak, under the light of truth. Only then can one speak of the lived experience of value. Scheler, however, is an exponent of a totally different view on this topic. The lived experience of value, he maintains, is a spontaneous function of the emotional life, and the cognition or feeling of value is an act of a unique emotional "intuition." It seems, however, that this is precisely where Schelerian emotionalism has covered up or simply "swallowed up" the whole rich structure and content of the spiritual life of the human person.

Since I do not agree with such an oversimplification and obfuscation of the essential contours of this whole issue, I will have to accept the thesis that the lived experience of a value is somehow connected with the positing of a value, that is, with some sort of evaluation of a good (in the purely existential sense), and that this evaluation once again consists in placing that good under the light of truth. Only then is there a place for the norm—including the ethical norm—in a philosophical system as a whole. By itself, the concept of value would exclude such a place in advance. Value is essentially already a consequence of some sort of evaluation, or, to use the language of St. Thomas, of some sort of subordination of the good to the true. Thus, once inside the framework of a system of values, we are in a sense already on the other side of norms and the positing of norms, and thus also beyond them. An "ethics of values" would, therefore, be an "ethics" of the ready-made fruits of norms and the positing of norms. The question then arises: in that case, would there still be any ethics at all?—a fundamental question.

This question is posed here a little more broadly than the sources upon which I based the analytical part of this essay would allow. At any rate, in the light of my analysis of the views of these two thinkers, St. Thomas Aquinas and Max Scheler, I am led to conclude that the concept of a norm is justified in a system of moral philosophy that proceeds from an existential view of the good and is not really justified in a system of the philosophy of values.

Obviously, there is a difference between positing a norm and positing a value. Still, they both have as a basic constituent the element of the truth of the good. And in this sense to posit a value is already somehow to posit a norm, although not in the full sense of the term. In the full sense of the term, to posit a norm does not just mean to determine the truth of the goodness of a human action, but also to direct that action in keeping with this truth.

NOTES

1. Thomas Aquinas, *Quaestiones disputatae de veritate* XXI, 2.
2. Thomas Aquinas, *Quaestiones disputatae de potentia Dei* III, 6; *Summa theologiae* I, 48, 1.
3. Thomas Aquinas, *Summa contra Gentiles* II, 41.
4. Thomas Aquinas, *Summa theol.* I–II, 18, 1; I–II, 18, 3 ad 3.
5. Thomas Aquinas, *Quaestiones disputatae de malo* I, 2; *Contra Gent.* III, 20; *Summa theol.* I, 5, 3 ad 3.
6. See Thomas Aquinas, *Summa theol.* I, 5, 5, and also I, 6, 3; I, 16, 3; I, 16, 4; I–II, 52, 1; *Contra Gent.* I, 40.
7. Thomas Aquinas, *Scriptum in IV Libros Sententiarum* I, 3, 2, 2.
8. Thomas Aquinas, *De veritate* XXI, 6.
9. Thomas Aquinas, *Quaestiones disputatae de virtutibus* I, 8, 12.
10. Thomas Aquinas, *Summa theol.* I–II, 85, 4.
11. Thomas Aquinas, *Summa theol.* I, 6, 1 ad 1.
12. Thomas Aquinas, *Sent.* I, 38, 1, 3.
13. Thomas Aquinas, *Summa theol.* I, 6, 1 ad 2; I, 23, 4 ad 5; I, 65, 2; *Contra Gent.* I, 40, 2; III, 20; III, 25, 5; *Sent.* I, 1, 2, 2, 2; *Quaestiones quodlibetales* X, 17.
14. Thomas Aquinas, *Summa theol.* I–II, 2, 6; I–II, 84, 4; I–II, 8, 7 ad 2; II–II, 73, 3; II–II, 85, 3 ad 2; II–II, 104, 3; II–II, 118, 5; II–II, 152, 2 ad 4; *Contra Gent.* III, 134, 4–5; *Sent.* I, 36, 4; *In Epistolam ad Ephesios* VI, 1.; etc.

15. Thomas Aquinas, *Summa theol.* I, 59, 2 ad 3; I, 87, 4 ad 2; I–II, 9, 1; I–II, 9, 1 ad 3; II–II, 109, 2 ad 1; *De virtutibus* I, 6, 5.

16. Thomas Aquinas, *Summa theol.* I, 16, 4 ad 1; I, 59, 2 ad 3; I, 79, 11 ad 2; I, 82, 3 ad 1; I, 82, 4 ad 1; *De veritate* III, 3, 9; *De malo* IX, 6.

17. Thomas Aquinas, *Summa theol.* II–II, 141, 1; *De Malo* I, 4.

18. Thomas Aquinas, *Summa theol.* I, 6, 4; II–II, 23, 2 ad 1; *De veritate* XXVI, 4.

19. Max Scheler, *Formalism in Ethics and Non-Formal Ethics of Values: A New Attempt Toward the Foundation of an Ethical Personalism*, trans. Manfred S. Frings and Roger L. Funk (Evanston: Northwestern UP, 1973) 48 ff., especially "The Non-Formal A Priori in Ethics" 81–110.

20. Scheler distinguishes *advice* from *counsel* in the following way: "There is still an *expression of will* in 'advice.' Advice is not a *mere* communication of what someone else should ideally do. In contrast to this, moral '*counsel*' is only an assist that helps one to see morally what should or should not be; it is *not* an expression of will" (*Formalism* 205). Despite their name, the evangelical counsels also fall into the category of advice (see *Formalism* 205). —Trans.

21. Scheler, "Variations in Ethos," *Formalism* 301–307.

22. Scheler, "The Relation of the Values 'Good' and 'Evil' to the Other Values and Goods," *Formalism* 23–30.

23. Saintly value, spiritual value, vital value, and sensory value are the values personified in the models of the saint, genius, hero, and epicure, respectively. Saintly values, or religious values, have to do with the holy and all it entails; spiritual values, or values of the spirit, with knowledge, beauty, and rightness; vital values, or life values, with the noble and whatever is conducive to life (health, vitality, strength, courage, etc.); and sensory values with the sensibly agreeable, the pleasant. See Scheler, *Formalism* 104–110 and 585–586. —Trans.

24. Scheler, "The Law of the Origin of the Prevailing Ethos. Model Persons," *Formalism* 572–583; "The Idea of Ordered Ranks among Pure Types of the Value-Person," *Formalism* 583–595.

6

Human Nature as the Basis of Ethical Formation

I

Ethical topics are always in lively demand; perhaps of all philosophical disciplines, ethics is the most intriguing to people in general. The concept of ethics is connected with a whole series of vital, practical problems. We are all familiar with these problems in one way or another from our own experience and observation. And because these are inner problems—from which they derive their mystery and intimacy—and, at the same time, critical, dramatic problems, we readily turn our thoughts to them. I should say right at the outset, however, that to speak of morality, even in a deep, intelligent, perceptive way, is one thing, and to pursue ethics is another. Ethics is a part of philosophy. This means that it has the same orientation as philosophy in general. This orientation of philosophy was described by Aristotle, who saw philosophy as a science that attempts to present and explain all problems in the light of the highest principles.

In addition, ethics has its own object. To illuminate this object, we would do best to proceed from the questions with which all ethical reflection—all philosophical reflection in the area of ethics—begins. These are the following two questions: 1) What makes the human being and human actions good, and what makes them bad? 2) What gives the human being complete goodness, i.e., happiness? These are two questions that we all

Karol Wojtyla, "Natura ludzka jako podstawa formacji etycznej," *Znak* 11 (1959): 693–697. A summary prepared by Wojtyla of a lecture he gave on 19 February 1959, during the Second Annual Philosophy Week at the Catholic University of Lublin.

in some way ask ourselves. Moral philosophers also begin from these same two questions, except that they develop the reflections that lead them to the answers not in a prescientific but in a philosophical way, employing methods used by philosophy. Ethics has the same orientation as philosophy in general. It tries to answer these two basic questions in the light of the highest principles. Its proper function is not to establish norms but to justify them. Ethics is not involved with passing sentence in the realm of behavior, any more than grammar, for example, is involved with passing sentence in the realm of language. The task of ethics is to justify norms, which are themselves something vital—one could say existential—for they are connected with really existing people and societies. The source of norms is found in natural law, which is not a written law. The believer finds the source of ethical norms in revelation, which to a significant degree confirms natural law. Revelation, moreover, is a written source.

II

The title of this talk is "Human Nature as the Basis of Ethical Formation." *Nature* is equivalent to a thing's essence, understood as the basis of the thing's activity. If we examine a really existing being with full regard for its essence, we will have to agree, on the one hand, that the activity of this being is an extension of its existence (*operari sequitur esse*), and, on the other, that the content of this activity is an expression or externalization of the being's essence. Thus we find the same two aspects in the being's activity as we find in the being itself. Activity as activity is a kind of extension of existence, a continuation of existence. Activity as the particular content that is realized in this activity is a kind of externalization or expression of the being's essence. And so when we say, for example that "an animal acts," this means something different from when we say that "a human being acts." This is understandable, since a different nature lies at the basis of the one activity and the other. The activity is different in terms of its content, but because essence is strictly connected with existence, the activity as an expression or continuation of existence is also different. In ethics, we are concerned with human actions (*actus humani*). We are not really interested—except perhaps only indirectly—in any *actus hominis*, that is, in any human activity that has a certain similarity to the activity of animals; in other words, we are only indirectly interested in phenomena having to do with the sensory and vegetative life of the human being.

To say that the human being is a rational being is also to say that the human being is a person. The human being is a person by nature. Boethius said that a person is an individual of a rational nature. Only such a nature—a rational nature—can be the basis of morality. And a person is an individual of a rational nature.

What does it mean "to be the basis of morality"? The concept of morality is connected with moral good and evil, with the occurrence of moral good and evil in a given subject, namely, a person. The person is not only the subject in which moral good and evil occur but also the efficient cause of that good and evil. This is the sense in which the person, an individual of a rational nature, is the basis of the fact—or, in a certain sense, of the phenomenon—of morality.

III

Why is only a person a subject of morality? Why is only a rational nature capable of being a basis of morality? Because reason is connected with being a person. Reason is not just the ability to form general concepts and make judgments. It is also the ability to know the truth; it is in some sense a natural relation to the truth. It is the ability to know—among other things—the truth with respect to the good and the truth with respect to goods.

The good is always related to appetitive powers, which differ completely from cognitive powers. Desire itself is blind to the truth; a relation to the truth does not exist for desire as desire. Even the will as an appetitive power does not have a relation to the truth. But although the will as a source of desire is blind to the truth, it is still susceptible to the truth, amenable to it. St. Thomas calls the will an *appetitus rationalis*, i.e., the kind of appetitive power that has a natural and most intimate connection with reason and its natural relation to the truth. And it is precisely this element—the presence of an *appetitus rationalis* in the human being—that from the structural point of view is decisive for the fact of morality.

Morality exists because of this possibility of subordinating to the truth the relation to various goods. The human being is by nature rational, is a person, an individual of a rational nature, and so morality is something natural and necessary in the human being. A human being must subordinate to the truth the various goods with which he or she is involved in acting, thereby also subordinating this activity itself to the truth. Morality is an irrevocable aspect of human acts (*actus humani*).

IV

Just as reason is a property of human nature, freedom is also a property of a rational nature. Both reason and freedom are signs of personality.

Freedom of will is a condition of morality because of its natural connection with reason. Reason is the ability to know the truth; it is a natural relation to the truth. Freedom of will is naturally and intimately connected with this relation to the truth. As a result, the will is faced with the "necessity" of choosing either a true good or a false good. Choice is an act of will because the will is an *appetitus rationalis*. And because reason (*ratio*) exists in a natural relation to the truth, it insinuates itself somehow into the object of choice. When the object of choice—when the object of a voluntary act of will—is a true good, then the human action is morally good. When the object of a conscious, voluntary act of will is a false good, then the human action becomes morally bad.

Because reason and will are properties of human nature and properties of every concrete human person, a whole separate region of truth opens up in the human being, namely, the truth with respect to the good. The content of a norm is basically the truth about a good, a proposition affirming that "*A* is good and *B* is evil." This affirmative proposition is directed to the will; it is, so to speak, addressed to the will. It, therefore, takes hold of the will's natural dynamism and thereby evokes a command or a prohibition.

The moral formation of the human being means a formation through moral good. The human being is formed through moral good. And one could say in a parallel way that the human being is deformed through moral evil. Moral formation has mainly positive overtones: it is connected with good. Its antithesis is deformation through moral evil. In saying that the human being is formed through moral good, we presuppose a certain property of the human person in general and of the will in particular. To be able to be formed by moral good, the human being must be in some way disposed toward this, must be susceptible to such formation, as well as to such deformation. Consequently, the human being must have a special potentiality that conditions and makes possible such formation and deformation. This potentiality will be primarily an attribute of the will. I believe we conceive the will too one-sidedly when we regard it only as an efficient power (as did, for example, Narziss Ach and similar psychologists), a power that is merely an initiator of activity. Moral facts and the moral life of the human being require us to view the will somewhat differently: the will is not only an efficient power, a power that gives rise to action, but also a kind of ability to become. Free will is that power of a concrete, individual human nature, that power of a person, by virtue of which the person becomes morally good or bad.

This becoming—or, if we wish to use a Latin derivative, this formation or deformation—of the will and of the person is realized to some extent through every separate human action that has a specific moral value: through each good act and each bad act. The will can become good or bad not only actually but also habitually. A particular good or evil moral value can become fixed in the will—and here we enter the realm of virtues and vices, an area that in St. Thomas' *Summa* comprised an extensive treatise, *De habitibus*. Moral good and moral evil can become crystalized in the will in a lasting, habitual way. The will can become formed or deformed in a lasting way. By becoming formed in a lasting way, the will acquires certain virtues; by becoming deformed, it acquires vices.

7

Ethics and Moral Theology

Let me begin with some general remarks about the meaning of certain terms basic to this discussion. Ethics for me will be neither a purely descriptive science of morality (ethology) nor a merely "moralistic" doctrine of morality. In other words, I am renouncing the two extreme tendencies in the way moral questions are approached. Both of these tendencies, though for different reasons, lose sight of the proper ethical problematic. I am, therefore, renouncing the science of morality,[1] which sacrifices normativeness for descriptiveness, and the "logic of norms," which is basically confined to the construction of internally coherent codes of rules of behavior and is less—or not at all—concerned with their ultimate justification. In contrast to both of these approaches, I will take ethics to mean a science that deals with morality in its normative, not just descriptive, aspect and that aims at "objectifying" norms, and thus above all at ultimately justifying them, not just presenting them.

Moral theology presently exists in two forms:

1) as *positive theology*, which makes use of the findings of various particular sciences, such as history, archaeology, and philology; this form of theology is an *exegesis* of the doctrine of Christian morality contained in revelation (scripture and tradition), in keeping with the magisterium of the Church;

2) as *speculative theology*, or theological ethics in the strict sense; this form of theology is an *interpretation* of scripture and tradition in keeping with the magisterium of the Church *by means of a particular philosophical system.*

Karol Wojtyla, "Etyka a teologia moralna," *Znak* 19 (1967): 1077–1082. A summary authorized by Wojtyla of a lecture he gave on 17 February 1967, during the Tenth Annual Philosophy Week at the Catholic University of Lublin.

An example of such speculative theology is the moral theology of St. Thomas Aquinas, which is widely known and used both in its original form and in various commentaries and textbooks. It is really the only example of this type of theology. Centuries of work had already gone into it long before St. Thomas. The entire reception of ancient philosophy—both Plato's and Aristotle's—by the Fathers and later by the Scholastics tended in this direction. Despite the many profound differences between Plato's and Aristotle's systems, they display a certain oneness of metaphysical orientation. It was just this feature that especially predisposed these two "philosophies" for use as tools in interpreting the data of revelation.

What is the significance of this "philosophization" that occurs in speculative theology?

1) Generally speaking, the significance and need of such theology in general, and of moral theology in particular, springs from the same sources from which the need and meaning of philosophy itself arises, namely, from our natural human aspiration as rational beings to "get to the bottom" of everything that affects us and everything we meet—in short, from our need to understand reality *per ultimas causas.* In a certain realm of reality, ethics as moral philosophy has the role of "getting to the bottom" of the reality of morality. In a way parallel and analogical to ethics, moral theology "gets to the bottom" of the reality of morality in the light of the teachings on morality contained in the sources of revelation. It stands to reason, then, that theology should derive the tools for an "ultimate" analysis of its own revealed contents from philosophy. In this respect, speculative moral theology is equally an expression and a realization of normal—though certainly very ambitious— cognitive aspirations on the part of those who, as Christians, want to get to the bottom of their Christian morality.

2) More specifically, moral theology in the Thomistic sense "gets to the bottom" of moral reality by explaining it on the basis of the ultimate end, which implies a particular concept of the good and a particular con- cept of being. It also implies a corresponding metaphysical concept of the human being, a concept in which a "person" is in a certain sense reducible to a "nature": *individua substantia rationalis naturae.* This con- cept of the human being, in turn, forms the basis of a very important part of St. Thomas' moral theology, namely, aretology, which is connected with the system of the faculties (*potentiae*) of human nature.

Thomistic moral theology viewed from the aspects distinguished above, both the more general aspect and the two more specific ones, appears as an intellectual synthesis that goes far beyond the threshold of exegesis (positive theology). Indeed, as an interpretation that throws light on the data of revelation and insightfully arranges them by means of metaphysical categories, it is a work of simply monumental proportions—not just for its own time but for ours as well, for it can still astonish anyone who only takes the trouble to learn how to see and appreciate it.

The admiration we have for this "summa," however, does not have to mean—and even should not mean—that we regard it as a work complete and perfect in every respect. The inner bond emphasized above that exists between speculative theology and philosophy directs us today to look at this remarkable work as a "fruit of its times," that is, to view it not only within the framework of the state of philosophy in St. Thomas' day but also from the perspective of the subsequent development of philosophy. This is all the more necessary given the fact that not everything in the subsequent development of philosophy—and thus in the development of this potential tool for interpreting revealed contents—would seem to be a mere deviation. In this context, the following question arises with regard to the process of the philosophization of the message of revelation: In what direction has it developed, is it developing, and should it develop?

It seems that in connection with the general direction of the development of philosophy, which is a movement away from the philosophy of being toward the philosophy of consciousness, the two previously mentioned interpretive elements in the structure of Thomistic theology have undergone—or at least should undergo—significant modifications.

a) "Getting to the bottom" of morality by explaining it on the basis of the ultimate end has given way to explaining and justifying morality on the basis of values and norms. We are concerned today not so much with determining the ultimate end of moral conduct as with giving an ultimate justification of the norms of morality. The credit for bringing about this change in how the central problem of ethics is posed and formulated undeniably goes to Kant. But to accept Kant's point of departure in ethics—that is, to regard the problem of the justification of norms as the chief ethical problem—is not necessarily to accept Kant's solution. Indeed, a search for the ultimate justification of moral norms may lead us straight to the ultimate end. This is not presupposed in advance in the point of departure. One thing, however, is presupposed right from the start: in the whole way ethics is treated, normative rather than teleological tendencies will prevail, even in the case of "teleological" conclusions.

The assimilation of this change in ethics by moral theology will proceed in the direction of an interpretation of the ethically relevant "facts and words" of revelation in a way that will fully disclose their normative content, in order that this content might, in turn, be provided with an ultimate justification. This process of the assimilation by moral theology of the "revolution" that has taken place in ethics, a process that I both foresee and encourage, is already to some extent an accomplished fact. Contemporary moral theology is less concerned with probing the eschatological and teleological meaning of the moral content of revelation (although it does not neglect this either) and more concerned with investigating the normative meaning of the "Incarnate Word," the exemplariness of the fact of the "God-Human," a living model for living people, a model for the here and now, *in via.*

b) The second element is anthropology. Together with the emergence of the philosophy of consciousness and the development of the cognitive tools proper to it (e.g., the phenomenological method), new conditions are taking shape for enriching the concept of the human person in terms of the whole subjective, "conscious" aspect, which had in some ways been leveled in metaphysical "naturalism." This whole enriched concept of the human person can and should be brought into the interpretation of revelation as well. In moral theology, we should likewise require that this "change," which in ethics is already to a large extent an accomplished fact, be increasingly absorbed. And, indeed, the efforts of moral theologians are heading in this direction as they enter into the spirit of the developmental trends taking place in philosophy. It is extremely important to become aware of these processes. An accurate assessment of the directions of the waxings and wanings, of all that in them is a symptom of crisis and all that is a genuine achievement, will make it possible to consciously direct the whole process of theological renewal (*aggiornamento*) in keeping with the adage: *vetera novis augere.*

Up to this point my remarks have had the character of general methodological observations. They should be supplemented with more specific observations dealing with content. In particular, we must ask what the main object of this type of "philosophization" in moral theology could and should be.

It seems that the best candidate in this regard is aretology. In St. Thomas' system of moral theology, aretology had a teleological and "naturalistic" character. This aretology arose from the Aristotelian concept of the person as a nature. The human being was treated somewhat on the model of a biological organism, in which everything is explained and acquires meaning from the point of view of "maturing" and attaining its end. Today we find this "naturalistic" concept of the human being rather inadequate. The aretology being developed today is taking on a normative and personalistic character. "Virtues" and "norms" themselves are not changing, but the way they are presented in the subject is.

They will no longer be presented on the basis of means to an end. And again it must be conceded that this new way of "presenting" virtues and norms is already an accomplished fact in ethics (see, for example, Max Scheler and Nicolai Hartmann). But what about the state of moral theology? Should we not speak here instead of a certain lagging behind?

When we shift from teleological ethics to normative ethics and attempt to reconstruct moral theology along the lines of the latter, we are faced with the question: what is the relation between the norms contained in revelation and the norms of natural law, between "revealed virtues" and "natural virtues"? Are any of these norms exclusively "revealed," such that they could not be known without revelation? The possibility seems to exist of arriving at a purely philosophical understanding and acceptance of the entire moral content of the evangelical message, especially the precept that persons are to be loved by reason of the dignity vested in them.

After all, according to revelation, particularly the teachings of St. Paul, the content of revealed precepts can also be known and is in fact known without revelation, in a natural way. This is also confirmed by general experience, which, in turn, stands at the basis of the current widespread call for dialogue. Obviously, such a purely rational interpretation of revealed norms involves a certain "compression" and "abbreviation" of them. A purely philosophical interpretation is not adequate. In order to arrive at a wholly adequate interpretation, we must turn to theology and draw upon the full content of revelation. Without theology, there is no way to give a fully adequate interpretation of moral norms or of the so-called theological virtues. I should emphasize that *all* the virtues and norms contained in revelation are "theological." If the term "theological" applies in a special way to the virtues of faith, hope, and charity, this is because these three virtues (or "norms") *express in a special way the relation—revealed through "facts and words"—of human beings to God.* The nature of this relation is such that our relation to God, to others, and to ourselves conforms, corresponds, and "is a response" to God's relation to us. This relation includes the plan of salvation and sanctification, together with its realization or history. Without revelation, we would know nothing of such a plan, and so we would know nothing of the fact of the intervention of the Incarnate God in human affairs. Not knowing this, we would also not be able to interpret adequately the moral contents of revelation (e.g., the precept of love) that are "in principle" accessible to reason.

The meaning of revealed normative contents ("virtues") can be adequately interpreted only theologically, for only theology unveils before us the whole truth concerning our relation to God, which is a "response" to God's relation to us. (This latter "is" has both an informative and a normative meaning. It concerns the *truth* of our relation to God.)

The above remarks show the intimate connection of moral theology with dogmatic theology, which includes the "revealed truth about the human being," or a kind of theological anthropology. The information about our "new existence," our "being in Christ," which has such great normative significance, finds here its proper source and foundation. This, in turn, gives rise to the methodological demand to do moral theology in strict connection with dogmatics. Another demand that should be put forth in the light of all that has been said here is the need to supplement the "theology of ultimate realities," which corresponds more to the teleological treatment of moral theology, with the moral aspect of a "theology of earthly realities," which corresponds more to the normative treatment of moral theology. Both of these demands are basically one: the demand for a more integral "theologization" of moral theology.

NOTES

1. While appreciating the need for a descriptive science of morality, I do not regard it, as some still do, as the only possible—or even the only necessary—scientific discipline for investigating morality. Without ethics in the strict sense, I believe that the science of morality would meet with insurmountable difficulties in defining its object and also, therefore, in methodologically establishing itself. Only ethics has at its disposal the proper cognitive tools for adequately distinguishing the sphere of the moral from the amoral.

8

The Problem of Experience in Ethics

1. ETHICS IN A STATE OF DIVISION

Contemporary scholars who deal with the area of morality are completely
at odds about ethics. It is hard to find a uniform answer among them to
the question: what is ethics? Many even totally reject the possibility of
its existence, responding negatively to the more fundamental question:
does ethics have any basis for existing as a science? can it exist as a
science at all?[1] This intellectual climate, however, in no way drives
scholars away from the area of morality or removes the need to treat
morality in a scientific way. This issue is ultimately related to the problem
of the scientific character of philosophy, with which ethics—like so many
other branches of science—was originally one. It is also explained by the
critical attitude toward human knowledge that has developed in philosophy
over the last few centuries. These two processes—the dissolution of the
original structural whole of the philosophical sciences into a multiplicity
of particular sciences governed by their own scientific criteria, and the
critical attitude toward human knowledge—gradually also determined the
state in which ethics has found itself. In this sense, this is a "critical"
state. It would be hard to describe it in any other way, if scholars who
deal with the realm of morality are asking themselves a question as basic
as "what is ethics?" and "does it even have a basis for existing as a
science?" Can ethics still exist as a science, given the current state of
intensified criticism in the theory of science?

The critical view of the sources and criteria of meaningful knowledge
gave rise among thinkers to two orientations that, although somewhat

Karol Wojtyla, "Problem doswiadczenia w etyce," *Roczniki Filozoficzne*
17.2 (1969): 5–24.

divergent, are not intrinsically incompatible, but when taken to an exclusive degree become antagonistic and mutually opposed. They are as though two extreme tendencies in the theory of science toward which modern and contemporary philosophical thought gravitates. The first pole is empiricism, and those who gravitate toward it go by the name of not just empiricists but also—for reasons that will be discussed later—radical empiricists. On account of the latter, it is not enough to say that we seek the grounds of meaningful knowledge in experience; we must also define more precisely what sort of experience is at issue. As we know, the concept of experience is not strictly univocal, and so the orientation in science called empiricism is also not uniform. It is precisely this lack of uniformity, as we shall see later, that creates the possibility of developing a certain cohesive and integral concept of experience, one that is also operative in the realm of ethics—something that seems impossible from the radical empiricist's point of view.

The other pole toward which contemporary philosophical thought is oriented can be defined as rationalism, and, in its more radical form, as apriorism. Because the term *rationalism* has many meanings, I should clarify that I am speaking here of the kind of orientation that, in striving to attain scientific certitude, seeks its point of departure in the immediate decisiveness of primary judgments. Sober empiricism basically does not take issue with such an account of the matter; its opponent and "deadly enemy" is not rationalism in general, but solely and exclusively rationalistic apriorism. Apriorism takes the position that those immediate and self-evident primary judgments have their source in reason alone, and not in experience. Empiricism, on the other hand, maintains that the basis—the source and criterion—of the objectivity of knowledge is experience.

This, then, is how the radical opposition between empiricism and apriorism looks when viewed against the broad background of contemporary philosophical thought. It is a split that allows for no reconciliation, a split in which the cohesiveness and unity of philosophy cannot survive. This split grows even wider when the empirical orientation becomes radically empirical and narrows experience down to the "purely sensory." Then this split of an epistemological nature also seems to indicate a kind of basic "astigmatism" of the human being in the realm of knowledge, which is perhaps ultimately the root of the inclination toward skepticism or agnosticism. After all, what sense can there be in speaking of the unity of human knowledge if the sources from which we derive it are so divergent?

Against this broader background, which brings into relief the state of a certain division in philosophy, it is also easier to understand the division that has taken place in ethics. The questions posed at the beginning concerning the essence of ethics (what really is ethics?) and the possibility of pursuing it in an objectively justified way spring from precisely the state in which ethics finds itself today. Against the background of the divergence between empiricism and apriorism, each of which displays a strong tendency "toward its own pole," the state of ethics has become even more complicated than that of the other philosophical disciplines. Its original unity within the framework of philosophy, as well as its unity in the area of its problematic, has undergone a deep split. Those who are aware of this situation find it hard to say what ethics really is and in what orientation it properly belongs. Does it belong in the realm of the science of morality, which attempts to respond to the demands of an empirical-inductive science, or in the realm of a strictly deductive science, which strives to determine the cognitive value of moral norms and then arrange them by specifying the logical relations among them? The latter corresponds to the tendencies of rationalism and even apriorism.

Here we are already dealing with the legacy of not just critical philosophy but also positivism, which gradually arose out of critical philosophy in the last century. Positivism turned its attention to the phenomena of morality (moral phenomena) and prescribed the descriptive method for investigating them. This description took two forms, the psychology of morality and the sociology of morality, since morality was regarded—for reasons easy to understand—as a manifestation of the psychic life of the individual and as a manifestation of social life.

In view of this assumption, the only question that the positivistic science of morality asks is: what does a given individual, a given society, or a given period in the history of that society regard as morally good or evil? It never goes beyond, nor can it go beyond, questions of this type. It also cannot raise and deliberately avoids raising the question proper to ethics: what is good and what is evil, and why? The science of morality—either as psychology or as sociology—is a science of norms, but it is not and cannot be a normative science. In this regard, it differs fundamentally from ethics. We have here a major consequence of the critique of human knowledge in science. Positivists are convinced that science cannot answer the question: what is morally good and what is morally evil, and why? And so they treat a norm exclusively as a fact—either a psychological fact or a sociological fact—but they are not interested in the issue of the ultimate justification of norms. Such a position has repercussions for the proper meaning of the whole logic of norms, which manifests a tendency to model the science of morality after the particular sciences, understanding the science of morality as a set of norms subordinated one to another by means of deduction. This deduction alone, however, does not resolve the basic question of ethics, the question of the normativeness of norms themselves, the question of their ethical basis. The logic of norms may remain wholly within the boundaries of the science of morality. It then functions as an auxiliary discipline in relation to that science, organizing the norms that *de facto* exist in a given morality.

Thus the state of division in which ethics has found itself as a result of the increasing tendencies of empiricism and apriorism implies something more as well, namely, a retreat from the basic and ambitious tasks that ethics initially set for itself and that were assigned to it—and, in fact, are still assigned to it—in the belief that it can and should accomplish them. Clearly, the answer to the question of moral good and evil, not only in the descriptive order but also especially in the normative order, is one of the most important needs of humanity. In keeping with our rational nature, science should help us meet this need. And yet ethics in its present state—a state of division—has as though backed away from such a possibility. Neither in the position of the science of morality nor in the position of the aprioristic "logic of norms" can we see any possibility of answering the basic question: what is morally good and what is morally evil, and why? Ethics has as though retreated to the margins of its great and age-old tasks.

2. ETHICS IN SEARCH OF ITS EXPERIENTIAL POINT OF DEPARTURE

The psychology and sociology of morality as forms of the science of morality that arose out of the assumptions of positivism nevertheless perform a very important role for the subsequent development of ethics, for they draw attention to the enormous significance of the fact of morality. Likewise, the deductive science of morality, which aims at a precise organization of norms, beginning with an establishment of their logical value, also has great importance for the development of ethics. I intend to return to this topic in an appropriate place. Here, however, I wish to examine the problem of the experiential point of departure, with reference to the two branches of the science of morality mentioned above.

Both the psychology and the sociology of morality appeal to the body of facts that make up the structural whole of the phenomenon of morality. The very concept of the phenomenon of morality must present a serious problem. In what sense is morality a phenomenon? Can one speak here of its being accessible to the senses—which for the concept of a phenomenon would seem to be essential? But this is not my main concern at the moment. Rather, it is that each of these sciences seems to deal with morality only *per accidens*—only through that aspect of the facts that corresponds to the respective science.

The psychology of morality is basically *quoad substantiam* psychology, and so it deals with experiential facts in terms of their psychological aspect, taking its point of departure from the experience of the psychic life of the human being. Psychology can approach morality only as a particular form of psychic life. While it cannot be denied that this is to some degree correct, there is also a certain danger here of converting morality *in aliud genus*. Morality has its own specific aspect, which arises in the human being on the basis of the spiritual life of the human person. This aspect is not completely reducible to the empirically accessible psyche and its dynamism. The study of the psychology of morality is certainly necessary, but it deals with a set of facts that underlie the moral fact, and not with the moral fact itself. The latter has its own specific aspect, which cannot be completely reduced to an object of psychology.

The same applies to the sociology of morality. It is basically *quoad substantiam* sociology and deals with its own set of facts. These facts make up the structural whole of social life and have their own specific aspect. Although morality is connected with these facts and with their specifically sociological aspect, it cannot be completely reduced to this aspect. Every attempt to do so is necessarily equivalent to a transference of morality *in aliud genus* and also, therefore, to a loss of the specific aspect proper to morality. A social (sociological) fact is not *per se* a moral (ethical) fact, any more than a psychic fact is a moral fact. Morality resides in each of these forms of experiential facts through its own specific aspect, which should be discovered and isolated—while, of course, preserving its whole real bond with the social reality and the psychic substrate. Nevertheless, the aspect proper to morality itself must be isolated. This alone can serve as the experiential point of departure for the science of morality.

We can see, then, that there is serious reason to suspect that the psychological and sociological forms of the science of morality, however well they may have demonstrated the need for an experiential point of departure, nevertheless in precisely this respect have departed—or at least could depart—from morality, from its own specific aspect, which in experience certainly constitutes a *proprium genus*. This *proprium genus* is what I shall be referring to in the subsequent course of this discussion as the experience of morality, denoting that through which every fact contained in human experience (understood here in the most general sense of the term) has an ethical property and is thus a moral—and not just a psychic or social—fact.

As we can see, therefore, there exists a need to homogenize ethics, and this problem emerges against the background of the historical division of ethics: the dissolution of the cohesive whole of ethics into two rather noncohesive wholes, one of which (the science of morality) is exclusively inductive and the other (the logic of norms) exclusively deductive. The problem of the homogenization of ethics is primarily connected with experience, for it seems that this is the area where ethics got off on heterogeneous tracks, turning into psychology or sociology and losing its essential contact with morality—with morality as such. Consequently, the demand for a homogeneous (authentic) experience of morality is perhaps one of the first that should be advanced. In making such a demand, I am by no means ruling out such sciences of morality as psychology and sociology. Of course, I believe that ethics is also a science of morality; it is one even *par excellence*. Moreover, ethics also has—as I will try to show—an empirical character, for it proceeds from facts that make up the structural whole of a completely unique reality. We call this reality morality, not abstracting from those facts, but, on the contrary, apprehending in each of them singly and all of them together that which is essential for morality—or, to put it another way, that which is essentially moral (ethical). The demand for homogenization is simply a call to apprehend that which is essential for morality—and not something else. I take the position that this apprehension initially takes place in experience itself, not in some subsequent abstraction or reflection. The point of departure in ethics is, therefore, the experience of morality. But the important thing here is to hit directly upon this and not some other thread of experience in this point of departure.

The problem of the heterogenization of ethics already in the experiential point of departure does not necessarily take the form of a deviation from the proper object, from that which constitutes the specific aspect of morality. It perhaps more often takes the form of a failure to arrive at this aspect.[2]

There is a certain perspective from which the human being and human activity is viewed that presupposes a blurring of the boundaries between morality and all the psycho-sociological contents connected with it. This perspective involves a system of assumptions—often tacitly accepted—that lead to a way of looking at the human being that is more of an overlooking.

In raising the issue of the experience of morality in the point of departure of ethics, I am also deciding in favor of a certain system of assumptions. This decision arises from a need to get out of the impasse of radical empiricism and apriorism and is equivalent to maintaining an experiential point of departure in ethics. This experience, of course, is *sui generis* and cannot be identified with the radically empirical concept of it.

Ethics for me, then, is a science of morality, although—to avoid misunderstanding and ambiguity—it would be better to call it a philosophical science of morality.

In this concept of ethics, the main "knowledge-generating" role will be played directly by an explanation of the data of experience. The proper method of ethics will, therefore, be the reductive rather than the deductive method (it is worth noting that the view that presents the greatest contrast to this concept of ethics is the radically aprioristic view, where the main role is played by the deductive method). Explanation here is a kind of intellectual "exploitation of experience." Its aim is to establish the adequate and, in this sense, ultimate reasons for the occurrence and intelligibility of the fact given to us in experience. The question of adequate and ultimate reasons—which for the time being may be formulated as the question: what is morally good and what is morally evil, and why?—delimits in the most general way the leading cognitive task with which we approach the sphere of morality. It should not be thought, however, that with this question we approach the sphere of morality entirely "from without." On the contrary, this question emerges—as will be shown later—out of experience itself; indeed, it lies within the very character of what we experience in morality. This circumstance alone already shows that it is impossible to confine ethics to a description of the content of moral experience, since the described content itself provokes questions that go beyond the content and the description of it.

3. THE PROPER MEANING OF THE EXPERIENCE OF MORALITY

I have said that experience should be placed at the very basis of the concept of ethics. This is also in keeping with trends in contemporary epistemology, which, of course, in this respect do not depart from the assumptions of all realistic thought in past ages. Experience as the point of departure for science has always been the first test of realism in the whole way science is pursued—and so it is also a test of the realism of the methods we use in a given science.[3]

In the case of the science whose proper object is morality, we must first determine in what sense one can speak of experience in its point of departure. The divergences and positivistic conceptions of the science of morality discussed above make it abundantly clear that the problem of the experience at the basis of ethics is intimately connected with the need to define the proper meaning of this experience. We have seen that when such concepts as the "phenomenon of morality" or the "moral fact" are treated in a certain way, ethics becomes impossible and only a descriptive science of morality remains. The concept of the "phenomenon of morality" can in a certain respect denote the experience in question, as I already mentioned earlier. This concept (perhaps even more than the concept of the "moral fact") may, therefore, assist us in illuminating the problem of experience itself and in grasping its proper meaning.

The term *phenomenon* signifies something that "manifests itself" to us, something that affects our cognitive powers in a perceptible way. I would be inclined to regard this perception of an object as the very heart of experience.[4] Experience is connected with the phenomenon—with the world of phenomena—in various ways. The perception of an object, though not always taken into account here, was often reduced to a purely sensory impression.[5] Kant, as we know, lent a special acuteness to this problem, which had already been raised prior to him. The reduction of experience to the purely sensory contents of perception, which was the main tenet of empiricists of a sensualistic bent, is what led Kant to view rational thought and its *a priori* laws as so radically opposed to sensory experience and its natural regularity.

I shall not go into the details of this historical process, which are already well known, but I do wish to point out that, if one accepts the assumptions of sensualistic empiricism, the concept of the experience of morality does not and cannot have any meaning.[6] When we speak of the "phenomenon of morality" or "moral facts" as experiential facts, it is certainly true that we find no counterparts of these terms—or, therefore, of their respective concepts—in the realm of "purely sensory impressions." At the same time, it would be difficult to deny that morality does in some way "manifest itself" to us and, therefore, that various moral facts are given to us in experience. Neither these facts nor morality itself as the fact that determines their specific aspect is constructed by anyone *a priori* in the mind or "mentally" imposed upon some set of "purely sensory" data.[7] And so one ought to maintain that experience is not limited to the perception of purely sensory contents alone, but includes the particular structure and essential content of that perception. We must take such a position if the term *phenomenon of morality* is to have any meaning at all—and likewise the term *moral fact*. Experience itself is what convinces us that these terms have meaning, because morality does indeed "manifest itself" to us in its own way. We have perceptual access to moral facts: we experience them.

Perhaps this would be a good place to examine the problem of experience a little more broadly, taking into consideration not just the experience of morality, but in some way all that the word *experience* entails—in its cognitive sense, of course, and not in any other sense (as I stated earlier). It seems that the fundamental meaning of experience must be firmly rooted not only in psychology but also in anthropology as a whole. In order to grasp this meaning, we must emphasize two elements of it that are in some way constitutive and at the same time intimately united into one organic whole. Appealing to psychology, we can define each of these elements as a certain "sense." This sense is not the same as consciousness, but is something even more concrete: it is a kind of *sensitivum*, although it is not "sensual." The first element of experience can be defined as a "sense of reality," placing the accent on *reality*—on the fact that something exists with an existence that is real and objectively independent of the cognizing subject and the subject's cognitive act, while at the same time existing as the object of that act. Because of this, the structural whole of experience also contains a second element, which can be defined as a "sense of knowing." This is a sense of a distinctive kind of relation to what exists in a real and objective way, together with a sense of a distinctive kind of contact or union with what exists and exists in such a way.

Within the dynamic structural whole we call experience, the sense of knowing differs from the sense of reality, while at the same time intimately corresponding to it. The latter is a sense of reality in and through knowing—and the former is a sense of knowing through reality, through what really and objectively exists with an existence independent of the cognitive act and, at the same time, in contact with that act. It is in just such contact and in just such an orientation that the sense of knowing ultimately manifests itself as a tendency toward that which really and objectively exists—a tendency toward an object—as true. Here the sensualistic meaning of experience is radically overcome. In view of the configuration of these senses that enter into the dynamic structural whole of experience, we cannot persist in the notion of "purely sensory" experience. This also follows from correct anthropological assumptions: there can be no purely sensory experience because we are not "purely sensory" beings. The sense of knowing contains as an essential and constitutive element a distinctive necessity to tend toward truth.

In this way, we define to some extent the nature of cognition itself (not just the nature of experience, although all human cognition is in some way experiential). At the same time, we also arrive at a deeper explanation of the sense of reality, because we see more clearly that this sense deals with a reality that is transcendent in relation to cognition. If reality were identical with cognition, if *esse* were equivalent to *percipi* (as the idealists maintained), then the necessity of cognition to tend toward truth would be completely unintelligible. One could say that it would have no "assignment." The truth of the fact of knowing would be exhaustively contained in each cognitive act (*percipi*). No necessity of tending toward truth would have a reason for being in this act, since *esse = percipi*. The only way to explain this necessity is through the ultimate transcendence of *esse* in relation to *percipi*. Cognition must go beyond itself because it is realized not through the truth of its own act (*percipi*) but through the truth of a transcendent object—something that exists (*esse*) with a real and objective existence independently of the act of knowing.

Of course, the subject, or self, can also be an object of this kind, since the subject also resides beyond the concrete *hinc et nunc* cognitive act and is transcendent in relation to it.

It seems to me that in this way we apprehend the basic, as well as the proper and full, meaning of experience, and this is extremely important in the point of departure of our discussion. By thus clearing the way to deal with the reality with which ethics has always dealt, I have shown that experience can serve as the basis for pursuing this discipline in a scientific way. Earlier I said that experience *must* form this basis if ethics is to be pursued as a science. I also showed, in drawing attention to the sense of reality as an element of every experience, that cognition does not in any way create "reality" (cognition does not create its own content), but arises within the context of the different kinds of content that are proper to it; in other words, cognition arises thanks to the various kinds of *esse*, thanks to the enormous richness and complexity of reality.

One of these realities or *esse*'s is morality. The fact of experience reveals that morality is a form of reality, a form of *esse*. This *esse* is what is ultimately at issue when we speak of the "phenomenon of morality." Experience could be said to be like an original and unceasing call of reality to our cognitive powers. Through this call, reality at the same time "defines itself" as transcendent in relation to every act of cognition. In this way, morality "defines itself" through the sheer fact that it is given in experience.

With regard to the experience of morality, it is worth emphasizing yet again that this call of reality does not terminate with a feeling in the senses (with an "impression"). It reaches immediately and simultaneously to the potentiality of the human intellect and, with its aid, evokes the distinctive perception of the reality that is morality. Thus the dynamism of the human intellect and the structure of human cognition are evident already in experience. Every experience is also a primordial understanding, and so it can serve as a point of departure for subsequent understandings and as a kind of provocation toward them. The tendency toward truth is essential for intellectual cognition, and this tendency is realized by way of increasingly more mature understandings. This "way" also passes through experience, or at least depends on it. I shall attempt below to apply this assertion to the understanding of morality. It is extremely important for ensuring the realistic character of ethics. If one were to rule out the experience of morality, one would thereby rule out the realism of ethics.

4. THE EXPERIENCE OF MORALITY AND MORAL EXPERIENCE

To speak of the experience of morality is to assert, above all, that morality is something human beings practice and experience in a personal way. The practice of morality is a fact, one made up of many individual facts, which have a basically internal—but also to some degree external—character. By reason of their internal, intrapersonal, and private character, these facts lie in the field of experience also known as *inner experience* or *introspection*. They are not, however, totally restricted to this field. They also have a distinctive intersubjective aspect, which in large measure derives from the circumstance that all normal human beings practice morality and experience moral good and evil personally, and so they are predisposed to perceiving such facts, and even such experiences, in others. Although the lived experience of moral good and evil in its full subjective content can be communicated externally only to a limited degree, it lends itself to being easily understood by others who are also capable of such experiences and carry them within. We are capable not only of experiencing moral good and evil personally, but also of participating in the similar experiences of others.

This intersubjectivity of moral facts is something different from their social character. Exactly where the boundary lies between the personal and the social character of human morality is not easy to determine. Nor is it my aim to do that here, apart from saying that morality has such a dual character. The social character of morality derives simply from the fact that people—each of whom, to the extent that he or she enjoys the normal use of reason, practices morality and experiences moral good and evil—live in communities and societies. Even though the intersubjectivity of moral facts cannot be identified with the social character of morality, it is nevertheless strictly connected with it. Since we participate in the practice of the morality of others, our own morality and personal experience of moral good and evil become somehow dependent on them. Without going into a detailed inquiry, it can at least be said that social morality is a result—or better, a side effect—of the various influences and interactions of individual moralities.

In speaking of social morality, I am abstracting for the time being from its axiological-normative aspect, from the whole problematic of the common good. My only concern is to show the scope of the experience we encounter in this sphere. One could say that this is not just an inner experience, but also an outer experience, although the latter occurs somehow through the former. The specific aspect of morality cannot be grasped anywhere but in the human person. Nevertheless, this inwardness is not the only field of our experience. The personal profile of morality emerges in our experience somehow simultaneously with its social profile.

The practice of morality, both in its personal and in its social profile, should more properly be called *moral experience*. The *experience of morality* is something else; it is a kind of second-level experience. In an immediate way, each of us as a person and as a member of society has a certain kind of moral experience. To say that this experience consists in the personal practice of morality and the personal experience of moral good or evil is also to say that every normal human being is here an authentic author and producer.[8] It is impossible to divorce moral reality from this authorship and productivity. Moral experience consists primarily in this. In a derivative sense, it can also be said that, by practicing morality and experiencing moral good and evil, the person acquires a certain kind of experience in this sphere.[9] Experience in this case also refers to the particular proficiency or state of moral life that develops as a result of numerous actions. But that is not my main concern at the moment. Moral experience in the sense in which I am attempting to establish it here may be connected even with a single act, with a one-time lived experience of moral good or evil. The person, as its author, is also simultaneously its witness—both in himself or herself and also somehow in others and in society as a whole. The person is equally an eye-witness and an immediate witness. Moral experience entails a two-fold involvement on the part of the person: as its author and as its witness.

Thus moral experience is in some sense identical with what I wish to express in using the term *moral fact*. Such a fact consists in the involvement of a person (or persons) in the authorship connected with the emergence and lived experience of moral good or moral evil. When, on the other hand, I speak of *moral experience*, I am drawing attention beyond this to the element of a certain witnessing—to the fact that the person is a witness to the moral good and evil that arises in the act together with its authorship. This may be either the person's own act or an act performed by another. In the latter case, being a witness presupposes some participation in the act and in the lived experience of moral good or evil, while in the former case the person is both an eye-witness and an immediate witness.

The experience of morality, as I said, is something different from moral experience: it is a kind of second-level experience.[10] First of all, then, we should note that there is not and cannot be an experience of morality without moral experience. We experience morality in moral facts, and to that extent even the distinction of these two experiences is superfluous. The experience of morality would be just another name (though perhaps a less precise one) for moral experience. Nevertheless, I believe this distinction is still worth retaining if only to emphasize the perceptible character of morality itself. Morality is what determines the specific aspect of individual moral facts. It is not an intellectual abstraction derived from those facts, but it is precisely that which we experience in each of them. Moral facts are the kind of facts in which we experience morality. Hence, the meaning of the term *experience of morality* is related to that of the term *moral experience* in a way that adds depth and precision. This has serious consequences for the whole concept of ethics, which not only as a science of moral facts but also as a science of morality has its own homogenous roots in experience.

In addition to this, the term *experience of morality* seems to have yet another meaning as well. We use the term *morality* to refer not only to that which determines the moral character of a given fact, but also to the body of moral facts—the distinctive totality or resultant of them—that characterizes a particular individual or social group. Thus, for example, we speak of the higher or lower morality of certain individuals or groups. Morality in this extended sense also seems to enter the realm of our experience. Of course, this meaning of the experience of morality is derivative in relation to the previous one, which presupposes a strict contact with moral experience. This meaning also differs from the previous one. In its primary sense, the meaning of the experience of morality, like the meaning of moral experience, presupposes either the direct authorship of an act and the personal experience of moral good and evil or some involvement in this authorship and experience, whereas the experience of morality in the social sense can occur as though from a certain distance. In the former case, one must be to some degree both an author and a witness of the moral fact, whereas in the latter case it suffices to be merely a witness. And yet this second meaning of morality is also not just an abstraction, but it is the fruit of experience, and so it should not be overlooked in the experiential point of departure of ethics. We experience morality, we come in contact with it experientially, also as the resultant of many facts that in a certain way prevails in the lives of individuals and societies—and sometimes weighs quite heavily upon them. Of course, such an extended perception of morality, a perception as though from a distance, presupposes that proper and immediate perception that has its basis in moral facts themselves.[11]

5. THE EXPERIENCE OF MORALITY AND THE EXPERIENCE OF THE HUMAN BEING

I should also, at least briefly, attempt to shed some light on a topic that is contained implicitly in the previous one, namely, the problem of the relation of the experience of morality to the experience of the human being. This problem was implied in the above discussion, since the experience of morality was intimately connected there with moral experience, whose subject (as well as object) is always a human being. Moral experience always resides within the experience of a human being, and in some sense even *is* this experience. The two experiences mutually and bilaterally imply one another. A human being experiences himself or herself both personally and empirically through morality, which forms a special basis for understanding humanity. On the other hand, the experience of morality—and the understanding of morality that comes with it—is impossible to divorce from the human being and humanity. There is an essential connection here. The essence of morality and humanity are inseparably linked. This assertion could also be tested empirically.[12]

The essential connection of morality with the human being (both as a person and as a member of society) seems evident, however, apart from any inductive investigations. At most it could be said that the discernment of morality by such means, especially as a result of ethnological research, strengthens indirectly—not fundamentally—our conviction concerning the essential connection between morality and humanity. This conviction is so basic that we regard the absence of morality in a person as a sign of abnormality. Normal people "exhibit" moral facts and experiences within the structural whole of their human existence. If someone is lacking in these facts and experiences, this means that the person is also lacking in those attributes that are proper to humanity. Our conviction regarding the strict and necessary connection of morality with humanity does not, however, have an *a priori* character. This conviction is clearly based upon the experience of the human being. It arises in us not in an *a priori* but in an *a posteriori* way, which, it must be acknowledged, does involve a certain kind of induction. Induction in this case, however, does not have the meaning ascribed to it by Mill and the positivists, but the meaning ascribed to it by Aristotle: it is not a method of generalizing a certain thesis, but simply a method of directly grasping a general truth in particular facts.

When it comes to the connection of morality with the human being in a given instance, we do not prove and we do not feel the need to prove that this connection occurs. We confine ourselves to affirming it on the basis of the experience of human beings in general. This experience discloses and attests to the strict connection of morality with humanity.[13] The testimony of experience is so unequivocal that seemingly contrary cases do not affect our belief. In fact, these cases make us even more convinced of the connection between morality and the human being. In each case in which we perceive a person to be lacking in certain moral facts and experiences, we also perceive that person to be lacking in either certain abilities proper to humanity, or—which is already a derivative matter—activities that flow from those abilities. This, however, does not occur—or at least not in a totally obvious way—in the case of moral insanity or in the case of a deterioration of the moral sense. In these cases, we are dealing with a normal humanity, one in which we find abilities proper to the human being, but at the same time a certain diminution of moral sensibility. If so, we also subject such cases to moral appraisal; we do not consider them beyond criticism, as we do in cases of authentic abnormality.

The problem of the connection of the experience of morality with the experience of the human being certainly belongs in the point of departure of ethics. I have already noted that the experience of the human being is necessarily implied by the experience of morality and cannot be divorced from it in the structure of moral facts. This also accounts for the close connection that has always existed between ethics and anthropology. This issue no doubt belongs to a subsequent stage, namely, to the interpretation of the experience of morality, but it should also be mentioned already in this first stage, where we raise the very problem of experience in the point of departure of ethics. We should also establish, as far as possible, the particular boundaries of experience. The experience of morality is not totally coextensive with the experience of the human being. In order to treat morality in a scientific way, we must consider the experience of the human being, but we cannot restrict ourselves to this completely, for that would lead to a loss of the experiential point of departure in ethics and would, in a sense, turn ethics into anthropology. We must, therefore, search very discerningly for morality and its proper aspect within the experience of the human being and apprehend the human being in terms of this aspect. In the point of departure of ethics, we are concerned with the experience of the human being as it relates to morality, and not as it relates to the human being.

Such a selective approach in no way diminishes or distorts the essence of experience. I pointed out earlier that there is always an element of understanding in human experience. Through this element, it becomes possible to organize experiences and arrange them in order of subsidiarity.

6. THE PROBLEM OF THE "MORAL SENSE"

One last topic that should be considered in the framework of this discussion is the problem of the so-called "moral sense." The concept of the moral sense arose in the context of sensualistic tendencies in anthropology and epistemology. David Hume may be regarded as the classical exponent of this concept. According to Hume, morality can be reduced to a distinctive sense that allows us to distinguish virtue from vice according to the particular pleasure that accompanies the former and the pain associated with the latter. This view paved the way for utilitarianism, which elevated the function of the moral sense to the level of a principle, one in which morality was said to be concerned with the maximization of pleasure and the minimization of pain: with the production of the maximum amount of pleasure, based on the function of the moral sense, and the reduction of pain to a minimum, based on this same function. In reaction to these views, Kant proposed an anthropology and ethics that radically excluded the moral sense and required morality to seek its grounds in the categorical imperative, which is an *a priori* form of practical reason. Kant simultaneously attacked utilitarianism and aposteriorism in ethics. This does not mean, however, that the understanding of morality he adopted was completely divorced from experience. Of course, Kant had—based on this experience—his own view, in the context of which he endorsed apriorism in morality. This apriorism in morality does not, however, signify a *de facto* break with the experiential point of departure in ethics as a science. This is not, then, an apriorism in the concept of ethics, but only in the concept of morality introduced by Kant's ethics.

Setting aside strictly historical considerations, we should at least briefly examine the problem of the moral sense in the context of these reflections on the problem of experience in ethics. It would be hard to deny that the concept of the moral sense entered ethics along with sensualism, but one also cannot fail to detect here a commendable desire to base ethics on experience and to emphasize more fully the experiential character of ethics in its point of departure. This took place in a period of growing empiricism, which, as a result of the identification of experience with a function of the senses, assumed a radically empirical form in this period. Such a form to a considerable degree also characterized the concept of the moral sense espoused by Hume, and even more so that of the 17th- and 18th-century utilitarians (Bentham and others). The concept of "purely sensory" experience, however, seems unacceptable in view of the type of analysis I attempted to carry out earlier.[14] The concept of "purely sensory" experience is especially unacceptable when applied to the sphere of morality, since the specific aspect of moral facts—that which determines the essence of the "phenomenon of morality"—is in no way accessible to the senses. The senses themselves apprehend nothing here. Even the pleasure and pain that, according to Hume, accompany morally good and evil acts are not accessible to the senses and cannot really be apprehended by the senses in terms of their specific aspect, i.e., as an object of the moral sense. In this regard, our knowledge in the area of the psychology of morality has been greatly enhanced by certain 20th-century phenomenologists, and perhaps especially by Max Scheler. There is no way to deny that human acts, precisely in terms of their moral value, i.e., the good or evil contained in them, are accompanied by very deep emotional experiences: by joy and spiritual contentment in the case of good and by depression and even despair in the case of evil. Still, the reduction of these experiences and feelings to the sensory categories of pleasure and pain is a gross oversimplification, one that results in a rudimentary impoverishment of the image of both the human being and the morality in the human being.

Consequently, the "purely sensory" concept of the moral sense had to be rejected in ethics not just because of Kant's radical critique, but perhaps even more because of the penetrating investigations in anthropology and psychology, which, among other things, resulted in a better understanding of the complexity and multidimensional structure of human emotional life. Despite this critique of the concept of the moral sense, it continued to survive in ethical terminology. The survival of this concept should be viewed as proper and useful. Although it is impossible to maintain that morality is an object of "purely sensory" experience, morality is nevertheless an object of experience, and so the senses must play some role in this experience, as they do in all human cognition. One great achievement of contemporary science, it seems to me, is that it drew attention to the involvement of the emotional element in the experience of morality. The reality of morality manifests itself to us through our feelings. By means of feeling, we become witnesses in a special way to both the moral value of our acts, witnesses to good and evil, and to the strict connection of this good and evil with ourselves as persons, with our own human essence, with our humanity.

The concept of the moral sense may, therefore, be retained in the terminology used by ethics—although the term *moral feeling* would correspond better to the meaningful intentions contained in this concept. Once we establish the basic and proper meaning of the experience of morality, this feeling and term serve to highlight that immediate contact with the reality that is morality. We describe such contact as experiential. The term *moral sense* points to the element of concreteness that appears in this contact. The moral sense allows us to arrive at individual moral facts and at the specific aspect of morality in each of those facts. This aspect, as we know, is not accessible to the senses. The apprehension of it must in each case be a function of understanding, a function of a certain intellectual intuition. This apprehension takes place, however, not in a general, abstract way, but in a particular and concrete way. It takes place within the framework of each and every moral fact. Viewed in this way, the function of the moral sense approximates the *ratio particularis* of which Thomas Aquinas spoke.

Feeling as an emotional function in a special way brings us closer to morality, to moral good and evil. Feeling is an important and usually a very rich component of the experience of this good and evil, one that causes moral values to be concretized in a particular way. I find it hard to accept, however, that the specific aspect of morality could only be felt, without at the same time being understood. It seems to me that feeling, emotional experience, has a kind of suggestive meaning for the apprehension of morality. One could say that moral values are as though "displayed" in the emotional sphere. One could also say that they come to be "indicated" through the particular reverberations connected with moral values. On the other hand, our apprehension of these values, and thus also our access to morality in its specific aspect, remains the work of a kind of intellectual insight.

All of this—in view of the concreteness and immediacy of the entire process—can perhaps also be described as a function of a distinctive "moral sense." This term, at the same time, emphasizes that there is an organic composition, not a radical dichotomy, in the human being.

NOTES

1. This is an almost unanimous view among contemporary logical empiricists.

2. We need only recall the place in Maria Ossowska's book *Wstep do nauki o moralnosci* [*Introduction to the Science of Morality*] where, after presenting many insightful and careful analyses, she says there is no way to determine what distinguishes the moral phenomenon from all the other phenomena connected with the life and activity of the human being.

3. As far as correct trends in contemporary epistemology and methodology are concerned, it is not a matter of somehow discovering experience in the point of departure of the individual sciences, but only perhaps of more fully accentuating it and also more fully reflecting on it, as a result of which experience as such becomes accentuated. We can, of course, rely on experience and make use of the data contained in it without being aware that we are doing so, and we can also be fully aware that we are doing so, such that the conscious identification of experience as the first step we take by means of cognition—and this is a fundamental step—is already somehow a passage from prescientific to scientific thought. This is also a—so to speak—"scientivization" of experience, an assignment of a specific function to it in the development of science. This may involve various measures aimed at taking fuller advantage of the experiential point of departure by making it more exact and expanding it in appropriate ways. We know that in some sciences experiences are expanded by conducting experiments.

4. I am, of course, using the term *experience* here in the strictly cognitive sense. This term can, as we know, have noncognitive meanings as well. We have the latter sense in mind when we say, for example, that someone has, in a difficult and painful way, become experienced at the hands of fate. We have a different sense in mind when we say that someone has experienced one thing or another—

then to some extent the cognitive meaning returns. The cognitive meaning of the term *experience* seems to be connected with its active use, but not with its passive use. [The example Wojtyla gives for the passive use of the term *experience—ze ktos zostal w przykry, bolesny sposob doswiadczony prez los*—does not translate well into English. Literally the phrase reads: "that someone has been in a difficult, painful way experienced by fate." In English we would not use the term *experienced* here, but would say instead that someone has been painfully *afflicted* or *tried* by fate. I can think of no instances in English where the term *experience* is used in a strictly passive sense. —Trans.]

5. This gets us into the realm of not just epistemology, but also psychology, and even to some extent anthropology.

6. Moral good and evil have no ontic status, and so they cannot be objects of knowledge or, therefore, of experience either. The terms *good* and *evil*, which tend to suggest that good and evil exist, do not function as designators, but are merely instruments for expressing the emotions of the speaker. This view, known as *emotivism*, was promulgated by A. J. Ayer, Charles Stevenson, and Hans Reichenbach. T. Geiger proposed calling this view *axiological nihilism*.

7. Kant, as we know, held such a view.

8. Wojtyla here uses the terms *sprawca* and *twórca*. He clarifies the meaning of these terms in *Osoba i czyn* [*Person and Action*] (Kraków: Polskie Tow. Teologiczne, 1969), where he defines an author (*sprawca*) as that which brings something into being and sustains it in existence, that which accounts for a thing's *fieri* and *esse* (69)—in short, as the efficient cause of a thing. A producer (*twórca*), on the other hand, is that which shapes or fashions (*uksztaltuje*) a thing. "To the essence of authoring," writes Wojtyla, "belongs causing the emergence and existence of an effect, while to the essence of producing belongs the shaping of the work" (72). —Trans.

9. In connection with this, one could distinguish the actual meaning and the habitual meaning of the term *moral experience*.

10. One could also use here respectively the terms *moral experience in the functional sense* (moral experience) and *moral experience in the objective sense* (the experience of morality).

11. As an aside to these reflections on moral experience and the experience of morality, it should be noted that experimentation does not and cannot have any meaning in ethics. As we know, this form of controlled experience plays a large role particularly in the natural sciences, and an even larger role in the technical sciences. Experimentation consists in creating the conditions under which a certain fact should arise. In the sphere of morality, however, such a creation of conditions would be directly contrary to the very essence of the moral fact, for to the essence of this fact belongs at least the possibility of independent authorship, which excludes artificial determination. The only empirical approach that seems possible here is to seek out the kinds of spontaneous manifestations of the authorship and lived experience of moral good and evil that tell us the most about the structure of moral facts and the specific aspect of morality.

12. One could investigate a variety of different people and a variety of different peoples—as ethnologists do—with a view to discovering the presence or absence of morality in each of them. It seems, however, that such a cognitive operation is not necessary. When ethnologists investigate the morality of different peoples, especially primitive peoples, it is not so much to discover the presence of morality in them as to discover the specific aspects of that morality. They do this by studying the prevailing systems of moral norms, which are expressed, among other ways, in the customs and traditions of those peoples.

13. By this I mean that a denial of the strict connection between the experience of morality and the experience of the human being would lead directly to a denial of the specific aspect of the content of morality and, consequently, also to a denial of the very occurrence or fact of this aspect as the proper object of the experience of morality.

14. See section 3 above.

9

The Problem of the Theory of Morality

1. EXPERIENCE AND INTERPRETATION: THE STARTING QUESTIONS

Following what I said in the previous chapter[1] on the topic of the experience of morality as the point of departure of ethics, I shall now turn to the interpretation of this experience. The experience of morality is connected with understanding, which is true of all experience in the basic structure and dynamism of human knowledge. Experience cannot be considered a function of the senses alone, since the senses function in human knowledge in conjunction with the intellect. Every feeling or emotion is permeated by some sort of intellectual content, which—as was shown earlier—takes a particular form in the experience of morality. The interpretation of morality is thus rooted in experience. Proceeding to this interpretation, we get an insight into that experience thanks to the understanding that is given to us together with the experience. The interpretation of morality consists in organizing the understandings that accompany the human experience of morality. Along with this organization, there comes about a deepening and expansion of those understandings. The essential function of the scientific method is to ensure that this organization, deepening, and expansion takes place on the basis of experience and in strict conformity with it.

Karol Wojtyla, "Problem teorii moralnosci," *W nurcie zagadnien posoborowych*, vol. 3 (Warszawa: Wydaw. Sióstr Loretanek-Benedyktynek, 1969) 217–249.

The organization and, in particular, the deepening and expansion of the understandings contained in the experience of morality are accomplished by means of questions we ask in connection with this experience—questions we must ask, because the process of understanding depends on them. These questions result from the process of understanding and, at the same time, carry it forward. In them we observe the age-old dialectical trait of human knowledge, which has particular significance as a science-generating trait. I already mentioned in the previous chapter that, in connection with the experience of morality and in strict dependence on this experience, there arises the question of moral good and evil.

This question occurs on two levels. On the first level, it can be formulated in two ways: "What is morally good and what is morally evil in human actions?" or "What makes human actions morally good or evil?" This first question directly gives rise to a second-level question: since human actions have the property of being morally good or evil, we ask why they have this property. The first-level question in the form, "What makes human actions morally good or evil?" already in some way entails a passage to the second-level question. When we ask, "What makes them so?" we are already asking, "Why?" I mentioned that these questions that arise in the point of departure of ethics, despite their simplicity and rudimentariness, point the way to the ultimate explanations sought by the human intellect with regard to morality as an experiential reality. Hence, these questions also determine the ultimate structure and proper character of ethics.

For the interpretation of morality as given in experience, these questions have an ultimately binding significance. This is related to the philosophical character of ethics. Philosophy's task, as conceived by Aristotle, is to explain reality in the light of ultimate reasons (*per ultimas causas*). In the case of the reality that is morality, our minds are directed to these ultimate reasons by those very simple and elementary questions mentioned above.

These questions are in a sense prescientific: everyone can ask them. They are intimately connected with the experience of morality and simultaneously point to that which is of ultimate concern in the understanding of morality. What is the meaning of this understanding and what is its goal? With regard to morality as an experiential reality whose specific aspect is formed by the moral good and evil of human actions, we inquire into the ultimate basis of this good and evil. If we manage to discover this ultimate basis, we have then completed the task of interpretation, we have "gotten to the bottom" of the matter, which is the special hallmark of philosophy. In the present case, this is the special hallmark of ethics as a separate branch of philosophy and philosophizing.

It seems that the form of ethics that ultimately emerges from the initial and basic questions mentioned above will be a *normative* form. When we ask, "What makes human actions morally good or evil?" we all know that what makes them so is their relation to norms. When we ask the further question, "Why?" we are then inquiring into the ethical foundation of the norms upon which the moral good or evil of human actions rests. To put it another way, we are inquiring into their rightness.

This seems to be the direction in which those initial and basic questions that arise together with the experience of morality point the interpretation, namely, in the direction of a search for the dependence of moral good and evil on the norms of morality and, beyond this, in the direction of a search for the rightness or ethical foundation of the norms themselves. The form of ethics that emerges from these questions by means of interpretation will be a *normative* form.

At the moment, I am not concerned with describing this form in detail, but only with presenting the prospect of it. It would also perhaps be well to recall that ethics as conceived by such distinguished thinkers as Aristotle and Thomas Aquinas takes a teleological form, one having to do with ends. In presenting the prospect of a normative ethics through the starting questions, I cannot at this time take up the question of the relation between these two forms of ethics, these two views of the philosophical interpretation of morality: the teleological and the normative. I raise this problem here as a side issue, one to which I shall attempt to return in my subsequent development of the concept of ethics, but for now I shall leave it aside.

I should, however, note that, in addition to the questions posited above, which point the interpretation of morality as given in experience in the direction of ethics, still another question suggests itself already in the point of departure of interpretation, namely, the question: "What is morality?" This question arises not just in addition to the other questions, but somehow together with them, as a question inseparable from those other questions. This question lies in the point of departure not so much of ethics as of the theory of morality. For a fuller description of the theory of morality and its relation to ethics, we must analyze the mutual relation of their starting questions.

2. AN ANALYSIS OF THE MUTUAL RELATION OF THE STARTING QUESTIONS

The question, "What is morality?" is more directly related to the experience of morality and more plainly aimed at the interpretation of it. Normally, when we come in contact with any reality, the first question we ask is: "What is it?" This is also true in the case of morality. It may even seem strange that we have already raised questions that somehow presuppose that we know what morality is. We asked, "What makes human actions morally good or evil?" and in posing the question in this way, we assumed not only that morality was already experientially apprehended in its proper perspective, but also that it was intellectually objectified. Since the question asks about actions that are *morally* good or evil, one would presume that we already know what morality is. We know—or we think we know. It seems that more often than not the latter has tended to be the case in views of ethics. Even the psychology and sociology of morality have helped us see that this assumption was not entirely warranted.

Ethical questions—questions of the type, "What is morally good and what is morally evil in human actions?"—already in a way concern a subsequent issue. We are not asking in them about morality as such; we are not trying to understand this morality; rather, we are asking—on the basis of some previous understanding of morality—about a distinction fundamental to morality, the distinction between good and evil, and about the basis of this distinction. We are asking about this especially when our question takes the form that goes still further ("What makes human actions morally good or evil?") and enters the realm of the basis of moral norms themselves ("Why is what is morally good or evil that way?"). Thus, not only do ethical questions go beyond the simple question, "What is morality?" which must suggest itself to us in connection with the experience of morality, but they also, so to speak, "begin farther down the line."

If in the present study, in speaking of going from the experience of morality to the interpretation of it by means of questions, I posed these other questions first, it was because of their vital, existential meaning. As can easily be seen from my discussion of the experience of morality, this is a realm in which human life and human existence find eloquent expression. In this context, ethical questions, questions concerning moral good and evil and their basis, are more pressing than the theoretical question, "What is morality?" Ethics responds more to the needs of human existence than does the theory of morality, and this should certainly be reflected in science.

Still, science cannot ignore questions that are less pressing from a vital or existential point of view, but are not for that reason any less important from a scientific point of view. This applies in a special way to the question of the essence of morality, for this question, as I already mentioned, conditions the very meaning of those other questions. To put it another way, the question of the essence of morality ensures that the questions concerning moral good and evil are posed in a homogeneous way with respect to the experience of morality. The experience of morality, as I showed in the previous chapter, allows us to come in contact with the essence of morality, and, in direct relation to this, the question arises, "What is morality?" In this question, we are seeking the intellectual objectification of that which is given in the experience of morality. Thus the theory of morality arises by means of knowledge of morality as the factor that accounts for the homogeneity of ethical knowledge. The theory of morality, which is the most basic and comprehensive response possible to the question, "What is morality?" should form the foundation of ethics. I am using the term *foundation* here not just in the sense of a substructure, but also in the sense of something that permeates a given structure "from the bottom up." If we think of ethics as a structure in the context of which human thought correctly arrives at ultimate answers to questions concerning moral good and evil, then this structure should be permeated throughout by a proper theory of morality. In this view, the sequence of tasks is as follows: first we should work on the theory of morality, so that we might later go on to ethics. This is the order I intend to follow in this essay.

At the same time, however, we know that the theory of morality somehow presupposes everything that we deal with in the framework of ethics. The vital and existential questions about moral good and evil that give rise to the proper structure of ethics must constantly somehow run across the field of experience upon which we base our theory of morality. Morality is essentially something dynamic and existential. We may for methodological reasons suspend those questions that are proper to ethics itself—but we cannot shake off the sense that they correspond in a most profound and definitive way to the experiential content of morality. Theoretical reflection, reflection that seeks to answer the question concerning the essence of morality, must constantly operate "above" those fundamental ethical questions, for they are the questions that remain in living and existential contact with the very essence of morality—which is not primarily an abstract system, but a distinctive mode of human life and existence. The theory of morality must as though "from above" encompass the whole process that gives rise to ethical questions (and also somehow shapes those questions). Logically speaking, the question, "What is morality?" should be asked before the question concerning the basis of moral good and evil, "What makes human actions morally good or evil?" but it is *de facto* asked after that question. And this is not merely for want of logic on the part of the questioner.

Thus, by beginning this study of the concept and methodology of ethics with the theory of morality, I am proceeding correctly, but I am doing so by means of a certain abstraction: I am abstracting from that which determines the essential vitality of the area under consideration, from that which determines its existential dynamism—the dynamism to which ethical questions directly refer. On the other hand, I will attempt to capture this vitality in my theory of morality and in this way simultaneously create a homogeneous foundation for ethics.

3. THE THEORY OF MORALITY AS AN OBJECTIFICATION OF THE CONTENT OF THE EXPERIENCE OF MORALITY

Now that I have shown how the starting questions are interrelated, I can go on to explain how I understand the content of morality. This is a problem proper to the theory of morality. When we ask, "What is morality?" we are asking about that which forms the essential content of the reality given in experience as morality. Clearly, the content at issue here is not the content of the *experience* of morality, but the content of *morality* as given in experience. Ethical questions presuppose this content, and they also grasp it in the form in which it actually occurs, for they ask about the moral good and evil that occurs in human actions. And it is precisely here—in human actions—that moral good and evil are realized; it is here that they take on a real, existential form. In actions, this moral good or evil—or, to put it differently, this moral value—becomes a reality in human beings. Only in human beings is moral value a reality, and only in them can it be a reality. Beyond human beings we do not find moral value anywhere. When we ask about the content of morality as given to us in experience, we are trying to objectify that which constitutes the essential structure of the moral fact.

To objectify means to stand beyond experience, to pull away from the subjective context that the experience of morality always involves. Moral value—good or evil—always occurs in a subjective context. It is a living, existential content. The transposition of this content to the theoretical order must not obliterate its existential expression, but must accentuate it in a special way. It seems that we achieve this in the theory of morality when we examine moral value—good or evil—in strict dependence on norms, and also when we attempt to understand norms and to grasp their strictly ethical aspect by means of moral value. As we know, the concept of a norm has many meanings and of itself does not yet point to the specific aspect of morality. By a moral norm—or a norm in the ethical sense—I mean a norm that forms the basis of moral value, and not some other kind of value. Characteristic of moral value is that it arises in the form of good or evil, a division that has both its objective and subjective source in norms. Not only are norms the basis of moral value, but they are also the source of the division into good and evil of the whole sphere known as moral value. Thus, for example, because there is a norm of truthfulness ("do not bear false witness"), there arises in human actions the characteristic differentiation into the good of telling the truth and the evil of lying. This differentiation is a characteristic attribute of morality. Thomas Aquinas defined moral good and evil as two species of the same genus, which is morality (*moralitas*)—or, one could also say, which is moral value.

This differentiation or, so to speak, splitting of morality into good and evil finds its basis and source in a norm. In calling this a *moral norm* (strictly speaking, we should say a *norm of morality*), we are referring precisely to the function of a basis and—in some sense—a source of moral good and evil. A relation arises here that has an objective character, which is extremely evident in subjective lived experience. This relation—the relation between moral value as split into good and evil and a norm of morality—determines the essential structure of every moral fact. Objectification in the realm of these facts conforms in the strictest sense to experience understood as lived experience. On the basis of this conformity, we also establish the essential content of morality as a reality given in experience. This content forms the central element of the theory of morality. It is an axiological content—because morality is indisputably a sphere of value with a characteristic differentiation into good and evil, a differentiation that, moreover, has its roots in a norm of morality. A norm is an even more profound and fundamental expression of morality than a value. Moral value belongs immediately to the phenomenon of morality. But even in the realm of phenomenology, morality reveals a further dependence, a dependence on a norm—for where else could that split into good and evil within moral value come from?

Phenomenologists place too little importance on this, and so their resulting studies apprehend morality somewhat one-sidedly as an axiological content, whereas this content is actually axiological-normative. A normative profile runs through the very center of the field of values in morality. A detachment from norms as the distinctive source of the phenomenon of morality—a source that, so to speak, beats within the heart of the unique and dynamic reality of morality—would rob morality of the dynamism proper to it. The task of the theory of morality, which basically conforms to experience and together with it forms an indisputable whole, is to capture this dynamism and to objectify it as adequately as possible. Hence, it is not enough to apprehend morality merely as an axiological content, as a distinctive "world (or set) of values." Such a view would ultimately be static, whereas morality—moral value—has a corresponding and entirely unique dynamism. This is the dynamism of ethical norms, which is strictly connected with the dynamism of human actions, and indirectly with the dynamism of the human person. Thus, to apprehend dynamic good and evil as mutually opposing moral values requires an insight into the dynamism of ethical norms that is connected with the dynamism of human actions. This fundamental trait has an essential meaning for the theory of morality as a whole.

In such a view, the theory of morality develops not just as a certain abstraction in relation to the living, existential reality of human morality, having its dialectical counterpart in ethical questions, but—as can be seen—it goes straight to the dynamic core of moral facts and seeks to give them the form of an intellectual objectification. This theory can, therefore, perform the function of a connecting link between the experience of morality and the normative structure of ethics. I am becoming more and more convinced that such a function is both proper and indispensable for the homogeneity of this structure.

4. THE THEORY OF MORALITY AS AN OBJECTIFICATION OF THE CONTENT OF THE EXPERIENCE OF MORALITY: AN ILLUMINATING EXAMPLE

Let me try now to illuminate this in a more concrete way. To do so, I shall consider the experience of guilt, which seems to be a particularly suggestive moral fact—one given in countless experiences. This also accounts for why this fact has become a theme for artistic creativity. This fact also gives rise to certain consequences in people's mental attitude, consequences that take the form of so-called ethical negativism—as though morality were primarily concerned with evil and its avoidance. In this respect, the Thomistic theory of evil is quite a revelation, because it views evil as the lack of an appropriate good, and not just its opposite. In this view, good is something ordinary and "natural" because it conforms to the nature of the human being and the world; evil, on the other hand, is always baffling because it conflicts with this nature. Perhaps this also explains why in literature and moral instruction more attention is paid to evil than to good. At any rate, it would be hard to deny that in the experience of morality as a distinctive and central dimension of human life moral evil tends to be more emphatic. And this is also why I am focusing here on the experience of guilt as a way of throwing additional light on what I said earlier concerning the experience of morality in the aspect of content.

The experience of guilt is in its essential core an experience of moral evil. This evil is contained in a human act, in a conscious and free action whose author is a human being—or, one could say, a concrete human self. If this self is the subject of moral evil, it is solely because this self is the author of an action that is evil. This is the basis of the lived experience of guilt. Guilt is the lived experience of a moral evil of which I myself am the author. If this evil were to reside in me only as, say, an innate inclination or an involuntary reaction and I were in no way its author, then there would be no talk of guilt. The experience of guilt always involves the efficacy of my personal self. If, therefore, the objectification of moral value is to conform to experience, to lived experience, it cannot detach that value from action, and, more precisely, from the conscious efficacy of the person. In order to define moral value in all its realism, this requirement is of fundamental importance. Moral value does not appear "on the margin" of human action, as though it were a side product of this action. Experience testifies that this value becomes real "in action," within the dynamic structure of action as an *actus personae*. As a result, moral value somehow "makes its abode" in the person: it roots itself in the person and becomes a quality of the person. This is clearly seen in the lived experience of guilt. As the author of an action that is morally evil, I myself become morally evil. Evil, so to speak, passes from my action to me as a person. Hence, the tasks of objectification are clear: it must apprehend moral value—in this case, evil—in the position it really holds in relation to the human being. This is a clear requirement for the theory of morality.

But this is not the end of the matter. In the lived experience of guilt—which is presented here to assist in bringing to light the proper content of morality—something more appears besides the element of value. I do not just experience the moral evil of which I am the author. This evil manifests itself and makes its abode in me in distinct dependence on yet another factor in addition to my own efficacy. Combined with my personal efficacy is a clear and distinctive element that can be called the element of a *principle*. Evil arises in an action, inside an action, and permeates my personal self because my conscious and voluntary action does not conform to this principle but stands opposed to it. The force of this principle, its sovereignty in relation to the action, comes to light in the lived experience of guilt. No dynamism of action can manage to obscure this distinctive force or place it beyond the pale of the realm of actions and persons. On the contrary—we see that human action includes it and draws its essential quality from it. From the force of this principle, too, comes the fact that the person through this action is actualized as good or evil—in the case of guilt, as evil.

The force of principles, their sovereignty in relation to action, a sovereignty that announces itself in a particular way in the lived experience of guilt, must find expression in the theory of morality. The structure of the moral fact clearly indicates that within this fact values are dependent on principles. Principles have a fundamental significance and determining power with respect to values. To apprehend the content of morality in a theoretical form means to apprehend this dependence and determination that occurs within the very being of the person as a result of consciousness and efficacy. What I am here—in this analysis of the lived experience of guilt—calling a principle appears within that lived experience in the form of conscience. Conscience is simply the lived experience of the principles of moral good and evil. As long as we continue to operate on the level of lived experience, principles take the form of conscience. Nevertheless, objectification can—without being in any way inconsistent with experience—consider the principles of good and evil to some extent beyond the lived experience of them. Such an inquiry also contributes to a better understanding of the lived experience of the principles of moral good and evil, that is, to a better understanding of conscience in terms of its structure and content. For the time being, I shall confine myself to saying that lived experience and objectification must conform to one another in a basic point: an inquiry into the principles of moral good and evil cannot entirely abstract from the lived experience of these principles, from conscience. This is important for the whole problematic of the norms of ethics and the norms of morality—for *norm*, in the most general sense of the term, is the name we give to a principle of moral good and evil.

At the moment, I am only concerned with establishing the presence of norms in the structure of the moral fact. The existence of norms is particularly evident in the lived experience of guilt. Moral evil tends to bring conscience more out into the open; along with conscience, the sovereignty of the norms of morality in a person also becomes more apparent. In this respect, moral good tends to be more discreet. The relation between values and norms that characterizes the inner structure of the moral fact is not as noticeable in moral good. The sovereignty of norms in a person, a sovereignty that moral evil—guilt—reveals though a distinctive inner conflict, is also less pronounced in moral good. The conflict I experience when I feel guilty is a conflict of me with myself. There would be no such conflict if the norms of morality had a merely external or even a heteronomous character: if they expressed a law whose rightness I did not perceive. The lived experience of guilt involves not only a conflict with a law, but also a conflict with conscience, which both perceives and participates in the rightness of the principle expressed by the law. This superior rightness stands in opposition to the action performed against it. It becomes in me the judge and indictor of the action. If such an inner division—a division of me against myself—is difficult and even painful, at least one must admit that it is creative and thoroughly human. It corresponds to my proper dynamism as a person; it is for me, and indirectly for others as well, testimony to an existence proper to a person. The existence proper to a person is an existence in truth, an existence in dynamic relation to truth. And that is why persons exist and act, actualizing their *esse* and their *operari*, not just on the level of values, but also on the level of principles. Morality is the dynamic and existential coordination of these levels.

For my own purposes here, this entire—admittedly cursory—analysis of the lived experience of guilt is important because it brings to light the type of content that must find expression in the theory of morality.

5. A PRELIMINARY REFLECTION ON THE MEANING OF MORAL VALUE

In attempting to formulate this content in a way that is consistent with experience, we must pause at the very first stage—at the very first step, so to speak. The method of science requires well considered steps. Its precision and certainty depends on this. The first step of an interpretation of the experience of morality that aims at constructing a theory of morality would seem to be simply to properly name the different elements of morality as a reality given to us in experience. To a certain degree, I have already done this; I have already named the different elements of the experience of morality, although I tried to do this very sparingly, as though anticipating that this step itself would still need to be inspected. What I want to do now is carry out such a preliminary, critical reflection on the terminology employed.

This applies first of all to the term *moral value* itself. The theory of morality focuses on the moral values given to us in experience as good or evil. Hence, the term *moral value* basically corresponds to an experience, for it emphasizes the axiological dimension of morality, which is the most obvious feature of morality. The term *moral value* expresses the essential content of morality in precisely this dimension. There can be no doubt that through moral value human actions and the people who perform them display a distinctive quality: they are virtuous or sinful, just, cruel, kind, brave, or steadfast. The term *moral value* seems to refer to just such qualities of actions and the people who perform them. Value belongs to the category of quality. We should note, however, that the use of the term *moral value* to designate this quality that occurs in people and their actions comes up against a very serious difficulty. It is easy enough to admit that good is a moral value, but in what sense can we predicate value of evil? Someone might say that we can predicate it in a negative sense. It is difficult, however, not to detect a basic contradiction in the concept of a *negative value*, since the term *value* essentially points to something positive. To avoid this contradiction, axiologists sometimes use the term *anti-value* to designate moral evil. This term assumes its proper meaning in conjunction with *value*; thus, moral good and evil occur always in the conjunction and opposition: value—anti-value.

Still, it is hard to resist the impression that there is something artificial about such a terminological solution and that it does not really correspond to the content of the experience of morality. Moral evil does not seem to be either solely or primarily the contrary of good; at least, that is not how we experience it. The term *anti-value*, therefore, leaves something to be desired as an expresssion for the reality of moral evil. As I already said in the preceding analysis, which examined the experience of guilt, moral evil primarily brings to light a conflict with a principle of morality, with conscience, with a norm. The opposition to moral good appears in it only secondarily: it appears precisely in the context of a relation to a principle—to conscience or a law; it appears somehow through this relation. Consequently, the reality of morality cannot be expressed in axiological terms alone. The problems surrounding the term *moral value* are in this respect very symptomatic. This leads me to conclude that this term only partially expresses the concept central to moral good and evil. Moral good and evil are intrinsically richer and more complex realities than the term *moral value* is able to convey.

I already mentioned this complexity and richness earlier. The complexity of moral good and evil arises 1) from their relation to a principle of morality, a norm, and 2) from their relation to action and the person who performs this action. Both of these relations should be adequately reflected in the theory of morality. The relation of moral good and evil to a norm will be discussed later. First I will consider the content of moral value—good and evil—in relation to action and to the person performing that action. Obviously this relation cannot really be divorced from the relation to a norm, and particularly to conscience. Together they determine the structure of the moral fact. I have chosen to deal with the relation to action and to the person as its author first for purely heuristic reasons. The integrity of the structure of the moral fact must, however, be kept in mind. Otherwise one could easily fall into the particular error of interpretation that characterizes the various expressions of psychologism in the theory of morality. This error of psychologism does not arise merely from a one-sided apprehension of the relation of moral value to the subject, without ultimately considering the dependence of this value on a norm. This error to a significant degree also arises from the way in which the subject—i.e., the person—and the action of the subject is apprehended. Thus, for example, an apprehension of the person in the aspect of consciousness alone, as though consciousness *were* the acting subject, is conducive to psychologism. So, too, is the treatment of individual psychic or psychosomatic functions in separation from the dynamic structural whole of the human person. In this regard, I detect psychologism in the assumptions of both idealistic subjectivism and positivism in their respective interpretations of morality.

A conception of the human being, anthropology, is an important cofactor of the theory of morality, as is evident from my earlier treatment of the connection of the experience of morality with the experience of the human being.[2] In the light of that treatment, one could say that a conception of the human being, a mature theory of the person, implies morality as a reality that corresponds in a fundamental way to the human person. In a sense, then, anthropology, the theory of the person, arises through an analysis of morality. At the same time, however, the theory of morality presupposes anthropology, a theory of the person. In particular, it presupposes a proper theory of the dynamism of the person, a correct view of activity, of the action of the person. Upon this also rests to a significant degree the proper interpretation of the content of moral value—the proper interpretation of the axiological content of morality. Let us now examine this in a little more detail.

6. THE PROPER INTERPRETATION OF MORAL VALUE

Psychologism in the theory of morality certainly stands at the basis of the conversion I mentioned earlier[3]—the conversion of ethics into the psychology of morality, and indirectly into the sociology of morality as well. I said that this conversion transfers us *in aliud genus*, that it constitutes a certain kind of "heterogenization" in relation to the authentic, essential content of the experience of morality. This experience shows that moral value (I am continuing to use this concept despite the problems surrounding its application to the species of moral good and evil) appears in the human being not just in the sense that the human being is its subject. If we say that moral good and evil are subjectified in the human being and human actions, we then express to some degree the content of the experience of morality, but we do not express its whole content. We do not say all that could be said about the relation of moral value to the subject, which is the human being. I said earlier that this results from an incomplete anthropology, from a too fragmented view of the subject and its activity. Basically, when "human being" is in some sense equated (=) with "consciousness" in the interpretation of morality, no other way of objectifying moral good or evil seems possible. It can only be understood as a content subjectified in the human being and human activity.

This content would be the specific content that corresponds to the human psyche, "psychic" content, in separation from all that corresponds to the somatic. A certain dualism, but above all a bifurcation of the apprehension of the phenomena proper to the human being, emerges in this view. Morality, moral value, is restricted here to the phenomenal dimension. The assertion that moral good or evil appears in the human being as a subject in connection with the human being's activity is as far as this phenomenalistic interpretation can go.

It seems, however, that this interpretation does not correspond to the full experience of morality, for it does not express what is contained in the objective—or, for that matter, even in the subjective—structure of the moral fact. It also seems that the proper and adequate interpretation in this regard is one that apprehends moral value in the context of the being and becoming (*esse* and *fieri*) of the human being through action. Through his or her actions, a human being becomes morally good or bad, depending on whether these actions are morally good or bad. This is not to deny that such objectification also includes subjectivity (the human being and human activity is the subject of moral value), but not just subjectivity. In the reality given to us experientially as morality, more than just subjectivity and subjectification come into view. In addition to subjectivity, the experience of morality also reveals the efficacy of the human being and, in strict connection with this efficacy, the *fieri* of the human being— the subject's becoming morally good or bad. We see, then, that the phenomenalistic interpretation, an interpretation that is limited exclusively to the "phenomenon," does not suffice here. One could say that such an interpretation is unable to adequately exploit the "phenomenon" understood as the full phenomenon. The phenomenon reveals that the subject "human being" becomes morally good or bad as a result of the efficient involvement of that subject, that personal self, whereas the phenomenalistic interpretation speaks solely and exclusively of "subjectification." One could say, therefore, that the phenomenalistic interpretation bypasses the phenomenon.

Thus only an interpretation that is able to objectify the human being as a being and, on this basis, is able to objectify the particular *fieri*, the becoming, that morality (moral good and evil) brings to the human being as a being, conforms to the experience of morality in this undeniably basic and key element. I do not wish to presuppose in advance that such an interpretation must have a metaphysical character, since the whole view I am developing here arises primarily from the perspective of experience, and not primarily from the perspective of ready-made philosophical assumptions. Hence, it is not on the basis of such assumptions, but on the basis of experience, on the basis of its eloquence, so to speak, that I affirm that only an interpretation that is able to grasp the subject of morality—the human being and human activity—in the aspect of being and becoming is able to formulate an adequate theory of morality. And only such an interpretation allows us to grasp the proper meaning of moral value.

I define moral value in the generic sense (abstracting for the time being from the duality implied in moral good and evil) as that through which the human being as a human being becomes and is good or evil. Of course, the generic meaning includes the two specific meanings. And so I define moral good as that through which the human being becomes and is good, and moral evil as that through which the human being becomes and is evil. Moral value, both good and evil, is something original and irreducible to any further, more general category. This originality manifests itself in the phenomenological realm as a distinctive kind of self-evidence: moral value as moral is self-evident, and its irreducibility to any other category is also self-evident. That, however, which for phenomenology is something immediately self-evident, an immediate perception of an essence (*Wertschau*), so to speak, for the positivistic mentality already implies something else. The positivistic mentality is not content with the immediate self-evidence of the character of moral value, but seeks a further explanation—which, given its concept of experience, it cannot find. The positivist is unable to accept that *esse* and *fieri*, being and becoming, can become an object of experience. And yet, the only possibility of explaining moral value—which, from the phenomenological perspective, is correctly regarded as something perceptible (*Wertschau*) and, in that sense, immediately self-evident—takes place through a reduction to the being and becoming of the human being as such.

The only possible explanation of moral value, of good and evil, lies in this direction. If someone asks, "What is moral value, or good and evil?" we can reply either by simply saying that it is the content of an intuition characterized by immediate self-evidence or by explaining that moral good is that through which the human being as a human being becomes and is good, and moral evil that through which the human being as a human being becomes and is evil. This explanation is to a certain degree a content of prescientific knowledge. Moral good and evil are universally and commonly understood in just this way and not some other. The scientific method does not really change this content at all, but only helps to "verify" it and provides us with a more detailed description of the grounds of this "verification." In this sense, our prescientific views of moral good and evil acquire a scientific dimension. The basic, essential identity of the content of scientific knowledge and prescientific knowledge in this regard is easily explained. After all, morality is first and foremost a sphere of human life and practice. It is not primarily a reality to be discovered, as is the case with so many other spheres of knowledge. Science's main role here is to give a precise description of this reality that so intimately belongs to every human being, that is so near to each of us because we live and practice it. This feature is important for a proper evaluation of both ethics and the theory of morality. In scientific work in this area, the object is not so much to discover an unfamiliar reality as to give a precise description of a reality that is familiar and proper to each of us as human beings, a reality that is, so to speak, our very own.

To say that moral value—good or evil—is that which makes the human being good or evil as a human being, that through which the human being as a human being becomes good or evil, is, in a sense, to reduce moral value to humanity. "The human being as a human being" is good or evil solely and exclusively through moral value. No other value accounts for this. Other values only account for a human being's becoming and being good in one respect or another—for example, a good mathematician, a good dancer, a good athlete, or, more generally speaking, a good performer—but only moral value accounts for a human being's being good or bad as a human being. This clearly shows that an apprehension of the relation of moral value to the human being as merely a subjectification of this value in the human being and human action is far too weak, insufficient, and inadequate with regard to the reality given to experience. The human being cannot be objectified in the theory of morality merely as the subject of moral values, because these values so obviously determine what the human being is as a human being, because, as we can see, these values so obviously determine the kind of human being he or she is, because the very humanity of the human being is the only key to understanding these values and the only possible way of explaining them. Moral values are explained through the human being as a human being, and, at the same time, the human being as a human being is explained through moral values. Humanity is in some sense presupposed in them, and, at the same time, they bring humanity most clearly into view. This is why moral value, or morality, cannot be interpreted without the human being, and "the human being as a human being" cannot be interpreted without morality. Morality is a necessary key to understanding the human being.

Since, in explaining moral values, I have used the term "human being as a human being" (a moral value is that through which the human being as a human being becomes and is good or bad), it seems that I could also say "human being as a person." And it also seems that such a formulation might give this important idea even more precision. When we call a human being a person, we are then referring not so much to the material integrity of humanity, but to that through which the human being—on the basis of this integral humanity—is a human being. By the concept "person" we mean something more than an "individual." It is not the quantitative element with respect to humanity, in the sense of the nature proper and common to all people, but the essential element that then comes to the fore. That which is denoted by "human being as a human being" is included in the concept of person. Hence, the reduction of moral value to the human being as a person would seem to be particularly justified. Moral good is that through which the human being as a person is good (is a good person), and moral evil that through which the human being as a person is evil (is a bad person). Such a formulation could be regarded as a fundamental tenet of personalism in ethics.

This personalism must not be confused with individualism. The human being is not a person, on the one hand, and a member of society, on the other. The human being as a person is simultaneously a member of society. The concept of person is neither opposed to this membership nor places the human being beyond it. At most one could say that what is opposed to society, understood as a certain multiplicity of people, is the human individual. But this is a purely quantitative opposition. And so in thinking of moral value as that through which the human being as a person is good or bad, we do not in the human being separate individuality and membership in a society, but we think them both together. A human being, precisely because he or she is a person, thanks to moral value, thanks to moral good or evil, becomes good or evil both as an individual and as a member of society.

7. THE POSSIBILITY OF A TELEOLOGICAL INTERPRETATION

Now that we have an explanation of the proper meaning of moral value, we should, within the framework of the theory of morality, seek a suitable expression for objectifying the content of the experience formed by the relation between the moral value of an action and the human being performing that action. The possibility of a teleological interpretation suggests itself here, if only because such an interpretation merited the right of inclusion in ethics beginning with Aristotle and, to a certain degree, still has that right—at least for those who follow in the tradition of the Stagirite and Thomas Aquinas. The historical view, however, cannot be decisive here. I also do not intend to deal in this place with teleological ethics as a complete ethical system, since my discussion—as can be seen—is chiefly concerned with the theory of morality. In the framework of that theory, I am interested at the moment in the relation of moral values, of good and evil, to the human being. In this realm, the possibility of a teleological interpretation arises insofar as moral value can be understood as an end.

I should immediately point out that this does not capture the main thought of the ethics of either Aristotle or Thomas Aquinas. That main thought is the notion that, through the moral value of our actions, we can either move toward or away from the end proper to human life. The end in question here is chiefly the ultimate end, to which we draw near through moral good, or virtue, and from which we distance ourselves through moral evil, or sin. My treatment of the theory of morality in this section does not extend to that issue. I am concerned only with a teleological interpretation of the relation of morality to the human person, to the human being, who is the author of actions and the subject of morality. I want to investigate whether and in what way moral value itself is an end. This is obviously a different problem from the one raised by Aristotle and Thomas Aquinas within the structure of their ethical systems. Nevertheless, this problem must in some way stand at the basis of that structure. Teleological ethics has meaning only insofar as it arises from the teleology of morality itself. Otherwise it would contain a basic incompatibility with experience. It would not be an objectification of the content that is really contained in the experience of morality. Does morality itself have a purposive, teleological character? Aristotle, as we know, proceeded from the premise that activity has such a character (*omne agens agit propter finem*). This would favor a teleological theory of action, a praxiology constructed upon the principle of finality. But does morality have the same kind of character? Between praxiology (the theory of action) and the theory of morality, we cannot place an equal sign. And that is why I am asking whether and in what sense moral value has the character of an end. This is the question of the possibility of a teleological interpretation of morality.

A positive answer suggests itself, which I will try to formulate here. An *end* has always been understood to mean an *object of an aim*: that at which we aim or that by reason of which we aim at something. (The more complete and proper concept of an end is the latter, which is in a sense contained in the former and only needs to be deduced from it.) Is moral value such an end for human beings? Is it an object of human endeavor? This would be impossible to deny. People not only want goods, but also want to be good. To want or not to want—therein lies the elementary core of morality. I cannot totally agree with the view that moral value appears somehow on the margin of striving for various other values—objective values. This would be pure psychologism, reducible to the one-sided assumption that human beings only "want goods," an assumption that fails to perceive that people in a no less real way also "want to be good." Of course, the view that moral values appear as though only "alongside" or "on the margin of" striving for various objective values does contain a partial truth. The realization of moral good or evil in a concrete action occurs always through striving for some objective value. One could say that it occurs always in the context of such striving; one could even say in this regard that moral value appears "alongside" the objective value that happens to be the end of an aim, as though on its margin. None of this means, however, that moral value itself is not an object of the will, that people do not aim toward moral value itself in their actions. I find it difficult to agree with the kind of completely ateleological theory of morality proposed, for example, by Scheler. It seems to me, instead, that moral value is also an end, although in a way different from any objective value of human activity. In human actions, a striving for moral value pervades the various wantings of various goods. In wanting various goods, people, in the course of these wantings, also want to be good—or else resign from this desire and do not want to be good. The latter involves moral evil. If someone wants to be bad, this is an expression of the extreme attitude that he or she does not want to be good. Moral evil basically consists in this: that a human being, in wanting some good, does not want to be good.

It is clear from this analysis that in the theory of morality we cannot give up the notion that moral value is an end. At the same time, however, we cannot place the purposiveness proper to moral value on the same level as the purposiveness of objective values. The difference lies both in the character of the values themselves and in the character of the aiming, the wanting. To want a good and to want to be good—these are two dynamic realities that occur on different levels in the subject "human being." They are actualizations of the will that are connected with this subject in different ways. In wanting any good whatsoever, the human self goes out toward a valuable object, whereas in wanting to be good the same subjective self in a sense confers value upon itself. This is not just a going out toward a value as an object, but a value-generating objectification of one's own self as a subject. And it is in this sense that we must accept a distinctive teleology of morality.

The statement that moral value is also an end for human beings and human actions is verified even more fully when we take a different concept of end, namely, when we view it not simply as the object of a particular aim but as that which fulfills—is conducive to the fulfillment of—the subject and its activity. I should add that the concept of fulfillment perhaps most properly corresponds to the Latin *actus*. We know how important *actus* is in Aristotelian and Thomistic philosophy and ethics. In this regard, it seems that moral value determines the fulfillment of actions proper to persons and also determines the fulfillment of the persons themselves in such actions. In acting, we either fulfill ourselves or do not fulfill ourselves. This depends precisely on moral value. Moral good is that through which we fulfill ourselves in action, and evil the opposite. In this view, morality appears as something proper to the human person, corresponding to the person's dynamic sphere of fulfillments and unfulfillments. Fulfillment reaches all the way to the potentiality of the person, as does unfulfillment. In relation to this potentiality essential to the human person, fulfillment is a good and unfulfillment is an evil—the lack of a good to which the person is "by nature" disposed. Fulfillment can also be defined as self-realization. I have presented a detailed analysis of this problem in my book *The Acting Person*.[4] In any case, the fulfillment of oneself in action, or self-realization, is also the attainment of the end proper to a human being as a person (a human being as a human being), and herein lies the essence of moral good. The essence of evil, on the other hand, consists in failing to achieve this end that is proper to a human being as a person (a human being as a human being).

As can be seen, the teleological interpretation is a dynamic development of the proper meaning of moral value. We have grasped this meaning in strict connection with the human being as a person: moral good is that through which the human being as a human being—as a person—becomes and is good, and moral evil that through which the human being as a human being—as a person—becomes and is evil. The teleological interpretation refers directly to this becoming, this *fieri*, proper to the human being as a person. In this *fieri* is also contained the whole dynamic of autoteleology that corresponds to the human being by reason of being a person.

I believe I have thus shown the possibility of a teleological interpretation, and perhaps even the indispensability of such an interpretation, in the theory of morality. The teleological interpretation is indispensable to the extent that without it we cannot objectify the basic content of the experience of morality expressed in the fact, "I want to be good" or, conversely, "I do not want to be good." At the same time, however, there is the danger of a certain one-sidedness in the use of this interpretation, namely, the danger of psychologism in the theory of morality, which I referred to earlier. I call this a danger here because I am constantly aware that the proper content of morality is an experientially given reality that awaits a homogeneous objectification. It seems—and certain phenomenological interpretations substantiate this—that we fail to achieve such an objectification when we do not distinguish between the relation of the human being to an objective value ("I want a good") and the relation of the human being to his or her own moral value ("I want to be good"). This observation has a bearing on anthropology and the theory of the person, as well as on the theory of morality and, indirectly, ethics.

8. THE NECESSITY OF INTRODUCING THE ELEMENT OF DUTY

It is precisely here that the need arises to introduce the element of duty as an integral component of the reality of morality. The relation of the subject "human being" to moral value emerges in every conscious activity, in and through every action. The foregoing analysis of this relation has revealed the specific aspect of moral values, their—so to speak—specific position in the human being. This required keeping a lookout for signs or possibilities of psychologism, which could prevent us from grasping the position proper to moral values in the human being. The possibilities of sociologism are of a similar type and form a kind of extension of the former. Sociologism is a particular kind of psychologism, with the qualification that sociologism mainly emphasizes the dependence of human wantings directed toward various objective values on a person's membership in a particular society, social group, or community. In the conception of the objectification of morality, however, our attention can be directed only secondarily and "materially," as it were, toward the wanting of objective values and any determinants of this wanting. Primarily and "formally," it must be directed toward the reality "I want—or I don't want—to be good," which forms the very core of morality and its essential property.

The reality "I want—or I don't want—to be good" not only involves the wanting of a certain objective value but also involves, as a necessary factor decisive for the very essence of morality, the element of duty. Duty denotes the distinctive *constitutivum* of the lived experience to which we ascribe a moral character in the proper sense of the term. Duty is more decisive for morality than is value. At least in this point I must concede that Kant comes closer to the truth than Scheler, although for other more basic reasons I cannot agree with Kant. The opposition of the ethics of values to the ethics of duty—an opposition that has attained special prominence since the end of the 19th century—seems to entail a kind of split in the experience of morality and also to accentuate artificially one of the aspects of the reality of morality at the expense of another. The task of the theory of morality in this case consists in correctly integrating these aspects, in keeping with how they appear in experience.

The specific aspect of morality is, as we have seen, contained in the experience "I want to be good," an experience that permeates human actions and their respective strivings or wantings directed toward various goods, toward various objective values. Duty seems to be the mode of such permeation proper to morality. It may be expressed as follows:

"If you want to be good, you should—or you must—behave this way or not behave that way." (The latter may be expressed in still other ways: "You ought not behave that way," "You may not behave that way," etc.) By *behavior* here I mean activity, human actions, together with their respective aims toward certain objective values. As can be seen, we express duty by means of a variety of phrases. In addition to those mentioned above, we also use other more impersonal forms, e.g., "one should" or "one ought"—and possibly even "it is fitting that," which expresses a lesser degree of intensity than that essential for duty. Here, however, I will leave aside the impersonal phrases, because I am concerned with duty not as an abstraction but as a concrete reality given in the concrete lived experience of duty. The most proper expressions, therefore, seem to be "you should," "you ought," or "you must." These expressions signify that there enters into the activity, or, more precisely, into that activity's aim toward an objective value, into the wanting of that value, a new content, a new dynamism.

This dynamism is intimately connected with the lived experience: "I want to be good," and with the "value-generating objectification" of one's own self: "If I want to be good, I should, I must..." Duty is unquestionably linked to the autoteleology—the element of fulfillment or unfulfillment—that we discovered at the core of the reality of morality. It arises from the structure of a personal being, a being capable of self-realization, and is based on a potentiality proper to such a being. This potentiality is the spiritual potentiality of the will, the potentiality of freedom, which in a rational being—and the person is such a being—reveals a dynamic ordination to truth. Duty arises in this context. A being devoid of such freedom—a freedom that is to be realized (actualized) in a dynamic ordination to truth—would be incapable of experiencing duty. This lived experience "reveals" the human being as a person; it discloses the very essence of the human being and makes visible the main aspect of the dynamism proper to the spirituality of the human being. From this perspective, duty is a kind of concentration of spiritual energy, in which we find something more than just a wanting of or striving for various objective values. Characteristic for duty is the lived experience "I must"—an inner coercion that constitutes a distinctive modification of the experience "I want." This inner coercion arises, like every "I want," from one's own self, but it differs as an experience and as an act of will from this "I want" in more than just the intensity of the striving. "I must" differs from "I want" by virtue of the value that corresponds to it. Wherever an "I must" occurs on the part of the will, wherever moral duty occurs in the proper sense of the term, an unconditional value is at stake.

No mere "I want" points to such a value. From the perspective of the subject and the will, moral duty signifies a transcendence of the threshold of the relativity of the good toward a kind of unconditionality of the good. This unconditionality of the good (or, to put it another way, this unconditionality of value) requires a fuller explanation. Such unconditionality seems to exist only at a given moment; it is a kind of situational unconditionality, one connected with a given *hic et nunc* of conscious activity. Hence, the unconditionality of the good that arises together with moral duty—and takes the form of a concrete obligation—cannot be identified with unconditional good in the ontological sense, i.e., with "the good in every respect." This would be a very great error in the theory of morality, one that could be described as an ontological error. The unconditionality of moral values occurs always in the context of the experience "I want to be good;" it thus occurs within a basic conditionality, in relation to the person performing an action. The unconditionality that corresponds to moral duty—which is also the kind of unconditionality that Kant had in mind in using the concept of the "categorical imperative" in connection with moral duty—is an entirely distinctive unconditionality. It results from the essence of morality, from the opposition of good and evil, which are mutually exclusive: if good, then not evil—if not evil, then good; if not good, then evil—if evil, then not good.

Moral duty as a lived experience reflects in a way the whole system in which good and evil mutually oppose and mutually exclude one another—and this is what accounts for that distinctive unconditionality, which encompasses within its scope both the moral value contained in a concrete action and the objective values toward which that action is directed. This also explains why moral duty is directly expressed primarily in the form of commands, prohibitions, and other related norms. I am speaking here of linguistic forms behind which lie conceptual forms. The various norms of morality are most readily and properly clothed in such forms. Every moral duty is a subjective and experiential correlate of some norm of morality. The norms of morality, in turn, involve various objectifications of moral duties. In the next chapter,[5] I shall deal with norms as a separate topic—basically still within the context of the theory of morality. First, however, I shall attempt to apprehend moral duty itself and the unconditionality of the value corresponding to it, which, as I said, encompasses within its scope both the moral value of the action and—by reason of the moral value—objective values as well.

If, for example, we express a concrete duty by the prohibition: "Do not commit adultery," this prohibition refers "materially" to a whole set of objective values that can be or are realized in concrete actions. In this case, they are the values associated with the area of sexuality and with the kind of sexual relations proper to human beings, namely, sexual relations on the level of persons and, therefore, embraced by the institution of marriage, in consequence of which a particular husband or wife is "mine" and not "another's," etc. All of this determines the material scope of the duty. The "formal" or essential element is always the moral value itself. It unites the material scope of the duty and forms the point around which the unconditionality that this duty brings to the whole of that system of values actually revolves. In the case in question, this unconditionality is expressed by the prohibition: "Do not commit adultery"—"If you want to be good (if you do not want to be bad), do not commit adultery." Unconditionality is proper to this whole system. This unconditionality determines the system's ethical meaning as its proper meaning; moral value is thus the center and source of the distinctive unconditionality of the good expressed by duty. Moral value is ultimately both the source and the outcome of duty. In realizing moral value in action, the person proceeds *hic et nunc* from the lived experience of duty and from the scope of the unconditionality of the good experienced in duty.

This lived experience not only provides a basis for objectifying moral duty in the form of the various norms of morality, but also provides—by means of an appropriate abstraction—a basis for objectifying moral value. We then, as it were, detach this value from all the concrete actions of concrete human beings, where it is moral value in the existential sense as moral good or evil, and we apprehend it somehow in itself, *in se*. Thus, for example, we can apprehend *in se* the moral good of marital fidelity by opposing it to the moral evil of adultery. The objectivity of the moral value in the one case and the other allows us to speak of an objective moral order, which in no way obscures the subjectivity that characterizes morality in the existential sense. The moral order that exists as a kind of abstract vision in human minds exists in them in strict reference to morality in the existential sense, to the living human reality given in experience as morality. The former exists in dependence on the latter. This dependence needs to be more fully investigated, particularly within the context of investigations—beginning with a theoretical investigation— of the norms of morality, a task I shall defer to the next chapter.[6]

9. IMPLICATIONS OF THE THEORY OF MORALITY FOR ANTHROPOLOGY

Before going on to the topic of norms, I should say a few words about certain elements of the theory of morality that are rather clearly implied in what I have said thus far. These implications need to be made more explicit, both for the sake of the clarity of the whole and on account of their importance. One such implication of the theory of morality presented here is certainly a view of the human being. I have already alluded to this several times along the way, but it deserves a somewhat fuller treatment—though not so full that a complete anthropology would arise within the context of the theory of morality. Here I am deliberately restricting my treatment of anthropology, which I have placed instead in a separate work entitled *The Acting Person*. Nevertheless, certain matters should be added here for the sake of completeness. They arise particularly in the light of the preceding analysis of duty.

The reality of morality, and especially duty, reveals that at the basis of morality is found the human being as a person. Morality is properly and fundamentally a correlate of personality: "the human being as a human being" means "the human being as a person." If we wish to abide by the profound eloquence of the experience of morality, we cannot put anyone else or anything else in this place. We cannot put any society, even the most universal (humankind) or the most interpersonal (the family), at the root of morality in place of the human being as a person. We also cannot put the world or the universe at the basis of morality. At the basis of morality and also at its true center resides only the human being as a person. Moral good is that through which the human being as a human being becomes and is good, and moral evil that through which the human being as a human being becomes and is evil. Morality of its essence is, so to speak, a sphere of the human being's authentic transcendence. This is also expressed through the distinctive unconditionality of moral good and—by contrast—moral evil. Moral value reveals that both the world and society are ordered to the human being as a person and that they ought to be subordinated to the human being as a person. Moral value is the point in which the whole realm of values accessible to our experience within the dimensions of the world attains its aspect of unconditionality, its distinctive absolute. This is not, of course, an absolute in the ontological sense.

This distinctive absolute, this aspect of the unconditionality of the good, belongs to the human being through morality—or, to put it more subjectively and experientially, through conscience. Through this aspect the human being as a person stands as though above the world. The human being as a person also stands above society, understood as a multiplicity of people joined together by various bonds into social units. These units cannot replace the human being in the position of the personal subject of morality; they cannot supplant the human being in this position. This position is just as inaccessible (*alter incommunicabilis*) as personality itself. By personality I understand here the pure fact of being a person. An expression of this transcendence of the person through morality, which has the person alone as its proper and substantial subject and center, is the principle of the freedom of conscience, a principle recognized in social life on its various levels. Today this principle in precisely this form is universally proclaimed by law. It defines the person's right to the transcendence most proper to the person, namely, transcendence through morality. This principle also demonstrates that no social group—no state, nation, social class, or even family—wishes to put itself in the position of the proper and substantial subject of moral values in place of the person.

Instead, all such societies and social groups acknowledge that this subject is solely and exclusively the human being as a person. Only the human being as a person is the true center of morality, whereas every society and social group bases its morality on the human being as a person and derives its morality from this source. The concept of social morality is, of course, something very real and continually evolving, but it in no way represents an attempt to substitute society for the human person as the substantial subject of moral values and the proper center of morality. Rather, the concept of social morality points to another aspect of the discussion, namely, to the increasingly new areas of moral duty that arise as a result of the expansion and diversification of social bonds among human beings. This does not change the subject and true center of morality, but it does enrich the relationships in which people must carry out their activity and fulfill their existence, which they do through the moral values corresponding to those relationships.

While taking this aspect of the content of morality fully into account in the theory of morality and in ethics, we must never lose sight of that which—according to experience—is decisive for the essence of morality. The core of morality, as I have already shown, is humanistic and personalistic through and through. The distinctive unconditionality of the good, which determines the personal transcendence of the human being, must neither be lost nor be transferred *in aliud genus*. The true measure of the greatness of any human being lies in morality; through morality, we each write our own most intimate and personal history. Any attempt to place the theory of morality outside this basic dimension creates an imminent occasion for alienation. Alienation, when it occurs in life, is a deprivation of that which properly belongs to a particular subject—in this case, the human person. When it occurs in theory, on the other hand, alienation is a type of error: a faulty exploitation of experience, a faulty interpretation. In the problematic of morality, it is very easy to make such an error, given the enormous complexity and number of aspects involved. It is certainly possible, therefore, to lose the human being as a human being, together with the subjectivity and ethical transcendence that belong inseparably to this being, in the multiplicity represented by various societies and social groups. The human being then appears as an individual against the background of this multiplicity, a human individual subordinate to the human multiplicity, estranged from his or her rightful position as a subject and convertible to an object of the processes proper to this multiplicity. This transformation of the subject into an object is equivalent to either significantly limiting or simply eliminating the position that the experience of morality tells us belongs to the subject. This experience also tells us that the activity of the human being as a person must not be lost in the development of the world—even though this world is transformed and developed by the human being. None of the effects of the human activity directed toward the world, toward transforming and developing it—indeed, toward "humanizing" it, toward adapting it to human needs—contain the element of the unconditionality of the good or the element of transcendence proper to the human being as a person. These elements are found only in morality. The theory of morality should bring this out.

The theory of morality thus discloses the position and ethical transcendence proper to the person by reason of the element of the unconditionality of the good. At the same time, however, the theory of morality—by reason of this very same element—cannot help but perceive another aspect of the human being, one that seems directly opposed to the former, namely, a certain profound contingency. This contingency is equivalent to ontic nonnecessity: the possibility of existence and nonexistence. Morality discloses the sheer possibility of good and evil within one and the same personal subject as the fruit of that subject's efficacy and self-determination. To the extent that good is the fulfillment of this subject, evil is its unfulfillment. Unfulfillment implies a certain nonexistence. In any case, unfulfillment is the nonrealization of that which not just *could* become a reality but in fact *should* become one. The element of duty reveals the unconditionality of the good as a kind of absolute residing in the human person; at the same time, however, it also reveals in a particular way the contingency of that person. This is contingency in the ethical, not the ontic, sense; it is the contingency of moral good and evil, and yet it does have a bearing on contingency in the ontic sense. That which can be fulfilled or not be fulfilled, or which even unconditionally should be fulfilled or not be fulfilled, is not in itself already fulfilled and complete. It resides in the dimensions of contingency and not necessity. The experience of morality certainly assists us in the definition of our status as human beings, including our ontological status. By the same token, this experience also indicates that the ontic explanation of our human essence enters the realm of the discipline that is, so to speak, *per se* sensitive to the contingency of everything that in any way exists.

This definition remains in a strict connection with the experience whose inseparable subject and true center is the human being: the human being as a human being, the human being as a person. Consequently, it has particular significance and profundity. As human beings, we experience the unconditionality of the good, and in this way we encounter the element of the absolute within ourselves, yet we ourselves are not the absolute, for we are constantly oscillating between the possibility of good and evil.

This also explains why in the realm of morality there arises an encounter with the Absolute, with God. The ability to experience the element of the absolute within ourselves while simultaneously being aware of our own contingency, including our ethical contingency as the constant possibility of good and evil, evokes in us a relation to the Absolute in both the ontic and the ethical sense. Religion and morality are mutually related to one another by a very deep bond. I will not, however, go into this problem here; I merely wish to draw attention to it.

10. IMPLICATIONS OF THE THEORY OF MORALITY FOR AXIOLOGY

The theory of morality is the description and interpretation of the experience of morality within the limits defined by the answer to the question: what is morality? In formulating this answer, we attempt to exploit experience, seeking an expression that allows us to objectify the content of this experience in the most suitable way possible. Although we do not proceed from a ready-made system in the framework of which this objectification has already been accomplished over the course of the history of human thought, yet at every step we cannot help but encounter elements of previously constructed objectifications of the experience of morality, objectifications both in the theory of morality and in ethics. I believe that no theory of morality or ethics has ever been developed in separation from the experience of morality, although this process has perhaps not been sufficiently recognized and made explicit. For this reason, too, however, even the very naming of the different elements of the experience of morality follows along the lines of previously constructed objectifications. This applies especially to the interpretation of morality as a particular axiological reality, a particular sphere of the good or value.

Here it is important to bear in mind that over the course of the history of philosophy a significant change of orientation took place, one that—to put it rather simply—led away from the philosophy of being toward the philosophy of consciousness. This change of orientation also has a fundamental significance for axiology, for the conception of the good or value. In the framework of the philosophy of being, the good was identified with being, accentuating only a difference of aspects. Good is equivalent to being as an object of activity, as an end. Such a view of the good pervades the whole ethics of Aristotle and Thomas Aquinas, a point already mentioned above. In the context of the philosophy of consciousness, this orientation changed. No longer was the concern about what the good is objectively, what it is in itself (that it is identifiable with being in the aspect of finality), but about the kind of content of consciousness it is and the sort of acts of consciousness to which it corresponds. Here, then, in the point of departure, was found the lived experience of value as a completely original intentional act, having—as many hold—a primarily emotional character, directed toward a completely original content. Neither this lived experience (act) nor the content corresponding to it can be reduced to anything else: they are totally original and elementary.

The interpretation of the experience of morality that I have presented in this chapter from the perspective of its axiological content must constantly be viewed in relation to each of these orientations. If on the level of their mutually exclusive epistemological assumptions these two orientations are not merely divergent but directly contradictory, then by omitting these assumptions they can appear convergent and complementary. My interpretation does not extend to the realm of epistemological assumptions. I am focusing on morality as a reality given in experience—and attempting to understand and interpret it in the deepest possible way. I maintain that morality as a value has objective meaning in and through the human being and that there is no way to apprehend this meaning apart from the categories of being and becoming: *esse* and *fieri*. In other words, moral good is that through which the human being as a human being becomes and is good, and moral evil that through which the human being as a human being becomes and is evil. This becoming (*fieri*) resides in the dynamism of human action (*actus humanus*); it cannot be properly objectified on the basis of consciousness alone, but only on the basis of the human being as a conscious being. It follows, too, that good or evil as a property of a conscious being is itself also a being and not just a content of consciousness. This does not, however, obscure the fact that it—good or evil—is, at the same time, a content of consciousness, that it is given in lived experience as a specific value, namely, moral value. Proceeding from the two different orientations in philosophy, it seems that we can arrive in the theory of morality at a complementary view of this same reality. Moral value points directly to that through which the human being as a human being is good or evil (I have already discussed the terminological difficulties connected with this opposition). The fact, in turn, that the human being experiences this good or evil, that the human being experiences himself or herself as the author of moral value and as its dynamic subject, is simply the experiential and conscious confirmation of this reality, which we can objectify in a completely adequate way only in the categories of being and becoming: *esse* and *fieri*.

I believe, then, that my analysis and interpretation of the experience of morality, when viewed in relation to these two great and divergent—and in some sense even mutually contradictory— orientations in philosophy, and thus also in axiology, can itself avoid contradiction. I am thinking here mainly of the charge of a certain contradiction, or at least a lack of philosophical convergence, with regard to such basic terms as *good* and *value*. I believe, moreover, that my analysis and interpretation can lead—as I have already attempted to show—to the discovery of a basic convergence between these orientations. This convergence occurs in the human being, in whom we cannot totally separate being from consciousness. This is especially evident in the sphere of morality. Here moral value is an essential expression of the good that determines the human being as a human being, the human being as a person. Consequently, in speaking of moral value, we always ultimately point to this reality of the good—and also of evil, since moral value appears to us in both of these mutually opposing axiological forms.

The theory of morality lies at the root of ethics. It is, as we have seen, a theory of human beings as persons who are good or bad beings, each within his or her own personal essence. At the same time, it is a theory of human beings as persons who experience their own moral value, who experience that they themselves become and are—as persons—good or evil. These are the two aspects of the theory of morality, and they seem to be inseparable. Any attempt to separate them will be connected with somehow absolutizing one aspect or the other. And so it will involve an error of theory.

Might we say that the theory of morality, and then ethics, is a kind of science subordinated (*scientia subalternata*) to the theory of the good—to axiology? I think that this would be an oversimplification. The concept of a subordinate science implies the notion of the application of ready-made concepts and judgments that are at the disposal of a superior science (*scientia subalternans*). But the theory of morality, and then ethics, proceeds from a thoroughly original experience. This experience contains a thoroughly original relation of human beings as subjects and authors to values, especially to moral values. The direct application of the general concepts and judgments proper to axiology—according to either of the contemporary orientations—cannot explain much here. Instead, we must seek our own methods of interpretation in this area, ones suitable to it. In doing so, however, I believe that our science of values in general will be indirectly greatly enriched. Thus, rather than speaking of subordination, we should speak of a certain mutual ordination of axiology and ethics.

NOTES

1. See Karol Wojtyla, "The Problem of Experience in Ethics" 107–127 above. These two articles—"The Problem of Experience in Ethics" and "The Problem of the Theory of Morality"—are the first and second chapters of an unfinished work entitled *The Conception and Methodology of Ethics*. —Trans.

2. See section 5 of "The Problem of Experience in Ethics" 120–122 above. —Trans.

3. See section 2 of "The Problem of Experience in Ethics" 110–113 above. —Trans.

4. Karol Wojtyla, *The Acting Person*, trans. Andrzej Potocki, ed. Anna-Teresa Tymieniecka (Boston: Reidel, 1979); originally published in Polish as *Osoba i czyn* (Krakow: Polskie Tow. Teologiczne, 1969; rev. ed. 1985). —Trans.

5. This chapter, which would have formed the third chapter of *The Conception and Methodology of Ethics* (see note 1 above), was never published. —Trans.

6. See note 5 above. —Trans.

PART TWO

Personalism

10

Thomistic Personalism

1. INTRODUCTORY REMARKS

St. Thomas was familiar with the concept of person and defined it very clearly. This is not to say, however, that he was equally familiar with the problem of personalism or that he presented it as clearly as the problem of the person. We would, however, be correct in thinking that, since he presented the problem of the person so clearly, he also provided at least a point of departure for personalism in general. And although the problem of personalism was formulated much later—in any case, my concern with it here is in the form it takes in contemporary thought and life—still, St. Thomas' overall philosophy and theology allows us to speak of Thomistic personalism. We find in his system not just a point of departure, but also a whole series of additional constitutive elements that allow us to examine the problem of personalism in the categories of St. Thomas' philosophy and theology. It is just these elements that I shall attempt to set forth here.

This will, of course, be only a sketch or an outline of the problem, which obviously lends itself to an extensive treatment. Here at the very outset I should mention one more thing. Personalism is not primarily a theory of the person or a theoretical science of the person. Its meaning is largely practical and ethical: it is concerned with the person as a subject and an object of activity, as a subject of rights, etc. And so in this sketch I will draw largely upon the practical philosophy and ethics of St. Thomas and also of those students of his who extracted the doctrine of personalism from St. Thomas' works and formulated it into an independent whole.

Karol Wojtyla, "Personalizm tomistyczny," *Znak* 13 (1961): 664–675. A paper presented by Wojtyla on 17 February 1961, during the Fourth Annual Philosophy Week at the Catholic University of Lublin.

2. THE THEOLOGICAL HISTORY OF THE QUESTION

The concept of person that we find in the philosophy and above all in the theology of St. Thomas has a history of its own going back many centuries. This history is connected with the work of theologians of the patristic period, who sought to clarify, or at least more precisely define, the main truths of our faith. They were concerned primarily with two truths: the mystery of the Trinity and the mystery of the Incarnation of the Second Divine Person, which involves a hypostatic union of two natures, divine and human. Both of these truths are mysteries of faith in the strict sense, and so even after they have been revealed by God human reason is not capable of fully and completely understanding their essence. Nevertheless, attempts to understand them are perfectly legitimate. Such attempts were made in speculative theology. The Church had to try to clarify these truths in a manner that would exclude faulty ways of understanding them. As we know, most of the heresies in the early centuries of Christianity arose precisely on the basis of a faulty understanding of the mystery of the Trinity and the mystery of the Incarnation of the Son of God. In order to present these mysteries, and particularly in order to give them greater speculative clarity and depth, what was especially needed was a concept of person and an understanding of the relation that occurs between person and nature. Consequently, in the works of theologians of the patristic period the concept of person was very thoroughly examined. St. Thomas had here, then, a prepared ground.

But this is also why in St. Thomas' system the person performs more of a theological function. In Christian thought, theological personalism is prior to humanistic personalism; this may also easily be said of St. Thomas' thought. We encounter the word *persona* mainly in his treatises on the Trinity and the Incarnation, whereas it is all but absent from his treatise on the human being. Nevertheless, St. Thomas presents the matter in the following way: whatever is a true perfection in the created world must be found in the highest degree in God, and so the person, too, which signifies the highest perfection in the world of creatures, must be realized in an incomparably more perfect degree in God. As we can see, then, St. Thomas not only analyzes the problem of the Trinity of Divine Persons, a truth known to us from revelation, and therefore a matter for theological reflection, but he also discovers a philosophical access to the concept of a personal God, based upon an analysis of created reality. In this case, he follows the same method he used in arriving at knowledge of the divine essence. Creatures provide the basis for our knowledge of this essence, since whatever is a true perfection in the created world must in some incomparably more perfect way be found in God. St. Thomas takes precisely this occasion to assert that in the created world the person is the highest perfection: the person is *perfectissimum ens*. And this forms the basis for St. Thomas' conception of a personal God. This conception is something separate from theological speculation on the Trinity. The latter has its entire basis in revelation, in the scriptures and tradition, whereas the former is the product of philosophical reflection, based on an analysis of reality accessible to human reason itself.

As we can see, then, St. Thomas' doctrine of person appears in strong connection with revelation, and therefore belongs to the realm of theology, and yet it also has a proper place of its own in the philosophical speculation of this great thinker.

3. THE DEFINITION OF PERSON AND THE GENERAL CHARACTERISTICS OF ST. THOMAS' VIEW OF THE PERSON

The best proof of this is the fact that St. Thomas continually has recourse to a definition of the person. This is the well known and widely used definition formulated by Boethius: *persona est rationalis naturae individua substantia*. St. Thomas frequently analyzes this philosophical definition, using it in his theological speculations on the Trinity and the hypostatic union. The definition itself, however, is philosophical; the basis upon which it is constructed is a fundamental understanding of the human being. The human being is an individual (*individua substantia*) of a rational nature. A rational nature does not possess its own subsistence as a nature, but subsists in a person. The person is a subsistent subject of existence and action—which can in no way be said of a rational nature. That is why God must be a personal being. In the visible world, every human being is such a created being. St. Thomas says that this being is objectively the most perfect being. Its perfection is undeniably the result of its rational, and thus spiritual, nature, which finds its natural complement in freedom. Both of these spiritual properties of the nature—reason and freedom—are concretized in the person, where they become properties of a concrete being, which exists and acts on the level of a nature that has such properties. The person, therefore, is always a rational and free concrete being, capable of all those activities that reason and freedom alone make possible. I shall analyze these activities in somewhat greater detail below.

St. Thomas, as I said, uses the term *persona* mainly in his purely theological treatises on the Trinity and the hypostatic union. In his treatise on the human being, on the other hand, he adopts a hylomorphic view, that is, he regards the human being as a composition of matter and form. In his analysis of this *compositum humanum*, St. Thomas presents an especially profound analysis of the human soul, which in this *compositum* performs the role of the substantial form. This is a rational soul (*anima rationalis*), the principle and source of the whole spirituality of the human being, and, therefore, also that by virtue of which the human being may properly be ascribed the character of a person. Later Thomists devoted numerous investigations and speculations to the problem of the so-called *constitutivum personae*, that is, to explaining the metaphysical basis of personality. We can, however, set aside those investigations here and concentrate more on the analysis of the soul that we find in St. Thomas. In this way, the point of view of our reflections will shift from personality in the metaphysical sense to personality in the psychological sense.

The human person is, like every other person (e.g., a Divine Person or an angelic person, both of whom are purely spiritual), an individual of a rational nature. This definition is verified in every person. What is peculiar to the human person, however, is that this person has a rational nature only because of a spiritual soul, which is the substantial form of the body. This fact is of basic importance for understanding the whole uniqueness of the human person, as well as for explaining the structure of the human person. Consequently, in attempting to explain the structure represented by the human person, we would perhaps do well to have recourse to the most comprehensive analysis possible of the human soul, following what St. Thomas left us in the first part of his *Summa*.

The human soul is a spiritual substance, whose natural properties are reason and freedom. The human soul is the principle of the life and activity of the human being; it operates, in turn, through the mediation of faculties. The faculties that express and actualize the soul's spirituality, and thus the human being's spirituality, are reason and free will. They are also the principal means, so to speak, whereby the human person is actualized; based on their activity, the whole psychological and moral personality takes shape. But these are not the only faculties of the human soul. As the substantial form of the body, the soul also has, in addition to spiritual faculties, faculties that are intrinsically dependent on matter. These are primarily sensory faculties, both cognitive and appetitive. These faculties, as belonging to the concrete human being, are likewise found in the person and contribute in their own way to the shaping of the psychological and moral personality. St. Thomas is well aware of this reality and formulates his characterization of the spirituality of the human being accordingly. This spiritual aspect, he says, is eminently suited to unite into a substantial whole with the corporeal, and thus also with the sensory. This union must, therefore, also play a special role in shaping the human personality. According to St. Thomas, all the faculties of the human soul work to perfect the human being, and so they all contribute to the development of the person. This position differs in a fundamental way from the Platonic position and also—though for different reasons—from the Cartesian position.

4. THE RELATION OF THE OBJECTIVE ELEMENT (BEING) TO THE SUBJECTIVE ELEMENT (CONSCIOUSNESS)

It is time now, in this presentation of St. Thomas' view of the human person, to compare it to the view of the person that we encounter especially in modern, post-Cartesian philosophy. A hallmark of Descartes' view is his splitting of the human being into an extended substance (the body) and a thinking substance (the soul), which are related to one another in a parallel way and do not form an undivided whole, one substantial *compositum humanum*. We can observe in philosophy a gradual process of a kind of hypostatization of consciousness: consciousness becomes an independent subject of activity, and indirectly of existence, occurring somehow alongside the body, which is a material structure subject to the laws of nature, to natural determinism. Against the background of such parallelism, combined with a simultaneous hypostatization of consciousness, the tendency arises to identify the person with consciousness. The person is primarily—if not exclusively—consciousness, a consciousness that is in some way subsistent, existing against the background of the organism, which Descartes regarded as a special kind of mechanism. Consciousness is an object of inner experience, of introspection, whereas the body, like all other bodies in the natural world, is accessible to observation and external experience. This view lacks a sufficient basis for including the body, the organism, within the structural whole of the person's life and activity; it lacks the notion of a spiritual soul as the substantial form of that body and as the principle of the whole life and activity of the human being.

The modern view of the person proceeds by way of an analysis of the consciousness, and particularly the self-consciousness, that belongs to the human being. Along with consciousness, freedom is also emphasized, but this freedom, which is conceived in an indeterministic way as total independence, is more of a postulate than a property. Freedom as a property of the person, freedom as an attribute of the will, disappears completely from the subjectivistic view of the person that, in various forms, we encounter in modern philosophy. And this is perhaps the most characteristic feature of such philosophy: its subjectivism, its absolutizing of the subjective element, namely, lived experience, together with consciousness as a permanent component of such experience. The person is not a substance, an objective being with its own proper subsistence—subsistence in a rational nature. The person is merely a certain property of lived experiences and can be distinguished by means of those experiences, for they are conscious and self-conscious experiences; hence, consciousness and self-consciousness constitute the essence of the person. This is a completely different treatment from the one we find in St. Thomas. According to St. Thomas, consciousness and self-consciousness are something derivative, a kind of fruit of the rational nature that subsists in the person, a nature crystalized in a unitary rational and free being, and not something subsistent in themselves. If consciousness and self-consciousness characterize the person, then they do so only in the accidental order, as derived from the rational nature on the basis of which the person acts. The person acts consciously because the person is rational. Self-consciousness, in turn, is connected with freedom, which is actualized in the activity of the will. Through the will, the human being is the master of his or her actions, and self-consciousness in a special way reflects this mastery over actions.

We can see here how very objectivistic St. Thomas' view of the person is. It almost seems as though there is no place in it for an analysis of consciousness and self-consciousness as totally unique manifestations of the person as a subject. For St. Thomas, the person is, of course, a subject—a very distinctive subject of existence and activity—because the person has subsistence in a rational nature, and this is what makes the person capable of consciousness and self-consciousness. St. Thomas, however, mainly presents this disposition of the human person to consciousness and self-consciousness. On the other hand, when it comes to analyzing consciousness and self-consciousness—which is what chiefly interested modern philosophy and psychology—there seems to be no place for it in St. Thomas' objectivistic view of reality. In any case, that in which the person's subjectivity is most apparent is presented by St. Thomas in an exclusively—or almost exclusively—objective way. He shows us the particular faculties, both spiritual and sensory, thanks to which the whole of human consciousness and self-consciousness—the human personality in the psychological and moral sense—takes shape, but that is also where he stops. Thus St. Thomas gives us an excellent view of the objective existence and activity of the person, but it would be difficult to speak in his view of the lived experiences of the person.

5. THE ACTIVITY OF THE PERSON

THOUGHT AS THE BASIS OF CREATIVITY

The person in St. Thomas' view is always a concrete being, one in which the potentiality proper to a rational nature is realized. This potentiality is realized, first of all, by means of thought. It would be difficult here to present the complete Thomistic analysis of thought in all of its psychological and logical dimensions. This is a separate and extremely large issue. I only wish to draw attention here to what in thought is most characteristic for the person. Human thought has a creative character; it is the basis of creativity and the source of culture. This does not mean that by thinking we create a world of ideas and judgments separate from and independent of reality. Quite the contrary. Human thought has a very realistic and objective character. It is also, however, the basis for deriving new truths from existing reality and for controlling reality. We gain mastery of reality by coming to know it more and more thoroughly. The better we know the world, the more we are able to subordinate it to ourselves and make use of the new resources and riches we discover in it. Something similar can be said of our self-knowledge: the better we know ourselves—our possibilities, capabilities, and talents—the more we are able to derive from ourselves and the more we are able to create, making use of the raw material we find in ourselves.

We are by nature creators, not just consumers. We are creators because we think. And because our thought (our rational nature) is also the basis of our personalities, one could say that we are creators because we are persons. Creativity is realized in action. When we act in a manner proper to a person, we always create something: we create something either outside ourselves in the surrounding world or within ourselves—or outside and within ourselves at the same time. Creating as derived from thinking is so characteristic of a person that it is always an infallible sign of a person, a proof of a person's existence or presence. In creating, we also fill the external material world around us with our own thought and being.

There is a certain similarity here between ourselves and God, for the whole of creation is an expression of God's own thought and being.

FREE WILL AS THE BASIS OF MORALITY

Although thought is the basis of the creativity in which we express ourselves as persons, this creativity neither ends nor culminates in thought. That which is most characteristic of a person, that in which a person (at least in the natural order) is most fully and properly realized, is morality. Morality is not the most strictly connected with thought; thought is merely a condition of morality. Directly, however, morality is connected with freedom, and therefore with the will. The object of the will is the good. There are a variety of goods that we can will. The point is to will a true good. Such an act of will makes us good human beings. To be morally good, we must not only will something good, but we must also will it in a good way. If we will it in a bad way, we ourselves will become morally bad. Morality, therefore, presupposes knowledge, the truth concerning the good, but it is realized by willing, by choice, by decision. In this way, not only does our will become good or evil, but our whole person also becomes good or evil. Thanks to our will, we are masters of ourselves and of our actions, but because of this the value of these actions of our will qualifies our whole person positively or negatively.

Clearly, then, freedom of will is not just an exceptional property but also a difficult one. In any case, according to St. Thomas, freedom is not given to us as an end in itself, but as a means to a greater end. Freedom for freedom's sake has no justification in the Thomistic view of the cosmos; freedom exists for the sake of morality and, together with morality, for the sake of a higher spiritual law and order of existence—the kind of order that most strictly corresponds to rational beings, which are persons.

6. THE PERSON AS A SUBJECT AND OBJECT OF LOVE

According to St. Thomas, love is basically a certain natural force that draws together and unites everything in existence. On the level of sensory beings, this love corresponds to the nature of such beings. This is also true on the level of persons—persons are capable of spiritual love. Although human beings are intellectual-sensory, spiritual-material composites, as a result of which energies of sensory love also operate in them, the love proper to human beings is spiritual love. Such love is directed in a special way toward other persons, for in them we find an object commensurate with ourselves. True love, the kind of love of others worthy of a human person, is that in which our sensory energies and desires are subordinated to a basic understanding of the true worth of the object of our love.

This truth, which is also a principle, explains a great deal in human life and coexistence. Love in St. Thomas' view is, on the one hand, a kind of need of nature, and, on the other, a demand and even an ideal of morality. Love brings about the union of persons and their harmonious coexistence. Love makes it possible for people mutually to enjoy the good that each person is, as well as the good comprised by their union, which love itself engenders. This is the good of spiritual harmony and peace. In this atmosphere, a kind of mutual sharing of self becomes possible, which leads to a deepening on both sides. Hence, the whole of human coexistence should be based on love. The evangelical counsel to love one's neighbor is a thoroughly personalistic principle. This principle takes on special meaning in every community, especially in the smallest and therefore most intimately related, where people are more dependent on other people, persons on other persons. Personalism is very much at the basis of all conjugal and familial morality; it explains the meaning and points to the means of education and self-education, all of which is based on a deep understanding of the value of the person, as well as on an understanding of love, whose proper object and subject is the person.

This relation between human persons goes in a horizontal direction. Theology, however, which is the terrain proper to St. Thomas' reflections, shows us this relation in the vertical direction: between God and people. God is a subject of love, whose object includes human beings—and human beings, in turn, are subjects of love, whose object includes God. Christianity involves an extremely personalistic understanding of religion, and St. Thomas presents a profound interpretation of this understanding.

7. THE PERSON AND SOCIETY: THE PRINCIPLE OF THE CORRELATION BETWEEN THE GOOD OF THE PERSON AND THE COMMON GOOD

The relation of the person to society and of society to the person forms a separate chapter in Thomistic personalism. The human being is always an individual within the human species. But this individual is a person, and the species is a collection of persons—though not a chaotic collection, but one formed naturally into various societies and communities. People are social beings, and so they have an innate tendency not only to form interpersonal relationships but also to create societies and communities. This is an effect of the operation of an elementary law of nature, which, however, in the case of human beings does not operate with blind necessity, but allows for the full involvement of consciousness and freedom. Consequently, the relation of the human being to society and of society to the human being is subordinate to morality, just as individual life and interpersonal relationships are. The basic question that must be resolved in social morality is how to create a system of relations between the individual and society that results in the fullest possible correlation between the person's true good and the common good that society naturally seeks. To attain this correlation in practice is no easy matter. On the one hand, persons may easily place their own individual good above the common good of the collectivity, attempting to subordinate the collectivity to themselves and use it for their individual good. This is the error of individualism, which gave rise to liberalism in modern history and to capitalism in economics. On the other hand, society, in aiming at the alleged good of the whole, may attempt to subordinate persons to itself in such a way that the true good of persons is excluded and they themselves fall prey to the collectivity. This is the error of totalitarianism, which in modern times has borne the worst possible fruit.

Thomistic personalism maintains that the individual good of persons should be by nature subordinate to the common good at which the collectivity, or society, aims—but this subordination may under no circumstances exclude and devalue the persons themselves. There are certain rights that every society must guarantee to persons, for without these rights the life and development proper to persons is impossible. One of these basic rights is the right to freedom of conscience. This right is always violated by so-called objective totalitarianism, which holds that the human person should be completely subordinate to society in all things. In contrast, Thomistic personalism maintains that the person should be subordinate to society in all that is indispensable for the realization of the common good, but that the true common good never threatens the good of the person, even though it may demand considerable sacrifice of a person.

8. THE PERSON AND ETERNITY

In connection with the above, we should also note that society as such is always a temporal product, whereas the person as such is destined to live on forever. The eternity of the person is strictly connected with the spirituality of the rational nature in which the person subsists. That which is spiritual cannot undergo disintegration, destruction, or death. The truth of the immortality of the soul is simultaneously the truth of the indestructibility of the person. Immortality, however, is not synonymous with eternity, for eternity is an existence not subject to limits with respect to time. No created existence is eternal in this sense; such eternity is solely and exclusively an attribute of God. Eternity belongs to the person, however, in the sense that whatever is spiritual is indestructible, that is, by nature capable of lasting without end.

This is one aspect of the eternity of the person, and it is connected with another aspect. The values by which the person as such lives are by nature transtemporal, and even atemporal. Such values include truth, goodness, and beauty, as well as justice and love, and, in general, all the values by which the person as such continually lives. One can say, therefore, that the very content of the person's life points to the eternity of the person. These values demand a more complete realization than they find in temporal life within the confines of the person's bodily existence. In fact, since these values are themselves absolute, they demand some sort of more complete and definitive realization in dimensions of the Absolute. The person is not the Absolute; the human being is a creature, a contingent being. God alone is the Absolute. An analysis of the spiritual life of the human person from the perspective of the values that appear in it and that determine its whole character indicates that, for the full attainment of that spiritual life, the person must exist beyond the bodily conditions of human existence—in the dimensions of God.

This particular need of the personal existence of the human being is addressed by the Gospel in the revealed doctrine of the beatific vision. The explication of this doctrine is a task for theology. While it is true that Thomistic personalism is a philosophical view, it would be hard to deny that this supernatural perspective not only corresponds to it extremely well, but also even ultimately explains everything that, when viewed in the light of reason alone, must remain a deep and impenetrable mystery of human existence.

11

On the Dignity of the Human Person

The human person is an element of the doctrine of the Second Vatican Council. Although none of the completed constitutions or directives has the human person as its specific topic, the person lies deep within the entire conciliar teaching that is slowly emerging from our labors, already in progress a number of years. The Council expresses itself directly in its teaching. Teaching is its proper function. This teaching, in turn, should permeate the consciousness of the Church and find expression in the work of the Church. The human person must find a suitable place in the Council's teaching, whence will flow the proper place of the person in the work of the Church. And this will be an enormous contribution, as far as the pastoral aim of the Council is concerned.

An attitude toward the human being as a person is emerging at the Council on the basis of experience and revelation. This experience seems enormous, even if we overlook its historical dimension, and thus all the past centuries of the Church's existence, and consider only the present age and all the priestly ministers whose basic vocation consists in dealing with human persons. One can safely say that through these ministers the Council is listening to contemporary people from practically every nation, as well as from an enormous variety of economic, social, and political systems. There are eyes enough at the Council to see humanity in the whole diversity of its contemporary existence. All of these eyes yearn in

Karol Wojtyla, "O godnosci osoby ludzkiej," *Notificationes a Curia Principis Metropolitae Cracoviensis* (1964): 287–289. A talk broadcast in Polish over Vatican Radio, 19 October 1964, at the time of the Second Vatican Council.

some way to extend the gaze of Christ, once directed upon the human person. This is, after all, a fundamental condition for proclaiming the Gospel and for making it a reality in our day. On this is based the *accomodata renovatio*—the renewal of the Church in keeping with the needs and possibilities of contemporary human beings.

The assertion that the human being is a person has profound theoretical significance. I do not have time to consider it here in detail. I should mention, however, that, despite differences in worldviews, everyone in some way agrees with this assertion. In a sense, it marks out the position proper to the human being in the world. It speaks of the human being's natural greatness. The human being holds a position superior to the whole of nature and stands above everything else in the visible world. This conviction is rooted in experience. From there it finds its way into both the human individual and the human community, conceived in the broadest possible sense. For both the one and the other, this conviction is constantly verified. Our distinctiveness and superiority as human beings in relation to other creatures is constantly verified by each one of us, regardless of how inferior we might feel because of our physical or spiritual deficiencies. In the latter case, the superiority and natural dignity of the person is confirmed as though by contrast. It is also verified by the whole of humanity in its ongoing experience: in the experience of history, culture, technology, creativity, and production. The effects of human activity in various communities testify to this dignity. A being that continually transforms nature, raising it in some sense to that being's own level, must feel higher than nature—and must *be* higher than it.

In this way, the constant confrontation of our own being with nature leads us to the threshold of understanding the person and the dignity of the person.

We must, however, go beyond this threshold and seek the basis of this dignity within the human being. When we speak of the human person, we are not just thinking of superiority, which involves a relation to other creatures, but we are thinking above all of what—or rather *who*—the human being essentially is. Who the human being essentially is derives primarily from within that being. All externalizations—activity and creativity, works and products—have here their origin and their cause.

This cause is what we mainly have in mind. And this cause shows itself to be, through its effects, a rational and free being. Intellect and freedom are essential and irrevocable properties of the person. Herein also lies the whole natural basis of the dignity of the person.

To acknowledge the dignity of the human being means to place people higher than anything derived from them in the visible world. All the human works and products crystalized in civilizations and cultures are only a world of means employed by people in the pursuit of their own proper end. Human beings do not live for the sake of technology, civilization, or even culture; they live by means of these things, always preserving their own purpose. This purpose is intimately connected with truth, because the human being is a rational being, and also with the good, because the good is the proper object of free will.

There is no way to acknowledge the dignity of the human being without taking this purpose and its thoroughly spiritual character into account. Neither the concept of *homo faber* nor the concept of *homo sapiens*, understood in a purely functional way, will suffice here. It follows that the matter of the dignity of the human person is always more of a call and a demand than an already accomplished fact, or rather it is a fact worked out by human beings, both in the collective and in the individual sense. It is very easy here for quantity to prevail over quality. How easy it is to think and judge on the basis of people *en masse*. And yet we must transvalue every numerical aggregate of people according to the principle of the person and the dignity of the person.

This task is often difficult beyond words.

The Council and the Church are attempting to undertake this task. They regard the call concerning the dignity of the human person as the most important voice of our age. This is eloquently expressed in the encyclicals of John XXIII and Paul VI, as well as in the entire work of the Council, especially in the declaration on religious freedom and the schema on the relation of the Church to the modern world, which is currently under discussion.

In undertaking this important task, the Council proceeds not only from experience but also—and above all—from revelation. The Council is charged with teaching divine truth, which has a supernatural, not just a natural, meaning. The dignity of the human person finds its full confirmation in the very fact of revelation, for this fact signifies the establishment of contact between God and the human being. To the human being, created in "the image and likeness of God," God communicates God's own thoughts and plans. But this is not all. God also "becomes a human being;" God enters into the drama of human existence through the redemption and permeates the human being with divine grace.

For those of us who are believers, this is where the dignity of the human person finds its fullest confirmation; this is where it is, so to speak, brought to the surface. Religion, as Paul VI points out, is a dialogue: through religion God confirms the personal dignity of the human being.

The believer finds this confirmation in religion. This may be described as a confirmation "from above."

In addition, religion dictates another direction as well: a confirmation of the dignity of the person as though "from below." The latter is important also for those who do not acknowledge a religious reality and do not find the fullest confirmation of the dignity of the human person in such a reality, those for whom the human being is confirmed only from below: in relation to the visible world, in the economy, technology, and civilization. But here there appears a whole series of conditions either produced by nature or created by people. These conditions are to a certain extent inescapable. A basic question and a basic task arises for us all: how, in the midst of these numerous conditions, can the dignity of the human person be most fully preserved? For it must be preserved! Otherwise we shall find ourselves in conflict with the very purpose of human existence. And then our whole pursuit of means will be of no avail whatsoever; they may all the more readily become means of self-destruction.

We can see why the matter of the dignity of the human person is one of the fundamental elements in the Council's reflections. It is certainly an ecumenical element, an element common to all people of genuinely good will. Without grasping this element, there can be no talk of real progress.

Tomorrow, on the feast of St. John Cantius, as I celebrate Mass in the council hall, I wish to ask God in a special way for one of the gifts of the Holy Spirit, the gift often referred to as the gift of piety—in essence, the gift of the reverence due each creature for the sake of God. May we, with the help of this gift, know how to realize in the modern world the basic good of collective and individual life: the dignity of the person.

12

The Human Person and Natural Law

Under the topic "The Human Person and Natural Law," I shall first of all explain and then try to resolve the conflict that exists between the person and natural law. In the first part of this essay I would like to describe as briefly as possible the extent to which this conflict is illusory. It is the fashion nowadays to revolt against natural law, to reject natural law. We should, therefore, at least try to understand why this is happening. I think that those who spontaneously reject natural law are spontaneously rising up in defense of the special character of human action, in defense of the reality of both the action of the person and the person as such. I say spontaneously, because they are not always justified in doing so. And I would now like to show the extent to which this conflict, which is so widespread and spontaneous, is an illusory conflict. To do so, I shall have to examine a very basic and elementary concept, the concept of nature, and its relation to the concept of person (since these are the two concepts I am comparing here, though not, of course, as concepts for their own sake, but as signs of reality).

In comparing these two realities, the one designated by the concept of person and the other by the concept of nature, we should note that the concept of nature has at least two meanings. We in the Thomistic school, the school of "perennial philosophy," are accustomed to primarily or ex-

Karol Wojtyla, "Osoba ludzka a prawo naturalne," *Roczniki Filozoficzne* **18.2** (1970): 53–59. A paper presented on 11 April 1969 at a conference held in conjunction with the celebration of the 50th anniversary of the Catholic University of Lublin.

clusively one meaning—nature in the metaphysical sense, which is more or less equivalent to the essence of a thing taken as the basis of all the actualization of the thing. I emphasize *all*, because this will come in handy in a moment when I try to show that nature can also have another meaning. This will certainly be the meaning given it by phenomenalists, but also perhaps by phenomenologists as well. Within their field of vision, nature is equivalent to the subject of instinctive actualization, and so it has a narrower, more limited meaning. When we say that something happens by nature, we are immediately emphasizing that it *happens*, that it *is actualized*, and not that someone performs an action or that someone acts. In a certain way, nature in this sense excludes the person as an acting subject, as the author of action, because nature in this sense points to a thing's being actualized, and to its being actualized in a ready-made realm, without the efficient involvement of anyone—any subject who is a person.

On the other hand, nature in what we might call its traditional sense, the metaphysical sense, is the essence of a thing taken as the basis of all actualization. The word *all* here, of course, excludes the kind of limitation mentioned above. Nature in the metaphysical sense is integrated in the person. Boethius, and the whole Thomistic school after him, defined the person in the following way: *persona est rationalis naturae individua substantia*. Nature in this sense is integrated in the person.

Thus the conflict between person and nature appears only when we understand nature in the sense in which the phenomenologists understand it, namely, as the subject of instinctive actualization, as the subject of what merely happens. A conflict between person and nature does arise here in a certain sense: nature as the source of such actualization excludes the person. The person, in turn, as the source of a particular kind of actualization, and, concretely, as the source of actions or deeds, stands above nature and is in a certain sense opposed to nature.

This conflict is a philosophical conflict, even an epistemological conflict, because it exists only to the extent that a certain theory of knowledge and a certain method of philosophical cognition exists. This particular conflict between person and nature was extended and somehow transposed into a conflict between person and natural law. Given what I have already said, we are perhaps within a step of asserting that this conflict is an illusory conflict, for it exists only between person and nature understood in a certain way. There can be no talk of a conflict between person and natural law anywhere in this discussion; if there is talk of anything, it can at most be of merely certain regularities in the actualization of nature that we observe in the natural world—in the animal world, the plant world, and also the human world.

Certainly on the somatic and even the psychic level in the human being we are constantly observing the sort of actualization of nature—the sort of different *happenings*—in which the efficient, creative agency of the person is lacking. We are well aware of this, and philosophy and ethics have always felt the need to distinguish between *actus humanum* and some other thing, which is not too felicitously referred to as *actus hominis*. We may be dealing here with the particular regularity with which nature is actualized, with which certain things happen in a subject—and, if this subject is a human being, in the somatic and even psychic nature of this subject. Ultimately, even with regard to the emotional life of the human being, I believe a great deal happens without the participation of free will—happens in the person, but is not an action of the person. All of this merely strengthens my conviction that we cannot be dealing here with a conflict between person and law. When we understand the opposition between person and nature phenomenologically, or even phenomenlistically, there is no basis for asserting a conflict between person and natural law. Of course, this kind of shifting or transposing of concepts and meanings goes on all the time.

We saw this occur just recently with regard to the encyclical *Humanae Vitae*, when a discussion arose in the press—and not only in the press—concerning the extent to which natural law can serve as a norm or as the basis of a norm for the person. In this discussion, natural law was taken to mean merely the biological regularity we find in people in the area of sexual actualization. This was said to be natural law. Authors of various articles and publications spoke out in behalf of such a misguided concept, and they in turn imposed upon the Holy Father, and along with him upon the magisterium of the Church, an understanding of natural law that in no way corresponds to the Church's understanding of it.

So much for the first topic—the illusory conflict between person and natural law. This conflict will appear even more illusory as I attempt to establish in an elementary way the proper meanings of person and natural law, in order to view the affinity existing between them in the light of these meanings. First some definitions:

- The person is "an individual substance of a rational nature" (*rationalis naturae individua substantia*).
- Law is "an ordinance of reason for the common good, promulgated by one who has care of the community" (*quaedam rationis ordinatio ad bonum commune ab eo qui curam communitatis habet promulgata*).
- Natural law is "the participation of the eternal law in a rational creature" (*participatio legis aeternae in rationali creatura*).

In this light, we see what natural law is according to St. Thomas' philosophy and, in an indirect sense, also according to the Catholic worldview. We should note, first of all, that natural law is something that intimately corresponds to the human being as a person and that is proper to the person. For if the person is an "individual substance of a rational nature," it is hard to deny that an "ordinance of reason" corresponds to and is proper to the person. Here we should certainly remove ourselves far from the understanding connected with the phenomenalistic or phenomenological concept of nature; we should maintain a necessary distance. An "ordinance of reason" is something proper to the human being as a rational individual, as a person. Rationality serves here as a sufficient reason, and once this has been established the matter becomes transparent. There can be no doubt that a rational ordinance corresponds to a rational being.

From these elementary tenets, we see that law does not imply some sort of arbitrary interference of subjective reason in the objective world, but rather implies a basic orientation toward this objective order. This order is the order of values. Reason's orientation toward this objective order is expressed in its discovery and definition of that order. Consequently, this is not a subjective interference of reason in objective reality, in the sense that reason would impose its own categories on reality, as was ultimately the case in Kant's anthropological view, but a completely different orientation and attitude: the attitude of reason discerning, grasping, defining, and affirming, in relation to an order that is objective and prior to human reason itself. I emphasize *to human reason*, since it should be noted at once that through the orientation of human reason toward the objective order, which is itself an actual component of this orientation or "ordinance of reason," a singular encounter with the divine source of law takes place. This is brought out very strongly in the Thomistic definition of natural law. The encounter of human reason in its orientation toward the objective order is an encounter with the divine source of law. This encounter is very profound, for it involves participation in the eternal law, which is in some sense identical with God, with divine reason.

These are the elementary contents that, in the light of our worldview and in the light of Catholic teaching (or, more precisely, the teaching of St. Thomas), are contained in the concept of natural law. We see that when the matter is formulated in this manner there is no opposition, no discord, but only affinity. Natural law corresponds to the person. Moreover, not only does natural law correspond to the person, but it also in a particular way establishes persons in their proper place in the whole objective order of the world. Next, it places them in a special relation to the source of law, namely, God. Through natural law, human beings participate in God, in God's reason, in God's relation to the whole of reality created by God.

I would say that what is most important for this elementary analysis is that such a conception of natural law suggests an integral conception of the human person. Once we become aware of the affinity between the person and natural law, we can see the true nature of the conflict between the person and natural law. The real conflict lies in another sphere—in the tenet concerning the basic character of the human being. We have seen that an affinity between the person and natural law is possible only if we accept a certain metaphysics of the human person, which also entails a certain subordination of the human person in relation to God, a subordination that is, after all, very honorable. On the other hand, if we do not accept such a view of the human being, then a conflict is unavoidable, and this is a real conflict.

If we regard the human being as some sort of pure consciousness, such a philosophical stance immediately presents us with an image of the human being as a kind of absolute affirmed on the intellectual plane, and we then proceed to all the consequences of this initial intellectual act. The same applies, though even more so, to the concept of human freedom. If we understand human freedom in an entirely indeterministic way, as complete independence unlimited by anything whatsoever, then this concept, of course, already excludes all natural law: natural law loses its meaning.

I wanted to outline the problem of the person and natural law from the point of view of its difficulty, for we know that this difficulty exists. It is certainly a difficulty for people who are not too well educated, but it is also one for those who are highly educated, especially one-sidedly, and hold a certain view of philosophy. In the context of such assumptions, this difficulty exists. I attempted to do one thing in this essay: to distinguish the seeming difficulty from the real difficulty, to show where this seeming difficulty lies so as better to show where the real difficulty lies. My own resolution of this matter is found in the second part of this essay, where I dealt with the question of the affinity that exists between the concept of the human person and the concept of natural law, between the reality of the human person and the reality of natural law.

13

The Personal Structure of
Self-Determination

I

In this paper, I wish not only to discuss a question that seems to me to be crucial for the concept of the human person and for the creative continuation of St. Thomas' thought in this area in relation to different schools of contemporary thought, especially phenomenology, but also to inform you of the state of this question among Catholic philosophers in Poland today. My point of departure here will be a discussion that arose following the publication of my book *The Acting Person*.[1] This discussion began with a meeting of philosophy professors at the Catholic University of Lublin in December 1970; it continued on, however, through a number of written responses (about twenty in all), which are to be published in the 1973 volume of *Analecta Cracoviensia*.[2] Taking part in this discussion were representatives of several Catholic scholarly circles, principally from Lublin, Warsaw, and Krakow, reflecting somewhat different philosophical orientations. The discussion placed a heavy emphasis on the methodological side of the question, although there was no lack of comments on the theory of the person itself, and even on the application of this theory to contemporary ministry, pedagogy, and psychiatry. Simplifying the matter somewhat, I would say that the philosophers from Lublin were chiefly interested in the methodological precision of my presentation of St. Thomas' thought, in this case in my attempt to translate this thought into

Karol Wojtyla, "Osobowa struktura samostanowienia," *Roczniki Filozoficzne* **29.2 (1981): 5–12. A paper presented at an international conference on St. Thomas Aquinas, Rome—Naples, 17–24 April 1974.**

contemporary language, while those from Krakow were more interested in the possibility itself of a contemporary interpretation of St. Thomas' thought by means of a properly understood phenomenology. (My book *The Acting Person* also elicited some interest among Marxist writers, who have commented on it from time to time, although they did not take part in the discussion mentioned above.)

The preceding information may also serve as a certain introduction to the problem I wish to present here, for the problem of the personal structure of self-determination lies at the very heart of my study *The Acting Person*. In presenting this problem here, I also wish at the outset to emphasize its connection with my native Polish philosophical milieu, with its interests and creative inquiries, which are distinctly connected with overall trends in European thought. While participating in those trends, Polish scholarship has its own native profile, which from time to time makes itself known on the wider "market" of philosophical productivity (as was true, for example, of the work of the logicians of the Lwow-Warsaw School and of the Krakow phenomenologist Roman Ingarden), but more often in some way daily shapes Polish intellectual culture at home.

II

With these introductory remarks, I will get straight to the topic. In order to grasp the personal structure of self-determination, we must start from the experience of the human being. This experience obviously cannot be understood phenomenalistically, for such an understanding presupposes a theory of cognition that accepts an inner division between the functions of the senses and the intellect and also between sensory and intellectual contents. While not denying that these functions and their respective contents differ, I must insist that human cognition forms an organic (not just an organizational) whole. Experience is always the first and most basic stage of human cognition, and this experience, in keeping with the dual structure of the cognizing subject, contains not only a sensory but also an intellectual element. For this reason, one could say that human experience is already always a kind of understanding. It is thus also the origin of the whole process of understanding, which develops in ways proper to itself, but always in relation to this first stage, namely, experience. Otherwise I see no possibility of a consistent realism in philosophy and science. The image of the world that we produce in them could then be basically at odds with reality.

This also applies to the human being as the object of philosophical anthropology. The basis for understanding the human being must be sought in experience—in experience that is complete and comprehensive and free of all systemic *a priories*. The point of departure for an analysis of the personal structure of self-determination is the kind of experience of human action that includes the lived experience of moral good and evil as an essential and especially important element; this experience can be separately defined as the experience of morality. These two experiences—the experience of the human being and the experience of morality—can really never be completely separated, although we can, in the context of the overall process of reflection, focus more on one or the other. In the case of the former, philosophical reflection will lead us in the direction of anthropology; in the case of the latter, in the direction of ethics.

The experience of human action refers to the lived experience of the fact "I act." This fact is in each instance completely original, unique, and unrepeatable. And yet all facts of the type "I act" have a certain similarity both in the lived experience of the same person and in intersubjective dimensions. The lived experience of the fact "I act" differs from all facts that merely "happen" in a personal subject. This clear difference between something that "happens" in the subject and an "activity" or action of the subject allows us, in turn, to identify an element in the comprehensive experience of the human being that decisively distinguishes the activity or action of a person from all that merely happens in the person. I define this element as *self-determination.*

This first definition of self-determination in the experience of human action involves a sense of efficacy on the part of the personal self: "I act" means "I am the efficient cause" of my action and of my self-actualization as a subject, which is not the case when something merely "happens" in me, for then I do not experience the efficacy of my personal self. My sense of efficacy as an acting subject in relation to my activity is intimately connected with a sense of responsibility for that activity; the latter refers mainly to the axiological and ethical content of the act. All of this in some way enters organically into the experience of self-determination, although it is disclosed in this experience in varying degrees, depending to some extent on the personal maturity of the action. The greater this maturity, the more vividly I experience self-determination. And the more vividly I experience self-determination, the more pronounced in my experience and awareness become my efficacy and responsibility.

Self-determination as a property of human action that comes to light in experience directs the attention of one who analyzes such action to the will. The will is the person's power of the self-determination. This becomes evident upon closer examination of the person's acts, both the simple act of will, "I will," and the complex act, or the process of will (as it is called by psychologists such as Ach, Michotte, and, in Poland, Dybowski). Self-determination manifests itself both in elementary willing ("I will") and in choice and decision, which arise from an awareness of values, a weighing of motives, and also not infrequently a struggle and conflict of motives within an individual. If one compares the works of the above psychologists with St. Thomas' view of the complex and mature act of will, one will detect a rather significant convergence in their positions.

At the moment, however, I am not concerned with a comparative analysis of the act of will. When I say that the will is the power of self-determination, I do not have in mind the will all alone, in some sort of methodical isolation intended to disclose the will's own dynamism. Rather, I necessarily have in mind here the whole person. Self-determination takes place through acts of will, through this central power of the human soul. And yet self-determination is not identical with these acts in any of their forms, since it is a property of the person as such. Although my whole discussion here takes place on the phenomenological plane of experience, still, in the light of this discussion, St. Thomas' distinction between substance and accident and between the soul and its powers (in this case, the will), becomes especially apparent. My analysis, however brief, shows that self-determination is a property of the person, who, as the familiar definition says, is a *naturae rationalis individua substantia.* This property is realized through the will, which is an accident. Self-determination—or, in other words, freedom—is not limited to the accidental dimension, but belongs to the substantial dimension of the person: it is the person's freedom, and not just the will's freedom, although it is undeniably the person's freedom through the will.

III

In connection with my observation that the self-determination given in the complete experience of the human being directs one's analysis toward the act of will, I should also note that an analysis that conceives this reality in the phenomenological categories of intentional act is inadequate.

To conceive the will merely as a "wanting" that is directed toward a corresponding object (i.e., toward a value that is also an end) does not fully explain its dynamism. Such an analysis points to only one aspect of the will and one aspect of the transcendence proper to it. An act of will is an act of a subject directed toward an object; more precisely, it is an act of a faculty of the subject directed toward a value that is willed as an end and that is also, therefore, an object of endeavor. Such an active directing (which, it should be noted, distinguishes an act of will from the various "wantings" or "wishings" that arise in the subject) also implies the transcendence of this subject toward the value and end: the subject actively "goes out" beyond itself toward this value. This transcendence may be described as horizontal. In psychology, the analysis of the act of will seems to be somehow exhausted in the aspect of intentionality and "horizontal" transcendence. This aspect is often emphasized in a somewhat one-sided way in the presentation of St. Thomas' teaching on the act of will.

I believe, however, that, with the aid of the comprehensive experience of the human being and human action, we can more fully apprehend the dynamism of the will and in this way come closer to the complete view handed down by St. Thomas. It is precisely the reality of self-determination that brings this to light. Self-determination reveals that what takes place in an act of will is not just an active directing of the subject toward a value. Something more takes place as well: when I am directed by an act of will toward a particular value, I myself not only determine this directing, but through it I simultaneously determine myself as well. The concept of self-determination involves more than just the concept of efficacy: I am not only the efficient cause of my acts, but through them I am also in some sense the "creator of myself." Action accompanies becoming; moreover, action is organically linked to becoming. Self-determination, therefore, and not just the efficacy of the personal self, explains the reality of moral values: it explains the reality that by my actions I become "good" or "bad," and that then I am also "good" or "bad" as a human being—as St. Thomas so eminently perceived. If we were to stop at an analysis of the will as an intentional act, acknowledging only its horizontal transcendence, then this realism of moral values, this good and evil in the human being, would be completely inexplicable.

We must, therefore, acknowledge the personal structure of self-determination. This self-determination, which expresses itself in particular willings, transcends the pure intentionality of those willings (regardless of whether they are simple willings or complex processes of the will). Intentionality points as though outward—toward an object, which, by being a value, attracts the will to itself. Self-determination, on the other hand, points as though inward—toward the subject, which, by willing this value, by choosing it, simultaneously defines itself as a value: the subject becomes "good" or "bad." Human beings not only determine their own activity but also determine themselves in terms of a most essential quality. Self-determination thus corresponds to the becoming of a human being as a human being. Through self-determination, the human being becomes increasingly more of a "someone" in the ethical sense, although in the ontological sense the human being is a "someone" from the very beginning. I might add here that the pronoun "someone" as the antonym of the pronoun "something" very succinctly captures the uniquely personal character of the human being.

The experience of self-determination—with its basically phenomenological character—would seem to lead us to an increasingly deeper understanding of the reality that St. Thomas defined as *actus humanus* or, alternately, as *voluntarium*. If we acknowledge, as Thomas did, the full reality of moral value in the subject "human being," we must also acknowledge that this subject, in the act of self-determination, becomes a particular object. Self-determination objectifies the acting subject in the subject's own activity. This objectification of the person is in no sense a "reification" of the person: I cannot become a thing for myself, although I myself am the first and most basic object that I determine. In this determination of myself, my subjectivity is revealed in its deepest possibilities, in the essential qualifications that testify to what is both human (*humanum*) and personal.

By revealing that I am an object of my own subject, self-determination also brings to light the particular composition that is proper to me as a person. St. Thomas, along with the whole subsequent tradition of Christian thought, emphasizes that *persona est sui iuris et alteri incommunicabilis.* In the light of the experience of the human being, a key element of which is self-determination, the cogency of these traditional descriptions is immediately apparent. Self-determination in some sense points to self-possession and self-governance as the structure proper to a person. If I determine myself, I must possess myself and govern myself. These realities mutually explain one another because they also mutually imply one another. Each of them reveals the unique composition that is proper to a human being as a person. (The Thomistic adage also emphasizes that we are dealing here with a person: *persona est sui iuris et alteri incommunicabilis.*) This is not the metaphysical composition of body and soul (the composition of prime matter and substantial form) proper to the human being as a being, but a more "phenomenological" composition. In phenomenological experience, I appear as someone who possesses myself and who is simultaneously possessed by myself. I also appear as someone who governs myself and who is simultaneously governed by myself. Both the one and the other are revealed by self-determination; they are implied by self-determination and also enrich its content. Through self-possession and self-governance, the personal structure of self-determination comes to light in its whole proper fullness.

In determining myself—and this takes place through an act of will—I become aware and also testify to others that I possess myself and govern myself. In this way, my acts give me a unique insight into myself as a person. By virtue of self-determination, I experience in the relatively most immediate way that I am a person. Of course, the path from this experience to an understanding that would qualify as a complete theory of the person must lead through metaphysical analysis. Still, experience is the indispensable beginning of this path, and the lived experience of self-determination seems to be the nucleus of this beginning. In any case, if a full affirmation of the personal value of human acts requires a theory of the person as its basis, the construction of this theory seems impossible without an analytic insight into the dynamic reality of action, and above all into the structure of the self-determination essential for action, a structure that from the very beginning presents itself in some sense as a personal structure.

IV

In Vatican II's Pastoral Constitution *Gaudium et Spes*, we read that "the human being, who is the only creature on earth that God willed for itself, cannot fully find himself or herself except through a disinterested gift of himself or herself" (24). The document of the last Council seems in these words to sum up the age-old traditions and inquiries of Christian anthropology, for which divine revelation became a liberating light. The anthropology of St. Thomas Aquinas is deeply rooted in these traditions, while also being open to all the achievements of human thought that in various ways supplement the Thomistic view of the person and confirm its realistic character. The words of Vatican II cited above seem chiefly to accentuate the axiological aspect, speaking of the person as a being of special intrinsic worth, who is, therefore, specially qualified to make a gift of self. Beneath this axiological aspect, however, we can easily discern a deeper, ontological aspect. The ontology of the person suggested by this text seems again to coincide closely with the experience discussed above. In other words, if we wish to accentuate fully the truth concerning the human person brought out by *Gaudium et Spes*, we must once again look to the personal structure of self-determination.

As I said earlier, in the experience of self-determination the human person stands revealed before us as a distinctive structure of self-possession and self-governance. Neither the one nor the other, however, implies being closed in on oneself. On the contrary, both self-possession and self-governance imply a special disposition to make a "gift of oneself," and this a "disinterested" gift. Only if one possesses oneself can one give oneself and do this in a disinterested way. And only if one governs oneself can one make a gift of oneself, and this again a disinterested gift. The problematic of disinterestedness certainly deserves a separate analysis, which it is not my intention to present here. An understanding of the person in categories of gift, which the teaching of Vatican II reemphasizes, seems to reach even more deeply into those dimensions brought to light by the foregoing analysis. Such an understanding seems to disclose even more fully the personal structure of self-determination.

Only if one can determine oneself—as I attempted to show earlier—can one also become a gift for others. The Council's statement that "the human being...cannot fully find himself or herself except through a disinterested gift of himself or herself" allows us to conclude that it is precisely when one becomes a gift for others that one most fully becomes oneself. This "law of the gift," if it may be so designated, is inscribed deep within the dynamic structure of the person. The text of Vatican II certainly draws its inspiration from revelation, in the light of which it paints this portrait of the human being as a person. One could say that this is a portrait in which the person is depicted as a being willed by God "for itself" and, at the same time, as a being turned "toward" others. This relational portrait of the person, however, necessarily presupposes the immanent (and indirectly "substantial") portrait that unfolds before us from an analysis of the personal structure of self-determination.

As far as this last issue is concerned, I shall have to confine myself here to merely drawing attention to it. In concluding this examination of the personal structure of self-determination, I should add that it was necessarily brief and left out many points that deserve a more extensive analysis (which I present in my book *The Acting Person*, mentioned at the beginning). I have attempted, however, even in this short presentation, to stress the very real need for a confrontation of the metaphysical view of the person that we find in St. Thomas and in the traditions of Thomistic philosophy with the comprehensive experience of the human being. Such a confrontation will throw more light on the cognitive sources from which the Angelic Doctor derived his metaphysical view. The full richness of those sources will then become visible. At the same time, perhaps we will better be able to perceive points of possible convergence with contemporary thought, as well as points of irrevocable divergence from it in the interests of the truth about reality.

NOTES

1. Karol Wojtyla, *The Acting Person*, trans. Andrzej Potocki, ed. Anna-Teresa Tymieniecka (Boston: Reidel, 1979); originally published in Polish as *Osoba i czyn* (Krakow: Polskie Tow. Teologiczne, 1969; rev. ed. 1985). —Trans.

2. The papers ended up filling two volumes of this annual journal (see *Analecta Cracoviensia* 5–6 (1973–1974): 49–263). For a complete list of the published papers, see Karol Wojtyla, "The Person: Subject and Community," note 3, 258–259 below. —Trans.

14

Participation or Alienation?

1. INTRODUCTORY REMARKS

I wish to add my thoughts to those of all who will be taking part in this conference, which has as its theme *"Soi et autrui"* ("I and the Other"[1]). My remarks here will be related to my previous reflections in the area of philosophical anthropology, particularly to those that find expression in my book *Osoba i czyn*,[2] which has not yet been translated from Polish.[3] Since, therefore, the distinguished participants at this conference will not be familiar with my book, I have taken the liberty of translating the last two sections of it and including them with this paper.[4] They concern—in the broad sense of the term—the meaning of the evangelical commandment to love one's neighbor, viewed from the perspective of a personalistic interpretation of human action. The first section presents an analysis of the meaning of the concept "neighbor" as distinct from the concept "member of a community" (in the sense of any community whatsoever, any society or social group). The second section looks at the commandment of love in relation to the concept of alienation as it has come to be understood in contemporary anthropology, especially as a result of Marxism. It seems to me, however, that the second section is more of a supplement (both with respect to this conference and even with respect to my book); the basic problematic seems to lie in my reflections on the topic of neighbor. What I intend to say here is a kind of commentary on the two sections of *Osoba i czyn* enclosed in translation.

Karol Wojtyla, "Uczestnictwo czy alienacja," *Summarium* 7.27 (1978): 7–16. A paper sent in French translation to the Fourth International Phenomenology Conference in Fribourg, Switzerland (24–28 January 1975), and also presented by invitation to the Philosophy Department at the University of Fribourg (27 February 1975).

2. THE NEED TO ESTABLISH THE POINT OF DEPARTURE

It seems that in the very positing of the problem *I—other* (*soi—autrui*) we proceed simultaneously from two cognitive situations. One is the ascertainment of the fact of the existence and activity of a concrete human being, designated by the pronoun *I*, who exists and acts in common with other human beings. The *other* is one of them, someone who lives alongside me, and who is both *another* and *one of the others* who exists and acts in common with me. For the sake of precision, I should immediately add that the circle of *others* is as broad as the sum of human beings in general. Everyone of them can be an *other*. In reality, however, an *other* is always someone in an actual—i.e., some sort of experiential—relationship to me. Here we are already approaching the other cognitive situation, which must in turn be more precisely defined. Its basis is not so much consciousness as self-consciousness, conditioning the whole structure of the lived experience of the self, the concrete *I*.[5] This consciousness from its own perspective constitutes that entire world that is simultaneously given to us as a fact. In this world, consciousness constitutes all human beings, each and every one of them, both near and far. It constitutes them as *different* from me. It constitutes the *other* among them, who is both *another* and *one of the others*, thus also defining the other's relation to me, to my *I*.

We must necessarily take both of these cognitive situations into consideration in the point of departure of our reflections, because the *I—other* problematic is not limited to the ascertainment of being, or existence, alone, but also requires an analysis of lived experience. At the same time, however, this is lived experience in the relationship of two really existing and acting subjects. Here I wish to explore the *I—other* problematic from the perspective of action.

3. THE *I*: SELF-DETERMINATION AND SELF-POSSESSION

Action is what most fully and profoundly reveals the human being as an *I*—and, indeed, as a person, for that which we express in categories of being by the concept "person" is given in experience precisely as a self (*soi*), as an *I*. Consciousness alone is not yet that *I*, but it conditions the full manifestation of the *I* through action. Through action, my own *I* is fully manifested for my *I*'s consciousness. This would require a separate analysis of consciousness itself in relation to action, which I attempted to present in *Osoba i czyn*. Here, however, I wish to set that issue aside and focus primarily on the element of action, of conscious activity, for the constitution of the human *I*, or self. This is also a constitution in consciousness, although not by consciousness alone. Although consciousness for its part conditions action as conscious activity, consciousness itself does not produce or shape action. Instead, action is produced and shaped from different bases, from other sources of human potentiality. The essential potentiality that constitutes action as such and gives action its whole actual reality is the will. I am merely asserting this here, for I shall not be discussing action as an act of will, since I have already done so a number of times.

It would be helpful, however, to have a basic notion of what it is about action that allows it somehow to reveal the wholeness, originality, and unrepeatability of each human being and to disclose our own acting *I*, or self, in a way different from self-consciousness—in what might be called a more profound and ultimate way. An essential element for every action consciously performed by a concrete human being is self-determination. And what appears to stand out as most essential in this element is the will as a property of the person and of the person's potentiality—not the will taken as a power in itself, but the will as a property of the person and of the person's essential potentiality. I can determine myself by my will, and I determine myself as often as I bring myself to act. I am the author of the act, and my agency in this act, that is, my will ("I will"), turns out to be self-determination.

Self-determination, which reveals the freedom of the will and the freedom of the human being in the most direct and complete way, also allows us to define what makes each individual his or her own *I*. It allows us as if to touch what is expressed in the concept "self." Through the aspect of the self-determination manifested in my action, I who am the subject of that action discover and simultaneously confirm myself as a person in possession of myself. To the essence of my *I*, or self, belongs not just self-consciousness, but more importantly self-possession. Self-consciousness conditions self-possession, which manifests itself primarily in action. Thus action leads us into the very depths of the human *I*, or self.[6] This takes place through experience.

4. THE *OTHER*

The *other* (*autrui*) lies beyond the field of this experience. Self-consciousness, like self-possession, as the name itself suggests, is not transferable beyond the individual concrete *I*, or self, that experiences itself and consequently understands itself in this manner. Although I cannot experientially transfer what constitutes my own *I* beyond myself, this does not mean that I cannot understand that the *other* is constituted in a similar fashion—that the *other* is also an *I*. For the *other* to be so constituted, self-possession conditioned by the other's own self-determination will be essential. An understanding of this truth defines to some extent the relation of my own concrete *I* to all other human beings. They are not just *others* in relation to my *I*; each of them is also another *I*. The *other* is always one of those *I*'s, another individual *I*, related experientially in some way to my own *I*.

The consciousness that the *other* is another *I* stands at the basis of what in *Osoba i czyn* I defined as participation, a concept I would like to make even more precise here. In my book, the concept of participation basically serves to express the property by virtue of which we as persons exist and act together with others, while not ceasing to be ourselves or to fulfill ourselves in action, in our own acts. This notion of participation does not have much in common with the Platonic or Scholastic notion. It serves, instead, to specify and express what it is that safeguards us as persons along with the personalistic nature and value of our activity as we exist and act together with others in different systems of social life. That is precisely what I meant by participation in *Osoba i czyn*, namely, the ability to exist and act together with others in such a way that in this existing and acting we remain ourselves and actualize ourselves, which means our own *I*'s.

At the end of my analysis in the book, in the sections I mentioned earlier, an even deeper property and an even more basic meaning of participation come into view. As human beings, we are capable of participating in the very humanity of other people, and because of this every human being can be our *neighbor*. This is the point at which what I said in the book converges with my reflections here concerning the *other*. "The *other*" does not just signify that the being existing next to me or even acting in common with me in some system of activities is the same kind of being as I am. Within the context of this real situation, "the *other*" also signifies my no less real—though primarily subjective—participation in that being's humanity, a participation arising from my awareness that this being is another *I*, which means "also an *I*."

Thus the reality of the *other* does not result principally from categorial knowledge, from humanity as the conceptualized essence "human being," but from an even richer lived experience, one in which I as though transfer what is given to me as my own *I* beyond myself to *one of the others*, who, as a result, appears primarily as a different *I*, another *I*, my *neigh-*

bor.[7] Another person is a neighbor to me not just because we share a like humanity, but chiefly because the other is another *I*.

5. THE *I—OTHER* RELATIONSHIP: ITS POTENTIALITY AND ACTUALIZATION

This, then, is how the *I—other* relationship looks when delineated in its proper structure. As can be seen, this is not a purely ontic structure, but a conscious and experiential one as well. It is this structure that I am understanding here as participation. Participation in the humanity of other people, of *others* and *neighbors*, does not arise primarily from an understanding of the essence "human being," which is by nature general and does not bring us close enough to the human being as a concrete *I*. Rather, participation arises from consciously becoming close to another, a process that starts from the lived experience of one's own *I*. This does not mean that understanding the essence "human being" is of no consequence for participation, that it is foreign or even opposed to participation. Far from it. An understanding of this essence opens the way to participation, but it does not itself determine participation. It also does not itself give rise to an *I—other* relationship. This relationship does not emerge from having a universal concept of the human being, a concept that embraces all people without exception. The *I—other* relationship is not universal but always interhuman, unique and unrepeatable in each and every instance—both when viewed as a one-way relationship proceeding from the *I* and when viewed as a reciprocal relationship (the *other*, after all, is also an *I* for whom I can be an *other*).

The universality of the concept "human being" brings into clear relief the problem of both the potentiality for *I—other* relationships and the need to actualize participation, through which such relationships properly emerge. There is, as we know, an enormous amount of people living and acting in the world, and all of them are apprehended conceptually by anyone who thinks "human being." In this concept, however, none of them is yet an *other* in relation to an *I*. The concept "human being" does not itself create this relationship. Does it, then, merely suggest the possibility of such a relationship? It seems to do something more, namely, it seems to constitute the first potentiality of such a relationship: it basically makes such a relationship possible. And it makes such a relationship possible with respect to all human beings without exception—with respect to every single human being. The concept "human being" basically opens the way for me to experience as another *I* everyone who is included in this concept in the same way as my own *I* is included in it—and precisely because my own *I* is included in it. Thus the first requirement for an *I—other* relationship is an awareness of the fact that both partners in this relationship are human beings.

How is participation actualized? It is certainly not already a full-blown reality merely as a result of my conceptualizing or becoming aware of the fact of another's humanity. In order for me to regard the *other* or a *neighbor* as another *I* (and only this qualifies as participation in another's concrete humanity), I must become aware of and experience, among the overall properties of that other "human being," the same kind of property that determines my own *I*, for this will determine my relationship to the other as an *I*. The lived experience of my own *I*—of the human being that I am as a self—is determined, as I said before, not only by self-consciousness but also and to a far greater degree by the self-possession conditioned by self-consciousness. Self-possession is connected more with the will than with knowledge. I possess myself not so much by knowing myself as by determining myself. Self-possession brings to light both my full subjectivity and the objective unity that exists between my activities and the being that I am as the subject of those activities. Self-possession thus testifies to my own *I* as a person. The category of the person objectifies and expresses in philosophical language (and in everyday language as well) what is given in experience as the *I*.

The actualization of the *I—other* relationship starts by my becoming aware of the fact of the humanity of a specific human being apart from myself, one of the others, but it takes place by my experiencing that other *I* as a person. Participation signifies a basic personalization of the relationship of one human being to another. I cannot experience another as I experience myself, because my own *I* as such is nontransferable. When I experience another as a person, I come as close as I can to what determines the other's *I* as the unique and unrepeatable reality of that human being.

6. PARTICIPATION AS A TASK

The foregoing analysis leads me to conclude that although we may live and act in common with others in various societies, communities, and social groups, and although this life and activity may be accompanied by a basic awareness of each other's humanity, this alone does not actualize participation in that humanity. The actualization of participation in relation to every other human being arises before each of us as a task. It also seems that this is how we ought to explain the basic need for the commandment contained in the Gospel, a commandment whose complete validity—i.e., key ethical significance—people tend to accept regardless of their professed religion or worldview. On the basic, elementary, pre-ethical level, so to speak, the commandment of love is simply the call to experience another human being as another *I*, the call to participate in another's humanity, which is concretized in the person of the other just as mine is in my person.

The *I—other* relationship, as I pointed out earlier, does not exist in us as an already accomplished fact; only the potentiality for it exists. Experience shows that a certain impulse is needed to actualize this relationship. Although this impulse has been expressed in a commandment, this does not mean that it may remain merely on the outside. It must arise from within. The commandment of love prescribes only this: that each of us must continually set ourselves the task of actually participating in the humanity of others, of experiencing the other as an *I*, as a person. Thus the impulse that the commandment expresses from without must in each instance arise from within. Is this inner impulse purely emotional, as Max Scheler seems to suggest? And does it have an exclusively spontaneous character?

It would be difficult to deny the significance of human spontaneity and emotions in the development of interpersonal relationships. Certainly such factors are enormous resources, variously distributed among people and also variously influencing the development of *I—other* relationships. Scheler's analysis[8] also provides an additional argument for maintaining that people have some sort of basic, innate disposition to participate in humanity as a value, to spontaneously open up to others. This seems to contradict Sartre, whose analysis of consciousness leads him to conclude that the subject is closed in relation to others.[9]

While in no way detracting from the importance of emotions and spontaneity in the development of authentic *I—other* relationships, it would be hard to deny that, since the *other* stands before us as a specific *task*, the actualization of such relationships always depends to a basic degree on the will. Experiencing another human being, one of the others, as another *I* always involves a discreet choice. First of all, it involves choosing this particular human being among the others, which simply means that this particular one from among the others is *hic et nunc* given to me and assigned to me. The choice here consists in my acceptance of this particular individual's *I*, my affirmation of the person. I thus in a sense

choose this person in myself—in my own *I*—for I have no other access
to another human being as an *I* except through my own *I*. An emotional
disposition and a purely emotional spontaneity may facilitate this choice—
but may also impede it. I have purposely used the term "emotional spontaneity" here because we must acknowledge the existence of another kind
of spontaneity as well, namely, that of the will. The choice here seems
to lie on the plane of the spontaneity of the will. The constitution of the
I of another in my consciousness and will is not the result of choosing
among people, among others; it is a matter, as I said, of choosing the
human being who is *hic et nunc* given to me and assigned to me. This
is also why I do not experience this choice as a choice. Rather, it is a
matter of simply identifying one of the others as another *I*, which does
not require a more prolonged process of the will—assent or conflict of
motives, etc.

This, however, in no way alters the fact that we are dealing here with
a certain choice and that participation in the humanity of others is a certain
task. This task can and should be placed at the basis of the strictly ethical
order and strictly ethical appraisal. And although this task seems to have
a primarily personalistic meaning, the strictly ethical order of values
nevertheless depends in large part upon it. Kant's second categorical imperative[10] may be regarded as a confirmation of this thesis.

7. THE VERIFICATION OF PARTICIPATION

The assertion that the *I—other* relationship is neither an already accomplished fact nor an entirely spontaneous one, but rather a specific
task, certainly helps us interpret such realities as friendship or a *communio
personarum*. *Communio*, which is essentially an *I—other* relationship inwardly maturing into an interpersonal *I—thou* relationship, should be
clearly distinguished from *communitas*, which embraces a larger number
of persons. Friendship has already been analyzed many times. There can
be no doubt that friendship is based upon the relationship of one human
being as an *I* to another as an *I*. Friendship is simply an evolution of this
relationship and an expression of its richness in proportion to the love
that two people are capable of bringing to it. This matter was already
explained to a considerable degree by Aristotle.[11]

In addition to these *positive* verifications of participation, we should
also consider its *negative* verifications. They may, in fact, speak even
more plainly of the kind of reality participation in the humanity of another

human being is. Such feelings or attitudes as hatred, animosity, aggression, and jealousy, when their subjective complexity is more deeply analyzed, show that they are based on nothing other than the lived experience of another human being as another *I*—not the human being I grasp in the abstract concept, but the one I in some sense "choose in my *I*" ("choose on the basis of my *I*"). Only this can explain the spiritual oppressiveness of such feelings or attitudes as animosity, hatred, aggression, and jealousy. The torment associated with them shows at least that I am not indifferent to the human being as another *I*. Perhaps these negative feelings or attitudes bring into even sharper relief the very elementary reality of my participation in the humanity of the other and reveal how deeply I am bound—inwardly bound—to that person in myself.

The Gospel also suggests this by using not the word *other* but the word *neighbor*.

8. ALIENATION

The concept of alienation, which was introduced into philosophy in the 19th century and adopted by Marx, seems to be making a great come-back today. This is not a very sharp concept, much less an unambiguous one, which is probably why contemporary Marxists have so much trouble with it. I do not intend here to recount their difficulties or to remove the ambiguity from the concept. Despite its weaknesses, however, the concept of alienation seems needed in the philosophy of the human being. It is warranted by the condition of human existence, by the contingency and limitation of every particular realization of a concrete *I*, or person. The concept of alienation, when properly applied, can aid in the analysis of human reality—not primarily on the plane of external influences from the extra-human world, but mainly in the realm of specifically human and interhuman relationships—and, therefore, in the analysis of the *I—other* relationship.

According to Marx's philosophy, human beings are alienated by their products: their economic and political systems, their property, and their work. Marx also included religion in this category. Such a formulation of the problem leads, of course, to the conclusion that all we have to do is transform the world of products, change the economic and political systems, and rally against religion—and then the age of alienation will come to an end and a "reign of freedom" will ensue, bringing with it complete self-actualization for one and all. Even apart from what the experience of our age will show—and is already showing—to be the case in this regard, we should notice that such a conception of alienation actually transfers the problem beyond ourselves to what could be called the structures of our social existence, while ignoring what is essential. What is essential is how we relate to one another, even somehow despite the structures. We know, for example, that in the concentration camps there were people who managed to relate to others as other *I*'s, as *neighbors*—often to a heroic degree.

This does not mean that there is no need to transform the structures of the social existence of human beings in the conditions of modern civilization. It only means that the fundamental issue remains always the participation of every human being in the humanity of another human being, other people. This is also the plane upon which we must seek the roots and primary seeds of alienation. Alienation basically means the negation of participation, for it renders participation difficult or even impossible. It devastates the *I—other* relationship, weakens the ability to experience another human being as another *I*, and inhibits the possibility of friendship and the spontaneous powers of community (*communio personarum*). Transposing the problem of alienation to the sphere of human products and structures may even contribute to its development, as certain contemporary Marxists have already observed.[12] The structures of the social existence of human beings in the conditions of modern civilization, and even this civilization itself and its so-called progress, absolutely must be evaluated in the light of this basic criterion: Do they create the conditions—for this is their only real function—for the development of participation? Do they enable and help us to experience other human beings as other *I*'s? Or do they do just the opposite? Do they obstruct participation and ravage and destroy this basic fabric of human existence and activity, which must always be realized in common with others? The central problem of life for humanity in our times, perhaps in all times, is this: *participation or alienation?* This problem seems to take on sharper contours today. It is also one that is very much alive in people's minds.

NOTES

1. *"Ja i drugi."* *Soi* is translated as "I" here in keeping with the Polish convention of using the personal pronoun "I" (*ja*) to refer to what in English is called "the self." —Trans.

2. Karol Wojtyla, *Osoba i czyn* [*Person and Action*] (Krakow: Polskie Tow. Teologiczne, 1969, rev. ed. 1985).

3. This book has since appeared in a somewhat controversial English translation under the title *The Acting Person*, trans. Andrzej Potocki, ed. Anna-Teresa Tymieniecka (Boston: Reidel, 1979). There are several reliable translations of *Osoba i czyn* in other languages. These include the German edition, *Person und Tat* (Freiburg: Herder, 1981); the Italian, *Persona e atto* (Rome: Libreria Editrice Vaticana, 1980); the French, *Personne et acte* (Paris: Centurion, 1983); and the Spanish, *Persona y acción* (Madrid: Biblioteca de autores cristianos, 1982). —Trans.

4. The two sections of *Osoba i czyn* that Wojtyla sent to the conference in French translation are "Fellow Member and Neighbor" and "The Commandment of Love," *The Acting Person* 348–357. —Trans.

5. It should be clear from this that I am understanding *soi* as the *I*; this is already an attempt of sorts to restore the unity of the two cognitive situations under discussion.

6. See my essay "The Personal Structure of Self-Determination" 187–195 above.

7. This lived experience might perhaps even more accurately be described as "regarding another person as another *I*." It seems, however, that such "regarding" does not take place without reference to one's own *I*, which may also more precisely define the meaning of transference.

8. See especially Max Scheler's *Formalism in Ethics and Non-Formal Ethics of Values: A New Attempt Toward the Foundation of an Ethical Personalism*, trans. Manfred S. Frings and Roger L. Funk (Evanston: Northwestern UP, 1973), and *The Nature of Sympathy*, trans. Peter Heath (New Haven: Yale UP, 1954), among other works.

9. See Jean-Paul Sartre, *Being and Nothingness*, trans. Hazel E. Barnes (New York: Washington Square, 1966).

10. See Kant's *Critique of Practical Reason*, trans. Lewis White Beck (Indianapolis: Bobbs, 1956), pt. 1, bk. 1, ch. 3, and *Foundations of the Metaphysics of Morals*, trans. Lewis White Beck (Indianapolis: Bobbs, 1959).

11. See Aristotle, *Nicomachean Ethics*, trans. Martin Ostwald (Indianapolis: Bobbs, 1962), especially Book 8.

12. See Adam Schaff, *Marxism and the Human Individual*, trans. Olgierd Wojtasiewicz, ed. Robert S. Cohen (New York: McGraw, 1970).

15

Subjectivity and the Irreducible in the Human Being

1. THE STATE OF THE QUESTION

The problem of the subjectivity of the human being seems today to be the focal point of a variety of concerns. It would be difficult to explain in just a few words exactly why and how this situation has arisen. No doubt it owes its emergence to numerous causes, not all of which should be sought in the realm of philosophy or science. Nevertheless, philosophy—especially philosophical anthropology and ethics—is a privileged place when it comes to clarifying and objectifying this problem. And this is precisely where the heart of the issue lies. *Today more than ever before we feel the need—and also see a greater possibility—of objectifying the problem of the subjectivity of the human being.*

In this regard, contemporary thought seems to have more or less set aside the old antinomies that arose primarily in the area of the theory of knowledge (epistemology) and that formed an as though inviolable line of demarcation between the basic orientations in philosophy. The antinomy of subjectivism vs. objectivism, along with the underlying antinomy of idealism vs. realism, created conditions that discouraged dealing with human subjectivity—for fear that this would lead inevitably to subjectivism. These fears, which existed among thinkers who subscribed to realism and epistemological objectivism, were in some sense warranted by the subjectivistic and idealistic character—or at least overtones—of

Karol Wojtyla, "Podmiotowosci i 'to, co nieredukowalne' w czlowieku," *Ethos* 1.2–3 (1988): 21–28. A paper sent to an international conference in Paris (13–14 June 1975).

analyses conducted within the realm of "pure consciousness." This only served to strengthen the line of demarcation in philosophy and the opposition between the "objective" view of the human being, which was also an ontological view (the human being as a *being*), and the "subjective" view, which seemed inevitably to sever the human being from this reality.

Today we are seeing a breakdown of that line of demarcation—and for some of the same reasons that gave rise to it in the first place. By "some of the same reasons" I mean that this is also happening as a result of phenomenological analyses conducted in the realm of "pure consciousness" using Husserl's *epoché*: bracketing the existence, or reality, of the conscious subject. I am convinced that *the line of demarcation between the subjectivistic (idealistic) and objectivistic (realistic) views in anthropology and ethics must break down and is in fact breaking down on the basis of the experience of the human being.* This experience automatically frees us from pure consciousness as the subject conceived and assumed *a priori* and leads us to the full concrete existence of the human being, to the reality of the conscious subject. With all the phenomenological analyses in the realm of that assumed subject (pure consciousness) now at our disposal, we can no longer go on treating the human being exclusively as an objective being, but we must also somehow treat the human being as a subject in the dimension in which the specifically human subjectivity of the human being is determined by consciousness.

And that dimension would seem to be none other than *personal* subjectivity.

2. THE HISTORY OF THE QUESTION

This matter requires a fuller examination, in the course of which we must consider the question of the irreducible in the human being—the question of that which is original and essentially human, that which accounts for the human being's complete uniqueness in the world.

Traditional Aristotelian anthropology was based, as we know, on the definition ο ανθρωπος ζωον νοητικον, *homo est animal rationale*. This definition fulfills Aristotle's requirements for defining the species (human being) through its proximate genus (living being) and the feature that distinguishes the given species in that genus (endowed with reason). At the same time, however, the definition is constructed in such a way that it excludes—when taken simply and directly—the possibility of accentuating the irreducible in the human being. It implies—at least at first glance—a belief in the reducibility of the human being to the world. The reason for maintaining such reducibility has always been the need to understand the human being. This type of understanding could be defined as cosmological.

The usefulness of the Aristotelian definition is unquestionable. It became the dominant view in metaphysical anthropology and spawned a variety of particular sciences, which likewise understood the human being as an *animal* with the distinguishing feature of reason. The whole scientific tradition concerning the composition of human nature, the spiritual-material *compositum humanum*—a tradition that came down from the Greeks through the Scholastics to Descartes—moved within the framework of this definition and, consequently, within the context of the belief that the essentially human is basically reducible to the world. It cannot be denied that vast regions of experience and scientific knowledge based on that experience reflect this belief and work to confirm it.

On the other hand, a *belief in the primordial uniqueness of the human being, and thus in the basic irreducibility of the human being to the natural world*, seems just as old as the need for reduction expressed in Aristotle's definition. This belief stands at the basis of understanding the human being as a *person*, which has an equally long tenure in the history of philosophy; it also accounts today for the growing emphasis on the person as a subject and for the numerous efforts aimed at interpreting the personal subjectivity of the human being.[1]

In the philosophical and scientific tradition that grew out of the definition *homo est animal rationale*, the human being was mainly an *object*, one of the objects in the world to which the human being visibly and physically belongs. Objectivity in this sense was connected with the general assumption of the reducibility of the human being. Subjectivity, on the other hand, is, as it were, a term proclaiming that the human being's proper essence cannot be totally reduced to and explained by the proximate genus and specific difference. *Subjectivity is, then, a kind of synonym for the irreducible in the human being.* If there is an opposition here, it is not between objectivism and subjectivism, but only between two philosophical (as well as everyday and practical) methods of treating the human being: as an object and as a subject. At the same time, we must not forget that the subjectivity of the human person is also something objective.[2]

I should also emphasize that the method of treating the human being as an object does not result directly from the Aristotelian definition itself, nor does it belong to the metaphysical conception of the human being in the Aristotelian tradition. As we know, the objectivity of the conception of the human being as a *being* itself required the postulate that the human being is 1) a separate *suppositum* (a subject of existence and action) and 2) a person (*persona*). Still, the traditional view of the human being as a person, which understood the person in terms of the Boethian definition as *rationalis naturae individua substantia*, expressed the individuality of the human being as a substantial being with a rational (spiritual) nature, rather than the uniqueness of the subjectivity essential to the human being as a person. Thus the Boethian definition mainly marked out the "metaphysical terrain"—the dimension of being—in which personal human subjectivity is realized, creating, in a sense, a condition for "building upon" this terrain on the basis of experience.

3. LIVED EXPERIENCE AS AN ELEMENT IN INTERPRETATION

The category to which we must go in order to do this "building" seems to be that of lived experience. This is a category foreign to Aristotle's metaphysics. The Aristotelian categories that may appear relatively closest to lived experience—those of *agere* and *pati*—cannot be identified with it. These categories serve to describe the dynamism of a being, and they also do a good job of differentiating what merely *happens* in the human being from what the human being *does*.[3] But when the dynamic reality of the human being is interpreted in Aristotelian categories, there is in each case (including in the case of *agere* and *pati*) an aspect not directly apprehended by such a metaphysical interpretation or reduction, namely, the aspect of lived experience as the irreducible, as the element that defies reduction. From the point of view of the meta-physical structure of being and acting, and thus also from the point of view of the dynamism of the human being understood meta-physically, the apprehension of this element may seem unnecessary. Even without it, we obtain an adequate understanding of the human being and of the fact that the human being *acts* and that things *happen* in the human being. Such an understanding formed the basis of the entire edifice of anthropology and ethics for many centuries.

But as the need increases to understand the human being as a unique and unrepeatable person, especially in terms of the whole dynamism of action and inner happenings proper to the human being—in other words, as the need increases to understand the personal subjectivity of the human being—the category of lived experience takes on greater significance, and, in fact, key significance. For then the issue is not just the metaphysical objectification of the human being as an acting subject, as the agent of acts, but the revelation of the person as a subject *experiencing* its acts and inner happenings, and with them its own subjectivity. From the moment the need to interpret the acting human being (*l'home agissant*) is expressed, the category of lived experience must have a place in anthropology and ethics—and even somehow be at the center of their respective interpretations.[4]

One might immediately ask whether, by giving lived experience such a key function in the interpretation of the human being as a personal subject, we are not inevitably condemned to *subjectivism*. Without going into a detailed response, I would simply say that, so long as in this interpretation we maintain a firm enough connection with the integral experience of the human being, not only are we not doomed to subjectivism, but we will also safeguard the authentic personal subjectivity of the human being in the realistic interpretation of human existence.

4. THE NECESSITY OF PAUSING AT THE IRREDUCIBLE

In order to interpret the human being in the context of lived experience, the aspect of *consciousness* must be introduced into the analysis of human existence. The human being is then given to us not merely as a being defined according to species, but as a concrete self, a self-experiencing subject. Our own subjective being and the existence proper to it (that of a *suppositum*) appear to us in experience precisely as a self-experiencing subject. If we pause here, this being discloses the structures that determine it as a concrete self. The disclosure of these structures constituting the human self need in no way signify a break with reduction and the species definition of the human being— rather, it signifies the kind of methodological operation that may be described as *pausing at the irreducible*. We should pause in the process of reduction, which leads us in the direction of understanding the human being in the world (a *cosmological* type of understanding), in order to understand the human being inwardly. This latter type of understanding may be called *personalistic*. The personalistic type of understanding the human being is not the antinomy of the cosmological type but its complement. As I mentioned earlier, the definition of the person formulated by Boethius only marks out the "metaphysical terrain" for interpreting the personal subjectivity of the human being.

The experience of the human being cannot be derived by way of cosmological reduction; we must pause at the irreducible, at that which is unique and unrepeatable in each human being, by virtue of which he or she is not just *a particular human being*—an individual of a certain species—but *a personal subject*. Only then do we get a true and complete picture of the human being. We cannot complete this picture through reduction alone; we also cannot remain within the framework of the irreducible alone (for then we would be unable to get beyond the pure self). The one must be cognitively supplemented with the other. Nevertheless, given the variety of circumstances of the real existence of human beings, we must always leave the greater space in this cognitive effort for the irreducible; we must, as it were, give the irreducible the upper hand when thinking about the human being, both in theory and in practice. For the irreducible also refers to everything in the human being that is invisible and wholly internal and whereby each human being, myself included, is an "eyewitness" of his or her own self—of his or her own humanity and person.

My lived experience discloses not only my *actions* but also my inner *happenings* in their profoundest dependence on my own self. It also discloses my whole personal structure of *self-determination*, in which I discover my self as that through which I possess myself and govern myself—or, at any rate, *should* possess myself and govern myself. The dynamic structure of self-determination reveals to me that I am given to myself and assigned to myself. This is precisely how I appear to myself in my acts and in my inner decisions of conscience: as permanently assigned to myself, as having continually to affirm and monitor myself, and thus, in a sense, as having continually to "achieve" this dynamic structure of my self, a structure that is given to me as self-possession and self-governance. At the same time, this is a completely internal and totally immanent structure. It is a real endowment of the personal subject; in a sense, it *is* this subject. *In my lived experience of self-possession and self-governance, I experience that I am a person and that I am a subject.*

These structures of self-possession and self-governance, which are essential to every personal self and shape the personal subjectivity of every human being, are experienced by each of us in the lived experience of moral value—good and evil. And perhaps this reality is often revealed to us more intensely when it is threatened by evil than when—at least for the moment—nothing threatens it. In any case, experience teaches that the *morale* is very deeply rooted in the *humanum*, or, more precisely, in what should be defined as the *personale*. Morality defines the personalistic dimension of the human being in a fundamental way; it is subjectified in this dimension and can also be properly understood only in it. At the same time, however, the *morale* is a basic expression of the transcendence proper to the personal self. Our decisions of conscience at each step reveal us as persons who fulfill ourselves by going beyond ourselves toward values accepted in truth and realized, therefore, with a deep sense of responsibility.

5. A CHALLENGING PERSPECTIVE

This topic has been the subject of many penetrating analyses, some already completed and others ongoing. While not continuing those analyses here, I wish only to state that, when it comes to understanding the human being, the whole rich and complex reality of lived experience is not so much an element or aspect as a dimension in its own right. And this is the dimension at which we must necessarily pause if the subjective structure—including the subjective personal structure—of the human being is to be fully delineated.

What does it mean to *pause cognitively at lived experience*? This "pausing" should be understood *in relation to the irreducible*. The traditions of philosophical anthropology would have us believe that we can, so to speak, pass right over this dimension, that we can cognitively omit it by means of an abstraction that provides us with a species definition of the human being as a being, or, in other words, with a cosmological type of reduction (*homo = animal rationale*). One might ask, however, whether in so defining the essence of the human being we do not in a sense leave out what is most human, since the *humanum* expresses and realizes itself as the *personale*. If so, then the irreducible would suggest that we cannot come to know and understand the human being in a reductive way alone. This is also what the contemporary philosophy of the subject seems to be telling the traditional philosophy of the object.

But that is not all. The irreducible signifies that which is essentially incapable of reduction, that which cannot be reduced but can only be *disclosed* or *revealed*. *Lived experience essentially defies reduction*. This does not mean, however, that it eludes our knowledge; it only means that *we must arrive at the knowledge of it differently*, namely, *by a method or means of analysis that merely reveals and discloses its essence*. The method of phenomenological analysis allows us to pause at lived experience as the irreducible. This method is not just a descriptive cataloging of individual phenomena (in the Kantian sense, i.e., phenomena as sense-perceptible contents). When we pause at the lived experience of the irreducible, we attempt to permeate cognitively the whole essence of this experience. We thus apprehend both the essentially subjective structure of lived experience and its structural relation to the subjectivity of the human being. Phenomenological analysis thus contributes to trans-phenomenal understanding; it also contributes to a disclosure of the richness proper to human existence in the whole complex *compositum humanum*.

Such a disclosure—the deepest possible disclosure—would seem to be an indispensable means for coming to know the human being as a personal subject. At the same time, this personal human subjectivity is a determinate *reality*: it is a reality when we strive to understand it within the *objective totality* that goes by the name *human being*. The same applies to the whole character of this method of understanding. After all, lived experience is also—and above all—a reality. A legitimate method of disclosing this reality can only enrich and deepen the whole realism of the conception of the human being. The personal profile of the human being then enters the sphere of cognitive vision, and the composition of human nature, far from being blurred, is even more distinctly accentuated. The thinker seeking the ultimate philosophical truth about the human being no longer moves in a "purely metaphysical terrain," but finds elements in abundance testifying to both the materiality and the spirituality of the human being, elements that bring both of these aspects into sharper relief. These elements then form the building blocks for further philosophical construction.

But certain questions always remain: Are these two types of understanding the human being—the cosmological and the personalitic—ultimately mutually exclusive? Where, if at all, do reduction and the disclosure of the irreducible in the human being converge? How is the philosophy of the subject to disclose the *objectivity* of the human being in the personal *subjectivity* of this being? These seem to be *the questions that today determine the perspective* for thinking about the human being, the perspective for contemporary anthropology and ethics. They are essential and burning questions. Anthropology and ethics must be pursued today within this challenging but promising perspective.

NOTES

1. One such effort is my book *Osoba i czyn* [*Person and Action*] (Krakow: Polskie Tow. Teologiczne, 1969; rev. ed. 1985). [English edition: *The Acting Person*, trans. Andrzej Potocki, ed. Anna-Teresa Tymieniecka (Boston: Reidel, 1979).] Another even more relevant work in this regard is my essay "The Person: Subject and Community" 219–261 below.

2. See the section entitled "Subjectivity and Subjectivism" in *The Acting Person* 56–59.

3. My work *The Acting Person* is in large measure constructed upon this basis.

4. One can observe this by comparing my book *The Acting Person* with Mieczyslaw A. Krapiec's book *I—Man: An Outline of Philosophical Anthropology*, trans. Marie Lescoe, Andrew Woznicki, Theresa Sandok et al. (New Britain: Mariel, 1983).

16

The Person: Subject and Community

All of the reflections I shall be presenting here refer to and are rooted in my book *The Acting Person*.[1] Based on the analyses in that book, I wish to reexamine the connection that exists between the subjectivity of the human person and the structure of human community. This problem was already outlined in *The Acting Person*, especially in the final section "Participation." Here I wish to develop that outline somewhat, beginning with the concept of person, which itself was rather extensively discussed in the book. Many of the analyses presented in *The Acting Person* are closely connected with the problem of the subjectivity of the human person; one might even say that they all in some way contribute to an understanding and disclosure of this subjectivity. It would be difficult here to reproduce them in full. Certain sections could be compiled as an appendix to this essay. In addition, I should also mention a discussion that took place in connection with *The Acting Person* at a meeting of professors of philosophy.[2] Taken as a whole, the papers from that discussion constitute an extensive contribution to Polish philosophical anthropology; it was also with this in mind that they were subsequently published in *Analecta Cracoviensia*.[3]

The problem of the subjectivity of the human being is a problem of paramount philosophical importance today. Divergent tendencies contend with one another over it; their cognitive assumptions and orientations often give it a diametrically opposed form and meaning. The philosophy of consciousness would have us believe that it first discovered the human

Karol Wojtyla, "Osoba: Podmiot i wspolnota," *Roczniki Filozoficzne* 24.2 (1976): 5–39.

subject. The philosophy of being is prepared to demonstrate that quite the opposite is true, that in fact an analysis of pure consciousness leads inevitably to an annihilation of the subject. The need arises to find the actual point at which phenomenological analyses based on the assumptions of the philosophy of consciousness begin to work in favor of an enrichment of the realistic image of the person. The need also arises to authenticate the foundations of such a philosophy of person.

In addition, the problem of the subjectivity of the person—particularly in relation to human community—imposes itself today as one of the central ideological issues that lie at the very basis of human praxis, morality (and thus also ethics), culture, civilization, and politics. Philosophy comes into play here in its essential function: philosophy as an expression of basic understandings and ultimate justifications. The need for such understandings and justifications always accompanies humankind in its sojourn on earth, but this need becomes especially intense in certain moments of history, namely, in moments of great crisis and confrontation. The present age is such a moment. It is a time of great controversy about the human being, controversy about the very meaning of human existence, and thus about the nature and significance of the human being. This is not the first time that Christian philosophy has been faced with a materialistic interpretation, but it is the first time that such an interpretation has had so many means at its disposal and has expressed itself in so many currents. This aptly describes the situation in Poland today with respect to the whole political reality that has arisen out of Marxism, out of dialectical materialism, and strives to win minds over to this ideology.

We know that such situations in history have frequently led to a deeper reflection on Christian truth as a whole, as well as on particular aspects of it. That is also the case today. The truth about the human being, in turn, has a distinctly privileged place in this whole process. After nearly twenty years of ideological debate in Poland, it has become clear that at the center of this debate is not cosmology or philosophy of nature but philosophical anthropology and ethics: the great and fundamental controversy about the human being.

From the point of view of Christian philosophy, and theology as well, such a turn of events (which was reflected in the entire teaching of the Second Vatican Council, especially in the constitution *Gaudium et Spes*) favors treating the topic of the human person from a variety of angles. (I have always to some extent taken this approach in my publications.[4]) The present work also develops in accord with this principle.

1. BETWEEN THE *SUPPOSITUM* AND THE HUMAN SELF: REFLECTIONS ON THE SUBJECTIVITY OF THE PERSON

1.1. THE EXPERIENCE OF THE HUMAN BEING

In the field of experience, the human being appears both as a particular *suppositum* and as a concrete self, in every instance unique and unrepeatable. This is an experience of the human being in two senses simultaneously, for the one having the experience is a human being and the one being experienced by the subject of this experience is also a human being. The human being is simultaneously its subject and object. Objectivity belongs to the essence of experience, for experience is always an experience of "something" or "somebody" (in this case, "somebody"). The tendency to retreat toward the "pure subjectivity" of experience is characteristic of the philosophy of consciousness, about which more will be said later. In reality, however, objectivity belongs to the essence of experience, and so the human being, who is the subject, is also given in experience in an objective way. Experience, so to speak, dispels the notion of "pure consciousness" from human knowledge, or rather it summons all that this notion has contributed to our knowledge of the human being to the dimensions of objective reality.

In experience, the human being is given to us as someone who exists and acts. I am such an existing and acting individual and so is everyone else. The experience of existing and acting is something that all human beings, both others and I, have in common; at the same time, all human beings, both others and I, are also the object of this experience. This occurs in different ways, because I experience my own self as existing and acting differently from how I experience others, and so does every other concrete self. Obviously, though, I must include both others and myself in the whole process of understanding the human being. I can proceed in this process either from others or from myself. Special attention to this self is particularly important for a full understanding of the subjectivity of the human being, because in no other object of the experience of the human being are the constitutive elements of this subjectivity given to me in such an immediate and evident way as in my own self.[5]

When I construct an image of the person as subject on the basis of the experience of the human being, I draw especially upon the experience of my own self, but never in isolation from or in opposition to others. All analyses aimed at illuminating human subjectivity have their "categorial" limits. We can neither go beyond those limits nor completely free ourselves from them, for they are strictly connected with the objectivity of experience. As soon as we begin to accept the notion of "pure consciousness" or the "pure subject," we abandon the very basis of the objectivity of the experience that allows us to understand and explain the subjectivity of the human being in a complete way—but then we are no longer interpreting the real subjectivity of the human being.

Nor are we interpreting it when we focus in a purely "phenomenal" or "symptomatic" way on individual functions or even on selective structural wholes within the human being, as do the different particular sciences that examine the human being in a variety of aspects. While it cannot be denied that through the use of this method these sciences gather more and more material for understanding the human person and human subjectivity, they themselves do not provide this understanding. On the other hand, because they do supply us with an ever increasing body of empirical knowledge about the human being, we must constantly renew (or, as it were, "reinterpret") philosophically the essential content of our image of the human being as a person. This need also increases along with the whole wealth of phenomenological analyses, which, in the interests of the objectivity of experience, must in some way be transposed from the plane of consciousness and integrated into the full reality of the person. There can be no doubt that these analyses are especially valuable and fruitful for the entire process of understanding and explaining the subjectivity of the person.

This state of research on the human being, and in particular its rather well-defined and differentiated approach to the basic source of knowledge of the human being, that is, to the full and multidimensional experience of the human being, allows us to accept completely the ancient concept of *suppositum* and, at the same time, to understand it a new way. To say that the human being—I and every other human being—is given in experience as a *suppositum* is to say that the whole experience of the human being, which reveals the human being to us as someone who exists and acts, both allows and legitimately requires us to conceive the human being as the subject of that existence and activity. And this is precisely what is contained in the concept of *suppositum*. This concept serves to express the subjectivity of the human being in the metaphysical sense. By "metaphysical," I mean not so much "beyond-the-phenomenal" as "through-the-phenomenal," or "trans-phenomenal." Through all the phenomena that in experience go to make up the whole human being as someone who exists and acts, we perceive—somehow we must perceive—the subject of that existence and activity. Or better, we perceive that the human being is—must be—that "sub-ject." Otherwise the whole existence and activity given to us in experience as the human being's existence and activity (and, in the concrete case of my own self, as *my* existence and activity) could not be the human being's (*my*) existence and activity. Metaphysical subjectivity, or the *suppositum*, as the transphenomenal and therefore fundamental expression of the experience of the human being, is also the guarantor of the identity of this human being in existence and activity.

By saying that the *suppositum* is the fundamental expression of the whole experience of the human being, I mean that this expression is in some sense an inviolable one: experience cannot be detached from it, and, at the same time, that it is open to everything that the experience of the human being, especially the experience of one's own self, can bring to the understanding of the subjectivity of the person. While recognizing the special and distinct character of metaphysical knowledge, I am not willing to let it be divorced from the rest of human knowledge. After all, all knowledge is metaphysical at root, for it reaches to being; this cannot, however, obscure the significance of the particular aspects of being for understanding it in its full richness.

1.2. *OPERARI SEQUITUR ESSE*

The discovery of the human *suppositum*, or human subjectivity in the metaphysical sense, also brings with it a basic understanding of the relation between existence and activity. This relation is expressed in the philosophical adage: *operari sequitur esse.*[6] Although the adage sounds as though it were referring to a unilateral relation, namely, to the causal dependence of activity on existence, it also implies yet another relation between *operari* and *esse*. If *operari* results from *esse*, then *operari* is also—proceeding in the opposite direction—the most proper avenue to knowledge of that *esse*. This is, therefore, a gnosiological dependence. From human *operari*, then, we discover not only that the human being is its "sub-ject," but also who the human being is as the subject of his or her activity. *Operari*, taken as the total dynamism of the human being, enables us to arrive at a more precise and proper understanding of the subjectivity of the human being. By subjectivity here, I am no longer referring to just the *suppositum* as the subject in the metaphysical sense; I am also referring to everything that, based upon this *suppositum*, makes the human being an individual, personal subject.

The dynamism proper to the human being is complex and differentiated. Abstracting for the moment from other differentiations, we should note that the structural whole of human dynamism (*operari* in the broadest sense of the term) includes everything that in some sense merely *happens* in the human being, along with everything that the human being *does*. The latter—i.e., action—is a distinct form of human *operari*; the human being is revealed as a person mainly in and through action. A complete analysis of human dynamism would give us a complete picture of human subjectivity. By a complete analysis, I mean an analysis not only of actions but also of everything that happens in the human being on both the somatic and the psychic level, or, more precisely, on both the somatic-reactive and the psychic-emotive level[7]—for there can be no doubt that human subjectivity reflects the complexity of human nature and is, therefore, in some sense multidimensional. A deeper analysis based on the relation *operari sequitur esse* and carried out always within the context of the human *suppositum*, or metaphysical subjectivity, would help reveal the nature of both the somatic and the psychic subjectivity of the human being; in other words, such an analysis would help show how human persons are subjects through their bodies and psyches. It would be difficult not at least to mention the enormous significance of the emotions for the development of a concrete human subjectivity, i.e., for the kind of subject that a concrete human being is, namely, both an individual and a person.

I shall, however, set aside that whole line of inquiry here, for I believe that the form of human *operari* that has the most basic and essential significance for grasping the subjectivity of the human being is *action*: conscious human activity, in which the freedom proper to the human person is simultaneously expressed and concretized. Thus, remaining always within the context of the *suppositum* (the *suppositum humanum*, of course), or subjectivity in the metaphysical and fundamental sense, we can arrive at a knowledge and explanation of subjectivity in the sense proper to the human being, namely, subjectivity in the personal sense. After all, metaphysical subjectivity in the sense of *suppositum* belongs to everything that in any way exists and acts; it belongs to different existing and acting beings according to an analogy of proportionality. We must, therefore, define more precisely the subjectivity proper to the human being, namely, personal subjectivity, taking as our basis the whole of human dynamism (*operari*), but especially the dynamism that may properly be called the activity of the human being as a person: the dynamism of action.

Beginning, then, with action, we cannot help but perceive that the personal subjectivity of the human being is a distinctive, rich structure, one that is brought to light by means of a comprehensive analysis of action. The human being as a person is constituted metaphysically as a being by the *suppositum*, and so from the very beginning the human being is someone who exists and acts, although fully human activity (*actus humanus*), or action, appears only at a certain stage of human development. This is a consequence of the complexity of human nature. The spiritual elements of cognition and consciousness, along with freedom and self-determination, gradually gain mastery over the somatic and rudimentary psychic dimensions of humanity. The individual's whole development, in turn, tends clearly toward the emergence of the person and personal subjectivity in the human *suppositum*. In this way, somehow on the basis of this *suppositum*, the human self gradually both discloses itself and constitutes itself—and it discloses itself also by constituting itself.

The self constitutes itself through action, through the *operari* proper to the human being as a person. It also constitutes itself through its entire psychosomatic dynamism, through the whole sphere of *operari* that simply happens in the subject but that nevertheless also somehow shapes the subjectivity of the individual. Of course, the human self is able to constitute itself in this manner only because it already is and has been constituted in an essential and fundamental way as a *suppositum*. The *suppositum humanum* must somehow manifest itself as a human self: metaphysical subjectivity must manifest itself as personal subjectivity.

This *must* is the strongest argument for the metaphysical conception of human nature. The human being is a person "by nature." The subjectivity proper to a person also belongs to the human being "by nature." The fact that the human *suppositum*, or metaphysical subjectivity, does not display the traits of personal subjectivity in certain cases (i.e., in cases of psychosomatic or purely psychological immaturity, in which either the normal human self has not developed or the self has developed in a distorted way) does not allow us to question the very foundations of this subjectivity, for they reside within the essentially human *suppositum*.

In what follows, I shall be considering the normally developed human self, for it is there that we find the authentic traits of the subjectivity proper to the person.

1.3. CONSCIOUSNESS AND LIVED EXPERIENCE

In singling out action, or human *operari*, as the form of human dynamism that best enables us to know the human being as a personal subject, the first thing we should note is that this action is conscious activity. In attempting to understand the subjectivity of the person by means of action, we also need to become aware of the special significance

consciousness has for this subjectivity. It must be conceded that this aspect
was not developed in the Scholastic tradition, where *actus humanus* was
subjected to a detailed analysis chiefly from the side of *voluntarium*.
Voluntarium, of course, could only occur on the basis of understanding—
mainly an understanding of goods and ends—since *voluntas* is simply
appetitus intellectivus expressed in *liberium arbitrium*. Consciousness,
however, is not the ordinary understanding that directs the will and activity. After Descartes, on the other hand, the aspect of consciousness
eventually assumed a kind of absolutization, which in the contemporary
era entered phenomenology by way of Husserl. The gnosiological attitude
in philosophy has replaced the metaphysical attitude: being is constituted
in and somehow through consciousness. The reality of the person, however, demands the restoration of the notion of conscious being, a being
that is not constituted in and through consciousness but that instead somehow constitutes consciousness. This also applies to the reality of action
as conscious activity.

While it may be granted that the person and action—or, to put it another
way, my own existing and acting self—is constituted in consciousness to
the extent that consciousness always reflects the existence (*esse*) and activity (*operari*) of that self, still the experience of the human being (and
especially the experience of my own self) clearly reveals that consciousness is always subjectified in the self and that its roots are always the
suppositum humanum. Consciousness is not an independent subject, although by means of a certain abstraction, or rather exclusion, which in
Husserlian terminology is called *epoché*, consciousness could be treated
as though it were a subject. This way of treating consciousness forms the
basis of all transcendental philosophy, which investigates acts of cognition
as intentional acts of consciousness, that is, as acts directed toward extra-
subjective, objective contents (phenomena). As long as this type of
analysis of consciousness retains the character of a cognitive method, it
can and does bear excellent fruit. And yet because this method is based
on the exclusion (*epoché*) of consciousness from reality, from really existing being, it cannot be regarded as a philosophy of that reality, and it
certainly cannot be regarded as a philosophy of the human being, the
human person. At the same time, however, there can be no doubt that
this method should be used extensively in the philosophy of the human
being.

Consciousness is not an independent subject, but it does play a key
role in understanding the personal subjectivity of the human being. It is
impossible to grasp and objectify the relation between the *suppositum*

humanum and the human self without taking into consideration consciousness and its function. The function of consciousness is not purely cognitive in the sense that this may be said of acts of human knowledge or even self-knowledge. While I can agree with Husserl that these acts are in consciousness, it is quite another thing to say that they are proper to consciousness and correspond genetically to its proper function. Consciousness, insofar as it undoubtedly reflects whatever is objectified cognitively by the human being, at the same time and above all endows this objectified content with the subjective dimension proper to the human being as a subject. Consciousness interiorizes all that the human being cognizes, including everything that the individual cognizes from within in acts of self-knowledge, and makes it all a content of the subject's lived experience.[8]

Being a subject (a *suppositum*) and experiencing oneself as a subject occur on two entirely different dimensions. Only in the latter do we come in contact with the actual reality of the human self. Consciousness plays a key and constitutive role in the formation of this latter dimension of personal human subjectivity. One could also say that the human *suppositum* becomes a human self and appears as one to itself because of consciousness. This in no way implies, however, that the human self is completely reducible to consciousness or self-consciousness. Rather, the self is constituted through the mediation of consciousness in the *suppositum humanum* within the context of the whole existence (*esse*) and activity (*operari*) proper to this *suppositum*. This should not be understood in the sense of individual acts or moments of consciousness, which, as we know, manifests itself as dynamic as well as discontinuous and oscillating (we need only consider periods of sleep), and also as connected with the subconscious in various ways.

Taking all of this into consideration, we still cannot fail to recognize that human beings are subjects—and even subjects completely *in actu*, so to speak—only when they experience themselves as subjects. And this presupposes consciousness. Clearly in such a view the very meaning of *subject* and *subjectivity* is not only enriched but also somewhat modified. The concept of subjectivity takes on a distinctive inwardness of activity and existence—an inwardness, but also an "in-selfness." Human beings exist "in themselves," and so their activities likewise have an "in-self," or "non-transitive," dimension. This in-selfness and inwardness of human activity and existence is simply a more precise—and no less philosophical—definition of what is contained virtually in the notion of *suppositum humanum*. To attain an image of the person as a concrete human self and, together with this, to arrive at the full meaning of personal human subjectivity, we must unravel this "virtualness" and explicate as fully as possible what is contained in the *suppositum humanum*. And that is precisely what an analysis of the human being from the perspective of consciousness and lived experience will help us do.

There are those who hold the view that by such an analysis we sever ourselves from metaphysical subjectivity and enter the realm of purely psychological subjectivity. This view ultimately appeals to the experience of the human being and to a manner of methodically examining that experience. It does not seem to me, however, that anything stands in the way of our analyzing the human being from the perspective of consciousness and lived experience so as better to understand the *suppositum humanum*, and especially this *suppositum* as a concrete and unrepeatable self, or person. After all, the reality of the person is not "extra-phenomenal," but only "trans-phenomenal." In other words, we must deeply and comprehensively explore the "phenomenon" of the human being in order fully to understand and objectify the human being.

1.4. EFFICACY AND SELF-DETERMINATION

Following these observations, we may now return to the form of human *operari* called action—conscious activity. Having considered the aspect of consciousness, which is essential for such activity, we are better prepared to understand the special connection between action and the personal subjectivity of the human being. Action, which in traditional terminology was called *actus humanus*, should really be called *actus personae*. The latter is a better name for action because of the element of efficacy that lies at the basis of action, for this is the efficacy of a person. A strict connection exists between a concrete human action and a particular self, a connection that has a causal and efficient character. Because of this connection, the action cannot be divorced from that self and attributed to someone else as its author. This connection is of a completely different kind from the one that occurs between the same human self and everything that merely happens in it. We attribute the action, the conscious activity, to this self as its likewise conscious author. Such efficacy involves the element of will, and therefore of freedom, which, in turn, brings with it the element of moral responsibility. And this takes us right into the essential dimension of the personal subjectivity of the human being.[9]

This dimension will have to be analyzed in successive stages, for it contains—and in some sense continues to accumulate—such a wealth of specifically human reality that it is impossible to examine all of its essential elements at once. Although an analysis of moral responsibility takes us even more deeply into the problematic of the will and of the freedom proper to the human being as a person, and thus in a certain sense makes our view of them even sharper, an analysis of personal efficacy should come first.

The concept of efficacy, though certainly grounded in the experience of the human being, is imprecise here insofar as efficacy may refer to the dependence of an external effect on a cause—an effect outside the authoring subject. Activity itself in that case has a transitive character, which, of course, is often true of human activities. Through our activity we are the authors of many effects outside ourselves; through it we shape our surrounding reality. This type of causal dependence also appears in the concept of action, but there it is not the most basic type of causal dependence. For action, another type of causal dependence is more basic, namely, that which connects conscious human activity with the subject of that activity. Obviously this other type of causal dependence, which has an intransitive character, is accessible in each particular instance only to introspection, to inner experience. This may be why even our linguistic conventions tend to link the concept of action and this basic dimension of it less strongly than is true in reality. In order to get a full sense of the reality of this dimension, we must considerably supplement external experience with internal experience. This dimension, in turn, is of great importance for an insight into the personal subjectivity of the human being.

Once we have a full sense of the reality of the inner dimension of the human being, we see that the efficacy so clearly manifested in the experience of action is not just efficacy but also self-determination. In acting consciously, not only am I the agent of the action and of its transitive and intransitive effects, but I also determine myself. Self-determination is a deeper and more basic dimension of the efficacy of the human self through which the acting human being is revealed as a personal subject. Efficacy alone—the causal dependence of an action on the self—does not tell us the whole story about personal subjectivity. If it did, then this subjectivity could be understood by analogy to other subjects of existence and activity (other *supposita*) in the world, subjects to which we also attribute efficacy and the effects of this efficacy according to their respective natures and powers. Such efficacy comes from the subject (*suppositum*), but it does not go back into the subject or return to it somehow, and it does not refer in the first place to the subject itself. It also does not exhibit the unique subjective structure that is revealed by action and by the personal efficacy contained in action. In contrast, the efficacy that is also self-determination fully discloses the person as a subjective structure of self-governance and self-possession.[10]

In human activity, or action, I turn toward a variety of ends, objects, and values. In turning toward those ends, objects, and values, however, I cannot help but also in my conscious activity turn toward myself as an end, for I cannot relate to different objects of activity and choose different values without thereby determining myself (thus becoming the primary object for myself as a subject) and my own value. The structure of human action is autoteleological in a special dimension. This is not merely the dimension of biological life and its respective instincts; it is also not merely the dimension of the elementary attraction and repulsion associated with various types of pleasure and pain. The self-determination contained in actions and in authentically human efficacy points to another dimension of autoteleology, one that is ultimately connected with the true and the good—the good in an unconditional and disinterested sense (*bonum honestum*). Human actions thus display a transcendence that is as if another name for the person. This transcendence is what brings to light the subjectivity proper to the human being. If this subjectivity is revealed through self-determination, it is because self-determination expresses the transcendent dimension of essentially human activity. This dimension stops at the person as a subject and cannot go beyond the person, for it finds its reason of being and its meaning primarily in the person. The efficacy of the person, therefore, ultimately brings to light the subjectivity proper to the person, and it does so every time it is exercised: in every action, choice, and decision, it somehow brings this subjectivity out of the dark and makes it a distinct "phenomenon" of human experience.

Here we are already touching upon other areas of the analysis. As I said before, we cannot do the whole analysis at once, but must develop it gradually and successively. At the same time, however, it is not easy in this analysis to separate the different areas and seal them off hermetically from one another. Before going on, then, let us dwell yet a moment on the structure of efficacy as self-determination. Through it, personal human subjectivity is not only disclosed to us cognitively but is also really constituted as a specific reality, one that is essentially different from all the other *supposita* we encounter in the surrounding world. This human *suppositum*, which is constituted and constitutes itself through acts of self-determination, is what we call a self, or an *I*. Of course, we say this primarily and properly of our own *suppositum*, but indirectly also of every other human *suppositum*.

I already mentioned earlier that the self is not reducible to consciousness alone, although it is constituted through consciousness. Consciousness, and especially self-consciousness, is an indispensable condition for the constitution of the human self. Nevertheless, the real constitution of this self within the framework of the human *suppositum* ultimately takes place as a result of acts of self-determination. In them, as I said before, the structure and profile of the self-possession and self-governance proper to a person are revealed. And they are revealed because in every act of self-determination this structure is somehow realized anew. It is in this realization of the structure of self-determination and self-governance that the person as a concrete human self is actually constituted. This also brings into clearer focus the intimate connection between the self and the *suppositum*. The self is nothing other than the concrete *suppositum humanum*, which, when given to itself by consciousness (self-consciousness) in the lived experience of action, is identical with the self-possession and self-governance that comes to light as a result of the dynamics of the personal efficacy that is self-determination.

The self, then, is not just self-consciousness, but it is also the self-possession and self-governance proper to a concrete human *suppositum*. These latter aspects of the self are manifested primarily through action. Earlier I said that the self cannot be reduced to self-consciousness alone; now, however, I should add that the full dimension of the human self, which includes self-possession and self-governance, is conditioned by self-consciousness. This dimension is also the basis of the full relation of the self to the personal subjectivity that is proper to a human being. Such subjectivity, as I said before, is not only the subjectivity of being but also the subjectivity of lived experience. Consciousness plays a fundamental role in the constitution of such subjectivity through its special function of internalization (in *The Acting Person*, I called this the reflexive function of consciousness). Thanks to this function, the experience of the human being (primarily as a determinate self) discloses the "inwardness" and "in-selfness" proper to concrete human *esse* and *operari*. These are, as I said, meanings of the subject and subjectivity that the concept of *suppositum* itself does not yet bring to light.

This "inwardness" and "in-selfness," as the full (experienced and lived) realization of the personal subjectivity of the human self, is both manifested and actualized in self-possession and self-governance, for I experience myself as a personal subject to the extent that I become aware that I possess myself and govern myself. The consciousness—or, more precisely, the self-consciousness—connected with action and with efficacy as self-determination conditions that lived experience. In this sense, we can say that both the concrete human self and the concrete personal human subjectivity corresponding to it are constituted though consciousness (with its help).

From the point of view of the person as a being that "exists and acts," the person as a *suppositum*, I do not see any fundamental flaws or shortcomings in this analysis. After all, the lived experience of our personal subjectivity is simply the full actualization of all that is contained virtually in our metaphysical subjectivity (*suppositum humanum*). It is also both the full and fundamental revelation of our metaphysical subjectivity and the full and fundamental actualization and realization of our being in lived experience. This also seems to be a possible—and in some sense even the philosophically definitive—meaning of the ancient adage *operari sequitur esse*. The *suppositum humanum* and the human self are but two poles of one and the same experience of the human being.

1.5. FULFILLMENT AND TRANSCENDENCE

The picture of personal human subjectivity that unveils itself before us in experience would be incomplete if we failed to include the element of fulfillment. If action is the avenue to knowledge of the person (*operari sequitur esse*), then we must necessarily examine the expression "to fulfill an action."[11] This expression seems in a most basic way to refer not just to the reality of the action, the *actus humanus*, but also to the reality of the human being, the subject who fulfills the action. This is not an accidental expression. Properly understood, it signifies a tendency away from what is incomplete toward an appropriate fullness. An action as an *actus humanus* is this actual fullness in the order of *operari*. The person, however, is always included within the compass of the action's fulfillment. The action as an *actus humanus* reveals the inwardness and in-selfness of the person and also activates the self-possession and self-governance proper to the structure of the person. In the light of this, we must ask: to what degree is the fulfillment of an action also the fulfillment of oneself, the fulfillment of the person who fulfills the action?[12]

This is a very real problem. In some sense, it is even the most profound and basic of all the problems that must be addressed in an analysis of the personal subjectivity of the human being. In the dynamic structure of this subjectivity, the tendency toward the fulfillment of oneself, a tendency that lies at the root of all human *operari*, particularly actions, testifies simultaneously to contingency and autoteleology. The tendency toward the fulfillment of oneself shows that this self is somehow incomplete, and although the incompleteness and contingency of this being are not synonymous, the former may be reduced to the latter. This same tendency also points to autoteleology, because the aim of this being—a *suppositum* that experiences itself as incomplete—is the fulfillment of itself: self-fulfillment. The disclosure of this tendency completes our picture of the human self, which constitutes itself in its actions by means of consciousness and self-consciousness. In these actions, through the element of self-determination, the human self is revealed to itself not only as self-possession and self-governance, but also as a tendency toward self-fulfillment. This shows conclusively that the personal subjectivity of the human being is not a closed-in structure. Neither self-consciousness nor self-possession encloses the human self within itself as a subject. Quite the contrary. The whole "turning toward itself" that consciousness and self-consciousness work to bring about is ultimately a source of the most expansive openness of the subject toward reality. In the human being, in the human self as a personal subject, self-fulfillment and transcendence are inseparably connected. I already mentioned earlier that, to the modern mind, transcendence is as if another name for the person.

In philosophy, the term "transcendence" has many meanings. In metaphysics, it signifies being as a reality surpassing all categories, while at the same time constituting their foundation; it also signifies the true and the good as transcendentals on the same level as being. In philosophical anthropology, transcendence—in keeping with its etymology *transcendere*—likewise signifies a surpassing (a going-out-beyond or a rising-above), to the extent that this is verifiable in the comprehensive experience of the human being, to the extent that this is revealed in the dynamic totality of human existence and activity, human *esse* and *operari*. The various manifestations of this transcendence ultimately converge in a single source, which constantly resounds within the human being as a subject, as a *suppositum*, and which in the final analysis testifies that the *suppositum humanum* is also of a spiritual nature. Transcendence is the spirituality of the human being revealing itself.

I do not intend here to present either a metaphysical analysis of this problem or a comprehensive treatment of the transcendence proper to the human person. I shall confine myself to discussing just one element of transcendence, namely, that which is revealed by the distinctive personal shape given to human actions by conscience. The profile of fulfillment, as strictly belonging to the personal subjectivity of the human being, is connected with this element of transcendence in an especially vivid way.

We often speak of moral subjectivity by analogy to psychological subjectivity when considering the aspects of consciousness and lived experience, but such distinctions must not be allowed to shatter the image of the basic unity of the personal subject. Personal subjectivity is the subjectivity that we experience as our own self in our own actions. This subjectivity is revealed to us in its true depth in the lived experience of moral value (good or evil), an experience always connected with the element of conscience in human actions.

Why does the element of conscience in action reveal the transcendence of the person? The answer to this question would require a whole series of analyses, which I attempted to carry out in *The Acting Person*.[13] Here, however, I shall keep my response brief. In conscience, truth presents itself as the source of moral duty, or "categorical" duty (as Kant would say). Truth presents itself as a constitutive condition of the freedom proper to action, in which this freedom manifests itself as the self-determination of the person. To be free means not only to *will*, but also to *choose* and to *decide*, and this already suggests a transcendent subordination of the good to the true in action. Conscience, however, is the proper place of this subordination. The person's authentic transcendence in action is realized in conscience, and the *actus humanus* takes shape as the willing and choosing of a "true good" thanks to conscience. Thus the element of conscience reveals both in action and in the efficient subject of action the transcendence of truth and freedom, for freedom is realized precisely through the willing and choosing of a true good.

"Do good and avoid evil" is the first principle of conscience as synderesis and also the elementary precept of all human praxis. To act in accord with this principle, I must in my conscience constantly go out beyond myself toward true good. This is the basic direction of the transcendence that is a property of the human person (*proprium personae*). Without this transcendence—without going out beyond myself and somehow rising above myself in the direction of truth and in the direction of a good willed and chosen in the light of truth—I as a person, I as a personal subject, in a sense am not myself. Consequently, when we analyze acts of knowledge, acts of will, or the world of values connected with them, we do not bring to light the personal property of the human being unless we bring to light the transcendence that resides in those acts, a transcendence they have by reason of their relation to the true and to the good as "true" (or as "befitting," *honestum*), i.e., as willed and chosen on the basis of truth.

An analysis of conscience also reveals the strict connection between transcendence and fulfillment. At issue here is not only the role of conscience in the dynamics of fulfilling an action, but also the fulfillment of the self in that action. In fulfilling an action, I fulfill myself in it if the action is "good," which means in accord with my conscience (assuming, of course, that this is a good conscience, a true conscience). By acting in this way, I myself *become* good and *am* good as a human being. The moral value reaches to the very depths of my ontic structure as a *suppositum humanum*. The opposite would be an action not in accord with my conscience, a morally evil action. I then *become* evil and *am* evil as a human being. In this case, the fulfillment of the action leads not to the fulfillment but to the unfulfillment of myself. The lived experience of the unfulfillment of myself corresponds to a negative moral value (which could also be called an anti-value, especially from the point of view of the judgment and verdict of conscience). Thus fulfillment of self and unfulfillment of self have two meanings: 1) a metaphysical meaning (I *become* and *am* good or evil as a human being) and 2) an experiential meaning (which is given in my awareness and lived experience of a moral value—good or evil). These two meanings really deserve a separate analysis, which I do not intend to present here. I wish, however, at least to draw attention to the special proximity of these two meanings. It serves as still another proof that the *suppositum humanum* and the human self are but two poles of one and the same experience of the human being.

Obviously fulfilling oneself is not identical with fulfilling an action, but depends on the moral value of that action. I fulfill myself not by the fact that I fulfill an action, but by the fact that I become good when that action is morally good. We see, then, that the fulfillment of a person is related to transcendence, to the transcendent dimension of the action, a dimension objectified in conscience. I fulfill myself through good, whereas evil brings me unfulfillment. Obviously, too, self-fulfillment is a distinct structure of the personal subject, a structure that differs from both self-possession and self-determination. This structure is actualized in the action through its moral value—through good—of course, only in the dimension of that action *per modum actus*. The experience of morality also reveals ways in which moral value, good or evil, may become rooted and ingrained in the subject. In this regard, the ethics of Aristotle and later that of Thomas Aquinas, as well as modern-day character studies, speak of habits (*de habitibus*) and also of moral proficiencies, of virtues and vices. These all involve different forms of the fulfillment or the unfulfillment of the self. Both the one and the other speak of the human being, the human self, as a personal subject.

The essential point in all this is that fulfillment as a subjective reality, a reality given to us in the lived experience of conscience, but clearly not limited to or reducible to that experience, is distinctly connected with transcendence. I fulfill myself, I realize the autoteleology of my personal self, through the transcendent dimension of my *operari*. The transcendence of truth and goodness has a decisive influence on the formation of the human self, on its development within the whole reality of the personal subject, as an analysis of conscience and morality so clearly reveals. Such an analysis also deepens our view of the contingency of the human being. It does this both by showing how essential it is for us as human beings to strive for self-fulfillment and especially by showing how in this striving we find ourselves always between good and evil, between fulfillment and unfulfillment, and how persistently we must overcome the forces operating both from without and from within against self-fulfillment.

This even partial self-fulfillment brought about by the moral good of an action is accompanied by the element of peace and happiness so essential for experiences of conscience (whereas moral evil manifests itself in the experience of conscience accompanied by depression and despair). This suggests that transcendence is in some sense a common perspective for self-fulfillment and happiness. I shall not, however, examine this issue here; I merely wish to draw attention to it.

2. THE DIFFERENT DIMENSIONS OF COMMUNITY

2.1. THE STATE OF THE QUESTION

The conjunction of *subject* and *community* in the title of this essay on the person does not presuppose in advance how these two topics will be joined in the analysis. The course of the preceding discussion—in keeping with the plan I outlined at the beginning—points this analysis in the direction of the connection that occurs between the subjectivity of the human being as a person and the structure of human community. Now I intend to reexamine that connection in relation to my previous examination of it in *The Acting Person*.[14] While this should be noted, I also wish to stress that the treatment in *The Acting Person* was in no way exhaustive, nor shall the present one be. Perhaps, however, I will manage to add a few new thoughts to what I have already said.

First of all, then, I should point out that *The Acting Person* does not contain a theory of community, but deals only with the elementary condition under which existence and activity "together with others" promotes the self-fulfillment of the human being as a person, or at least does not obstruct it. One cannot, after all, deny the facts involved. These facts—negative facts known to us from the history of humankind and the history of human societies—should be kept in mind when considering the problem of the personal subject in community. This problem is also the focus of the last part of *The Acting Person*. Although I do not present a full-blown theory of community there, certain elements of this theory are already implicitly contained in it. One such element in particular is the concept of *participation*, which I understand in the last part of *The Acting Person* in two ways. First of all, I view it as a property of the person, a property that expresses itself in the ability of human beings to endow their own existence and activity with a personal (personalistic) dimension when they exist and act together with others. Secondly, I conceive participation in *The Acting Person* as a positive relation to the humanity of others, understanding *humanity* here not as the abstract idea of the human being, but—in keeping with the whole vision of the human being in that book—as the personal self, in each instance unique and unrepeatable. Humanity is not an abstraction or a generality, but has in each human being the particular "specific gravity" of a personal being (clearly this "specific gravity" does not derive in this case solely from the concept of the species). To participate in the humanity of another human being means to be vitally related to the other as a particular human being, and not just related to what makes the other (*in abstracto*) a human being. This is ultimately the basis for the whole distinctive character of the evangelical concept of *neighbor*.

The first meaning of participation refers not to this positive relation to another's humanity, but to the property of the person by virtue of which human beings, while existing and acting together with others, are nevertheless capable of fulfilling themselves in this activity and existence. Such a formulation of the problem points to the irrevocable primacy of the personal subject in relation to community, a primacy in both the metaphysical (and hence factual) and the methodological sense. This means not only that people *de facto* exist and act together as a multiplicity of personal subjects, but also that we can say nothing essential about this coexistence and cooperation in the personalistic sense—we can say nothing essential about this multiplicity as a community—unless we proceed from the human being as a personal subject.[15]

In my opinion, the whole problematic of alienation is ultimately reducible to this as well. Alienation has relevance not for the human being as an individual of the human species but for the human being as a personal subject. The human being as an individual of the species is a human being and remains a human being regardless of the system of interpersonal or social relations. The human being as a personal subject, on the other hand, can experience alienation, or a kind of "dehumanization," in these relations. That is why in *The Acting Person* I treat participation primarily as a property by virtue of which human beings, while existing and acting together with others, that is, in various systems of interpersonal and social relations, are able to be themselves and to fulfill themselves. Participation is in a sense the antithesis of alienation. When I say in *The Acting Person* that participation is a distinctive property of the human being as a person, I mean that people tend toward participation, whereas they defend themselves against alienation, and that the basis for both participation and alienation is not people's essence as members of the human species but their personal subjectivity.

In reflecting on community, therefore, we should not attach fundamental significance to the "material" fact that people live and act "together with others." As a "material" fact, it still says nothing about community, but speaks only of a multiplicity of beings, of acting subjects, who are people. The "material" fact of a number of people existing and acting together, or—as I put it in my analyses in *The Acting Person*—of the human being existing and acting together with others, is still not a community. By community I understand not this multiplicity of subjects itself, but always the specific *unity* of this multiplicity. This unity is accidental with respect to each subject individually and to all of them together. It arises as the relation or sum of relations existing between them. These relations can be investigated as an objective reality that qualifies everyone jointly and singly in a particular multiplicity of people. We then speak of a society (or, using other terminology, of social groups, etc.). Only the individual people—the personal subjects—who are the members of this society are substantial subjects (*supposita*), each of them separately, whereas the society itself is simply a set of relations, and therefore an accidental being. In the notion of society, however, this accidental being in some sense comes to the fore and becomes the basis for predication concerning the people, the persons, who belong to the society. We then speak of a person from the point of view of his or her social membership, e.g., a Pole, a Catholic, a member of the middle-class, a blue-collar worker.

This same relation or set of relations through which a particular multiplicity of people—of personal subjects—forms a social unity may be examined not so much as an objective reality that qualifies everyone jointly and singly in this multiplicity, but rather from the perspective of the consciousness and lived experience of all its members and also in some sense each of them. Only then do we arrive at the reality of community and detect its proper meaning. There clearly occurs—both from the factual (and thus also metaphysical) and from the methodological point of view— a strict connection, correspondence, and conformity between community and personal human subjectivity, understanding subjectivity here in the sense presented in the first part of this essay. By analyzing only the multiplicity of human *supposita* and the unity of objective interpersonal and social relations that corresponds to them, we obtain a somewhat different picture from the one we get when we focus on personal subjectivity,[16] and thus on the consciousness and lived experience of interpersonal and social relations in a particular human multiplicity. Only the latter picture, it seems to me, corresponds to the concept of community.

We do in fact often use the terms *community* and *society* interchangeably. This is justifiable, even in the light of what was said above. At the same time, however, what was said above also gives us reason to distinguish them. A community is not simply a society, and a society is not simply a community. Even though the same elements may to a large extent go into the makeup of both realities, we apprehend them in different aspects, and this adds up to an important difference. In a sense, too, one could say that a society (a social group, etc.) is what it is by virtue of the community of its members. Community, therefore, seems to be the more essential reality, at least from the point of view of the personal subjectivity of all the members of a given society or social group. From this it also becomes clear that the social relations in a given (one and the same) society can become a source of alienation in proportion to the disappearance of community, that is, in proportion to the disappearance of the relations, bonds, and social unity perceived and experienced by the individual subjects.

The concept of community, as can be inferred even from what was said above, has both a real and an ideal meaning: it signifies both a certain reality and an idea or principle. This meaning is ontological as well as axiological, and hence also normative. It would be impossible here to go into a full discussion of all these meanings of community; the most I can do is simply mention them. The preceding analysis of personal subjectivity can to a certain degree assist us in understanding and explicating these different meanings of community. Community is an essential reality for human coexistence and cooperation, and in another sense it serves as a fundamental norm for such coexistence and cooperation. Clearly, then, there must be a special value of community, one that I do not think should simply be identified with the common good. We discover this value by observing the co-existence and co-operation of people as if from the perspective of the personal subjectivity of each of them. The common good, on the other hand, seems to be an objectification of the axiological meaning of each society, social group, etc. The discovery of the value of community may be considered a direct argument in support of the thesis concerning the social nature of human beings.

And it is precisely in this context that we encounter the problem of the relation between community (the value of community) and the autoteleology of the human being. That people fulfill themselves in and through community with others seems beyond doubt. But does this mean that we can somehow reduce the self-fulfillment of the person to community, or autoteleology to the teleology of one or more communities? I shall attempt to address this issue below by outlining the two—seemingly mutually irreducible—profiles or dimensions of human community. One is the dimension of interhuman and interpersonal relations, which may be symbolized by the relationship *I—thou*. The other, which may be symbolized by the relationship *we*, seems to involve not so much interhuman as social relations. In both of these relationships, the aspect of personal human subjectivity analyzed earlier must not only be subjected to further analysis, but also be gradually and, so to speak, retrospectively verified.

2.2. *I—THOU*: THE INTERPERSONAL DIMENSION OF COMMUNITY

In this and the following section of the analysis, I could use the term *profiles* of community, but I think it would be better to speak of *dimensions* of community. In each of the relationships I plan to analyze, community is a different fact. In addition, however, to its factual structure (to which the term *profile* seems to refer), community has an axiological and normative meaning as well, and so each of these relationships also presents us with a different dimension of community. In my analysis, I will also attempt to bring to light and to some extent describe the dimension of *I—thou* relationships, and then do the same for *we* relationships. These relationships arise in the context of the facts of human coexistence and cooperation. They are part of our human experience and of our original (prescientific and even to some degree prereflective) understanding of this experience. We come into being, begin life, and go through a relatively long period of development in *I—thou* and *we* relationships, and yet, although our whole existence is immersed in these profiles of community during this time, we do not reflect upon the meaning or structure of community. Studies in developmental psychology can throw a great deal of light on this issue. There can be no doubt that *I—thou* and *we* relationships as experiential facts, as facts given in our experience, occur in each of us much earlier than any attempt—especially any methodological attempt—on our part to reflectively objectify these relationships.

While fully appreciating this fact, or rather this rich and very influential set of facts, I prefer to base my analysis on a later situation, one that will allow me to speak of a sufficiently developed stage of personal subjectivity.

After all, this analysis is concerned throughout not just with the *suppositum humanum*, but also with the human *I*, or self. It seems that only from the perspective of a sufficiently developed personal subjectivity can we conduct a full analysis of the *I—thou* and *we* relationships with respect to the communal reality contained in them. It also seems that the profiles and dimensions of community contained in these relationships, when analyzed at the stage of a sufficiently developed personal subjectivity, should operate retrospectively to explain these relationships at earlier stages, and not conversely. Let us, then, first consider the *I—thou* relationship, which is the one in which we primarily detect (to a certain degree in contrast to the *we* relationship) the interhuman, interpersonal dimension of community.

It is sometimes said that the *I* is in a sense constituted by the *thou*.[17] This superb intellectual synopsis needs to be unraveled and developed, of course. In explicating it, we should not overlook the basic fact that this *thou*—like the *I*—is always a someone: the *thou* is some other *I*. And so in the very point of departure of the *I—thou* relationship we find a certain multiplicity of personal subjects. Although this is a minimal multiplicity (one + one), an analysis of the unity essential for the concept of community must be based on the assertion of this multiplicity. A *thou* is another *I*, one different from my own *I*. In thinking or speaking of a *thou*, I express a relation that somehow proceeds from me, but also returns to me. *"Thou"* is a term that expresses not only a separation, but also a connection. This term always contains a clear separation of one from many others. The separation need not necessarily be formal; it may be virtual. Nor does it have to comprise the "text" of the relation; it may belong to its "subtext." Nevertheless, in thinking or speaking of a *thou*, I always have some sense that the concrete human being whom I thus describe is one of many whom I could so describe, that at other times or in other situations I also describe (and experience) various other people in the same way, and that I could describe each of them in this way. Potentially, therefore, the *I—thou* relationship is directed away from me toward all human beings, while actually it always connects me with some one person. If it actually connects me with many, then it is no longer a relation to a *thou* but a relation to a *we*, although it can easily be resolved into a number of relations to *thou*'s.

The particular reflexivity of this relation is also revealed here. The relation to a *thou* is in its essential structure always a relation to another, and yet, because one member of this relation is an *I*, the relation—in a way peculiar to itself—demonstrates the ability to return to the *I* from which it proceeded. I am not referring here to the function of a counter-relation, where the *thou* as an *I* would be related in the same way to me (to my *I*) as a *thou*, and I would then be a *thou* for the other. I am referring to the very same relation that proceeds from my *I* to the *thou*, for this relation has a complementary function, which consists in returning to the *I* from which it proceeded.

Of course, all of this has its full meaning only in the context of consciousness and lived experience, in the same context, therefore, in which both the *I* and the *thou* as another *I* are constituted; it does not, however, have this same full meaning with respect to the metaphysical category of relation. Throughout this part of the analysis, I am speaking about the lived experience of relations, which presupposes the *I* and the *thou* as separate personal subjectivities, and not merely about relations as accidents subjectified in separate *supposita*, although I am in no way questioning this basic reality. What is essential for the present analysis, however, is the *I* and the *thou* as fully constituted, separate, personal subjects, along with all that comprises the personal subjectivity of each of them.

When the relation directed from my *I* to a *thou* returns to the *I* from which it proceeded, the reflexivity of this relation (which need not yet be a mutual relation involving the counter-relation *thou—I*) contains the element of specifically constituting my *I* through its relation to the *thou*. It seems, however, that this element still does not give rise to community; rather, it has meaning for a fuller experience of myself, of my own *I*, and in some sense for the verification of myself "in the light of another self." At the basis of this relation, there may also develop a process of the imitation of personal models, a process very important for education and self-education,[18] and ultimately, therefore, for that self-fulfillment whose original dynamism is rooted in every personal subjectivity, as was mentioned earlier. Leaving aside that possibility, however, it must be acknowledged that, in the normal course of events, the *thou* assists me in more fully discovering and even confirming my own *I*: the *thou* contributes to my self-affirmation. In its basic form, the *I—thou* relationship, far from leading me away from my subjectivity, in some sense more firmly grounds me in it. The structure of the relation is to some degree a confirmation of the structure of the subject and of the subject's priority with respect to the relation.[19]

Even the unilateral relation of an *I* to a *thou* is already a real experience of an interpersonal relationship, although the full experience of such a relationship occurs only when the *I—thou* relationship has a reciprocal character: when a *thou* that for me becomes a specific other, and thus "also another human being," simultaneously makes me its *thou*; when two people mutually become an *I* and a *thou* for each other and experience their relationship in this manner. Only then, it seems to me, do we observe the full character of the community proper to an interpersonal *I—thou* relationship. I wish to reemphasize, however, that even without such reciprocity the *I—thou* relationship is still a real experience of an interpersonal relationship. This experience can also serve as a basis for analyzing the participation that I described in *The Acting Person* as a participation in the very humanity of another human being. The *I—thou* relationship does not have to be reciprocal for such participation to occur. When the relationship is reciprocal, however, we can then say that it is precisely participation, and not something else, that forms the essential constituent of a community having an interhuman, interpersonal character.

I shall not go into an analysis of the individual forms and varieties of interpersonal *I—thou* relationships or the individual forms and varieties of community that develop within such relationships (and also through which such relationships develop, for community, as I have already said, is an essential element of such reciprocal relationships). Certain forms of interpersonal *I—thou* relationships, above all friendship and love, have, of course, been examined and explained many times and in many ways, and are always a favorite topic of reflection. In the present study, while omitting an analysis and description of *I—thou* relationships themselves, I wish to bring to light what is essential for the kind of community contained in them and do this from the point of view of the subjects themselves—or, more precisely, from the point of view of the mutuality of the subjects—of such concrete relationships of an *I* and a *thou* in their personal subjectivity. This will allow us to detect the element of a certain regularity that, in an analogous way, is common to all relationships in which two people are joined together as an *I* and a *thou*, regardless of the particular type of relationship it happens to be. I am concerned here with the interpersonal dimension of community proper to all *I—thou* relationships, regardless of their particular form. Hence this analysis embraces within its scope the *I—thou* of married or engaged couples, the *I—thou* of mother and child, and even the *I—thou* of two strangers who unexpectedly find themselves in such a relationship.

While leaving aside all the particular features of these relationships, there is one thing in this regard that needs to be recognized and emphasized. The human being—both the *I* and the *thou*—is not only an existing subject but also an acting subject, and in this acting the *thou* becomes at every step an object for the *I*. This objectivity, together with the whole relation, returns to the *I* by means of a special kind of interaction: the *I* becomes in a certain sense an object for itself in actions objectively directed toward a *thou*. This, of course, belongs somehow organically to the process of the distinctive way the *I* is constituted by the *thou*, which I already discussed. If the *I*, or self, is constituted by its actions (as was shown in the first part of this essay), and if the *thou* as another *I*, or self, is also constituted in the same way, then this is also the means by which the *I—thou* relationship, including the corresponding effects of this relationship in both of its subjects (the *I* and the *thou*) is constituted. The subject *I* experiences the relation to a *thou* in activity that has the *thou* as its object, and, of course, vice versa. Through this activity directed objectively toward the *thou*, the subject *I* not only experiences itself in relation to the *thou*, but also experiences itself in a new way in its own subjectivity. The objectivity of activity (action and interaction) serves to confirm the agent's own subjectivity, if only because the object of this activity is itself a subject and represents a personal subjectivity proper to itself.

Confining ourselves to the *I—thou* relationship in what could be called its elementary form, without any particular qualifications concerning how the two persons are mutually related, except to say that in this relationship the *I* is a subject of activities directed objectively toward the *thou* and vice versa, we can now describe the basic dimension of interpersonal community. This dimension is both a fact and a demand: it has both a metaphysical and a normative (ethical) meaning, in keeping with what was said earlier concerning the concept of community. This dimension is reducible to treating and really experiencing "the other as oneself" (to use an expression taken directly from the Gospel). This whole analysis, in turn, directs us back to what was said in the last part of *The Acting Person* concerning the meaning of *neighbor*.

To specify more precisely what distinguishes the dimension of community proper to interpersonal *I—thou* relationships, it should be noted that these are the relationships in which human beings mutually reveal themselves to one another in their personal human subjectivity and in all that goes to make up this subjectivity. The *thou* stands before my self as a true and complete "other self," which, like my own self, is characterized not only by self-determination, but also and above all by self-possession and self-governance. In this subjective structure, the *thou* as "another self" represents its own transcendence and its own tendency toward self-fulfillment. This whole structure of personal subjectivity proper to the *I* as a self and to the *thou* as another self is mutually revealed through the community proper to the *I—thou* relationship, since, by virtue of the mutuality of the *I—thou* relationship, *I* am simultaneously a *thou* for the *I* that is a *thou* for me. In this way, the *I—thou* relationship as a mutual relation of two subjects (*supposita*) not only takes on meaning but also truly becomes an authentic subjective community.

To say that such a community involves the mutual revelation of the partners in their personal human subjectivity is to point to the factual meaning of the community proper to an interpersonal *I—thou* relationship. We must not forget, however, that such a community has a normative meaning as well. From this point of view, we may say that, through the dimension of community proper to an interpersonal *I—thou* relationship, there *ought* to be a mutual self-revelation of persons: the partners *ought* to disclose themselves to each other in their personal subjectivity and in all that makes up this subjectivity. Through the *I—thou* relationship, they should reveal themselves to one another in their deepest structure of self-possession and self-governance. Above all, they should reveal themselves in their striving for self-fulfillment, which, culminating in acts of conscience, testifies to the transcendence proper to the human being as a person. In interpersonal *I—thou* relationships, the partners should not only unveil themselves before one another in the truth of their personal reality, but they should also accept and affirm one another in that truth. Such acceptance and affirmation is an expression of the moral (ethical) meaning of interpersonal community.

This meaning both shapes and—in another respect—verifies interpersonal community in its individual realizations and in the individual forms of these mutual relationships of a human *I* and *thou*, including those such as friendship and love. The more profound, integral, and intense the bond between the *I* and the *thou* in these mutual relationships, and the more it takes on the character of trust, a giving of oneself, and (to the extent possible in the relation of one person to another) a special kind of belonging, the greater the need for the mutual acceptance and affirmation of the

I by the *thou* in its personal subjectivity, in the whole structure of self-possession and in full harmony with the personal transcendence that expresses itself in acts of conscience. In this way, within the context of the *I—thou* relationship, by the very nature of interpersonal community, the persons also become mutually responsible for one another.[20] Such responsibility is a reflection of conscience and of the transcendence that for both the *I* and the *thou* constitutes the path to self-fulfillment and, at the same time, characterizes the proper, authentically personal dimension of community.

By "community" I understand "that which unites." In the *I—thou* relationship, an authentic interpersonal community develops (regardless of its form or variety) if the *I* and the *thou* abide in a mutual affirmation of the transcendent value of the person (a value that may also be called *dignity*) and confirm this by their acts. Only such a relationship seems to deserve the name *communio personarum*.[21]

2.3. *WE*: THE SOCIAL DIMENSION OF COMMUNITY

I believe it is extremely important to distinguish the social dimension of community from the interpersonal dimension. The need for this distinction is dictated by the different profiles of community, profiles that in a symbolic, but also very precise, way are expressed by the pronouns *I—thou* and *we*. *I* and *thou* refer only indirectly to the multiplicity of persons joined by the relation (one + one), whereas directly they refer to the persons themselves. *We*, on the other hand, refers directly to the multiplicity and indirectly to the persons belonging to this multiplicity. *We* primarily signifies a set—a set, of course, made up of people, of persons. This set, which may be called a society, a group, etc., is not itself a substantial being, and yet, as I said above, what results from accidents, from the relations between human persons, in some sense comes to the fore here, providing a basis for predication primarily with respect to all and secondarily with respect to each one in the set. This is precisely what is signified by the pronoun *we*.

Clearly, then, the *we* introduces us to another world of human relationships and refers to a another dimension of community, namely, the social dimension, which differs from the previous dimension, the interpersonal dimension of community found in *I—thou* relationships. In the following analysis of the social dimension of community, I shall take the position that community is particularly compatible with the person as a subject, with the personal subjectivity of the human being, with the fact that each human being is an *I* or a *thou*, and not merely a *he* or a *she*. *He* and *she* seem to refer primarily to people as objects, just as *they* does. I intend to analyze the social dimension of community not so much from the perspective of the *he, she,* or *they,* but—in a way parallel to the previous analysis—more from the perspective of the *I* and the *thou*. I also shall not be discussing society, but only the social dimension of human community, which is precisely what the pronoun *we* signifies. I should note right at the start of this analysis that not only does this pronoun refer to many subjects, to many human *I*'s, or selves, but it also refers to the unique subjectivity of this multiplicity. And in this respect a *we* differs from a *they*.

If a *we* is many human *I*'s, or selves, then—like the *I*, or self—it may be conceived and understood through activity. A *we* is many human beings, many subjects, who in some way exist and act together. Acting "together" (i.e., "in common") does not mean engaging in a number of activities that somehow go along side by side. Rather it means that these activities, along with the existence of those many *I*'s, are related to a single value, which, therefore, deserves to be called the *common good*. (By speaking in this way, I do not mean to use the concepts of *value* and *good* interchangeably, much less confuse them.) The relation of many *I*'s to a common good seems to be the very core of social community. By virtue of this relation, the people involved in it, while experiencing their personal subjectivity—the factual multiplicity of human *I*'s—are aware that they form a specific *we*, and they experience themselves in this new dimension. This is the social dimension, different from the *I—thou* dimension, although in it the persons remain themselves (they remain an *I* and a *thou*), but the direction of the relation is fundamentally changed. This direction is determined by the common good. In this relation the *I* and the *thou* also find their mutual relationship in a new dimension: they find their *I—thou* through the common good, which establishes a new union between them.

The best example of this is marriage, in which a clearly delineated *I—thou* relationship, an interpersonal relationship, takes on a social dimension when the spouses accept into this relationship the set of values that may be defined as the common good of marriage and—at least potentially—of family. In relation to this good, their community appears in activity and existence in a new profile and a new dimension, namely, the profile of a *we* and the social dimension of a couple (not just one + one). The couple do not cease being an *I* and a *thou*, and they also do not cease being in an interpersonal *I—thou* relationship. In fact, their *I—thou* relationship in its own way draws upon the *we* relationship and is enriched by it. This also means, of course, that their new social relationship imposes new duties and demands on the interpersonal *I—thou* relationship.

Now that we have a basic outline of the *we* relationship, we may ask, by analogy to the previous analysis: to what extent and in what sense is each *I* constituted by the *we* in a way similar to how the *I* is constituted by the *thou* in interpersonal relationships? Human experience confirms that this does happen. Of course, when speaking here of the constitution of the human *I*, I am assuming all that I said in the first part concerning the personal subjectivity of the human being. I am not referring to its constitution in the metaphysical sense, for in that sense every *I* is constituted in its own *suppositum*. In contrast, the constitution of a concrete *I* in its personal subjectivity takes place in a special way through activity and existence "together with others" in social communities, in the dimension of various *we*'s. It takes place differently from the way it occurs in the *I—thou* dimension, for in the *we* dimension the relationship has a decisive significance for the common good. Through this relationship, a human being, a concrete *I*, discovers different confirmations of his or her personal subjectivity from those that occur in interpersonal relationships. And yet this confirmation of the subject *I* in the community *we* agrees profoundly with the nature of this subject. Perhaps it is just such verification that lies at the basis of all that has ever been said concerning the social nature of the human being.

Essentially speaking, a *we* does not entail a diminution or distortion of the *I*. If *de facto* this sometimes happens (I dealt with this in *The Acting Person*), then the cause should be sought in the realm of the relation to the common good. This relation can be defective in various ways—both on the side of the human *I* (or many such *I*'s) and on the side of what is regarded as the common good for many *I*'s.

This topic comprises an extensive area of philosophy, and above all of social ethics, which I shall not go into here in any depth or detail. Similar to my analysis of interpersonal relationships (*I—thou*), I shall not discuss the different forms and varieties of social community—the different forms and varieties of social reality (societies, social groups, circles, etc.)—in which all human beings exist and act. In my analysis of the social dimension of community, I basically wish to grasp and illuminate the meaning of this dimension primarily in the aspect of the personal subjectivity of the human being—and thereby show the compatibility of personal subjectivity and community. In this aspect, where the autoteleology of the human being and the whole problematic of human self-fulfillment naturally comes to the fore, community, too, must present not only a factual, ontological (and thus meta-physical) meaning, but also a normative (and thus ethical) meaning.

First of all, then, the "common" relation of many *I*'s to a common good, by virtue of which this multiplicity of subjects appears to itself (and to others as well) as a specific *we* and *is* that *we*, is a particular expression of the transcendence proper to the human being as a person. In a particular way, too, the relation to the common good actualizes this transcendence. Here we should recall what was said in the first part of this essay with regard to transcendence and its strict connection with the self-fulfillment of the subjective self. Conscience, as a key element of the self-fulfillment of the personal self, points in a special way to transcendence and, so to speak, lies at its subjective center. Objectively, transcendence is realized in a relation to truth and to the good as "true" (as "befitting," *honestum*). The relation to the common good, a relation that unites the multiplicity of subjects into one *we*, should likewise be grounded in a relation to truth and to a "true" good.[22] The proper dimension of the common good then comes into view. The common good is essentially the good of many, and in its fullest dimension the good of all. This multiplicity can be quantitatively diverse: two in the case of marriage (no longer just one + one, but a couple), several in the case of a family, millions in the case of a particular nation, billions in the case of all humankind. Hence, the concept of the common good is an analogical concept, an analogy of proportionality, since the very reality of this good is subject to differentiation. The common good of a married couple or a family is one thing, that of a nation another, and that of humankind still another. The human *we* is also realized in them in an analogous way. In all of these realizations, however, the common good corresponds to the transcendence of the persons and forms the objective basis for their constitution as a social community—as a *we*.

The reality of the common good in the whole wealth of its analogies determines the direction of the transcendence that lies at root of the human *we*. This transcendence, however, belongs to the structure of the human *I*; it is not in principle opposed to the personal subjectivity of the human being, but in principle corresponds to it. This does not mean, of course, that social life is a realm free from conflict. We know only too well from experience that just the opposite is true. In *The Acting Person*, I attempted to point out some varieties of such conflict, merely indicating their different forms and scope.[23] Nevertheless, in principle the social dimension of community enters compatibly into the whole tendency toward self-fulfillment proper to human subjectivity. The common good, as the objective basis of this dimension, represents a greater fullness of value than the individual good of each separate *I* in a particular community. It, therefore, has a superior character—and in this character it corresponds to the subjective transcendence of the person. The common good's superior character and the greater fullness of value it represents derive ultimately from the fact that the good of each of the subjects of a community that calls itself a *we* is more fully expressed and more fully actualized in the common good. Through the common good, therefore, the human *I* more fully and more profoundly discovers itself precisely in a human *we*.

The common good is often a difficult good; perhaps it is even so in principle. We Poles know from our own history how much the common good we call "Poland" or "our homeland" has at times cost particular individuals and even whole generations of our countrymen and -women. The amount of effort expended in achieving the common good, the amount of sacrifice of individual goods—to the point of exile, imprisonment, and death—testifies to the greatness and superiority of this good. The situations mentioned here by way of example (and very telling ones indeed, especially the extreme situations) are convincing proof of the truth that the common good conditions the individual goods of the members of the community, the human *we*. In extreme situations, it seems as though in the lived experience of certain members of the community those individual goods tend to lose their reason of being without the common good. This does not mean, however, that the sacrifice of oneself or one's life for the common good comes down to a simple "tipping of the scales" in favor of the common good over the good of the individual in one community or another.

Because the common good appears as superior, and as such corresponds to the transcendence of the person, confronting the person's conscience and either agreeing with it or giving rise to conflict, the question of the common good must be a central issue for social ethics. The history of societies and the evolution of social systems show that we are constantly struggling to attain the "true" common good that corresponds to the essence of both the social community proper to the human *we* and the personal transcendence proper to the human *I*. The historical facts tell also, however, of the repeated emergence of various kinds of utilitarianism, totalitarianism, and social egoism. Already in the smallest and most basic human *we*, marriage and the family, we find signs of these different deviations—proportionate, of course, to this community and its particular nature. As the multiplicity of human *I*'s increases, social community, the unity proper to the human *we*, becomes more difficult, obviously on different levels. But I already said that the common good is a difficult good.

The privileged status of this good, the reason for its superiority in relation to individual goods, derives, as I said, from the fact that the good of each of the subjects of the community, which defines and experiences itself as a *we* on the basis of the common good, is more fully expressed and more fully actualized in that good. This also accounts for the fact of social community, the fact of the constitution of a *we* by many human *I*'s. In itself, this fact is essentially free from utilitarianism; it lies within the realm of the objective and authentically experienced truth of the good, which is also the truth of conscience. In behalf of this truth, human beings as members of a community embrace the hardships connected with the realization of the common good—at times even to the point of the extreme situations mentioned above. In behalf of the same truth of the common good, however, they also achieve all those values that go to make up the true and inviolable good of the person. This finds particular expression in our own day, as evidenced in numerous declarations and actions. Community, the human *we*, in its various dimensions, signifies a human multiplicity with the kind of structure in which the person as a subject is maximally actualized. This, too, will be the meaning of the common good in its various analogies, this the reason for its superiority, which is experienced by the personal subject at times dramatically, but always in a basically ethical way.

We—as I said at the outset—does not signify just the simple fact of a human multi-subjectivity. It refers not only to the multiplicity of human *I*'s, but also to the special subjectivity of this multiplicity, or at least to a decided tendency toward the achievement of such a subjectivity. This is obviously a diversified tendency, which should be understood and realized in proportion to the different *we*'s and in accord with the specific communal nature proper to each of them. This tendency, together with the resulting realization of the subjectivity of the multiplicity, develops in one way in the case of a *we* such as marriage or the family, in another in the case of a particular circle, association, or social group, and in still another in the case of a nation, a country, or, finally, all humankind (the term "human family" also speaks very eloquently in this regard). In these different dimensions, the human *I*'s display a readiness not only to think of themselves in categories of a *we* but also to realize whatever is essential for the *we*, for social community. In the context of such community, therefore, and in keeping with its human essence, they also display a readiness to realize the subjectivity of the many, and, in the universal dimension, the subjectivity of all—for this is what a complete realization of the human *we* entails. It seems that only on the basis of this kind of social community, one in which a factual multi-subjectivity develops in the direction of the subjectivity of the many, can we perceive in the human *we* an authentic *communio personarum*.

We all know, however, how many obstacles and counter-dispositions stand in the way of this readiness, prevailing over it from various sides. We also know how much we are continually on the road to realizing the human *we* in different realms, a road that in so many places winds both backward and forward, depending on what holds sway in different periods and on how the balance of the realization of the different *we*'s, and ultimately the universal *we*, evolves.

In any case, an analysis of social community points in this regard to a basic homogeneity of the personal subject and human community. That at which the development of the different *we*'s in the whole wealth of their analogies aims is a clear reflection of the human *I*, of personal human subjectivity, rather than something opposed to this subjectivity. And if it happens to be opposed, human beings as subjects must institute reforms. The social community of the *we* is given to us not only as a fact but also always as a task. All of this, in turn, confirms that the subject as a person has a distinctive priority in relation to community. Otherwise it would be impossible to defend not just the autoteleology of the human self, but even the teleology of the human being.

2.4. ALIENATION AS THE ANTITHESIS OF PARTICIPATION

The above analysis of interpersonal community and social community seems to entail a number of consequences. First of all, the concept of community cannot be used univocally, since it refers to different kinds of realities. The reality of social community cannot be completely reduced to the reality of interpersonal community, nor can the latter be reduced to the former. Between the *I—thou* relationship and the *we* relationship there exists a difference of profiles that seems to extend to the very roots of the two relationships. One can only say—and even should say—that the *I—thou* relationship exists within various *we* relationships, which do not and certainly should not annihilate the *I—thou* relationship, but should rather facilitate and promote it. Similarly, one can and should say that various types of *we* relationships run through the *I—thou* relationship. The social and interpersonal dimensions of community in various ways mutually permeate, imply, and even condition one another. Still, the profiles of these relationships remain basically different and separate. From the normative point of view, we should strive to develop, maintain, and expand *I—thou* and *we* relationships in their authentic forms. This means working to bring about the most harmonious disposition of communal and personal life possible, to which the well known principle of subsidiarity (*principium subsidiarietatis*) also refers.

Secondly, when viewed in the context of the preceding discussion, the meaning of participation and also of alienation as its antithesis takes on greater clarity. While noting the different kinds of community that occur in *I—thou* and in *we* relationships, the separate dimensions of interpersonal and social community, I have maintained throughout this analysis that the human being as a person serves as a basis of analogy with respect to them. Moreover, it seems that an analysis of community from the point of view of the personal subjectivity of the human being—as I presented (though merely in outline) above—allows us to establish certain basic tenets concerning community, i.e., concerning the discovery of the very patterns of communal reality. The reversal of this order seems not so much dangerous for the truth of the image in question as quite simply impossible. We can speak meaningfully of community only in the light of persons, which means only in the context of the person as the proper subject of existence and activity, both personal and communal, and only in relation to the personal subjectivity of the human being, because only this aspect allows us to grasp the essential property of human *I*'s and their relationships, both interpersonal and social. And that is precisely why the level of the subject (which is nevertheless an objective level from the epistemological and methodological point of view) would seem to allow for a fuller understanding of both participation and alienation.

In viewing alienation as the opposite or antithesis of participation, I have in mind the person and both dimensions of community, the *we* and the *I—thou*. In each of these dimensions, participation is connected with transcendence, and so it is grounded in the person as a subject and in the person's innate tendency toward self-actualization, toward self-fulfillment. We fulfill ourselves as persons through interpersonal *I—thou* relationships, as well as through a relation to the common good, which allows us to exist and act together with others as a *we*. These two different relations and their corresponding communal dimensions also entail two different profiles of participation, which I outlined at least partially in *The Acting Person*. That sketch, as I already mentioned, needs to be analyzed and developed in greater detail, which I have done to some extent in this essay.

The present analysis tends to confirm me in the conviction that participation should be seen as a property of human beings, corresponding to their personal subjectivity. This subjectivity does not enclose people within themselves or make them impenetrable monads, but—on the contrary—opens them up to others in a way proper to a person. Participation, then, both in the case of the interpersonal community *I—thou* and in the case of the social community *we*, can and should be seen as an authentic expression of personal transcendence and as a subjective confirmation of this transcendence in the person. It might seem as though transcendence toward a common good would lead us away from ourselves, or, more precisely, would lead us all away from the human being. A thorough analysis of this good, however, shows that the human being is deeply inscribed in the true meaning of the common good—the human being not as conceived in the species definition, but the human being as a person and subject. For this reason, too, the true meaning of the common good, its full "integrity" (*honestas*), is and must be in science a central issue for social ethics and in practice a matter of the greatest responsibility.

Although in their profiles *I—thou* and *we* communities are distinct and mutually irreducible to one another, in the experience and development of communal life they must permeate and mutually condition one another. The fully authentic human being, the human being as a person, the one whose personal identity is disclosed through *I—thou* relationships to the extent that those relationships have the profile of a genuine *communio personarum*, is the one who is and must be permanently inscribed in the true meaning of the common good if that good is to conform to its definition and essence. That is why in *The Acting Person* it seemed possible to define participation (in its social profile) as a property by virtue of which human beings tend (also) toward self-fulfillment and fulfill themselves by acting and existing together with others. Although this definition is based on the person as a subject rather than on community—on the *I* rather than on the *we*—and, consequently, seems partial and incomplete, it nevertheless allows us to discover the social profile of community equally well. Participation thus understood conditions the whole authenticity of the human *we*, a *we* that develops objectively on the basis of a relation to the common good but that also—on the basis of this same relation—tends toward the development of the true subjectivity of all who enter into the social community. The passage from multi-subjectivity to the subjectivity of the many is the proper and full meaning of the human *we*. Participation, understood as a property of each *I*, by virtue of which that *I* fulfills itself by existing and acting "together with others," is not opposed to such a meaning of social community. In fact, it seems that only when understood in this way can participation ensure both that meaning and, more importantly, the realization of social community: the realization of the human *we* in its full authenticity as the true subjectivity of the many.

Participation in this sense—as a property of the person, by virtue of which each person is and remains himself or herself in a social community—seems to be a necessary condition for an authentic *communio personarum*, both in *we* relationships and in interpersonal *I—thou* relationships. Both of these relationships involve openness, and both develop within the context of the transcendence proper to the person. An *I—thou* relationship opens one human being directly to another. To participate means in this case to turn toward another self in the context of personal transcendence and, therefore, to turn toward the full truth of that human being. In this sense, then, to participate means to turn toward humanity. This humanity is given in the *I—thou* relationship not as the abstract idea of the human being (in *The Acting Person*, I treat this problem as belonging instead to the epistemological foundations), but as a *thou* for an *I*. Participation in this relationship is equivalent to the realization of an interpersonal community in which the personal subjectivity of the *thou* reveals itself through the *I* (in some sense reciprocally as well). Most importantly, however, this is a community in which the personal subjectivity of both the *I* and the *thou* are anchored, safeguarded, and developed.

Alienation is the opposite of participation; it is its antithesis. The concept of alienation, as we know, was employed in Marxist philosophy, but even independently of this it has become an aspect of modern anthropology, of contemporary thought on the human being. What, then, is alienation? How should its essence be conceived? Regardless of all that has been said concerning what was or is a real or supposed form of alienation, it is always worthwhile and even fundamental to ask what alienation is in itself. In fact, only an answer to this question can validate our judgments concerning the actual forms of alienation, that is, our judgments concerning what was, is, or may be an instance of alienation.[24]

When I say that alienation is the antithesis of participation, this should be understood in the light of what I said earlier in formulating the state of the question of the second part of this essay on the person. I said there that the whole problematic of alienation refers not to the human being as an individual of the species, and thus not to the human being as conceived in the species definition, but to the human being as a personal subject. I take the position that alienation is essentially a personalistic problem, and, in this sense, clearly both a humanistic and an ethical one as well.

As the antithesis of participation, alienation contributes to or (depending on the alienating factor) creates an occasion for depriving people in some respect of the possibility of fulfilling themselves in community, either in the social community of a *we* or in the interpersonal community of an *I—thou*. Alienation can and in many ways does occur in both of these dimensions of community. In the social dimension, the presence of alienating factors is apparent when the multiplicity of human subjects, each of whom is a particular *I*, is unable to develop appropriately in the direction of an authentic *we*. The social process, which ought to lead to the genuine subjectivity of all, is then checked or even reversed, because human beings cannot find themselves as subjects in this process. Social life goes on as though beyond them—not so much in opposition to them but rather "at their expense." They, in turn, although existing and even acting "together with others," do not fulfill themselves in this life, either because they have estranged themselves or because the society, through some faulty structure, does not give them a basis for self-fulfillment or even denies them the rights needed for it. This, of course, is not a complete and exhaustive picture, but only an outline, suggesting an understanding of alienation as the antithesis of participation in the social sense. Depending on its proportions, this type of alienation constricts or even annihilates the human *we*. And it does so not just with respect to one *I* or another (as in the case of estrangement), but—as history and the contemporary era teach—in dimensions of whole social groups, societies, and classes, and even entire nations. I am not attempting here to analyze this social phenomenon; my only concern at the moment is to apprehend the feature that will allow us to formulate a more precise definition of the essence of alienation.

In an analogical form—but, of course, while preserving the whole distinctness of this relationship, which I discussed earlier—we can detect this feature in the interpersonal dimension of community, in relationships of the *I—thou* type. Although this dimension is generally not commensurate with the *we* dimension quantitatively, it is sometimes even more painful qualitatively, since human life is probably lived out more in *I—thou* dimensions than in *we* dimensions. In the *I—thou* dimension, alienation as the antithesis of participation signifies a constriction or annihilation of everything through which one human being is another self for another human being. This subverts the lived experience of the truth of the humanity, the truth of the essential worth of the person, in the human *thou*. The *I* remains severed and disconnected from the *thou*, and so it is not fully disclosed to itself either. In such interpersonal relationships, the "neighbor" also disappears and all that remains is the "other," or even a "stranger" or an outright "enemy." This, too, however, is only a kind of outline, suggesting the meaning of alienation in the interpersonal dimension. Community in this dimension becomes distorted and disappears in proportion to the disappearance of the lived experience of humanity, which is the experience that authentically draws people together and unites them.

By taking the position that in both dimensions of community alienation is the antithesis of participation, I wish to emphasize here from the negative side the same point that formed the crux of this entire analysis: that the reality of human community in both of its dimensions, the *I—thou* as well as the *we*, develops in the context of the personal subjectivity of the human being, and develops in relation to it specifically and primarily. Alienation as the antithesis of participation, and thus its opposite or negation, does not so much "dehumanize" the human being as an individual of the species as it threatens the person as a subject. On the other hand, participation as the antithesis of alienation confirms and emphasizes the person as a subject. In this sense, participation may also be regarded as a distinctive "property" of the person, for it fosters the person's self-fulfillment both in interhuman and in social relationships. In each dimension, it safeguards the transcendence proper to the person.

My reflections are drawing to a close. I do not intend to analyze alienation itself in this essay. What I said about alienation above is neither a description of the phenomenon nor an attempt to develop it systematically. As we know, a great deal has been written about this topic. The concept of alienation has become an important and even fundamental category of contemporary thought on the human being. At the same time, despite the numerous pronouncements concerning what alienation is—even those known from Marxist philosophy alone—there is no completely established view concerning what alienation is, or what constitutes its essence.

I have not dealt here with this topic *ex professo*. The real purpose of these analyses collected under the title "The Person: Subject and Community" was to investigate the relations that occur between community (interpersonal and social) and the personal subjectivity of the human being. Toward the end, however, I saw a possibility of proposing a reduction of the various current descriptions of alienation (which contain only an assertion or suggestion that alienation occurs in certain situations) to the realm of the person as subject and community. I believe that by means of such a reduction—and the present analysis can also serve as a tool to this end—the fuller essence of alienation is revealed. And only with a fuller grasp of what alienation essentially is do we have a basis for saying what it is in particular instances or situations, and why.

In the second part of this essay, I mentioned a number of times that we cannot speak of alienation on the basis of the species concept "human being," but only in relation to the personal subjectivity of the human being. This is a preliminary assertion, in a sense still intuitive. Nevertheless, I believe that this analysis of the personal subjectivity of the human being, carried out here in the context of the person as subject and community, can by means of this intuition also contribute to the investigation of the nature of alienation.

NOTES

1. This meeting took place on 16 December 1970 at the Catholic University of Lublin. For a brief account of the discussion, see the opening section of "The Personal Structure of Self-Determination" 187 ff. above. —Trans.

2. Karol Wojtyla, *The Acting Person*, trans. Andrzej Potocki, ed. Anna-Teresa Tymieniecka (Boston: Reidel, 1979); originally published in Polish as *Osoba i czyn* (Krakow: Polskie Tow. Teologiczne, 1969).

3. *Analecta Cracoviensia* 5–6 (1973–1974): 49–263. The articles include Andrzej Szostek, "Wprowadzenie" ["Introduction"] 49–51; Karol Wojtyla, "Wypowiedz wstepna w czasie dyskusji nad 'Osoba i czynem' w KUL 16 XII 1970" ["Introductory Remarks at the Discussion of *The Acting Person*, Catholic University of Lublin, 16 December 1970"] 53–55; Mieczyslaw A. Krapiec, "Ksiazka Kard. Karola Wojtyly monografia osoby jako podmiotu moralnosci" ["Card. Karol Wojtyla's Monograph on the Person as the Subject of Morality"] 57–61; Jerzy Kalinowski, "Metafizyka i fenomenologia osoby ludzkiej. Pytania wywolane przez 'Osobe i czyn'" ["The Metaphysics and Phenomenology of the Human Person: Questions Evoked by *The Acting Person*"] 63–71; Stanislaw Kaminski, "Jak filozofowac o czlowieku?" ["How Does One Philosophize About the Human Being?"] 73–79; Kazimierz Klosak, "Teoria doswiadczenia czlowieka w ujeciu Kard. Karola Wojtyly" ["The Theory of the Experience of the Human Being According to Card. Karol Wojtyla"] 81–84; Jozef Tischner, "Metodologiczna strona dziela 'Osoba i czyn'" ["The Methodological Side of *The Acting Person*"] 85–89; Marian Jaworski, "Koncepcja antropologii filozoficznej w ujeciu Kard. Karola Wojtyly. Proba odczytania w oparciu o studium 'Osoba i czyn'" ["An Attempt to Interpret Card. Karol Wojtyla's Conception of Philosophical Anthropology Based on *The Acting Person*"] 91–106; Tadeusz Styczen, "Metoda antropologii filozoficznej w 'Osobie i czynie' Kard. Karola Wojtyly" ["The Method of Philosophical Anthropology in Card. Karol Wojtyla's *The Acting Person*"] 107–115; Roman Forycki, "Antropologia w ujeciu Kard. Karola Wojtyly na podstawie ksiazki 'Osoba i czyn', Krakow 1969" ["The Anthroplogy of Card. Karol Wojtyla, Based on the Book *The Acting Person*, Krakow 1969"] 117–124; Mieczyslaw Gogacz, "Hermeneutyka 'Osoby i czynu'" ["The Hermeneutics of *The Acting Person*"] 125–138; S. Grygiel, "Hermeneutyka czynu oraz nowy model swiadomosci" ["A Hermeneutics of Action and a New Model of Consciousness"] 139–151; Antoni B. Stepien, "Fenomenologia tomizujaca w ksiazce 'Osoba i czyn'"

["Phenomenology Made Thomistic in the Book *The Acting Person*"] 153–157; Andrzej Poltawski, "Czlowiek a swiadomosc w zwiazku z ksiazka Kard. Karola Wojtyly 'Osoba i czyn'" ["The Human Being and Consciousness in Card. Karol Wojtyla's Book *The Acting Person*"] 159–175; Jerzy Galkowski, "Natura, osoba, wolnosc" ["Nature, Person, and Freedom,"] 177–182; Leszek Kuc, "Uczestnictwo w czlowieczenstwie 'innych'?" ["Participation in the Humanity of 'Others'?"] 183–190; Tadeusz Wojciechowski, "Jednosc duchowo-cielesna czlowieka w ksiazce 'Osoba i czyn'" ["The Spiritual-Physical Unity of the Human Being in the Book *The Acting Person*"] 191–199; Zofia J. Zdybicka, "Praktyczne aspekty dociekan przedstawionych w dziele 'Osoba i czyn'" ["The Practical Aspects of the Inquiries Presented in the Work *The Acting Person*"] 201–205; Jerzy Stroba, "Refleksje duszpasterskie" ["Pastoral Reflections"] 207–209; T. Kukolowicz, "'Osoba i czyn' a wychowanie w rodzinie" ["*The Acting Person* and Education in the Family"] 211–221; W. Poltawska, "Koncepcja samoposiadania—podstawa psychoterapii obiektywizujacej w swietle ksiazki 'Osoba i czyn'" ["The Concept of Self-Possession as the Basis for an Objectifying Form of Psychotherapy in Light of the Book *The Acting Person*"] 223–241; Karol Wojtyla, "Slowo koncowe" ["Concluding Remarks"] 243–263.

4. See, for example, "The Personal Structure of Self-Determination" 187–195 above, as well as "Czyn a przezycie" ["Action and Lived Experience"], presented at a symposium on "Phenomenology and Metaphysics" (typescript). See also "The Problem of the Separation of Experience from the Act in Ethics" 23–44 above.

5. See Mieczyslaw A. Krapiec, *I—Man: An Outline of Philosophical Anthropology*, trans. Marie Lescoe, Andrew Woznicki, Theresa Sandok et al. (New Britain: Mariel, 1983). In this work, the self, understood as a subsistent subject, is found in the point of departure and forms the basis of philosophical anthropology. Krapiec gives us an outline of a complete philosophy of the human being. In *The Acting Person*, on the other hand, I use analyses connected with the experience of the human self as a basis for bringing to light the human being as a person. Still another approach appears, for example, in Jozef Tischner's "Aksjologiczne podstawy doswiadczenia 'ja' jako calosci cielesno-przestrzennej" ["The Axiological Foundations of the Experience of the Self as a Physical-Spatial Whole"] *Logos i Ethos: Rozprawy filozoficzne*, ed. Marian Jaworski et al. (Krakow: Polskie Tow. Teologiczne, 1971) 33–82. Mieczyslaw Gogacz, one of the participants in the discussion on *The Acting Person*, presented a paper on the hermeneutics of *The Acting Person*. He later returned to this theme in a paper presented at an interdisciplinary symposium on "The Hermeneutics of Theological Anthropology," sponsored by the Warsaw Academy of Catholic Theology, 15–16 February 1973 (for the published version of this paper, see "Filozofia czlowieka wobec teologii" ["The Philosophy of the Human Being in Relation to Theology"], *Studia Theologica Varsaviensia* 12.1 [1974]: 177–192). In addition, Gogacz has published a number of essays in his book *Wokol problemu osoby* [*On the Problem of the Person*] (Warsaw, 1974), which also contains the *Analecta Cracoviensia* paper from the discussion on *The Acting Person*. Having followed the progression of his thought in these essays, and in the light of what I already said concerning his paper "A Hermeneutics of *The Acting Person*" in my "Concluding Remarks" to the discussion, I feel a need to reiterate my assessment of Gogacz's position. It seems to me that he has misinterpreted the basic idea in *The Acting Person*; this is especially evident in his book *Wokol problem osoby*. In his *Studia Theologica Varsaviensia* article on my book *The Acting Person*, we read as follows: "The person is, according to this book, the *subject* (my emphasis) of the

conscious and creative activities, or actions, of the human being, which manifest the person externally" (190). What I actually said in *The Acting Person* is that the person is principally the agent of action (see Chapter Two, "An Analysis of Efficacy in the Light of Human Dynamism" 60–101).

6. In its basic conception, the whole of *The Acting Person* is grounded on the premise that *operari sequitur esse*: the act of personal existence has its direct consequences in the activity of the person (i.e., in action). And so action, in turn, is the basis for disclosing and understanding the person. Without commenting on the schema according to which Gogacz divides theories of the person into existentialistic and essentialistic, I question only—as I did in my "Concluding Remarks" to the discussion—the legitimacy of his interpretation of *The Acting Person*.

7. See Chapter Five, "Integration and the Soma," and Chapter Six, "Personal Integration and the Psyche," of Part III, "The Integration of the Person in Action," *The Acting Person* 189–258.

8. See Chapter One, "The Acting Person in the Aspect of Consciousness," *The Acting Person* 25–59; and Andrzej Poltawski, "Czyn a swiadomosc" ["Action and Consciousness"], *Logos i Ethos* 83.

9. See Roman Ingarden, *Man and Value*, trans. Arthur Szylewicz (Washington: Catholic U of America P, 1983).

10. See Chapter Three, "The Personal Structure of Self-Determination," *The Acting Person* 105–148.

11. This expression sounds a little awkward in English. We would normally say "to perform an action." In Polish, however, the same verb (*spelniac*) is used in the phrases "to perform an action" (*spelniac czyn*) and "to fulfill oneself" (*spelniac siebie*). *Spelniac* literally means to bring to completion or fullness. Wojtyla here is playing on the similarity of the phrases to bring home his point that when we fulfill (perform) an action we simultaneously fulfill ourselves as well; in other words, two types of fulfillment are going on here. This nuance unfortunately gets lost when *spelniac czyn* is rendered as "to perform an action," which is how it would normally be translated. —Trans.

12. See Chapter Four, "Self-Determination and Fulfillment," *The Acting Person* 149–186.

13. See Part Two, "The Transcendence of the Person in the Action," *The Acting Person* 103–186.

14. See Chapter Seven, "Intersubjectivity by Participation," *The Acting Person* 261–300.

15. At the discussion of *The Acting Person*, Leszek Kuc presented a paper entitled "Participation in the Humanity of 'Others'?" (see also my "Concluding Remarks," in which I comment on this paper). At the moment, however, I am concerned with the view that Kuc represents with regard to the question of person as community, a view he expressed not only in the above paper, but also in "Przyczynek do konstrukcji tematyki antropologii chrzescijanskiej" ["A Contribution to the Construction of the Thematic of Christian Anthropology"], *Studia Theologica Varsaviensia* 12.1 (1974): 289–302), which he presented at the interdisciplinary symposium mentioned earlier, and in his article "Zagadnienia antropologii chrzescijanskiej" ["The Questions of Christian Anthropology"], *Studia Theologica Varsaviensia* 9.2 (1971): 95–109. In these works, Kuc tends more to hint at his position than to present a full account of it. For example, in the *Analecta Cracoviensia* article we read: "It is precisely here, in this presence of other human beings in the concrete person, that we find the reality, the ontic

basis, of community. One can and should, in my opinion, treat every human person simultaneously as a separate and autonomous person and as a really existing and acting community of persons" (187). I would like to add, however, that this in no way removes the need to investigate this community as an objective unity of a real multiplicity of personal subjects. Just as the personal subjectivity of the human being is an objective reality, so, too, is—in each given instance—the multiplicity of those subjects and their community or unity through the common good, primarily in relationships of the *we* type, as will be shown in the course of this analysis.

16. In this sense, we can also speak of that person-community nexus to which Kuc refers in the above mentioned articles.

17. Marian Jaworski, in the essay "Czlowiek a Bog. Zagadnienie relacji znaczeniowej pomiedzy osoba ludzka i Bogiem a problem ateizmu" ["The Human Being and God: The Question of a Meaningful Relation Between the Human Person and God, and the Problem of Atheism"], *Logos i Ethos*, writes: "Among the essential elements that distinguish a human person should be included a relation to a *thou*" (127). This entire article is devoted to the relation of the human being (the human *I*) to God as an unconditional *Thou* for the human *I* and as the basis of the human being's personal mode of existence. While taking note of this position, I wish to add that I shall not be analyzing this important relation in the present essay but shall confine my analysis to the area of interhuman relations.

18. I have dealt with this issue particularly in connection with my work on Max Scheler's ethics; see my *Ocena mozliwosci zbudowania etyki chrzescijanskiej przy zalozeniazch systemu Maksa Schelera* [*An Evaluation of the Possibility of Constructing a Christian Ethics on the Principles of Max Scheler's System*] (Lublin: Tow. Naukowe KUL, 1959); "System etyczny Maxa Schelera jako srodek do opracowania etyki chrzescijanskiej" ["Max Scheler's Ethical System as a Means of Developing Christian Ethics"], *Polonia Sacra* 6 (1953–1954): 143–161; "Ewangeliczna zasada nasladowania: Nauka objawienia a system etyczny Maxa Schelera" ["The Evangelical Basis of Imitation: The Teachings of Revelation and Max Scheler's Ethical System"], *Ateneum Kaplanski* 55 (1957): 57–67.

19. I discuss the formation of the *I-thou* relationship in an analytic way in my essay "Participation or Alienation?" 197–207 above.

20. This principle forms the basis of my ethical study *Love and Responsibility*, trans. H. T. Willetts (New York: Farrar, 1981), originally published in Polish as *Milosc i odpowiedzialnosc* (Lublin: Tow. Naukowe KUL, 1960).

21. See also *Gaudium et Spes* 12: "But God did not create the human being as a solitaire, for from the beginning 'male and female God created them' (Gen. 1:27), and their union is the primary form of a community of persons (*communio personarum*)."

22. See also *Gaudium et Spes* 24: "When the Lord Jesus prays to the Father 'that all may be one...as we are one' (John 17:21–22), opening inaccessible perspectives to human reason, he reveals that there is a certain likeness between the union of the divine persons and the union of the children of God joined in truth and love."

23. See especially "Individualism and Anti-Individualism" (271–276) and, for an analysis of attitudes, "'Authentic' Attitudes" (283–287) and "'Nonauthentic' Attitudes" (288–291), in Chapter Seven of *The Acting Person*.

24. See on this topic Zbigniew Majchrzyk's study, "Problem alienacji u polskich marksistow" ["The Problem of Alienation According to Polish Marxists"], diss., philosophy, Catholic University of Lublin.

17

The Problem of the Constitution of Culture Through Human Praxis

Let me begin by expressing my gratitude to the distinguished Rector of the Catholic University in Milan, Professor Giuseppe Lazzatti, and to the whole university community. Thank you for this invitation, which for me has more than just a personal significance. For I realize that I am standing here in a place that arose from the most authentic roots of Christianity and the Church: St. Ambrose and St. Charles Borromeo are among the milestones of its history. At the same time, I realize that I am standing here on a path of the great radiation of Christianity and of the culture for which Christianity forms an indispensable leaven (*fermentum*). Over the course of history, so many Poles have walked this path: Nicolas Copernicus, who had ties with the universities of Bologna and Padua, Stanislaw Hozjusz [Cardinal President of the Council of Trent], Jan Kochanowski, the greatest Polish poet of the Renaissance period, and so many others.

The Catholic University of the Sacred Heart in Milan is a contemporary expression of the fruition of the leaven (*fermentum*) that the Gospel, Christianity, and the Church continue to be for culture today. In saying this, I am also thinking of the Catholic University of Lublin, which was established at about the same time but which, due to adverse circumstances, was prevented from achieving the kind of expansion we see in Milan, and also in Rome, in Piacenza, and wherever separate branches of the Milanian *Cattolica* are found. Regardless of these facilitating or inhibiting

Karol Wojtyla, "Problem konstytuowania sie kultury poprzez ludzka *praxis,*" *Ethos* 2.8 (1989): 39–49. A paper presented at the Catholic University of the Sacred Heart, Milan, Italy, 18 March 1977.

factors, however, at the basis of both universities lies the same will to permeate with the Gospel the contemporary culture of societies that have behind them many centuries of this same living and life-giving tradition. As Bishop of the Church of Krakow, it would be hard for me not to mention here the traditions of the oldest university in Poland, the Jagiellonian University in Krakow, which traces its origin back to the year 1364. For many centuries, the Jagiellonian also operated the oldest school of theology in Poland. It was this university that was the center of the contacts I mentioned earlier. From it, here to Italy, came Copernicus and others, who marked out the historical paths of Christian and humanistic culture.

One cannot tread these paths without due piety. One cannot remain in these places without being moved. I wish at the beginning of my remarks to pay tribute to this great tradition that links us down through the centuries and also to convey expressions of unity from Catholic institutions in Poland.

1. THE CONTEMPORARY CONTROVERSY OVER THE *HUMANUM*

I have chosen the problem of the constitution of culture through human praxis as the topic of this talk largely for the reasons indicated above. Taking into consideration such motivation—at once situational and historical—I would like in addressing this topic to give expression to my main interests, which I have discussed not only in various publications in my native tongue, but also already here on Italian soil, where I have had the good fortune to be invited a number of times. Developing the themes of my Polish works, I spoke first at a conference in commemoration of the 700th anniversary of St. Thomas Aquinas (Rome—Naples 1974) on the topic of "The Personal Structure of Self-Determination,"[1] and then later I presented the inaugural lecture *"Teoria—praxis: un tema umano e cristiano"*[2] at an international conference in Genoa (September 1976). Those two presentations, especially perhaps the latter, may serve as a basis for my reflections here today on human praxis, which, I believe, provides us with the most direct route to understanding the *humanum* in its deepest plenitude, richness, and authenticity.

The effort to arrive at such an understanding of the *humanum* has perhaps never before been so central to the culture that unites us through common sources. We know that it is a Christian culture. The mission of

Europe throughout its two-thousand-year history is connected with this culture, a point that has been emphasized by Paul VI,[3] the 1974 Symposium of European Bishops,[4] and others as well. The Second Vatican Council in its Pastoral Constitution devoted a separate section to the question of culture (*Gaudium et Spes* 53–63), a fact that is but an epiphenomenon, a derivative manifestation, of all that Council did to articulate the Christian meaning of the *humanum*, to establish the truth concerning the human person and the universal vocation of the human being (see *Gaudium et Spes* 12–22).

In the early centuries of Christianity, the category of the person was introduced into the teachings of the Church as a means of achieving a somewhat more precise understanding of the revealed *divinum*. Today, so many centuries later, this category forms a key concept in the contemporary controversy over the *humanum*. This is not a controversy within the Church or within Christianity, or even within non-Christian religions. It is mainly a controversy with atheism, which most often denies the *divinum* in the name of the *humanum*. At the same time, while rejecting a relation to God as constitutive for the human person (who is an image of God), this atheism in its Marxist guise proposes a collective form of existence for the *humanum* as both the fundamental and the final form. Given this historical context, the category of the person must become a key concept in the controversy over the *humanum*, a controversy in which Christianity also has a role to play.

My reflections here on the constitution of culture through human praxis arise within the context of this controversy as well. They are intimately linked to an understanding of the human being as a person: a self-determining subject. Culture develops principally within this dimension, the dimension of self-determining subjects. Culture is basically oriented not so much toward the creation of human *products* as toward the creation of the human *self*, which then radiates out into the world of products.

2. HOW SHOULD THE PRIORITY OF THE HUMAN BEING WITH RESPECT TO PRAXIS BE UNDERSTOOD?

It will be helpful for me here to draw upon a basic element of St. Thomas' philosophy of activity. I referred to it already at the Genoa conference on the topic of "Teoria—Praxis" in showing that this topic is Christian because it is profoundly human. As I understand St. Thomas' thought, human activity (action) is simultaneously *transitive* and *intran-*

sitive.[5] It is transitive insofar as it tends *beyond the subject*, seeks an expression and effect in the external world, and is objectified in some product. It is intransitive, on the other hand, insofar as it *remains in the subject*, determines the subject's immanent quality or value, and constitutes the subject's essentially human *fieri*. In acting, we not only perform actions, but we also become ourselves through those actions—we fulfill ourselves in them.

The priority of the human being as the subject of activity has fundamental significance for the constitution of culture through human praxis. I should specify what I mean by this *priority*. I am not concerned here with the question of anthropogenesis. I am also not simply engaging in a direct critique of the Marxist thesis that work produces or is somehow the origin of the human being.[6] This must be resolved on the basis of the direct evidence. Work, or human praxis, is possible to the extent that the human being already exists: *operari sequitur esse*. The priority of the human being as the subject of essentially human activity—a priority in the metaphysical sense—belongs to the concept of praxis for the simple reason that the human being determines praxis. It would be absurd to understand the matter the other way around and accept some sort of subjectively indeterminate praxis, which would then define or determine its subject. It is also not possible to think of praxis in an *a priori* manner, as though this "quasi-absolute" category would give rise—by way of evolution—to the particular forms of activity that define their agent. If we accept as a basic premise that activity (praxis) most fully allows us to understand the agent, that action most fully reveals the human being as a person, then such an epistemological stance entails the conviction and certainty that the human being, or subject, has priority in relation to activity, or praxis, which, in turn, allows us most fully to understand the subject.

But this is not the only type of priority I have in mind here. I am thinking not only of priority in the metaphysical sense but also of priority in what might be called the praxiological sense. This is where the distinction between the transitive (*transitens*) and the intransitive (*intransitens*) in human action has key significance. Whatever we make in our action, whatever effects or products we bring about in it, we always simultaneously "make ourselves" in it as well (if I may be permitted to put it thus). We express ourselves, we in some way shape ourselves, we in a certain sense "create" ourselves. In acting, we actualize ourselves, we fulfill ourselves. We bring to a certain—albeit partial—fulfillment (*actus*) both what and who we are potentially (*in potentia*). From the perspective of experience and phenomenological insight, this is the meaning of the term action in the category of *actus*: *actus humanus*.[7] The priority of the human being in the metaphysical sense means that praxis presupposes the human being as its subject, and not vice versa. The priority of the human being in the praxiological sense requires us to reduce the very essence of praxis to the human being: the essence of praxis consists in realizing ourselves and, at the same time, in making the nonhuman reality outside ourselves more human. Only praxis understood in this sense provides a basis for speaking of culture as a connatural reality in relation to the human being.

If in our analysis of human praxis we wish to affirm this reality and not negate it (even while seeming to affirm it), we must radically reassess all formulations that speak of the transformation or modification of the world as the sole purpose of human praxis. More importantly, we must reassess all programs that view the whole of activity between the poles of production and consumption. While not denying the fundamentality of these categories as poles of economic thought, and even their great usefulness given appropriate assumptions, we must be careful in this way of thinking and speaking not to allow the human being to become an epiphenomenon and, in a sense, a product. If culture is to be constituted through human praxis, we cannot agree to such an epiphenomenal, economistic, or productionistic view of the human being and human action. We must ensure in this thought the priority of the human being both in the metaphysical and in the praxiological sense. Only with a strictly defined way of understanding human praxis can we speak of the constitution of culture through it.

Kant recognized this truth and expressed it in his famous second categorical imperative: *act in such a way that the person is always an end and never a means of your action*. It should be noted that Kant made this statement in the intellectual climate of the epoch that ushered in our own and that is especially fruitful in it. Kant's opposition to utilitarianism and its consequences, including its economistic ones, brings the personalism he expressed in the second imperative into proximity with a conviction that Christianity has always maintained. Vatican II gave classic expression to this conviction when it said that the human being is "the one creature on earth that God willed for itself" (*Gaudium et Spes* 24). Human beings, as willed by the Creator for themselves, may not be deprived of their autoteleology;[8] they may not be regarded as means or tools in their own praxis, but must preserve their own proper superiority in relation to it, their priority in the praxiological sense. This superiority is synonymous with regarding the intransitive in human activity as more important than the transitive. In other words, that which conditions the value of human beings and comprises the essentially human quality of their activity is more important than that which is objectified in some product or other and serves to "transform the world" or merely exploit it.

It follows from this that the "transformation of the world" of itself is still not the sense or dimension of human praxis through which culture is constituted. Of itself, it is only culture's raw material, the material element. The essential element is that which the Council expressed in the words "to make the world a more human place," or also "to make human existence in the world more human," an element in which, in the final analysis, we must ultimately discover the human being as the subject of every and all praxis. The fact that people, no matter who they are, each and every one of them, and thus as far as possible all of them, become more human—this fact is decisive for the constitution of culture through human praxis. The fact that the various processes of socialization, stimulated by industrialization, production, and consumption, correspond proportionally to the processes of personalization (to again use the language of *Gaudium et Spes*; see section 6)—this fact is decisive for the constitution of culture through human praxis.

This obviously requires a precise differentiation of the dimensions or aspects of praxis and, even more importantly, a proper coordination of them. We know full well that material means are a necessary condition for human existence and its "humanization." Used in the right measure, they help make people's lives truly human. The lack of such a measure reduces people to a level of life beneath that worthy of a human being. We must, however, very precisely distinguish that which is merely a condition for a truly human life from that which is decisive for such a life.

What I have called here the priority of the human being in the praxiological sense corresponds closely to Gabriel Marcel's distinction between *being* and *having*. Vatican II adopted this distinction and from it derived the basic principle that "human beings are more valuable for what they are than for what they have" (*Gaudium et Spes* 35). Culture (in the authentic and full sense of the word, and not as a set of substitutes and pretexts) is constituted through human praxis to the extent that through it people become more human, and not merely acquire more means.[9] In this regard, the contemporary situation of the *humanum* carries a dramatic challenge.[10] Alongside societies and people who have an overabundance of means there exist societies and people who suffer from a lack of them, from an insufficiency of means. It goes without saying that we should work toward a just distribution of goods. This is a self-evident principle. A departure from the realization of this principle is a threat to the *humanum*. One might ask, however, whether the threat is not greater where an overabundance of means, a superfluity of what people *have*, obscures who they *are* and who they ought to be.

This is an especially critical question, perhaps the most vexing one, for the future of culture in the Atlantic world.

3. CULTURE: PRAXIS THAT BESPEAKS A CONFRONTATION WITH THE NECESSITY OF DEATH

> *"For beauty exists that we might be enticed to work,*
> *And work, that we might be resurrected."*
>
> —CYPRIAN NORWID, Dialog I, *Promethidion*

I am taking the liberty of quoting a passage from the *Promethidion* of Cyprian Norwid, whom many regard as the most deeply reflective and authentically Catholic of Polish poets. I would like to use this passage as a transition to the final stage of these reflections on the constitution of culture through human praxis. The opinion expressed a moment ago concerning Norwid's deep Catholicism is particularly justified today in the light of the teachings of Vatican II. It would be impossible in this analysis not to appeal to the texts in which the Council—like Norwid— linked work, human praxis, to the paschal mystery (see *Gaudium et Spes* 38). Only this connection seems to bring out the full meaning of culture, in which the *humanum* encounters the *mysterium*. And this is just as it should be, since the human being in so many ways is a *mysterium*—a mystery.

There can be no doubt that culture is constituted through human praxis, through human activity that expresses and in some sense reveals humanity. This assumes, of course, that culture is constituted through work and its accompanying transformation of nature or modification of the world to the extent that this transformation or modification conforms to human reason and the objective order of nature, or the world. Such activity, such work, can then be said to involve a certain radiation of humanity, by virtue of which the effects of culture are properly inscribed in the effects of nature. Despite its distinctness, culture then forms a kind of organic whole with nature. It reveals the roots of our union with nature, but also of our superior encounter with the Creator in the eternal plan, a plan in which we participate by means of reason and wisdom (see, for example, *Apostolicam Actuositatem* 7 and *Gaudium et Spes* 34). There exists in nature, or the world, an anticipation of such human activity and such a radiation of humanity through praxis. There is also in nature, or the world, a kind of readiness to put itself at our disposal: to serve human needs, to welcome within it the superior scale of human ends, to enter in some way into the human dimension and participate in human existence in the world. Still, we must constantly ask ourselves whether and to what extent work, human praxis, is not encumbered in this regard by that "bondage to corruption" under which—as St. Paul writes—"all creation has been groaning and sighing until now" (Rom. 8:21–22). Does human work, in using the riches of creation, always and in all things bear the stamp of the rational order, the stamp of a radiation of humanity? Does it not at times turn into brute plunder—dictated, moreover, primarily by an intent to mutually destroy and dominate one another?[11]

The words of the Pastoral Constitution on this topic (see *Gaudium et Spes* 4–10) seem mild in comparison with what the experts are saying, at least in the renowned reports of the Club of Rome.[12]

When Norwid writes of beauty that it exists *"that we might be enticed to work,"* he is suggesting that there are other real dimensions of human praxis through which culture is constituted. Culture cannot be connected in a simplistic way—and perhaps even in a utilitarianized way by various totalitarian programs—with the element itself of work.

When the poet speaks of beauty and enticement, he is pointing to the eternal sources of culture that spring forth from the human soul. Christianity, conscious of these sources, has always tried to observe the right balance between *actio* and *contemplatio*, a topic that was also addressed in the documents of Vatican II (see, for example, *Sacrosanctum Concilium* 2 and *Lumen Gentium* 41). Culture is constituted through human praxis to the extent that we do not become slaves of activity and of accomplishing various works, but experience wonder and awe at reality (see *Gaudium et Spes* 56), to the extent that we attain within ourselves a strong sense of the cosmos, a strong sense of the order of the world, both the macro- and the microcosm, and make them a dominant feature of our understanding, rather than merely a grand, but somehow also brutal, instrument of our exploitation.[13]

It is necessary, therefore, to go beyond all the confines of the various kinds of utilitarianism and discover within the full richness of human praxis its deep relation to truth, goodness, and beauty, a relation that has a disinterested—pure and nonutilitarian—character. This disinterestedness of the relation essentially conditions the enticement of which Norwid writes: enticement, wonder, *contemplatio*, forms the essential basis of the constitution of culture through human praxis.[14] This does not take place beyond work, beyond human activity. In fact, this activity also has the dual character of being both transitive and intransitive at the same time, as St. Thomas pointed out. And yet that which is transitive in our culturally creative activity and is expressed externally as an effect, objectification, product, or work can be said to be a result of the particular intensity of that which is intransitive and remains within our disinterested communion with truth, goodness, and beauty. This communion, its intensity, degree, and depth, is something completely internal; it is an immanent activity of the human soul, and it leaves its mark and brings forth fruit in this same dimension. It is from this communion that we mature and grow inwardly.

At the same time, this disinterested inner communion with truth, goodness, and beauty is the source of the kind of praxis that involves a special radiation of humanity outward. This radiation gives rise to those deeds and works through which we most fully express ourselves as human beings. In them we transcend the confines of the merely useful and bring into the world, into the real arena of our lives, that which, apart from any *utile*, is purely and exclusively true, good, and beautiful—and assure it a genuine right to citizenship in our world. Culture as a distinctive social mode of being in the world, one that is essential for human beings, is constituted in human praxis on the basis of a disinterested wonder and admiration in relation to deeds and works that have originated in men and women on this same basis, in inner communion with truth, goodness, and beauty. Where the ability for such wonder is lacking, where the "social mandate" for it is lacking, and the focus of groups or societies does not extend beyond the *utile*, there culture as a social fact is also truly lacking, or at least in serious danger.[15] There, too, all human praxis in its function of "making human life more human" is endangered. For not only is culture constituted through praxis, but human praxis in its authentically human character is also constituted through culture. *"Beauty exists that we might be enticed to work..."*

Only given this assumption is the second part of Norwid's statement also true: *"...And work, that we might be resurrected."* Concealed within these words is the full truth about human death: only in humans is death not a simple and elementary occurrence, a fact and law of nature, but takes on a whole new meaning (see *Gaudium et Spes* 22). The meaning of human death emerges from its relation to immortality. Culture, as a profound human reality constituted through human praxis, encompasses and permeates this relation—this existential confrontation of death with our hope of immortality.[16] On the field of this confrontation with death as a natural necessity, both culture and the praxis through which culture is constituted in human life and history are uniquely expressed and tested.

After all, we are passing away, we are continually dying, in so much of our handiwork, in so many previous effects of our activity. That which is transitive, even based on the sound of the word alone, seems to speak of passing away and dying. So many works, so many products of human activity, are equally susceptible to this same necessity. For a while they sparkle in the arena of the human world, and then they grow dim and wither away. "For the form of this world is passing away" (1 Cor. 7:31). "Like a garment they shall all grow old; you shall change them like clothes, and they shall succumb to change" (Ps. 102:27). Some of these products bear the mark of something to be used up, something to be consumed, and cannot rise above this level in the hierarchy of values. A civilization that gives such products priority, a civilization that is somehow completely focused only on consumption, is a civilization of the "death of humanity."[17] Characteristic of human culture is the whole dynamism of this battle with death. Such a battle takes place in the context of human praxis, for praxis contains the power to transcend that which is merely *utile* (useful) and which, in being used up, is destined to die. The power and ability of disinterested communion with truth, goodness, and beauty gives birth to works that cannot be used up (*Gaudium et Spes* 57, 59). In them not only do their creators live on, whose names are remembered for generations on end, but also, and more importantly, men and women of different generations continually rediscover the intransitive within themselves: "intransitive" means, in a sense, "immortal."

Of course, this "intransitive," too, has "passed on" with those who managed to capture the transcendental dimension of goodness, truth, and beauty in works of culture. In dying, these concrete men and women have taken with them whatever was strictly internal and intransitive in all their activity. And yet not only do the traces of it that have remained in human culture themselves defy death, for they live on and reenliven ever new men and women, but they also seem to call for the immortality—and perhaps even testify to the personal immortality—of the human being, precisely by reason of what is intransitive in the human being. Culture is an unceasing experience and testimony that flies in the face of existential despair.[18]

Is not our continual resurrection in culture a confirmation of those most radical words that the poet said of work, of human praxis: *"Work [exists] that we might be resurrected"*?

The *Pastoral Constitution on the Church in the Modern World* concludes the chapter on "Human Activity in the World" with the following words:

"If in the spirit of the Lord and in keeping with His instructions we foster on earth the values of human dignity, familial community, and freedom, and, in short, all the goods of our nature and the fruits of our foresight, we will then find them anew, but purified of all stain, brightened and transformed, when Christ hands over to the Father 'an eternal and universal kingdom: a kingdom of truth and life, a kingdom of holiness and grace, a kingdom of justice, love, and peace' (Preface of the Feast of Christ the King). On this earth the Kingdom is already present in a mysterious way; it will be brought to fruition with the coming of the Lord" (*Gaudium et Spes* 39).

This is a declaration of hope, an optics of faith. These reflections on human praxis as the true place of the constitution of culture do not diverge from this optics and this hope, but converge with them. And it is in the name of this *patrimonium commune* that I have taken the liberty today of addressing so distinguished an audience.

NOTES

1. "The Personal Structure of Self-Determination" 187–195 above.

2. The inaugural lecture at a philosophy conference on "Teoria e prassi" (Genoa, 8 September 1976).

3. See, for example, "Il cammino spirituale dell'Europa verso il suo destino unitario," *L'Osservatore Romano*, 18 October 1975.

4. See, for example, "Les travaux du Symposium des évêques d'Europe," *La documentation catholique*, 16 November 1975: 992–994 (especially Bishop Alois Suster's remarks).

5. See, for example, *Summa theologiae* I, 23, 2 ad 1; I, 56, 1; I, 18, 3 ad 1; I, 85, 2; I–II, 31, 5; and I–II, 1, 6 ad 1.

6. Karl Marx, "Thesis on Feuerbach," *The Marx-Engels Reader*, ed. Robert C. Tucker (New York: Norton, 1972) 107–109. See also Tadueusz M. Jaroszewski, *Osobowosc i wspolnota* [*Personality and Community*] (Warsaw: Ksiazka i Wiedza, 1970) 39.

7. See my reflections on this topic in the chapter entitled "The Attempt to Discern Consciousness in the 'Human Act,'" *The Acting Person*, trans. Andrzej Potocki, ed. Anna-Teresa Tymieniecka (Boston: Reidel, 1979) 28–34.

8. See "L'autotelogia dell'uomo e la transcendenza della persona nell'atto," a paper sent *in scriptis* to the Sixth International Phenomenology Conference, sponsored by the Facoltà di lettere (Siena) and the Facoltà di magisteri (Arezzo), 1–5

June 1976, Arezzo. [This paper was published in English with the conference proceedings; see Karol Wojtyla, "The Transcendence of the Person in Action and Man's Self-Teleology," *Analecta Husserliana*, ed. Anna-Teresa Tymieniecka, vol. 9 (Boston: Reidel, 1979) 203–212. —Trans.]

9. "A world where techniques are paramount is a world given over to desire and fear; because every technique is there to serve some desire or some fear" (Gabriel Marcel, *Being and Having*, trans. Katharine Farrer [Westminster: Dacre Press, 1949] 76).

10. See Bernard J. James, *The Death of Progress* (New York: Knopf, 1973).

11. "Despite the achievements of technology, despite...the shrinking of distances between continents, the present age has brought with it a deep crisis of interpersonal communication... An increasing sense of isolation and powerlessness reveals the existence of a 'horizon of treason.' The other is someone who might betray me" (Jozef Tischner, *Swiat ludzkiej nadziei: Wybor szkicow filozoficznych* [*The World of Human Hope: Selected Philosophical Essays*] [Krakow 1975] 94). But what betrays and turns against us most of all is our own environment, the world of creatures so abused by us.

12. Donella H. Meadows, et al., *The Limits to Growth: A Report for the Club of Rome's Project on the Predicament of Mankind* (New York: 1972); Mihajlo D. Mesarovic and Eduard Pestel, *Mankind and the Turning Point: The Second Report to the Club of Rome* (New York: Dutton, 1974). "A serious and universal danger...threatens to destroy the whole human species... We should stop using technological innovations whose effects we cannot foresee and that are not indispensable for human survival" ("Apel uczonych wobec zagrozenia srodowiska czlowieku" ["An Appeal from Scientists on the Threat to the Human Environment"], *Biuletyn Polskiego Komitetu do Spraw UNESCO* 143 [1971]: 10–14).

13. See also:

> "And now imagine that there is a play of weary matter...
> and that beauty is whatever appeals to you
> through the egoism of the age or coterie;
> and then you find that some other beautiful person
> views the good egoistically, as well,
> and necessarily reduces it to convenience,
> and soon the globe will be too small for people."
> —CYPRIAN NORWID, Dialog I, *Promethidion*

14. "Objective knowledge is possible only where a love of the world has taught us disinterestedness in looking at the world... The 'originally holy' [*ursprünglich Heiligen*] person, endowed with an especially keen sense of the *Sacrum*, is for others a kind of model and also a stimulant in helping them become more 'sensitive' to the sacral aspect of the earth." "Magnanimity is an entirely unique way of respecting every good... Magnanimity is a way of purifying our hope of the temptations of utilitarianism... A deep theory of magnanimity could show us the great extent to which freedom is a condition of reason in us" (Max Scheler, qtd. in Tischner 244, 159).

15. "Curiosity, which Heidegger referred to fourteen [now fifteen] years ago as the greatest danger in relation to the growing supremacy of the image in means of mass communication, gains victory over reflection and concentration.

"Against culture is pitted counter-culture. It does not produce anything permanent... Curiosity is a powerful stimulant in a consumer society. The ultimate danger of the new European culture is that a culture without clear values and well-defined forms can very easily become a consumer good.

"We are faced with the possibility of a choice: either culture will be increasingly a realm in which we adopt conscious attitudes and forms of communication, or it will be swallowed up by the industrial system and become an object of production and consumption and, even worse, an instrument of manipulation and normalization in the hands of the ruling powers and classes" (M. J. M. Domenach, "Sytuacja kultury europejskiej" ["The Situation of European Culture"], a paper presented at the Third Symposium of European Bishops and published in *Ateneum Kaplanskie* 69 [1976]: 286).

Curiosity, which is insatiable and gives birth to counter-culture, may be opposed to contemplative, disinterested *wonder*, which stands at the basis of true culture.

16. "The Church...teaches that eschatological hope does not diminish the importance of temporal duties, but provides new incentives to aid in accomplishing them" (*Gaudium et Spes* 21).

17. "Nietzsche proclaimed the death of God. After God, the human being began to die. The image of the human being is gradually being erased from our culture, just as culture itself tends to disappear in an economic and political system where huge masses, bureaucracies, and gigantic machines predominate" (Domenach 288).

18. Culture is a cipher pointing to the Transcendent. According to Jaspers, "Everything in the world can be a cipher" (Karl Jaspers, *Philosophy of Existence*, trans. Richard F. Grabau [Philadelphia: U of Pennsylvania P, 1971] 85). Commenting on this view, Kowalczyk writes: "Whatever is real can be a cipher...the human being, consciousness, conscience, language, religion, art, the history of humanity... A cipher is something that lies between the Transcendent and existence; it is a sign pointing to a transcendent reality" (Stanislaw Kowalczyk, "Ambiwalencja absolutu Karla Jaspersa" ["The Ambivalence of Karl Jaspers' Absolute"], *Zeszyty Naukowe KUL* 14.4 [1971]: 32).

PART THREE

Marriage and the Family

18

The Problem of Catholic Sexual Ethics

Reflections and Postulates

1. GENERAL REFLECTIONS AND POSTULATES ARISING FROM THE CONCEPTION ITSELF OF MORAL THEOLOGY

I shall leave for a little later the question of the accuracy and suitability of the very name "Catholic sexual ethics," and particularly its qualifier. Recalling the treatises *de sexto* and also the treatises *de virtute castitatis*, which deal with the same issue but from a different angle, I accept without reservation that there is a part of moral theology that may be designated by such a name. Whether it ought to be so designated is something I shall yet consider. At the moment, however, I wish to address this part of moral theology from the perspective of the whole of moral theology—the scientific equivalent of Catholic ethics.

I favor defining moral theology in general as follows: *Moral theology is a science that, in the light of revelation, makes justified statements concerning the moral value, or goodness and badness, of human actions.* This definition seems to me to come closer to the situation in which ethics as a philosophical discipline finds itself today than the definition traditionally based on the teleological view of ethics. The teleological view owes its origin in philosophy to Aristotle and its crystalization in the realm of speculative theology to St. Thomas Aquinas. St. Thomas' transposition of ethical speculation into the realm of revelation and into the realm of the intellect illumined by faith, or into theology, was certainly the most complete transposition of its kind for the state of philosophical

Karol Wojtyla, "Zagadnienie katolickiej etyki seksualnej: Refleksje i postulaty," *Roczniki Filozoficzne* 13.2 (1965): 5–25.

thought at that time. To this day, the teleological view has not lost any of its metaphysical value, especially as far as theology is concerned. It would be impossible, however, not to detect a certain withdrawal from it on the part of contemporary thought. This withdrawal is caused, on the one hand, by a new, more critical attitude toward metaphysics, and, on the other—and this, in my opinion, is the more important cause—by a more basic grasp of moral facts themselves, by a reestablished contact with moral experience. In connection with this, ethics is pursued more as normative speculation than as teleological speculation.

It seems to me that moral theology can, without detriment to its inner structure, also assume this character. This does not, of course, exclude its traditional teleological character, but merely supplements the old with the new. If we wish to pursue moral theology—in keeping with the above definition—as a science that, in the light of revelation, makes justified statements concerning the moral value, or goodness and badness, of human actions, this in no way requires us to reject the teleological view, which sees moral theology as a science of the goodness or badness of human actions from the perspective of the ultimate end of the human being as known from revelation. This whole problem, of course, lends itself to a separate analysis; here I shall confine myself to the outline I need for my later discussion of the particular topic.

Moral theology as a normative science deals with the norms of morality contained in divine revelation and proclaimed by the magisterium of the Church in solemn and ordinary teachings. The task of moral theologians is to scientifically interpret these norms and, above all, to justify them in the light of reason and revelation. A justification of the norms of morality is more than an interpretation of them. This might also be expressed more clearly by saying that a complete and ultimate scientific (theological) interpretation of the norms of revealed (Catholic) morality is a justifying interpretation. To justify the norms of morality means to give reasons for their rightness. In performing this task, moral theologians should have before their eyes, as far as possible, the complete theoretical vision of reality contained in revelation, especially those elements of it that are indispensable for justifying the respective normative judgments. Normative judgments are based on value judgments, which, in turn, presuppose theoretical knowledge of the reality evaluated. In this view, normative theological ethics, or moral theology, is not a practical science in the direct sense, but then neither was teleological ethics. No science can be directly practical, since a practical judgment (*iudicium practico— practicum*) is always individual and particular, corresponding to what exists *hic et nunc*, whereas science is essentially general. The directly practical role in human knowledge is performed actually by conscience and habitually by the proficiency called prudence. Teleological ethics assists conscience and prudence with basic and scientific knowledge and the presentation of the ends of human activity. Normative ethics—including, of course, its theological form—assists conscience and prudence from another perspective by providing suitable premises for doing what is morally good, or virtuous, and avoiding what is morally evil, or sinful. What are these premises and where do they come from? They come from the whole scientific enterprise concerning the justification of norms: that which justifies a norm of morality serves also as an intellectual reason for virtue and against sin. The reasons supplied by moral theology, when based on revelation, basically affect the intellect of a person of faith. Of course, the intellect's acceptance of a reason may give rise to corresponding acts of the will under the immediate direction of conscience to the extent that this will truly wills what is morally good. Moral theology based on the teleological view regards this willing of what is morally good—and rightly so—as an expression of the will's tendency toward the ultimate end.

The task of Catholic sexual ethics, upon which I shall be focusing here in particular, is to justify the norms of revealed morality taught by the Church and, in so doing, to give the most basic grounds of moral good and evil in human behavior, especially in that part of it designated by the qualifier *sexual*.

2. REFLECTIONS AND POSTULATES CONCERNING THE MATERIAL OBJECT OF CATHOLIC SEXUAL ETHICS

We come now to the question of the name "Catholic sexual ethics," and especially its qualifier. This qualifier in an abbreviated way expresses the material object of our science. As we know, the material object of any science is that with which the science deals, that about which its propositions or theses speak, whereas the formal, or proper, object expresses the particular point of view from which the material object is considered. Sexual ethics deals with—speaking here in the most general sense—the problematic of sexuality from the point of view of morality (from the point of view of the moral good and evil proper to human action). Catholic sexual ethics deals with the same problematic and from the same point of view—with the added qualification that this problematic and point of view are given to us in revelation and in the teachings of the Church.

I should immediately note that the qualifier used in designating this branch of science as "Catholic sexual ethics" seems to transfer the property of the object to the subject. We know, after all, that it is not *ethics* that is sexual, but rather that with which ethics in this case deals as its material object. It would be more accurate to speak of "the ethics of sexual life" or "the ethics of sexual issues." I can, however, tolerate the mode of expression adopted at the outset, since no one doubts that it is the object and not the subject that is at issue here.

I mentioned above that the material object (*obiectum materiale*) of Catholic sexual ethics is, in the most general sense, the problematic of sexuality in human actions. Sexuality as a property of a being, or, more precisely, as a property of human nature, lies beyond the scope of moral appraisal. Moral appraisal has to do instead with sexuality as a factor involved in human actions. These actions arise for the most part—though not exclusively—on the basis of the various kinds of relations that occur between human beings in connection with the factor of sexuality. But not exclusively, since the factor of sexuality can also give rise to actions not related to other persons. It is easy to see, however, that the latter comprise a smaller portion of the actions at issue here.

The largest and decidedly most representative portion of human actions dealt with in sexual ethics, including Catholic sexual ethics, consists of actions connected with the relation—mutually oriented—between persons of the opposite sex, between a man and a woman. In this regard, the question arises of whether only actions connected with the sexual relation (sexual intercourse) itself, including all that leads up to or results from it, are the material object of sexual ethics, or whether this object is simply the relation between persons of the opposite sex, with particular attention to the sexual relation. This is an important question, because the selection and specification of the material object of sexual ethics already has a certain significance for the formal aspect of this science—for its overall style or manner of formulating and justifying norms. I will attempt to show this in the following sections. It will also become clear there why I regard as correct the second way of specifying the material object of Catholic sexual ethics, according to which we focus primarily on the relation between persons of the opposite sex and view the sexual relation in the context of the former, the interpersonal relation. I consider this to be the first condition of a personalistic approach to Catholic sexual ethics in general, as opposed to, say, a sexological approach. It is a condition that lies in the sphere of the material object.

I do not, however, believe that one can or even should regard marriage alone, much less the family alone, as the material object of Catholic sexual ethics. Consequently, I also do not believe that one can properly and adequately pursue this branch of ethical knowledge under the form of only the ethics of the family, or even just the ethics of marriage. Why? The family lies in the sphere of the effects of marriage, or, more precisely, the effects of the sexual relations of the spouses, and yet the family as such is not an object of sexual ethics but an object of social ethics, for the family is a genuine society. Marriage as such is not yet a society, but simply a very intimate interpersonal community ("two in one flesh"). If the norms of sexual morality apply to this community in a special way, this is, of course, because of the difference in sex found between the persons in marriage and because of the sexual relations that can legitimately be realized only within marriage.

The institution of marriage, with its character of an interpersonal community consisting of a man and a woman, speaks in the strongest way possible in favor of a personalistic approach to the material object of Catholic sexual ethics. In this regard, one could say that the element of the person with his or her natural sexual separateness (man—woman) is here by nature prior to the element of the institution. Marriage is possible and comes about because God "created them [human beings] male and female," because God endowed them with physical and psychological sexual properties and a sexual urge to go along with those properties. These properties and this urge are found in every human being outside of marriage as well, and so they need to be ordered from the perspective of the principles of morality not only within marriage but also outside of it. If Catholic sexual ethics were to be pursued merely as an ethics of marriage, then all the interpersonal relationships that result from the separateness of the sexes and lie outside of marriage would somehow be excluded from Catholic sexual ethics, or could be included in it only in a somewhat artificial way.

I believe that by specifying the relation between persons of the opposite sex as the material object of Catholic sexual ethics we attain the broadest and most comprehensive view of this object. We surely then also introduce it most effectively into the ethics of marriage—and, beyond that, into the ethics of the family as well. Couples should already be well disposed toward sexual morality when they enter into marriage. We know from experience how important the premarital period is in this regard and how fraught with consequences it can be. I believe, finally, that by specifying the relation between persons of the opposite sex as the object of Catholic sexual ethics—by already apprehending this science personalistically in this dimension—we open it up most profoundly and properly for its formal object, for the light of norms and of the values in which these norms find their respective justification.

3. PERSONALISM AND NATURALISM

I already mentioned above that the manner in which we specify the material object of Catholic sexual ethics indirectly affects the formal aspect of this science, or the manner in which we formulate and justify norms. With this in mind, I wish to compare two views of the object of sexual ethics, the personalistic view and the naturalistic view. I am not associating either of them with a specific approach or textbook, but rather I am considering them in the abstract. The works and textbooks on Catholic sexual ethics (e.g., treatises *de sexto*) with which I am familiar seem implicitly to contain elements of the personalistic view, but because they fail to explicate these elements they can sometimes give rise to naturalistic associations or suspicions. It is very easy to think of this area in naturalistic rather than personalistic categories. It is especially easy to do so when the sexual relation itself rather than the relation between persons of the opposite sex becomes the material object of the discourse. It is also easy because we become accustomed to this way of thinking from biological and medical sexology as a whole, not to mention the Freudian form of "sexological philosophy."

Before attempting to explain precisely how the naturalistic associations mentioned above are expressed, I should first point out that throughout the problematic of Catholic sexual ethics these two subjects—nature and person—continually intersect, somehow overlap, and mutually condition one another in our understanding of and reflection upon them. Consequently, there is no way to deal with this area of moral theology without touching upon them both.

The sexual properties of the human being—the fact that a human being is a woman or a man—and the sexual urge connected with these properties belong to human nature as accidents to a substance. We know, however, that human nature actually exists always in a concrete *suppositum* that is a person. Consequently, the sexual properties and the sexual urge in humans are always and in every instance attributes of a person. The mode of existence proper to them in a human being is a mode of existence in a person and on the level of a person. This has consequences for the mode of activity. Nature itself does not act; it is the *suppositum* that acts (*actiones sunt suppositorum*), and this *suppositum* is a person. Here we are interested in activity connected with sexual properties and the sexual urge. Our knowledge of the animal world convinces us that this urge has its own natural purpose, namely, to foster reproduction, or procreation. The sexual urge also operates in human beings for the same purpose. This is a purpose of nature. People do not create it, but find it already present in their total structure. But since human beings are persons, they must possess the sexual urge on the level of a person and use it in a manner proper to a person.

The social consequence of this fact is the institution of marriage, which has a bipersonal composition and an interpersonal structure. A person of one sex, who, in order to actualize the natural purpose of the sexual urge, needs a person of the opposite sex, unites with that person in matrimony. Marriage, however, according to the teachings revealed by God, is not just a sexual union of a man and a woman in which these persons use the urge to realize the ends of marriage, particularly its primary end—procreation. Marriage is also a genuine union of persons, a union that, according to revelation, bears the mark of indissolubility. This union arises from a mutual choice, and, according to Catholic teaching, the interpersonal relationship expressed and realized in this choice ought to be true love (I emphasize *ought to be*). In this view, the order of nature connected with the sexual urge and with its primarily procreative purpose is, in its human realization, conditioned by love. The realization of interpersonal love in marriage is also, however, conditioned by the spouses' acceptance—in an ongoing, systematic, habitual way—of the order of nature along with the purpose proper to it. This last point already takes us into the realm of normative considerations and their foundations.

Now that we have before us an outline of the system of reciprocal relations and dependencies between nature and person in the object of Catholic sexual ethics, I will attempt to show (I repeat, in the abstract) how such ethics may be given a naturalistic interpretation. More precisely, I will attempt to show how naturalistic associations may arise already in the way the material object of this science is conceived. Indirectly, this will also bring to light the elements of the exposition that require a clearer explanation in a spirit of personalism.

1) A man and a woman may be treated primarily as subjects who are bearers (*Träger*) of a sexual urge, whereas they ought to be treated primarily as conscious and free subjects, endowed with the ability to create genuine spiritual goods, particularly moral goods, in a variety of spheres, including the sexual.

2) The sexual urge itself may be treated too deterministically. Deterministic suggestions arise especially with regard to sexual responses in the somatic (physiological) sphere, as well as with regard to the accompanying psychological and emotional responses, all of which more or less "happen" in human beings. None of these facts, however, should obscure the human capacity for self-determination in the sexual sphere. Even with regard to the reactions mentioned above, people have some ability to shape them, or at least intervene in them.

3) In connection with naturalism and even more in connection with determinism in the sexual sphere, there seems to be a tendency to limit the possibility of virtue and magnify the "necessity of sin" in this sphere. Personalism, with its emphasis on self-determination, would entail the opposite tendency: where a more deterministically inclined naturalism would see the "necessity of sin" on account of the operation of the urge and its psychosomatic consequences, personalism would perceive the possibility of virtue, based on self-control and sublimation. A fuller discussion of this topic belongs in the section on education.

So as not to let this comparative discussion remain one-sided, I will try to achieve a kind of balance by pointing out the "dangers of personalism." These are not so much objective dangers of true personalism as they are associations attached to the personalistic view of the object of sexual ethics. Upon reflection, I am led to conclude that these "dangers" have less to do with the material object and more to do with the basis of positing norms. For example, by emphasizing that a man and woman are conscious and free subjects, endowed in their mutual love with the prerogative of self-determination, do we not accord them too exclusive a right to decide what is good and bad in their mutual relationship? Will they then still be subordinate to norms, or will they determine and create their own norms? Especially here, in this sphere, where human persons are left most to themselves amid the enormous intensity of impulses, reactions, and emotions? Does not personalism in sexual ethics lead to the danger of situationalism?

4. PROCEEDING FROM THE ORDER OF NATURE TO THE PERSONALISTIC NORM

The danger of situationalism arises only when we conceive the person in a totally subjectivistic way as pure consciousness. In such a view, the person is merely a "source" of experiences, and not really even a source, but just a background. The person then appears neither as a substantial subject (*suppositum*) of conscious and free acts nor as the basis of an objective norm. I mentioned earlier that norms (normative judgments) are based on appraisals (value judgments), which, in turn, are based on theoretical knowledge. Consequently, every being—or, more precisely, the essence, or nature, of every being—can serve as the basis of an ethical norm and of the positing of norms. A being's essence, or nature, determines how free we are to behave with respect to that being, how we should or ought to behave when that being is an object of our activity. This whole norm-generating aspect disappears when we conceive the person in a totally subjectivistic way as pure consciousness.

In Catholic ethics, including Catholic sexual ethics, we do not accept such a view of the person because it is extremely one-sided and incompatible with reality. The human person is not just a consciousness prolific in experiences of various content, but is basically a highly organized being, an individual of a spiritual nature composed into a single whole with the body (hence, a *suppositum humanum*). Every being is simultaneously a good of a higher or lower value, depending on the perfection of its nature. The human person, who is the most perfect being in the visible world, also, therefore, has the highest value. The value of the person is, in turn, the basis of the norm that should govern actions that have a person as their object. This norm may be called *personalistic* to distinguish it from other norms, which are based on the various natures of beings lower than the human being—nonpersonal natures. I shall not, however, call these other norms *naturalistic* for fear of evoking certain false and "demeaning" associations. All norms, including the personalistic norm, as based on the essences, or natures, of beings, are expressions of the order that governs the world. This order is intelligible to reason, to the person. Consequently, only the person is a *particeps legis aeternae et conscia legis naturae*, which means that the person is conscious of the normative force that flows from the essences, or natures, of all beings. In particular, the person is conscious of the normative force that flows from humanity, and this humanity in its individual form always appears as a person.

In the sphere of sexuality and sexual morality, nature and person (or rather the aspect of nature and the aspect of person), as I already mentioned, mutually intersect and condition one another in a special way. The use of the sexual urge is, normally speaking, intimately connected with a relationship to a person (of the opposite sex). One could also look at this the other way around and say that a relationship to a person of the opposite sex may at least involve the sexual urge. The sexual urge possesses its own nature and a purpose connected with this nature. It possesses this nature in animals on the level of nature and possesses it in humans on the level of the person. The nature and purpose of this urge in animals is one of the cofactors of the order of nature and is realized by way of instinct. The nature and purpose of this urge in humans is a cofactor of the order of nature by the fact that people grasp its normative meaning and grant it normative force in their behavior.

Because every normal and legitimate use of the sexual urge by human beings is intimately connected—in one and the same act—with a relationship to a person of the opposite sex, the norm that emerges from an understanding of the nature and purpose of the sexual urge must be supplemented with the personalistic norm. The necessity of combining these two norms into one—which involves, of course, the necessity of properly situating the norm that emerges from an understanding of the purpose of the sexual urge within the objective content of the personalistic norm—is indispensable for preserving the order of nature. And this also leads me to believe that to construct Catholic sexual ethics without an explanation of the personalistic element both in the sphere of the material object (as was already shown above) and, therefore, also in the sphere of norms and their justification leaves something to be desired even from the standpoint of natural law and its traditional interpretation. In integral theological (as well as philosophical) reasoning in Catholic sexual ethics, the aims of nature must always come together with the value of the person. Otherwise the reasoning will be incomplete, or even one-sided and partially flawed.

It follows from the above that there exists a norm that may be called personalistic and that this norm has a fundamental place in Catholic sexual ethics. But what is the content of this norm? Is it a general, overall content, like that which appeared at the beginning of this section when I said that the essence, or nature, of the person is the basis of the norm in any behavior having a person as its object? In other words, is the personalistic norm expressed in the duty to behave (in one way or another) toward a person in a manner demanded by the essence and value of that person?

In the light of the Gospel and of the whole tradition of the teachings of revealed morality, it seems that this general content of the personalistic norm can be supplemented by a more concrete content: the content of the commandment of love. The commandment of love in its evangelical form is not identical with the personalistic norm, for this commandment enjoins us to love God and neighbor—all human beings. It therefore commands us to love beings who are persons, although *expressis verbis* it neither speaks of loving persons nor formulates principles that prescribe love as the proper way of relating to persons. In other words, it does not say that persons deserve to be loved because they are persons. It seems, however, that from the concretely formulated commandment of love contained in the Gospel we can derive the more abstract principle that I referred to as the personalistic norm. For if Jesus Christ commanded us to love those beings who are persons, then love is the proper form of relating to persons: it is the form of behavior for which we should strive when our behavior has a person as its object, since this form is demanded by that person's essence, or nature.

The Gospel helps fill in the personalistic norm with positive, concrete content. Applying this to the sexual sphere, we must take the position that a human being uses the sexual urge legitimately in sexual activity only when the aims of the sexual urge are respected *and* love of the person is realized—for, as we know, there is no way to use the urge legitimately and normally without entering into a relationship with a person (of the opposite sex). I understand *love of the person* here not in the psychological but in the ethical sense, and therefore as a virtue—as a concretization (and also, of course, a realization) of the personalistic norm. To realize merely the ends of the urge without realizing the personalistic norm would not satisfy the normative principle of the order of nature. It would also in particular not satisfy the normative demands that Catholic sexual ethics must make concerning the concretization of the personalistic norm in the light of the commandment of love.

These two norms—the one derived from the nature of the sexual urge and demanding respect for its purpose and the other derived from the dignity of the person by virtue of which the person deserves to be loved—mutually imply and condition one another in every interpersonal relationship connected with the factor of sexuality. Of course, this applies above all to sexual relations between persons. The norm of the order of nature requiring respect for the purpose of the urge is more elementary and basic. The norm requiring a proper attitude toward the person in sexual relations is superior and performs a perfecting role—especially in its evangelical concretization. There can be no talk of fulfilling the personalistic norm, especially in its Christian and evangelical concretization, without respect for the purpose of the urge in a relationship with a person of the opposite sex. As for realizing the natural purpose of this urge, this demands the institution of marriage—and outside of the framework of marriage there can be no talk of fulfilling the personalistic norm in its evangelical concretization, and thus no talk of love in the realization of the sexual urge.

As can be seen, the ethical boundaries are delineated here quite clearly with respect to sexual love in general and conjugal love in particular. These boundaries are delineated on the basis of the natural order and the personalistic norm.

In addition to its positive content concretized by means of the commandment of love, the personalistic norm in interpersonal relationships based on the factor of sexuality can with relative ease also attain its requisite negative content. This negative content is the opposite of the positive. In interpersonal relationships based on the factor of sexuality, the positive content of the personalistic norm, namely, love of the person, is, as we have seen, conditioned by respect for—or, within the framework of the institution of marriage, the realization of—the purpose of the sexual urge. When the purpose of this urge is not respected (which may occur equally within or outside of marriage) or is not realized (which may only be considered within marriage) in such relationships, we then have the opposite of love of the person, which may be defined as *using the person*. An improper relation to the purpose of the urge either within or outside of marriage has repercussions on the plane of the personalistic norm. It results in making a person, who ought to be an object of love, merely an object of use. Treating a person as a loveless object of use places the entire interpersonal relationship based on the factor of sexuality beneath the objective demands of the personalistic norm. This is especially true when the relationship involves the exercise of the sexual urge.

The normative order delineated here, as far as Catholic sexual ethics is concerned, is merely an outline and requires further development both in its central points (e.g., the sense in which the personalistic norm is implied in the evangelical commandment of love) and in a number of lesser details. In any case, by explicating the personalistic element in the realm of the material object and in the normative order, we seem to bring sexual ethics more in line with the Gospel and surely also with human needs and expectations. It is significant that people tend to raise these issues always in some way together with love. And so there is a need to reflect upon them in the context of the commandment of love, in connection with love as a virtue. If the personalistic element is not grasped and included within the total structure of the question of sexuality in human life, we run a serious risk of slipping into the plane naturalism.

By naturalism here I am not referring to the order of nature in the sense presented earlier, but rather to a one-sided, "purely" naturalistic interpretation of the sexual facts in human beings and interpersonal relationships, an interpretation that does not take into account the basic fact that human beings are persons and that interpersonal relationships based on the factor of sexuality or connected with the sexual urge ought to measure up to the requirements of the personalistic norm. We meet with such a purely naturalistic interpretation of sexual facts in biological and medical sexology, whose claims, though often correct, cannot be introduced into sexual ethics without taking into consideration the whole personalistic context.

We should also be mindful of this context and the personalistic norm in understanding and presenting the Church's traditional teachings on the ends of marriage. The Church, in setting forth the principles of the order of nature (the natural law) confirmed by revelation, teaches that *mutuum adiutorium* and *remedium concupiscentiae* are secondary ends of marriage in relation to *procreatio*, which is its primary end. The Church has soundly rejected every attempt to alter this order. Obviously, it is impossible to maintain that a man and a woman (except in cases of acquired or innate sterility) are joined in matrimony primarily for the sake of mutually complementing or reciprocally supplementing one another (*mutuum adiutorium*), for this would not be in keeping with the plan of the Creator either in the order of nature and in the light of reason or in the order of grace and in the light of revelation. On the other hand, it is impossible to doubt that the realization of these two orders—in the light of reason and revelation—comes about by taking the personalistic norm into consideration. This could hardly be otherwise, because the man and woman are persons, and especially because—as Christians—they are aware of the normative force of the commandment of love. This commandment with its normative force must shape the realization of all the ends of marriage—and do so according to that objective hierarchy over which the Church keeps watch.

Mutuum adiutorium is sometimes translated as *love*. This is a very imprecise translation. We then, without further reflection, sometimes go on to list the ends of marriage as follows: first—offspring; second—love and the satisfaction of concupiscence (or we list the latter as third). Certainly, offspring are more important than love in the psychological and affective sense. Such love, however, must not be confused with the content of the greatest commandment of the Gospel, and especially with the normative force of this commandment, which should permeate the whole of human life and shape the realization of all the objective ends of marriage. This normative force should also somehow internally, in every concrete person and in every concrete marriage, keep watch over the preservation of the hierarchy of those ends, just as the Church through its magisterium keeps watch over their preservation externally.

5. THE PROBLEM OF THE JUSTIFICATION OF THE NORMS OF CATHOLIC SEXUAL ETHICS

The foregoing discussion addresses the most difficult and essential part of the question of Catholic sexual ethics. What I presented there—at least in outline—could be called an attempt to bring norms to light. Bringing norms to light is not the same as justifying them. The former is a preliminary and preparatory step in relation to latter. Bringing norms to light consists in revealing the "normative planes" that emerge from a fundamental analysis of the material object. The normative aspect of ethics and the proper method of justifying norms are intimately connected with the material object. Without this connection we would be doomed to normative apriorism. In the above discussion, these normative planes were defined as the plane of nature and the plane of the person. The individual norms, or rules of conduct, that we continually encounter in the Church's teachings on sexual morality are justified from these two planes. In other words, they are justified by appealing to the order of nature (natural law) and the personalistic norm. This also applies to any rules of conduct in the realm of sexual morality that can be deduced from those norms. The discipline that deals with the deduction of norms is moral science (*scientia moralis*), which often has a casuistic character.

Moral science is not the same as philosophical or theological ethics, which has to do with bringing to light and justifying the norms of Catholic sexual morality. Moral science, which is directly concerned with scientific moral doctrine, seeks to establish the content of the more general norms, or rules of conduct, so as then to be able to deduce from them the more particular rules, thereby also giving the whole doctrine of morality a more particular and scientifically precise character. This is, of course, a very necessary process in all areas of morality, including sexual morality, not only because the more particular norms, or precepts of conduct, make it easier to determine the moral value of the more particular cases of human activity (casuistics), but also because the more particular precepts of conduct may serve as intellectual premises for the more particular formation of actions and virtues—provided, of course, those precepts are thoroughly justified.

That is why I have decided to deal here with the problem of the justification of the norms, or rules of conduct, that appear in Catholic sexual morality. Such justification, as I said, takes place on the basis of the order of nature and the personalistic norm. I will attempt to show how this is done by means of an example. Let me take a rule that seems especially difficult in terms of both its justification and its practice. One such rule in Catholic sexual ethics seems to be the rule that permits, under certain conditions, the regulation of birth by natural means, but forbids the use of contraception. Married couples frequently express how difficult it is to practice this rule, and every confessor knows how hard it is to give a convincing argument for it. This is precisely the function of ethics, for the "argument" in question is nothing other than a justification of a particular norm, or precept of conduct, contained in revelation and official Church teaching.

I shall justify this precept by appealing to the order of nature and the personalistic norm. The course of the justification goes more or less as follows:

Part 1: A husband and wife who use the sexual urge within the framework of marriage are obliged, in order to preserve the order of nature, to comply with the nature of the urge and its procreative purpose. They most certainly violate the nature and purpose of this urge if they attempt to exclude by artificial means the possibility of procreation in their conjugal relations. When, on the other hand, they adapt themselves to the mode of operation of the urge and have sexual intercourse at a time when the woman is infertile, then, although they exclude the possibility of procreation (which in certain circumstances may be permissible or even obligatory), they certainly do not violate the nature of the urge, but only exercise rational control over its purpose. In this first part of the argument, I justify the particular norm (precept of conduct) by turning to the plane of nature and pointing in it to a principle of the natural order.

Part 2: Here I bring together the two planes—nature and person—by pointing to the person as a subject who is conscious of the order of nature and responsible for preserving it. The order of nature connected with using the sexual urge in accord with its nature and purpose has, in a sense, been turned over to human beings for conscious realization. This accounts for the possibility of regulating conception by taking advantage of the regularity of nature in the operation of the sexual urge—and human persons who do so (in appropriate circumstances, of course) somehow confirm themselves in their role as subjects conscious of the order of nature. On the other hand, by using a method of artificial contraception, they somehow compromise themselves in that role and degrade themselves as persons.

Part 3: Here I argue from a purely personalistic point of view, observing that in the act of artificial contraception the person who is the object of this act becomes for the person who is its subject an object of use and not of love, and such a way of relating to another person tends to ricochet back on the subject. For if we do not love the person in another human being, we thereby also degrade the person in ourselves.

Of course, Part 3 of my argument includes, or at least presupposes, Parts 1 and 2, because the planes of nature and person are closely intertwined here in the material object itself. The question of how much use to make of a particular part of this argument should depend in practice on the degree to which the partners are able to understand it and on the degree to which they are sensitive to the values connected with it.

I realize that the objective validity of an argument is one thing and its actual force or effectiveness in influencing beliefs and thus indirectly shaping actions and virtues is another. With regard to the area in question, the following circumstances work against an understanding of my argument: 1) the habit of thinking and judging in a utilitarian way; 2) the inclination to judge the value of an act solely on the basis of its effects; 3) the enormous pressure exerted by the subjective, emotional element; and 4) the whole set of difficulties, real and illusory, connected with the use of natural methods of birth control. All of these circumstances in various ways affect the force and practical effectiveness of my argument.

As far as the individual parts of the justification are concerned, the following points should be made:

1) With regard to Part 1, the argument from the order of nature, expressed here in the mode of operation and purpose of the sexual urge, is itself transparent and convincing. The difficulty lies in the lack of a clear connection with the person: the urge appears as something that merely "happens" in the human being.

2) This difficulty is removed in Part 2, where I stress the responsibility of the person that arises from an awareness of the order of nature. Perhaps it would also be well in connection with this point to forestall a certain danger connected with the autonomism expressed in the belief that people ought to impose their laws on nature. I should, therefore, add here that this "imposition of their laws on nature" is basically nothing other than a transformation of nature within the limits permitted by nature itself; in other words, it consists in taking advantage of nature's own potentiality. On the other hand, it never involves doing violence to nature and its purpose, for this would in principle turn against the human being.

3) As to Part 3, in which I contrast loving a person with treating a person as an object of use, this part of the argument depends largely upon emphasizing the whole personalistic side of the question, both in the realm

of the material object and also, therefore, in the realm of norms. With regard to the material object, I already mentioned that a relationship based on the factor of sexuality is in principle an interpersonal relationship, as is sexual intercourse itself. Perhaps of particular importance for Part 3 of my argument is what I earlier called "bringing norms to light," or revealing the personalistic plane of the question. This plane seems to be rather poorly objectified—to the detriment of the question. Against the background of an adequate objectification, the contrast between loving a person and treating a person as an object of use appears almost intuitively—and the act of moral appraisal likewise arises intuitively.

As far as the force and practical effectiveness of Part 3 of my argument is concerned, a lot depends here on the partners' subjective culture of the person, that is, on the manner and measure in which their consciousness is sensitive to the value of the person, specifically in relationships connected with the factor of sexuality. Without this, it will be difficult in practice to convince them that if a man and a woman have sexual relations in the framework of the institution of marriage and artificially exclude the possibility of procreation they treat each other merely as objects of sexual use and not as cocreators of an act that has the full objective value of an act of love. This difficulty arises especially when the partners are drawn together by a strong feeling of love or by a strong sensual passion. The latter in particular tends to obscure a clear view of the difference between legitimate conjugal relations and those that are deprived of their "naturalness" by the use of artificial means. "Naturalness" in this case is an expression of harmony not just with nature but also with the person. The lack of harmony with nature becomes the basis and source of treating the person as an object of use. In sexual activity—in the act of conjugal intercourse—a person is not an object of use to the extent that the act is in harmony with nature and, therefore, basically subordinated to its purpose. (It is important to note that the partners may basically subordinate the act to the purpose of nature without always actually intending a procreative effect.)

The argumentation in Part 3 is the most personalistic. It establishes a bond between the person and nature, which, of course, also occurs in Parts 1 and 2. The emphasis in Part 3, however, is placed on the element proper to the person, whereas the emphasis in Part 1, and even still in Part 2, is placed more on the element of nature itself and the order of nature. In any event, this whole argument, which proceeds from the planes of the order of nature and the personalistic norm, is the proper argument, or justification, for the particular norm (precept of conduct) of Catholic sexual morality under examination here. The sexological argument, regardless of how effective it may be in practice, performs only an auxiliary role. Such an argument, strictly speaking, takes into consideration only the good and evil of the organism in connection with its sexual functions, whereas moral good and evil is connected in this case with the interpersonal relationship based on the factor of sexuality. The good or evil of the organism is, in relation to the latter, a value *per accidens*.

In my presentation of the above argument, wherein I sought to justify a particular norm, or precept of conduct, contained in Catholic sexual ethics (on marriage), I was continually mindful not only of the objective validity of the reasoning but also of its practical force and effectiveness. Moral norms are valid independently of their effectiveness in practice, and yet the moralist, whose main task is to seek arguments for their objective validity, or correctness, cannot entirely neglect the aspect of their practical effectiveness. This opinion finds support in a whole variety of particular reasons, as well as in the overall experience of morality, where we constantly see norms coming to naught, even the most soundly justified.

From the foregoing discussion, it becomes quite clear that neither the personalistic norm nor the norm of the order of nature is itself one of the concrete precepts of conduct found in the teachings of Catholic sexual morality. These two norms are higher-level norms—the justifying norms, so to speak. Under them fall a whole series of justified norms, which, from the point of view of the structure of ethics, are lower-level norms. I used one of the latter as an example in showing how such norms are justified.

I should now add that neither the plane of the order of nature nor even the plane of the personalistic norm is yet an ultimate and complete basis for formulating a comprehensive justification of the norms of Catholic sexual ethics. We cannot justify everything with these basic norms, and above all, within the scope of them alone, we cannot obtain a complete view of the values that come into play in this rich and difficult area of human life and activity. Above the order of nature there is still the order of grace, which is connected in a most intimate way with the world of persons. The problematic of sexuality, which, as we have seen, is likewise deeply connected with the world of human persons, falls within the compass of the order of grace. The most eloquent proof of this is the sacrament of matrimony. The sacramental character of matrimony also provides a special occasion for reflecting upon the ethical problematic of the person and sexuality in supernatural categories. This will be important not only for the Catholic ethics of marriage, but also indirectly for Catholic sexual ethics in general.

It seems that the proper plane here will be not the personalistic norm, but a norm that, based on concepts contained in revelation, might be called the *norm of justification*. This issue would certainly require a thorough analysis. But unless we introduce the element of justification before God, a justification that is strictly connected with supernatural grace, there is no way we can formulate an ultimate interpretation and justification of Catholic ethical norms on marriage or on sexuality in general. We need only recall St. Paul's analogy between marriage and the union that exists between Christ and the Church to see the validity of this suggestion. I shall not, however, attempt to resolve this issue in the present article, but merely wish to call attention to it.

6. SOME REFLECTIONS AND POSTULATES OF A PRACTICAL AND EDUCATIONAL NATURE

By suggesting that we need to pursue Catholic sexual ethics from a normative point of view, I am not proposing that we abandon the whole enterprise of teleological ethics, for the latter also has an important role to play, especially in the realm of moral theology. Revealed knowledge concerning the ends of human existence points to the ultimate end, in relation to which the temporal end that finds expression in the perfection of the human person serves as a means. This perfection, the perfection proper to the human being as a person, is moral perfection. It consists in the possession and practice of a harmonious set of virtues that form a kind of coherent, organic whole in the inner life of the human being. Since everyone must acquire virtues, one of the tasks of pedagogy is to provide instruction in the practice of them. In the traditions of Catholic thought, sexual ethics and pedagogy are closely intertwined.

Catholic sexual pedagogy takes the position that educating people in the sexual sphere involves more than just providing them with sexological instruction. Education, after all, is not a function of knowledge alone, but is also a function of the will molding conduct by inwardly training the lower powers of the soul, powers that we know play a large role in interpersonal relationships based on the factor of sexuality. In the light of the foregoing discussion, Catholic sex education may be regarded as simply an integral, personalistic, education in the Christian spirit, one that properly takes into consideration all the values that the aspect of sexuality brings to human life, particularly to interhuman relations and to society.

Such a concept of education should allow us, on the one hand, to overcome (in content and in practice) Freudian pansexualism and, on the other, to take advantage of all that sound science, including biological and medical science, has to say on matters of sex. But the most essential (because the most Christian) and also—let us be honest about it—the most difficult task in the area of sex education is to incorporate properly all the contributions of science into the integral order of love. They should be incorporated from the very start and also in a progressive, ongoing way.

Without going into a whole lot of detail, I will attempt to formulate just some of the beliefs that should be instilled in consciousness and realized in practice if sex education is to have a personalistic character. We should instill in consciousness the conviction that 1) the value of the person is higher and more important than the sexual values connected with the person, and 2) love of the person, even when in some sense based on the factor of sexuality, is not synonymous with being sexually involved with someone. Experience suggests that people are rather poorly informed in theory and in practice about the different elements that essentially belong to love of the person, although some of these elements may appear only in relationships based on the aspect of sexuality. These are personal elements and can possess a thoroughly personal value if this value is competently disclosed and upheld. Otherwise they succumb to sexualization. We should in education particularly before marriage, and then later in marriage, find, as it were, more place for the person, for persons. Without this, marriage becomes empty except for a couple's sex life, as though a man and woman held no other value for each other apart from the value of sex.

In order to realize these beliefs in practice, training is needed in two directions: 1) self-control and 2) sublimation. The art of education—especially self-education—in matters of sex consists in the skill of combining these two elements, which both play an equally large role in interpersonal relationships based on the factor of sexuality. Self-control is indispensable for abstinence. Sublimation, on the other hand, refers to the particular effort involved in discovering a higher value where an average—or rather "degraded"—way of thinking, judging, and acting manages to find only the value of sex and the possibility of enjoyment. So as not to fall into an idealistic fiction or some sort of angelism, it should be added that sublimation presupposes self-control.

Only this path, it would seem, can lead to a conscious fulfillment in life of the contents contained in Catholic sexual ethics, one that also in some way brings happiness to human persons. Catholic sexual ethics is an indispensable introduction to the ethics of marriage and, from a further perspective, to the ethics of the family as well. We all know how important it is in this area to master the current conflict between education and morality and to continue to show new generations the validity, nobility, and effectiveness of eternal truths and solutions.

19

The Teaching of the Encyclical
Humanae Vitae on Love
An Analysis of the Text

1. INTRODUCTION

Paul VI's encyclical *Humanae Vitae* contains an extensive teaching on the topic of conjugal love. The encyclical takes its lead in this regard from an orientation that was clearly apparent at the Second Vatican Council both in its discussions and in the final draft of the document *Gaudium et Spes*; in the second part of this document, there is a whole chapter devoted to marriage and the family. In the discussions, the need was raised more than once for a deeper appreciation of the value of love as an end of marriage in relation to procreation. To consider the ethical issues of marriage in the context of love seems very fitting and proper, especially for psychological reasons, since this corresponds to a basic truth of human life. At the same time, this truth initiates us into a sphere of morality that is completely in line with the teachings of the Church, for the greatest commandment of the Gospel is the commandment of love. The Church, teaching through the Council or the Pope, seems to have a special right and responsibility *to speak out authoritatively on the topic of love and the proper meaning of love in human life—in this case, the life of marriage and the family.*

Karol Wojtyla, "Nauka encykliki 'Humanae vitae' o milosci," *Analecta Cracoviensia* 1 (1969): 341–356. A paper presented in September 1968 in Krakow at a theological conference on *Humanae Vitae*.

The Council, therefore, in one of its central documents, provides us with an extensive teaching on conjugal love, although I shall not be analyzing that teaching separately here. One could say, however, that it forms a kind of background for the subsequent teaching of Paul VI in his encyclical *Humanae Vitae*, a background that the Holy Father has before his eyes and to which he appeals in key elements. If I may here at the start make a general comparison, I would say that the conciliar constitution seems to be somewhat more descriptive and tends to place more emphasis on the *values* of marriage and the family, values connected with a love embraced in the spirit of the Gospel, whereas the encyclical places more emphasis on the *duties* corresponding to those values. The duties discussed in the encyclical, in keeping with its theme and intent, are mainly—though not exclusively—those connected with the transmission of life in marriage.

I should also point out at the very outset that neither the conciliar constitution nor the encyclical anywhere explicitly mentions the traditional view concerning the hierarchy of the ends of marriage. In that view, the primacy of *procreatio* (procreation) over *mutuum adiutorium* (which today we would call conjugal love) was always emphatically stressed. Neither the conciliar constitution nor the encyclical appeals to such a hierarchy of the ends of marriage, *much less places these ends in opposition to one another. Gaudium et Spes* (51) speaks of harmonizing conjugal love with a respect for human life; *Humanae Vitae*, of the inseparable connection between the two meanings of the conjugal act. I shall attempt to analyze this problem in some detail.

Finally, I should add that both the Council, as the author of the Pastoral Constitution, and Paul VI, as the author of *Humanae Vitae*, view the problematic of marriage in the context of love, and they are prompted to do so by an awareness of the significance such a view has for people today. "We can see," writes Paul VI, "certain changes...in the appreciation of the value of conjugal love and the meaning of conjugal relations for such love" (*Humanae Vitae* 2).

2. A THEOLOGY OF LOVE

The author of the encyclical *Humanae Vitae*, in his teaching on love in marriage, is concerned first of all with ensuring the integrity of this teaching in the theological sense. He, therefore, begins by explaining how we must think of love in general, and of conjugal love in particular, in the light of revelation: "Conjugal love most fully reveals its true nature and dignity when we consider that it takes its origin—as though from the highest source—from God, who 'is Love' and 'the Father from whom all fatherhood in heaven and on earth gets its name'" (*Humanae Vitae* 8). One could say that in this place the encyclical presents us with the very summit of the issue. The theological view of conjugal love must lead us to this summit.

Significant here is the deduction of this basic *proposition concerning conjugal love*, a theological proposition, from *two revealed truths about God* simultaneously: from the truth that God is Love and from the truth that God is Father. Paul VI writes that conjugal love derives its origin from God, which seems, therefore, to imply a dual order: the order of efficacy and the order of exemplariness. God, who is Love and Father, is both the exemplary and the efficient origin of all love and of all fatherhood in the world, and specifically in conjugal life. God perpetuates this love through the divine essence—through the very fact that God is Love and that God is Father. The exemplary origin is brought out very vividly with respect to fatherhood in the words of the Letter of St. Paul to the Ephesians (3:15).

But the Pope's words should be understood in the efficient sense as well, for in the same section we read of marriage that "God the Creator instituted it wisely and providentially in order to realize the divine plan of love in humankind" (*Humanae Vitae* 8). The spouses enter into this plan of love and realize it themselves by their conjugal love, for we read further: "For this reason the spouses, by making a mutual gift of self, proper and exclusive only to them, progress toward becoming a community of persons, that they might mutually perfect themselves in it, while also collaborating with God in bringing into the world and educating new human beings" (*Humanae Vitae* 8). This statement has a key meaning for other things the Pope has to say about conjugal love later in the encyclical; here, however, by its immediate context, it serves to *affirm both the exemplariness and the efficacy of God*. One could say that by means of this statement the Pope sets the whole human structure of conjugal love and the human meaning of this love firmly within a theological context. By doing this at the very beginning of his teaching on conjugal love, he is, in a sense, telling us to return continually to this foundation which forms the basis for everything he will later say about conjugal love.

To complete this theological foundation, Paul VI adds a statement on the *sacrament of matrimony*: "For the baptized, moreover, marriage assumes the dignity of a sacramental sign of grace, for it expresses the bond of Christ with the Church" (*Humanae Vitae* 8). Thus the theology of conjugal love, though only briefly outlined in the encyclical, contains all the essential elements that go into its makeup. The exemplariness and efficacy of God and the sacramentality of marriage are sufficient proof that the Pope wishes to give his teaching on conjugal love an *integral theological meaning*. The whole encyclical is about love in precisely this sense. Paul VI, responding to questions people are asking today, questions that he formulates very broadly and profoundly at the beginning of the encyclical, *responds basically to a single question*: what must conjugal love be like in order to discover God's eternal plan of love in it? under what conditions does conjugal love reflect its prime exemplar, God as Love and God as Father? This is the level upon which we must consider the entire encyclical and the teaching on conjugal love contained therein.

3. THE CHARACTERISTICS OF CONJUGAL LOVE

"When these matters are seen in the proper light," the Pope goes on to say, as though once again wishing to accentuate the exemplary order upon which his theology of conjugal love is based, "the characteristic traits and requirements of conjugal love come clearly into view" (*Humanae Vitae* 9). The characteristics of this love as a human community of two persons, a man and a woman, seem relatively succinct in relation to the statement contained in *Gaudium et Spes*. Paul VI, *in his very first words, emphasizes "traits and requirements,"* as though indicating in advance the direction he will take in his analysis of conjugal love, namely, that he will speak in it not only of values but also of the duties that must correspond to those values. If this were not the case, every word about love would be divested of its full realism. Essentially, the author of the encyclical presents all the characteristic traits of conjugal love from the point of view of the ethical integrity that such love ought to contain.

"This is first of all a thoroughly human love, and thus sensory and spiritual at the same time," we next read (*Humanae Vitae* 9). The Pope, with a full sense of reality, speaks of conjugal love as *human*. This flows from the simultaneous participation of sensuality and spirituality in the development of conjugal love. But this love, because it is human, makes clear demands upon the spouses: "It involves not just an ordinary impulse of instincts or feelings," we read further, "but also, and even principally, an act of free will, intended to ensure that this love, in the midst of the joys and sorrows of everyday life, might not merely endure but even grow, in such a way that the spouses might become as though one heart and one soul and together attain their human perfection" (*Humanae Vitae* 9). All of this ultimately determines and testifies to the true *humanness* of conjugal love. Such a joint involvement of spirituality and sensuality, and also—so very prominent here—of emotionality, of the heart, gives conjugal love a truly human expression and profile. Based on this characteristic trait of the love of the spouses, the fact that it is *human*, the Pope both sees and proclaims the *requirement of jointly striving for the human perfection* that such love entails.

Likewise in the case of the second characteristic trait of conjugal love. Paul VI teaches that such love should be *total love*, which he calls "a special form of personal friendship, through which the spouses generously share everything with one another without unfair exceptions and egoistic calculations. A spouse who truly loves his or her marriage partner does not love the partner only for what he or she receives from that partner, but loves the partner for the partner's self, glad to be able to enrich the partner with the gift of himself or herself" (*Humanae Vitae* 9). This is how, based on human experience and all the humanistic, personalistic, and ethical results of human thought, the Church understands that total love. This characteristic entails not just a one-sided pursuit, but special requirements. These are *the requirements that true friendship places upon human beings*, taking into consideration that special form of friendship that occurs in marriage, the special measure of the giving of self that is contained and realized in marriage and that should, of course, be properly reciprocated. The *measure* that must always be applied here *is that gift of the person*. This gift stands at the basis of all that the spouses "share with one another" and determines the depth of their community and oneness. The mutual gift of the person, a gift that is a fact in marriage, must also become—somehow on the basis of this fact—a requirement and a norm of action, if conjugal love is to be truly total.

Paul VI next characterizes this love as faithful and exclusive. "In addition," we read, "conjugal love is *faithful* and *exclusive* to the end of life, which means that it is the kind of love the spouses conceived it to be on the day they freely and with full awareness entered into the bonds of matrimony" (*Humanae Vitae* 9). The Pope connects fidelity and exclusivity as characteristic traits of conjugal love with the indissolubility of marriage, as can be seen from the words that follow in the text. These traits are intimately connected with the previously mentioned trait of total love and its personalistic interpretation. Thus we read: "Although this conjugal fidelity may at times encounter difficulties, no one may consider it impossible; on the contrary, it is always noble and meritorious. The example of so many spouses down through the ages shows not only that fidelity is in accord with the nature of marriage, but also that it is in some way a source of profound and lasting happiness." Here, precisely in these last words, the fidelity and exclusivity of conjugal love are shown to be an aspect, as it were, of the total love that was mentioned earlier—*the total love that results from the mutual gift of persons.* The form that this mutual gift takes in marriage presupposes exclusivity and, therefore, also mutual fidelity. It is upon this very basis that exclusivity and fidelity become a source of happiness. Happiness is explained both by the quality of the gift and by its endurance.

"Finally, this is a fruitful love," writes Paul VI, concluding his enumeration of the characteristics of conjugal love with this trait, "a love that is not exhausted in the community of the spouses, but tends also toward its own continuation and the awakening of new life" (*Humanae Vitae* 9). There follows a citation from *Gaudium et Spes* (50): "Children are also the most valuable gift of marriage and contribute greatly to the welfare of the parents themselves." The Pope then goes on to present specific reflections and observations concerning the requirements and duties that conjugal love entails by virtue of its characteristic and exceptional trait of being fruitful, and I shall follow this course of Paul VI's reflections as well. But first I would like to emphasize yet again the meaning that he gives to conjugal love by this enumeration of its main human traits. *In each of these traits, value converges with duty*—one could say that great value converges with grave duty—all of which is decisive for love. The Holy Father teaches of conjugal love with all the solemnity this topic demands. He instructs us about it by pointing to value and duty simultaneously. In this way, the teaching of the encyclical *Humanae Vitae*, in keeping with the Pope's mission and office, takes on an ethical meaning. *It is an authentic moral teaching.* Concern for integrity in the ethical sense goes hand in hand with concern for the theological integrity of the document, as I mentioned earlier.

4. A PERSONALISTIC VIEW OF CONJUGAL LOVE

Paul VI then goes on to discuss the central topic of the encyclical, a topic the constitution *Gaudium et Spes* (51) refers to as "harmonizing conjugal love with a respect for human life." The Council, in approving the constitution, was counting on the fact that the Pope would speak out in greater detail on this issue. The encyclical *Humanae Vitae* fulfills this expectation by taking an authoritative stance on responsible parenthood and contraception. If we wish to understand Paul VI's teaching on conjugal love in its entirety, we must become familiar with this position—not just for its own sake, but because it represents a *clear implication of his teaching on conjugal love*, in terms of both the theological and the ethical meaning of such love, which I have been discussing up to this point. Methodologists in the area of ethics and moral theology would do well to study this implication in terms of the process of presenting and justifying particular norms—in this case, the norms governing responsible parenthood and contraception—to the extent that this process is contained in the encyclical. This task should be left to methodologists. In this paper, however, I cannot omit Paul VI's position on responsible parenthood and contraception, since this position seems to be thoroughly rooted in his teaching on love—but here we may let the texts speak for themselves.

To bring out these implications, we must now, of course, following the progression of the encyclical, *proceed to an analysis of the concrete conjugal act and examine its internal order*. The conjugal act is a relation—a relation not only in the "sexual" sense but also in the ontological sense. Like every relation (*relatio*), the conjugal relation is realized in a dual aspect: it is realized in one person "relative" to another, and it is also realized "between them." Conjugal relations, as is true of conjugal love in general, are subject to ethical and theological appraisal, for they are genuine human acts, in which all the previously mentioned traits of love—not just fruitfulness—in a special way demand affirmation. The relevant passages of the encyclical must be thoroughly analyzed, because *from them the encyclical's teaching on love takes on an even more profound profile*. One could say that what is at stake here is the *real existence of conjugal love*, which always exists "in" persons—a husband and wife—and "between" persons, in keeping with its dual nature as a virtue (an inner attitude relative to another person) and as a relation. Love is always an interpersonal relation. The question here is: Under what conditions does the conjugal relation fulfill the requirements of love? Paul VI responds to this question by calling to mind the unchanging teaching of the Church concerning the dual function that the conjugal act signifies and performs—and the inseparable connection between these two functions.

This inseparable connection—we read in the encyclical—is established by God, and no human being may willfully break it (*Humanae Vitae* 12). The connection at issue here is that "between the twofold meaning of the conjugal act: the intended meaning of union and the intended meaning of parenthood." This is a very significant text. One could say that in it Paul VI passes the traditional and unchangeable moral teaching of the Church through the prism of those requirements that—in a primarily formal respect—contemporary psychology and anthropology set down in this regard concerning a basic ontology of love. One could also say that Paul VI brings fully to light this ontology of love and, to a large extent, uses it as a basis for the position he takes in the encyclical on responsible parenthood and contraception.

By appealing to the meaning of the conjugal act, the Pope places the whole discussion not only and not so much in the context of the nature of this act, but also and even more in the context of human awareness, in the context of the awareness that should correspond to this act on the part of both the man and the woman—the persons performing the act. One can detect in this part of the encyclical *a very significant passage from what some might call a "theology of nature" to a "theology of person."* To speak of the twofold meaning of the conjugal act would seem to correspond to the concept of nature: in the nature of the act, there is an expression of love and the possibility of fecundity. But the author of *Humanae Vitae* does not couch his thought in such formulations. Instead, when he writes of meaning here, he takes for granted that people understand the nature of the act.

Moreover, not only does he write of the meaning of the conjugal act that results from an understanding of its nature, *but he also writes of intended meaning and sign.* The personal subject of this act—a man or a woman—is not only aware of its meaning, but in performing this act can and should give it precisely this and not some other meaning, can and should signify only this and not something else by it. The conjugal act is conceived in the encyclical as a sign. We read: "For the conjugal act of its innermost essence, while uniting the husband and wife in a most intimate bond, at the same time enables them to bring forth new life, in keeping with laws inscribed in the very nature of the man and the woman. If these two essential elements of the conjugal act are preserved—the intended meaning of union and of parenthood—then there will also be fully preserved in it the meaning of mutual and authentic love and the relation to the sublime task of parenthood to which people are called." And, the Pope adds, "we believe that people in our day are particularly prepared to understand how compatible this teaching is with human reason" (*Humanae Vitae* 12). This final statement may be regarded as an appeal to natural law, which, however, is a separate issue.

For our purposes, this whole passage is important *from the point of view of an analysis of conjugal love*, whose theological and ethical aspects were in a general way outlined earlier. Here, as I said, we are considering the concrete existence of conjugal love, which exists always as a relation in and between persons. The conjugal act not so much *is* as *ought to be* a confirmation of this relation. The existence of love takes place between this *is* and this *ought to be*. Love cannot simply be identified with the conjugal act, but must be sought in the persons, in their awareness, choice, decision, and moral responsibility. The man and woman are aware of the meaning of the conjugal act. Moreover, in performing this act, they can and should intend by it precisely what it means essentially. It means both a special union of persons and, at the same time, the possibility (not the necessity!) of fecundity, of procreation. *If, in acting jointly, this is precisely what they intend to signify by their activity, then the activity is intrinsically true and free of falsification.* In the intentional sphere of meanings, they do not falsify the meaning that their joint activity—which is also an activity of each of them individually in this community of activity—has in the real sphere, has as the strictly defined reality of the conjugal act.

This particular passage from the encyclical seems especially important for bringing out the personalistic character of conjugal love—personalistic, of course, in the integral, ethical sense. In the more traditional view, one would speak of the conformity of the activity with reason, and the author of *Humanae Vitae* speaks of this as well. He does not stop, however, at an abstract expression of this conformity (or lack thereof), *but in some sense presents it as a lived experience of meaning, an experience that permeates the whole fiber of the human activity of the spouses*. When the Pope in this text of the encyclical speaks of meaning and intended meaning (and sign), he seeks thereby to express what for love is both the internal and the objective truth of the activities that make up the conjugal act. This truth is what determines whether an internal order or lack of order prevails in the act. This truth is what determines whether the conjugal act is or is not an act of love in the integral sense.

If the Church, teaching through *Humanae Vitae*, "regards it as licit for spouses to take periods of infertility into account" (which is known as the ethical regulation of birth) and yet "condemns as always illicit the use of means directly preventing conception" (which is how I am using the term contraception), it does this in the conviction that the former does not undermine the order of meanings contained in the conjugal act, whereas the latter does. The former—the ethical regulation of birth—does not violate the truth of the human activities that make up the conjugal act, whereas the latter—contraception—cannot help but violate this truth. *In the ethical regulation of birth, spouses can signify by their activity in*

the conjugal act what this activity essentially means, whereas contracep-
tion makes this impossible. For this reason, the Pope adds: "In reality,
there is an essential difference between these two methods of behavior"
(*Humanae Vitae* 16).

I am not concerned at the moment with the ethical regulation of birth
or with contraception as such. I only wish to show that this issue is an
implication of the teaching on conjugal love contained in *Humanae Vitae*.
This implication becomes even clearer in the context of a personalistic
view of such love, as I have attempted to show.

5. THE NEED FOR INTEGRATION

This personalism makes it easy to see the connection between the ethical meaning and the psychological meaning of conjugal love, and especially between the two meanings implied in the conjugal act. The
encyclical *Humanae Vitae* seems to *respect both of these meanings and
does not blur the boundary between them.* If contemporary views of the
"value of conjugal love and the meaning of conjugal relations" (*Humanae
Vitae* 2) seem to be marked by a one-sided psychologism, the encyclical
does not react to this with a one-sided moralism. In a certain sense, the
previously cited texts of the encyclical and their analysis have already
shown this.

The notion that the conjugal act should contribute to the spouses' union,
to their oneness, and that this act does not find its sole ethical justification
in its procreative purpose, is sufficient proof that the moral teaching contained in the encyclical is nevertheless free of a one-sided moralism. Certainly, too, the place that the encyclical leaves for the psychology of
conjugal love—although it does not, of course, become absorbed in this
aspect—is the fruit of the integral vision of the human being that Paul VI
has constantly before his eyes and to which he appeals at the very beginning of the doctrinal part of the encyclical (*Humanae Vitae* 7). This makes
me even more convinced that the entire view of conjugal love in *Humanae
Vitae* is basically personalistic, as I attempted to show earlier. This personalistic orientation is what explains the *relation between the psychological and the ethical meaning of love* that emerges in the texts of the
encyclical.

Thus, for example, concerning the earlier mentioned topic of the internal order that ought to prevail in the conjugal act, Paul VI says that
"sexual intercourse forced upon one's marital partner without regard for

his or her condition and legitimate wishes is not a true act of love, and is therefore contrary to what the moral order in the mutual ties between the spouses rightfully demands" (*Humanae Vitae* 13). The Pope affirms that the moral order requires love, and he states explicitly that a conjugal act may not be an act of love. This leads to the need to distinguish, both in the realm of individual conjugal acts and certainly also in the realm of whole attitudes, *that which is love from that which is not love.* Perhaps the terms "good love" and "bad love" find a certain justification here.

The Pope continues his thought in the following way: "Likewise, if the matter is well considered, one must acknowledge that a mutual act of love performed in such a way that it interferes with the capacity to transmit life—which God the Creator of all things has joined to this act by special laws—contradicts both the divine plan according to which marriage was instituted and the will of the original Creator of life. To use this divine gift while depriving it, even if only partially, of its proper meaning and purpose is to act contrary to the nature of both the man and the woman and also contrary to their intimate union" (*Humanae Vitae* 13).

This text is extremely significant. The Pope speaks here simultaneously of the nature and purpose of the conjugal act and of its integral meaning. He seems to take into account not only the objective meaning of the act, inscribed in its nature, but also to some degree *its subjective, experiential meaning for the spouses.* The ethical aspect and the psychological aspect appear in this view as two meanings that need to be mutually integrated within the same subject—or rather subjects, the man and the woman. The Pope writes of "a mutual act of love performed in such a way that it interferes with the capacity to transmit life" as an act of love—as if not wishing to deny that in this act there is basically always a desire to express and display conjugal love, that it responds to a psychological need for such love. At the same time, however, from the point of view of that love, even in the aspect of the actual lived experience of it, the active undermining of the "meaning and purpose" that corresponds to the plan of the Creator *must work against the "intimate union" of the spouses.* One could say, as a way of interpreting this thought, that the conjugal act *then lacks the value of a true union of persons.* In the undermining of the internal order of the conjugal act with respect to the "capacity to transmit life," Paul VI also sees—and this, in a sense, goes even deeper—an undermining of the very truth of personal love. The mode of conjugal life is also not irrelevant for this truth.

Consequently, Paul VI, in another place in the encyclical, writing of spouses who in their conjugal life practice periodic abstinence, says: "By behaving in this way, they bear witness to a truly and completely honest love" (*Humanae Vitae* 16). We see here that the concept of love must be made, as it were, explicitly unambiguous from the ethical point of view ("completely honest love"), since its psychological meaning alone does not resolve whether it is an "honest" or a "dishonest" love. Similarly, the conjugal act alone does not resolve whether it is a true act of love or not. For it to be a true act of love, its psychological value must be integrated with its ethical value. This integration extends even deeper—to the very theology of love: "To make use of the gift of conjugal love while respecting the laws of the transmission of life is to acknowledge that one is not the master of the sources of life, but rather a servant of the plan established by the Creator" (*Humanae Vitae* 13). In the theology of love outlined at the beginning of the encyclical, *God as Love and God as Father* is what gives conjugal love and its specific acts their ultimate and highest meaning. This theology of love, as I said earlier, permeates the entire teaching on conjugal love contained in the encyclical *Humanae Vitae*.

This is an authentic teaching of the Gospel. Paul VI stresses that the Church is always mindful of its responsibility "to proclaim with humility and firmness the entire moral law, both natural and evangelical" (*Humanae Vitae* 18). The evangelical law, or commandment of love, is not only inviting but also difficult, which becomes clear in—among other ways—the teaching on conjugal love. The definition of the true meaning of conjugal love, and particularly the strict and responsible teaching on how such love is to be realized in conjugal acts, frequently meets with resistance. This resistance is an indirect criterion of the truth contained in the teaching, which does not have a merely theoretical or abstract meaning, *but is directed toward human life and behavior*. In this regard, conjugal love in its proper evangelical sense must be attained by people—in this case, married people—as a good that is also difficult. "There is no doubt," we read in *Humanae Vitae*, "that the rational and free control of one's urges requires asceticism—something especially necessary for observing periodic abstinence—so that the signs of love proper to conjugal life might be in harmony with the ethical order. And yet this self-control in which conjugal chastity finds expression, far from harming conjugal love, instills new human values in that love. It demands almost constant effort, but thanks to its beneficial influence the spouses fully develop their personalities, being enriched with spiritual values" (*Humanae Vitae* 21).

The practical *confirmation that conjugal love corresponds to the greatest commandment of the Gospel* comes when the spouses regard the values of this love as in some sense a task to be achieved, one that requires a certain ascetic effort. This is what brings about the practical—existential and experiential—integration of this love. Abstinence also enters into the overall structure of the asceticism of love, and conjugal chastity then becomes a kind of integrating factor. In this way, too, *conjugal love also becomes a fruit of grace*, "which makes the human being a new creature, capable of conforming in love and true freedom to the divine plan of the Creator and Savior and of sensing the sweetness of Christ's yoke" (*Humanae Vitae* 25). In this grace is manifested the supernatural power of the sacrament of matrimony, which "in a certain sense consecrates the spouses for faithfully carrying out their responsibilities, for bringing their vocation to its proper perfection, and for giving, as befits them, Christian witness before the world" (*Humanae Vitae* 25).

6. THE MEANING OF *HUMANAE VITAE* FOR MORAL THEOLOGIANS AND PASTORAL MINISTERS

It is time now to summarize the content of this analysis, which aimed at presenting a closer reading of the teaching on love contained in *Humanae Vitae*. In the light of the somewhat exegetical character of this article, I should mention that this teaching has emerged as though "along the way," in the course of my analysis and in conjunction with it. Here at the end, it will perhaps suffice to add that the Pope approaches his magisterial teaching on conjugal love—which is an authoritative Christian moral teaching (with a practical and pastoral orientation)—as though from two sides. On the one hand, he presents an overall view of the meaning of conjugal love, a view that has a simultaneously theological and ethical character. On the other, he teaches of conjugal love through a deep analysis of the conjugal act. This two-sided approach to the issue helps us get a better insight into the reality of love itself, a reality that is confirmed and more fully reveals its essence in specific acts, in the entire human activity of the spouses, and, in a special way, in the conjugal act itself. This opens up a wide field for specialized studies.

Paul VI's teaching on conjugal love in the encyclical *Humanae Vitae* suggests that the whole problematic of Christian conjugal morality must be based more firmly on an ontology of marriage. The traditional schema, which sets forth the hierarchy of the ends of marriage mentioned at the beginning, is not called into question either in *Gaudium et Spes* or in *Humanae Vitae*. Rather, the message these documents have for theologians and pastoral ministers alike is that *the theology of marriage expressed in that schema needs to be grounded in a solid ontology*. A comprehensive ontology of marriage, an integral vision of the human being, a vision of man and woman as persons, is what best contributes to a true coordination of the ends of marriage. It also contributes to the presentation and justification of the norms that in marriage apply always to persons. In this respect, the encyclical *Humanae Vitae*, and particularly its teaching on love, is very significant. One could say that it points to the possibility, and even necessity, of in some way transforming the optics of the issue, while at the same time preserving—*and even for the sake preserving*—a more precise identity of doctrine.

In this way, too, the encyclical *Humanae Vitae* responds to the need raised by the Council for a deeper appreciation of conjugal love; it also makes the meaning of conjugal love more precise in the Church's moral teaching on marriage.

20

The Family as a Community of Persons

1. INTRODUCTION

This article is concerned with understanding the divine plan for the family in its *human interpretation* and also in its *human realization*. The family is a distinctly human reality. Human beings realize this reality by understanding its essence and meaning, but they also understand its essence and meaning by living it out and realizing it. The profoundly human meaning of marriage and the family also corresponds to the divine plan. This is brought to light by biblical and patristic studies; it is also the quintessence of the Church's contemporary teaching found in the Pastoral Constitution *Gaudium et Spes*. In the section of this document entitled "Fostering the Dignity of Marriage and the Family," the Second Vatican Council situates the whole heritage of the Church's doctrinal and pastoral tradition regarding marriage and the family in the context of our times. It states: "The power and strength of the institution of marriage and the family can also be seen in the fact that the profound changes in modern society, despite the difficulties that arise from them, time and again and in various ways reveal the true character of this institution" (*Gaudium et Spes* 47).

This statement suggests at least one optimistic conclusion: despite all the deviations, and even to some extent by virtue of them, the true meaning of the marriage covenant and of the family bonds that arise from it continues to be more fully revealed and confirmed. Errors in realization, distortions in practice, do not dim the divine light, but allow it in some sense to shine forth even more brightly in human minds and consciences.

Karol Wojtyla, "Rodzina jako 'communio personarum'" *Ateneum Kaplanskie* **66** (1974): 347–361. This is a companion article to the following essay, "Parenthood as a Community of Persons" 329–342.

The whole text of the Pastoral Constitution seems to point to a certain *organic development of the theology of the family*. This development consists in a deeper understanding of the interrelations and interdependencies that occur between the reality of human procreation, or the transmission of life, and the community of persons that ought to form around this reality, a reality that is in each instance extraordinary, and yet, in another sense, so very ordinary, running into millions of statistical facts.

This contrast between the ordinariness of all the facts of the birth of human beings in human families and the extraordinariness and unrepeatability of each of those facts leads us to another contrast, one that highlights the meaning of each concrete family as a community of persons. It is precisely for such a community that the fact of the birth of a human being is extraordinary and in each instance unique, as well as both personal and communal. Beyond this dimension, beyond the boundaries of the family, it loses this character and becomes a statistical fact, something to be subjected to various sorts of objectifications, up to the point of becoming merely a statistical entry. *The family is the place in which each human being appears in his or her own uniqueness and unrepeatability.* It is—and should be—the kind of special system of forces in which each person is important and needed because that person exists and because of who that person is. It is a profoundly *human* system, constructed upon the value of the person and concentrated entirely around this value.

2. THE HUMAN BEING AS PERSON AND GIFT

Vatican II's teaching on the human being is a synthesis of a long heritage of thought that seeks its light in revelation. The Council proclaims that "the human being, who is the only creature on earth that God willed for itself, cannot fully find himself or herself except through a disinterested gift of himself or herself" (*Gaudium et Spes* 24).

This teaching on the human being, this theological anthropology, captures as though the very essence of the human reality of the family. No matter how we view it, we must place the human being at the basis of this reality. *Every human being* takes his or her beginning from the family—and precisely as a "creature...*that God willed for itself.*" Everyone, too, in and through the family, seeks to realize that truth about himself or herself expressed in the words cited above. A married couple, a husband and wife, seek this somehow at their own stage of human development, as mature persons capable of transmitting life. But every child who receives life from them also seeks this, coming into its parents' lives—from the very moment of conception—as a human being, as a "creature...that God willed for itself." The whole decisiveness that Christian ethics ought to display in this area is an affirmation of such anthropology, in which this ethics also finds its roots.

Let us examine this passage from *Gaudium et Spes* 24 a little more closely. It contains a *theological truth about the human being*. This is shown by its proximate context, which refers to Christ's words from his archpriestly prayer at the last supper: "When the Lord Jesus prays to the Father 'that all may be one...as we are one' (John 17:21–22), opening inaccessible perspectives to human reason, he indicates that there is a certain likeness between the union of the divine persons and the union of the children of God joined in truth and love" (*Gaudium et Spes* 24). And, the text continues, it is "this likeness [that] reveals that the human being, who is the only creature on earth that God willed for itself, cannot fully find himself or herself except through a disinterested gift of himself or herself."

That is how the whole text sounds in context. The anthropology that should form the basis of the theology of the family is, of course, theological anthropology. The plane upon which the thought and investigations of such anthropology proceed is characterized by this fundamental truth about the human being, a truth we find in the very first pages of the Book of Genesis—*the truth concerning the human being's likeness to God*. This likeness is based not only on having a rational and free nature—as we are told by the whole tradition of Christian thought, together with various schools of non-Christian thought that also hold this view of human nature, of the human being—but also on being a person, a personal being. This is why the human being is the only creature on earth that God, in each and every instance, "wills for itself." This formulation expresses the fact of being a person, which, in turn, presupposes reason and freedom. Because of this, the human being is capable of self-determination and self-possession: the human being is a being capable of existing and acting "for itself," that is, capable of a certain *autoteleology*, which means capable not only of determining its own ends but also of becoming an end for itself. This distinguishes the human being as a person from the rest of the world. In a certain sense, every human being is a "world"—a microcosm—unto himself or herself, not only because the various ontic levels found in the beings that comprise the world are somehow concentrated in and built into the makeup of each human being, but also and especially because of the human being's own unique finality, or autoteleology, which characterizes the level and dynamism of a personal being.

Likeness to God, however, is reflected not just in the *rational and free nature*—the spiritual nature—of the human person. The passage from *Gaudium et Spes* 24 cited above, which, as I said, contains a rather concise synthesis of thought with regard to the human being in the light of revelation and the Gospel, also emphasizes that the human being's likeness to God occurs *by reason of a relation that unites persons.* The text speaks of a "certain likeness between the union of the divine persons and the union of the children of God joined in truth and love." It thus draws attention to the trinitarian dimension of the fundamental truth about human beings that we find at the very beginning of Sacred Scripture and that characterizes the theological plane of Christian anthropology. The conciliar text sharply emphasizes the remoteness of the analogy that occurs here, speaking of a "certain" likeness and noting at once that Christ's words "that all may be one...as we are one" open up "inaccessible perspectives to human reason." In other words, we are dealing here with a mystery in the strict sense of the term, for such is the unity of the three divine persons in one Godhead. In any case, this likeness of human beings to God in the trinitarian dimension was already suggested in the Gospel, and a whole theological tradition follows upon it. Human beings are like unto God not only by reason of their spiritual nature, which accounts for their existence as persons, but also by reason of their *capacity for community with other persons.*

If we were to say that the actualization of this capacity and the confirmation of this truth about human beings is social life, this would be true, but it still would not capture the full depth that is proper and specific to this truth. Likewise, it would also be true to say that the family is a society, the smallest social unit, but this still would not tell us much about the family and would fall short of the full ontological depth that we ought to discover and accentuate here.

Following the development of the passage from *Gaudium et Spes* 24, we should reflect next on the statement that "the human being, who is the only creature on earth that God willed for itself, cannot fully find himself or herself *except through a disinterested gift of himself or herself.*" At the basis of all human societies and social units, and at the basis of the family first and foremost, lies the human being, whose inner structure is that of a personal being. While it is true that this text seems to refer primarily to a certain order of activity (*operari*), which consists in the giving of oneself, this order of activity is itself rooted in the order of existence, in the personal being (*esse*) of the human being. In this sense, activity always follows being (*operari sequitur esse*). If the "gift of oneself" characterizes human activity, human conduct, it does so always because of this personal *esse*, which is capable of a disinterested gift of itself.

This gift rests entirely upon the dynamism of personal *esse*, upon the autoteleology proper to it, for we read that a human being "cannot fully find himself or herself except through a disinterested gift of himself or herself." Each of us is capable of such a gift because each of us is a person, and the structure proper to a person is the structure of self-possession and self-governance. Hence, we are capable of giving ourselves because we possess ourselves and also because we are our own masters in the dimension of ourselves as subjects. This in no way encroaches upon the Creator's *dominium altum* in relation to us, similar to other creatures, but, in fact, arises from this divine *dominium altum*. I have discussed these matters elsewhere in a more detailed and analytic way (see *The Acting Person*).

Taking all of this into consideration, it follows that the human being as a person is capable of community with others in the sense of *rational community* as *communio*. Such an ability is recognized by the tradition of Christian thought, which is based on revelation. This is, therefore, a theological tradition, and the teaching of Vatican II cited above is a convincing confirmation of this tradition.

This is not the place to undertake a detailed comparative analysis. I should note, however, that there is a certain difference between saying, on the one hand, that the human being, who is a person, also has a social nature and, on the other, that the human being as a person has the capacity for rational community as *communio*.

This does not mean that the two views are mutually opposed to one another. On the contrary, one could even say that they mutually contain and somehow imply one another. One of the things that makes human beings social beings is their capacity for rational community as *communio*. This capacity, however, is something deeper than merely the social property of human nature. *Communio* is far more indicative of the personal and interpersonal dimension of all social systems.

Clearly, then, a *theological analysis of the family* must proceed from the communal reality, *from the category of* communio, and not merely from the category of society, or "the smallest social unit," as the family is often called. This in no way implies a denial of that other category. Society, however, lies at the analysis' point of arrival rather than at its point of departure. At the point of departure, we must perceive *communio* as that reality that Vatican II expresses in the passage from the Pastoral Constitution, following the whole tradition of Christian thought concerning the human being, the tradition of theological anthropology.

3. COMMUNIO

I shall put off for the moment the question of the extent to which this theological anthropology is solely a fruit of revelation and faith and the extent to which it is also an object of natural knowledge based on human experience. I wish instead to turn now to an analysis of the reality of *communio*, proceeding from the insight contained in *Gaudium et Spes* 24. Perhaps it would also be helpful at this point to introduce a passage that occurs a little earlier in the Pastoral Constitution, one that pertains even more directly to the theology of the family: "But God did not create the human being as a solitaire, for from the beginning 'male and female God created them' (Gen. 1:27), and their union is the primary form of a community of persons. For by their innermost nature human beings are social beings, and unless they relate to others they can neither live nor develop their potential" (*Gaudium et Spes* 12).

When analyzing the concept of *communio*, we should always bear in mind that we are dealing with a personal and interpersonal reality, as well as with a human social structure (society), based on human beings as persons (see in this regard the last section of *The Acting Person*, entitled "Participation"). For Christians in general, the concept of *communio* itself has a primarily *religious and sacral meaning, one connected with the Eucharist*, which is a *sacramentum communionis* between Christ and his disciples—between God and human beings. By transposing this meaning to the human and interhuman plane, we do not venture to weaken or diminish it. In fact, such a transposition may indirectly even increase our appreciation for the profundity of the mystery of the Incarnation. The category of *communio* may be applied analogously to different kinds of interpersonal structures and relationships, both those between God and human beings and those between human beings themselves.

From the point of view of its Latin etymology, the term *communio* may refer to either 1) the confirmation and reinforcement that is a result of the unity and bond of a group of people when they exist and act together (to which the prefix *cum* points) or 2) the confirmation and reinforcement—the mutual affirmation—that is a property of the bond by which those people are united. The first meaning is closer to that of the adjective *communis*, which has to do more with the effects of a certain manner or mode of being and acting, whereas the second meaning defines that mode of being and acting itself. This mode of being and acting is an exclusive property of persons, for we do not apply the concept of *communio* to nonpersonal beings such as animals, for example. I should perhaps also add that this concept has no exact equivalent in the Polish language, and so for us it is in a sense untranslatable. The term *wspolnota*, which is used in the Polish edition of the conciliar documents to render the Latin *communio*, does not mean exactly the same thing. The term *wspolnota* lies on the same semantic plane as the adjective *communis*. The concept of *communio*, however, does not refer just to something common, to community as a certain effect or even expression of the being and acting of persons. It refers rather to the very mode of being and acting of those persons, which is *a mode of being and acting in mutual relation to one another* (not just "in common" with one another) *such that through this being and acting they mutually confirm and affirm one another as persons.*

As can be seen from this analysis, *communio* also refers to community as an effect, although this is not its primary meaning. *Communio* in the primary sense refers to community as a mode of being and acting (in common, of course) through which the persons involved mutually confirm and affirm one another, a mode of being and acting that promotes the personal fulfillment of each of them by virtue of their mutual relationship.

Such an understanding of the concept and term *communio* corresponds perfectly to the content of the conciliar statement concerning the human being, because it takes into account both that the human being is "the only creature on earth that God willed for itself" and that the human being "cannot fully find himself or herself except through a disinterested gift of himself or herself." These two parts of the Vatican II statement form a single, cohesive whole, in which the first part cannot be understood (because it also cannot be realized) without the second part, or the second without the first.

That is just the point I wanted to make in the above analysis of the concept of *communio*. Once we understand the *strict codependence* of these two parts of the Vatican II statement, we can also define precisely how one ought to conceive that *disinterested gift of self* without which the human person cannot achieve the fulfillment proper to a person, that is to say, cannot achieve the finality proper to the human being by virtue of being a person, or, as the conciliar text puts it, *"cannot fully find himself or herself."* I call the finality that is proper to the person *auto-teleology*: self-fulfillment, like self-possession and self-governance, is proper to the person.

In the communal relationship that occurs between persons, this self-fulfillment is realized through the mutual gift of self, a gift that has a disinterested character. As I mentioned earlier, the person is capable of such a gift because of the property of self-possession: only a being that possesses itself can give itself. At the same time, this gift has a disinterested character, which is why it fully deserves the name *gift*. If it were to serve some "interest" on one side or the other, it would no longer be a gift. It might perhaps be beneficial and even useful, but it would not be gratuitous. The whole tradition of Christian thought defends the *transutilitarian* dimension of human activity and existence. This is closely connected with the evangelical teaching on love and grace. Grace, in the final analysis (as well as in the primary and basic sense), is a disinterested gift of God to human beings, who both realize and manifest this transutilitarian dimension of the existence and activity proper to the world of persons. In interhuman relationships, therefore, the disinterested gift of self (of the person) stands at the basis of the whole order of love and the whole authenticity of love.

The human being as a person is capable of such a gift. Moreover, a personal gift of this nature does not impoverish but enriches the giver. Personal development takes place through the disinterested gift of self—and this development also involves the development of love in and between people. The disinterested gift of self initiates a relationship, in some way creates a relationship, by the mere fact of being directed toward another person or persons. Whether it is directed toward one or more persons ultimately depends upon the form the gift takes. In certain forms, this disinterested gift of self may only be directed toward one person and may only be legitimately received by one person; in other forms, the gift of the person may be directed toward many persons and may be received by many. In every case, however, if this disinterested gift of self is to be a gift and is to be realized as a gift in an interpersonal relationship or many such relationships, the nature of a community of persons demands that this gift be not only *given* but also *received in the whole of its truth and authenticity*. When a person gives himself or herself by making a gift of self or by doing something in which this gift is expressed, a condition of the functioning of the gift, a condition of its realization in an interpersonal relationship or relationships, is the genuine reception of the gift or of the act through which the gift of the person is expressed. One may not divorce the person from the gift he or she brings; one may not strip away from this giving of self who the person truly is and what the person truly intends to express by his or her activity.

These are the elementary conditions of the realization of communion between persons. Now that I have sketched out the general contours of the problem, I shall present it in a more particular way by analyzing the reality of the family. For if it is true that the concept of *communio* forms the elementary key to understanding this reality and interpreting it theologically, it is also true that an analysis of the interpersonal relationships proper to familial community will lead us to a clearer and deeper understanding of the concept of *communio* itself. Of all systems of relationships, the family is the one in which we can perhaps most easily and fully perceive not only the common but also the specifically communal character of human existence.

4. THE MARRIAGE COVENANT

The basis of the family is *marriage*. Marriage is not just a partnership, but it is—and ought to be—a real *communio personarum*, as we read in the Latin text of *Gaudium et Spes*. "Ought to be," because a *communio personarum* is always an ethical reality. Understood in the light of revelation, marriage presupposes the whole theological anthropology we find expressed in *Gaudium et Spes* 24. This is, as we have seen, an anthropology of person and gift: as "the only creature on earth that God willed for itself," the human being strives to find himself or herself in the full sense "through a disinterested gift of himself or herself." This gift of self lies at the basis of the marriage covenant, bringing to it the special dimension of love that we find in the concept of *married love*. The husband and wife are mutually each other's beloved when they enter into the marriage covenant, and this covenant—also as a legal act—testifies that they have both made a mutual gift of themselves. The Council speaks here explicitly of a covenant, whereas the *Code of Canon Law* defines marriage as a contract. The conciliar term is more profound, theological, and personalistic, although the legal aspect is not lost in it. "The deep community of married life and love has been established by the Creator and qualified by the Creator's laws. It is consolidated in the marriage covenant by irrevocable personal consent. In this way, by the personal act though which the spouses mutually give themselves to and accept each other, there arises by divine will, and in the eyes of society as well, a lasting institution" (*Gaudium et Spes* 48).

In marriage, therefore, there are in a sense *three dimensions*, which mutually imply one another: institution, covenant, and *communio*. I plan to conduct this whole analysis on the plane of *communio*, in keeping with what I said earlier, since this is the deepest plane; the other two are realized in it and, therefore, also emerge from it. According to Vatican II, then, *covenant* seems to signify both a *contract*, because it is entered into "by irrevocable personal consent," and at least the beginning of a community in the sense of a *communio personarum*, because by this personal act "the spouses mutually give themselves to and accept each other."

Let me say at once that to approach the problem of the family—and first of all marriage—on the plane of the reality of *communio* has a *twofold significance*: 1) it implies an acknowledgment of the whole personal and interpersonal depth of the relationship that Vatican II defined in the biblical spirit as a "covenant," but 2) it also implies a certain set of requirements, which apply first of all to marriage, and then to the family, precisely because it is a particular realization of a communion of persons. Even just based on the previous analysis of the concept of *communio*, it is easy to see that this concept not only has the character of an interpersonal relationship but also entails obligations: it sets particular requirements for this relationship. I shall, however, discuss the requirements, or *ethos*, of marriage and the family later. At the moment, I am trying to establish the content, or *logos*, of the *communio* that arises between persons by reason of the marriage covenant and that gives rise to the family.

The category of *gift* (the disinterested gift of self) takes on special meaning in the marriage covenant. The spouses "mutually give themselves to and accept each other" in a manner proper to the marriage covenant, a manner that presupposes their *difference in body and sex* and, at the same time, their *union* in and through this difference. This is a relationship that can be analyzed and interpreted in a variety of ways; the category of gift, however, has a key meaning here. Without it, there would be no way to properly understand and interpret either the marriage relationship as a whole or the acts of conjugal intercourse that are part of this relationship and have a strict causal connection to the emergence of the family. We all know that the family is based on procreation, that it is a community of persons connected in an active or passive way with the reality of human procreation as the elementary bond of this community. Procreation in the active sense occurs on the side of the parents, the spouses who transmit life to their children; procreation in the passive sense occurs on the side of the children, for they are born and thereby give *new meaning* to the marital bond itself: the *marital bond* then becomes a *parental bond*.

We cannot properly understand or explain the community of persons, the *communio personarum*, that arises and endures between a man and a woman as husband and wife without having before our eyes the full finality of the marital bond, which consists precisely in the achievement of marital parenthood. The fact that the marital bond becomes—and properly ought to become—a parental bond has fundamental significance for bringing to light the true dimensions of this community of persons, this *communio personarum*, which must first be a marriage so that it might later also be a family. Fifteen years ago, in my book *Love and Responsibility*, I presented a personalistic interpretation of marriage—an interpretation that, it would seem, has found its way into Vatican II's Pastoral Constitution *Gaudium et Spes*. That book lies in some way at the basis of the reflections on the theology of the family that I wish to present here. The *gift of self* is essential for the special *communio personarum* that takes the form of marital and familial community, and this gift would be difficult to comprehend without *first comprehending the very being and goodness of each person*. Without the mutual giving and receiving that Vatican II sees in the marriage covenant, one cannot help but arrive at a superficial understanding of marriage and divest it of the force of its ethical consequences. Here, however, I am concerned with illuminating the *logos* of marriage and the family in a way that will provide a firm foundation for their *ethos*. The categories of *communio*, person, and gift each have a certain greatness and specific import of their own, in the absence of which their functioning in the world of thought must necessarily be defective.

This applies first of all to conjugal intercourse. We grasp the objective reality and the objective criterion of this relationship when we perceive that it involves the realization of a true *communio personarum*, a union of persons and not just of bodies—not just sexual intercourse but a real union of persons, one in which the spouses mutually become a gift for each other, mutually give themselves to and accept one another.

This is not an idealistic picture, but a realistic one. The Gospel in a special way demands such realism of us in our appraisal of the marital bond. Man and woman were created as they were (according to the Book of Genesis), different in body and sex, so that through this difference they would be able *to make a gift to one another of the specific richness of their respective humanity*. We need only recall the primeval situation before original sin, as described in the Book of Genesis. The mutual bestowal of themselves, the category of *gift*, was inscribed in the human existence of man and woman from the very beginning. The body belongs to this system, and so it falls within the category of gift and within the relationship of mutual bestowal—the body as an expression of a distinctiveness that is not just sexual but wholistic, and therefore personal as well. Original sin did not fundamentally destroy this system, but merely disturbed it.

Moreover, man and woman after original sin find themselves not only in a fallen state (*in statu naturae lapsae*), but also in a redeemed state (*in statu naturae redemptae*). In this state, marriage became a sacrament. It was established as a sacrament by Jesus Christ in order to realize the redemption in those who enter into the community of married life. "Christians...having come to resemble the image of the Son, who is the firstborn among many brothers and sisters, receive 'the firstfruits of the Spirit' (Rom. 8:23) by which they become capable of discharging the new law of love. Through this Spirit, who is 'the pledge of our inheritance' (Eph. 1:14), the whole human being is inwardly renewed, even to the point of 'the redemption of the body' (Rom. 8:23)"—we read in the Pastoral Constitution (*Gaudium et Spes* 22). Although these words were said in the context of the law of death and the hope of resurrection, at which time, as Christ himself said, people will no longer get married (Matt. 22:30), *the "redemption of the body" is already an aspect of human life on earth*. This redemption is not just an eschatological reality but a historical one as well. It shapes the history of the salvation of concrete living people, and, in a special way, of those people who in the sacrament of matrimony are called as spouses and parents to become "one flesh" (Gen. 2:24), in keeping with the intent of the Creator announced to the first parents before their fall.

Thus the *status naturae creatae—lapsae* and *redemptae*—requires a special theological synthesis, a special theology of the body, so to speak, one that properly and adequately interprets this basic fact of marital community, this unique *communio personarum*, to which the sacrament of matrimony ultimately gives rise.

The theological dimension of the question foreshadows its ethical dimension. The fact that the spouses who "mutually give themselves to and accept each other" are persons endows their conjugal relations, their bodily and sexual intercourse, with the status of a genuine *communio personarum*; it also carries the "specific gravity" of a mutual gift of one person to another.

But this fact also makes obligatory—*must make obligatory*, and in a very strict way—*the kinds of principles that fundamentally protect* this status and specific gravity from anything that could destroy either the marital bond itself or the parenthood that has its origin in this bond. "Yet the dignity of this institution is not everywhere reflected with equal clarity," we read in this same Pastoral Constitution, "for polygamy, the plague of divorce, so-called free love, and other disfigurements obscure it. In addition, married love is often profaned by egoism, hedonism, and illicit means of preventing conception" (*Gaudium et Spes* 47).

In all of this, in different ways and in varying degrees, the interpersonal system that forms the essential content of the marriage covenant is violated and distorted. In all of this, too, it appears that we must in some sense and with some precision apply the category of *communio personarum* to the different areas of married life, including bodily and sexual intercourse, and judge their true value according to this category. A man and woman who are united by such a very intimate community of life and calling, one in which the mutual gift of themselves is expressed by a bodily union based on the difference of sex, *may not in any way violate* those profound laws that govern the union of persons and condition their true communion. These are objective laws, deeper than the whole somatic or emotional reality, laws that have their basis and justification in the very being and value of the person. If it is true that marriage may also be a *remedium concupiscentiae* (cf. St. Paul: "It is better to marry than to burn"— 1 Cor. 7:9), then this must be understood in the integral sense given it by the Christian Scriptures, which also teach of the "redemption of the body" (Rom. 8:23) and point to the sacrament of matrimony as a way of realizing this redemption.

Communio as a mutual, interpersonal relationship, together with the bond arising from this relationship, must in marriage promote the kind of confirmation of the person, the kind of mutual affirmation, that is demanded by the very nature of this bond. Consequently, anything that makes one person an object of use for the other is contrary to the nature of the marital bond as a *communio personarum* (this was the main subject of my analyses in *Love and Responsibility*).

We know, too, that the marital bond is brought to fruition by parenthood. In this way, a child, children, come into the two-person community of a man and a woman. In each act of procreation, a new human being, a *new person*, is introduced into the original *marital community of persons*. Marriage as a *communio personarum* is by nature open to these new persons, and through them it attains its proper fullness, not just in the biological or sociological sense, but precisely as a community with a truly communal character, a community that exists and acts on the basis of the bestowal of humanity and the mutual exchange of gifts.

21

Parenthood as a Community of Persons

1. MARRIAGE AND PARENTHOOD

The spouses' mutual bestowal of humanity, which determines the authentically personal character and plane of their marital community, leads, by means of the conjugal act of sexual intercourse, to parenthood. Parenthood is expressed in the conception of a child and in the subsequent birth of the child into the world. This external fruit and expression of parenthood, however, is intimately connected with an internal effect. *Parenthood* is an *internal fact* in the husband and wife as father and mother; by conceiving and giving birth to a child, they acquire a new property and a new state. This state also has a social meaning: they become parents in the eyes of society: in the eyes of the Church, nation, state, parish, and local community. Nevertheless, the social character of the parental state has its primary basis and meaning in the parents themselves.

Both spouses, each in his or her own way, the man as father and the woman as mother, are internally marked and defined by their parenthood, which also unites and fulfills them. Because this union and fulfillment through parenthood occurs in the man thanks to the woman and in the woman thanks to the man, the entire structure of their *communio personarum* takes on a whole new shape, a whole new dimension. It attains a new depth and a new level of affirmation, but it also imposes new demands to ensure that the mutual bestowal of humanity is not jeopardized.

Experience and practice are very eloquent teachers in this regard. This also brings us to the very heart of the problem of what is known as

Karol Wojtyla, "Rodzicielstwo jako 'communio personarum,'" *Ateneum Kaplanskie* 67 (1975): 17–31. This is a companion article to the preceding essay, "The Family as a Community of Persons" 315–327.

responsible parenthood. There can be no doubt that the *state of parenthood* in the man as father and in the woman as mother objectively produces *a new dimension, a new qualification, in their personal and social life*. This objective dimension, however, should be accompanied by subjective awareness and experience—in every single instance, in each conception and birth. Otherwise the *communio personarum* is disrupted, and this disruption must be directly proportional to the demands imposed by the very nature of the marital and parental system as a communal system in which a man and a woman "mutually give themselves to and accept each other" (*Gaudium et Spes* 48). The giving must find a response of acceptance— especially an acceptance of the motherhood of the woman by the man who is the father, regardless of how undesirable this motherhood may be, even to the woman herself. Of course, the same applies analogously to the fatherhood of the man.

The very essence of this social and communal system (this *communio personarum*) lies in the fact that the man's fatherhood always occurs through the woman's motherhood and, vice versa, the woman's motherhood through the man's fatherhood. This is an internally closed and objectively necessary system. It is important, however, for both spouses to enter into this system with full awareness and responsibility. Otherwise their *communio personarum* will be imperiled. If, for example, the man views the woman's motherhood as some sort of "fault" on her part—which, of course, will lead her to react by blaming the man (an understandable and somewhat legitimate reaction)—then the proper personal level of the mutual relationship of the spouses as "compulsory" parents is threatened in an especially sensitive area. *Parenthood* as a property and state, particularly that of the woman, *needs to be affirmed in a special way* on the basis of the *communio personarum*. This involves something more than just a joint sense of responsibility for the fact of conception, although such a sense of responsibility must also seek its basis and justification in the community of persons as a *communio personarum*.

This whole discussion, which finds empirical support in psychological and psychiatric studies, clearly suggests that the very manner in which marriage is conceived must be from the start, to the greatest extent possible, freed from purely impulse-oriented, naturalistic presuppositions and shaped personalistically. This follows from the theological essence of marriage, although it can also be justified using a purely rational method proper to the nontheological sciences. The principle *fides quaerens intellectum* finds broad application here. A genuine understanding of the reality of marriage and parenthood in the context of faith requires the inclusion of an anthropology of person and gift; it also requires the criterion of a community of persons (*communio personarum*) if it is to measure up to the demands of faith, which is organically connected with the principles of marital and parental morality. A purely naturalistic view of marriage, one that regards the sexual urge as the leading reality, can easily obscure these *principles of marital and familial morality* in which Christians must discern the *call of their faith*. This also applies to the essential theological meaning of the principles of marital morality.

In practice, this does not signify a tendency to minimize the function of the sexual urge, but simply to view it in the context of the integral reality of the human person and the communal property inscribed therein. This truth must somehow prevail in our view of the whole matter of marriage and parenthood; it must ultimately prevail. For this, a kind of spiritual purification is needed—purification in the realm of concepts, values, feelings, and actions. Christian morality in the area of matters of sex and the body is organically connected with the beatitude that speaks of "the pure of heart, for they shall see God" (Matt. 5:8). And this is the principle upon which Christian morality shapes all human judgment and action in the area of marriage and parenthood.

The demands that a *communio personarum* places upon a man and a women in connection with bringing their marriage to fruition by parenthood also seem to be *in basic agreement with the principle of the ethical regulation of birth by means of periodic abstinence*. This holds true, of course, only when such regulation and abstinence are understood and practiced in an entirely ethical way. It is possible, after all, to understand and practice the regulation of birth, which, when based on periodic abstinence, has an ethical qualification, in a purely "technical" way. I have already dealt with this problem in *Love and Responsibility*, and so there is no need to repeat that discussion here. I only want to point out that such a problem exists. And this is also why the method of the ethical regulation of birth may (and we know in fact does) give rise to reservations and even objections, which arise either from not understanding its basic principles or from not knowing how to put them into practice. A *communio personarum* always *requires the affirmation of parenthood* in conjugal intercourse—at least potential parenthood. The spouses in their sexual relations must bring to this act both an awareness and a readiness that expresses itself as "I could become a father," "I could become a mother." The rejection of such an awareness and readiness endangers their interpersonal relationship, their *communio personarum*, which—as I have been attempting to show from the start—forms the very essence of their mutual relationship, but also imposes serious demands to ensure that this inter-personal, communal relationship is realized in every aspect of their married life and sexual relations.

The set of demands that makes up the Catholic ethics of marriage and the family serves to ensure, in particular, that the parental aspect of the spouses, their fatherhood and motherhood, both within and between them, as well as in social life as a whole, is a transparent value and reflects the qualification that objectively belongs to it.

2. THE BESTOWAL OF HUMANITY

Having briefly considered the meaning of parenthood from the side of the spouses, we should now, at least in a cursory way, examine its meaning *from the side of the emerging family community*. This community, as I said earlier, arises when a new human being—in each instance, a new person—is brought into the original marital community of persons. "By their very nature, the institutions of matrimony and married love are disposed toward the birth and education of offspring, which are as though their crowning achievement. In this way, a man and a woman, who by the marriage covenant 'are no longer two, but one flesh' (Matt. 19:6), through the intimate union of their persons and actions render each other mutual help and service and experience the meaning of their oneness, which increases day by day. This deep bond arising from the mutual gift of self of two persons, as well as the good of the children, requires the total fidelity of the spouses and calls for the indissoluble oneness of their life together" (*Gaudium et Spes* 48).

This conciliar text makes it perfectly clear that parenthood constitutes the central meaning of marital community. In the birth and education of offspring, the spouses "experience the meaning of their oneness, which increases day by day." The meaning of the marital *communio personarum* and all it involves, particularly conjugal intercourse, is the child. In other words, the meaning of marriage is the family. One of the reasons children come into the marital community of husband and wife is to confirm, strengthen, and deepen this community. In this way, the spouses' own interpersonal life, their *communio personarum*, is enriched. It is enriched by a new person, who arises entirely from them both and thanks to them both. This statement is completely true from the biological point of view, but it should also be true from the personalistic point of view. The transmission of life as a biological process "happens" in the body, in the organism, and above all in the organism of the woman, the mother. The parents have a causal influence on the very beginning of this process. The proper form of this efficacy, however, must find expression in the whole consciousness and attitude of the father and mother, shaping them both before and after the birth of the child. Throughout this process, the new person who comes into their marital community is already operative and immediately *extends the circle of the community of persons* that has arisen around their marriage.

It is significant that the child—although deprived for a long time of the personal fullness of activity—nevertheless enters at once into the community as a person, as someone capable not only of receiving but also of giving. From the very beginning, the tiny new member of the family makes a gift of its humanity to its parents, and also, if it is not the first child, to its siblings as well. It extends the circle of giving that existed before its birth and brings to this circle a new and wholly unique content. The parents are perhaps even less aware that the child is their mutual gift to one another, whereas they tend to be more aware that the child is "theirs." It is difficult to say whether the latter awareness is connected mainly with a sense of ownership. This sense is always associated with an object or thing. In any event, the parents, who are deeply aware that the child *belongs to them*, also from the first moment *accept the child into their personal community as a new subject* of this relationship and this *communio* that allows people to mutually give themselves, give their humanity, to one another in a most intimate way. This giving does not attain its full truth and authenticity until the gift of the person is accepted by another person or persons with the complete affirmation it deserves.

If it is true that each child from the very beginning—not just from the moment of birth, but right from the moment of conception—presents itself as a person and a gift, then it is all the more true that this gift is fully given to the parents, and in another sense to the siblings as well, only when it is also given as a task. The real introduction to the family community, to the *communio personarum*, occurs when the parents fully *discover* in their child the *task* that together with the child presents itself to their love. In order for this task to be fully discovered and carried out, it must be discovered gradually and carried out gradually. "Gradually" here means proportionate to the development of the new member of the family community. This applies to the parents; it also applies in a different but no less real way to the siblings as well. The whole family community develops as a *communio personarum* as though in stages, and this development in each of its stages includes the development of each person who comes into the community. This development, in turn, is simply an increasingly more complete and mature actualization of the human being, who, as Vatican II tells us, in keeping with the whole Christian tradition, "is the only creature on earth that God willed for itself," and who "cannot fully find himself or herself except through a disinterested gift of himself or herself" (*Gaudium et Spes* 24).

This law of the development of the person applies in a special way to the spouses, who through parenthood can and should find themselves in the gift that children are for them. It would be difficult here, in a discussion having a general and basic character, to go into the various aspects of the process of education (this will be a separate topic). I should, however, point out what lies at the basis of this process and constitutes its essential meaning and significance. The whole task that the parents discover in their child from the very beginning and throughout the years of the child's development is reducible simply to the exigency of *making a gift of mature humanity to this little person, this gradually developing human being*. One could say that, from the perspective of the communal structure of the family, childhood signifies the passive need for such giving, and parenthood, the active potentiality—the readiness and capacity—for such giving. This applies first of all to the fact of birth itself, and then to the whole process of education, to the vast and varied set of facts and activities that go to make up this process. Perhaps, too, nowhere more than here is the ethical meaning of the metaphysical adage *operari sequitur esse* borne out. Education is not reducible merely to a set or system of activities, but through them it reaches to a more basic reality, to a whole "system of being." Education then takes place more through who and what one is than through the different educational endeavors themselves in separation from this basis.

This thesis is not meant to downplay the value and purpose of special or even quite specialized educational endeavors or to gloss over the entire educational aspect of activities (with which pedagogy deals), but simply attempts to show their indispensable basis. It also tends to verify the notion of the bestowal of humanity, which I mentioned earlier in discussing the structure of the familial *communio personarum*. The complete process of education obviously includes a whole series of endeavors and activities aimed at *creating the external conditions* for this process, activities such as, for example, all those undertaken to provide for the material welfare of the family, e.g., professional work. These activities are also indispensable from the point of view of education itself; they are at least indirectly educational if they express the parents' concern for the whole family community. But these activities, at least in terms of the way work is organized in today's society, take place outside the family and do not directly contribute to the development of family ties, as was (and partly still is) true of work that took place in a family environment, e.g., work on the farm or in the crafts. In the latter cases, activity undertaken to provide for the family's material welfare was able to be connected with education in a more direct way.

It seems, however, that, although there may be some orientational value in describing certain activities of the parents as *indirectly* or *directly* educational, such classifications do not strictly distinguish these activities in the "material" sense. After all, any activity of the parents, whether it is performed in the home or outside the home, whether it is done in relation to the children or without a direct (material) relation to them, may have an educational value or lack such a value. This once again confirms the thesis that the basis of the process of education should be sought more deeply than in certain types of activities and endeavors, that ultimately what is at issue here is the bestowal of mature humanity upon those to whom the parents have given human life—their own children. Anything opposed to this, even in areas seemingly removed from the direct educational process, must also have adverse educational effects. The family as a *communio personarum*, and parenthood as a particular element of it, requires the gift of the whole human being, a gift that is in some sense indivisible. This should be kept in mind especially in today's social conditions, which, for various reasons, tend to be less family-oriented than in the past.

3. THE ORGANIZATION AND FORMATION OF THE FAMILY

I have outlined above the interpersonal system that emerges with each fact of birth and the entry of new human beings into the marital community of a man and woman. For such a system to retain the character of an authentic *communio personarum* and fulfill its proper task, *a certain organization of the family*, along with *a certain inner formation* that fosters an appropriate attitude on the part of all members of the family community, is indispensable. These two parts of the question must be understood together, since the realization of family life is possible only when what I am defining here as the *organization* of the family is and continues to be genuinely coupled with a proper *attitude* on the part of all family members. Without this attitude and the formation that gives rise to it, the family has no real organization. The organization of the family cannot be prescribed or regulated by external laws; at most, such laws can indirectly assure that this organization takes shape in an appropriate way and does not become distorted. In itself, however, the internal structure of a family society is something natural; it arises and develops to some extent spontaneously. At the same time, this structure is very strictly dependent upon the proper acceptance and fulfillment of the particular functions that in this society fall to the father, the mother, and the children at different periods in their life. As the children mature, the task of *education* turns into *self-education*. The parents, in turn, who are their children's natural educators, also themselves continue to be educated by their children as they carry out their parental functions at the different stages of their children's development.

The issue of the organization of the family and its strict connection with the formation of all the family members is a theological topic first of all in the sense that it finds extensive *expression in divine revelation*, both in the Old and in the New Testament. The particular exegesis of this question belongs to scripture scholars. Thanks to such exegesis, we have come to recognize a certain historical evolution in the organization of the family society, an evolution that certainly also resulted from concrete social, economic, and political conditions. These conditions underwent change not just in the historical times of the Old and New Testament but thereafter as well. They also continue to change today, as is noted by the Pastoral Constitution, which presents a broad discussion of these matters in its introductory statement entitled "The Situation of the Human Being in the Modern World." Amid these changing external conditions, however, certain principles remain immutable, namely, those that define in a necessary way the essential conditions for the creation and formation of the family community as a unique kind of *communio personarum*.

Perusing Sacred Scripture, we find *a number of such principles* whose relevance for the proper formation of family life *never becomes obsolete* and remains constant despite otherwise changing conditions. Thus, for example, when we read in the classic text of the Letter to the Ephesians, "Husbands should love their wives as their own bodies. He who loves his wife loves himself" (Eph. 5:28), "Children, obey your parents in the Lord, for this is right" (Eph. 6:1), "And you, fathers, do not provoke your children to anger, but bring them up in the discipline and instruction of the Lord" (Eph. 6:4), we come in contact with those immutable laws without which it would be impossible in any age to form a familial community and society. In these passages, St. Paul is, of course, alluding to the Old Testament, to the Book of Genesis and the Ten Commandments, in order to emphasize the continuity and immutability of divine teaching on the organization of the family and the attitudes that in an indispensable way condition the realization of the familial *communio personarum*, regardless of changing circumstances. Among these immutable principles of the ethos of the family we should include, following St. Paul, the mutual love of the spouses, the mutual love of parents and children, and the obedience of children to their parents in keeping with the Fourth Commandment and also in the spirit of the parents' full sensitivity to the developing personalities of their children.

All of this, which we find in just this one text of the New Testament, gives us a sufficient indication of the whole "organizational" aspect of a family society in which *parents discharge their authority*, or "rule over" their children (*potestas domestica*, in contrast to *potestas civilis et iurisdictionis*). This authority, however, has an entirely distinctive character and scope. There is no way to understand it in legal categories alone, even though parenthood brings with it unquestionable rights and responsibilities on the part of the parents and children. The whole aspect of authority in the family, along with its correlative aspect of obedience, is entirely unique and much more profound than in any other human society. Such authority and obedience presuppose the closest ties, the most intimate interpersonal relationships, that can exist among human beings; both of them are based upon these relationships and also strive to respond to them and foster them. Consequently, we get a much better understanding of authority and obedience in the family when we think of it *in categories of the influence of parents and the compliance of children* than when we think of it in legal categories alone, which assume, on the one hand, an abstract power to give orders and, on the other, the responsibility to carry them out. In any case, it is clear that this obedience, which according to both divine revelation and human experience is an indispensable component of family morality, must be understood in an analogous way. The obedience of children to their parents prior to the time when children attain the use of reason is one thing, and that of older children in a family is another. The former is a more "blind," unconditional, and uncritical obedience, whereas the obedience of teenage or adult children depends in large part on what the parents have to say to them not only through their words but also through their lives. St. Paul seems to have had all of this in mind in the passages cited above from his Letter to the Ephesians.

The institutions of marriage and the family, as well as the organization of the family, must certainly be understood in legal categories (both civil and ecclesial) as well. "Let civil authority regard it as a sacred duty to acknowledge the authentic nature of these institutions and to protect and support them," we read in the Pastoral Constitution. "The right of parents to beget children and to educate them in the bosom of the family should be safeguarded" (*Gaudium et Spes* 52). None of these legal provisions, however, shape the *inner organization* of the family, although *they condition it externally*. Internally, on the other hand, the whole cohesiveness of the family community is conditioned and its proper organization assured by the attitudes and virtues that shape and develop the familial *communio personarum* into a fully authentic and harmonious community.

"The family is a school of more mature humanity. But in order for the family to attain the fullness of its life and mission, it needs the friendly communication and mutual sharing of thoughts between the spouses, as well as the solicitous cooperation of the parents in the education of their children" (*Gaudium et Spes* 52). These words can be taken as a modern expression of the same truth concerning the family that St. Paul expressed in his Letter to the Ephesians. Although this expression is adapted to the circumstances of modern life, it presents the same unchanging elements of the ethos of the family. "The active presence of the father," the document continues, "is very beneficial to their [i.e., the children's] formation; but the care of the mother at home, which is needed especially by the younger children, should be ensured. This ought not, however, impede the legitimate social advancement of women." There is certainly a new modern element here that does not appear in St. Paul's epistle, but this does not change the basic line of teaching on the morality of the family. Another truth that does not change is one we read a little further on in the conciliar text: "Thus *the family*, in which different generations come together and help one another to grow in practical wisdom and to harmonize the rights of individual persons with the requirements of social life, *is the foundation of society*" (*Gaudium et Spes* 52).

Returning to the point of departure, I wish to stress again that the organization of the family is ultimately reducible to the persons who comprise it and are capable of making a mutual gift of their humanity in keeping with the potentialities that reside in the vocation of father and mother, as well as in the vocation of children, who, with the help of their parents, mature toward fuller personal independence. These vocations also involve the ability to *identify fully with one's function and task in the family society*. Under these conditions, the family becomes "a school of more mature humanity" (*Gaudium et Spes* 52), and its organization ultimately fosters the development of fully authentic human beings. Thus the organization of the family is brought about by formation, by education broadly understood, through which basic human values are instilled in each new person who comes into the family.

4. THE FAMILY IS IRREPLACEABLE

And in this regard the family is irreplaceable. The significance of this statement manifests itself in different ways in different eras. It also has a special significance in our own era. We are currently witnessing an enormous growth in the human population, particularly in some parts of the world. The family, with its procreative function, obviously stands at the root of this process. There is a strict connection between the birth rate and demographics, and an indirect connection between it and the economy. In this regard, we must ask about the family—we must pose the question of the family just as it was posed in the encyclical *Humanae Vitae*—both in relation to those societies in which the family performs its procreative function to a seemingly excessive degree and in relation to those (and this currently includes our own Polish society) in which it performs this function to a deficient degree. This aspect, however, does not exhaust the contemporary problem of the family. Demographics and the economy are not the only key to opening the door to this problem, although they are certainly a vital key. The *procreative function of the family* was very strongly accentuated in the history of human salvation revealed in the pages of Sacred Scripture, beginning with the Creator's own words instructing the first human couple to "increase and multiply" (Gen. 1:28).

Accepting as a basic and self-evident truth that the family is irreplaceable from the point of view of its procreative function, we must, however, in a theological context, examine this truth more deeply and confront it with the whole experience of the modern age. The family is a community of persons united around the reality of birth, and so it is a strictly delimited society. We call this a natural society, bearing in mind that the term *nature* has many meanings. *Nature* here means that which "cannot be otherwise," but "must be as it is." Obviously birth, or the transmission of new life to others, cannot take place except through the conjugal union of a man and a woman. One could say that this is the *natural* foundation, as well as the ontological core, of the family. Upon this necessary element, however, there arises an interpersonal relationship and society that is, in each of its individual realizations, the result of a free decision and an expression of personal being. The adjective *natural*, when applied to the family as a society, does not refer to the kind of natural necessity that characterizes the operation of instinct (see, in this regard, my analyses in *Love and Responsibility* and *The Acting Person*). It signifies only that the institution of the family is not a result of the human will alone, and that the family is not an "artificial" or arbitrary society, left entirely up to the human will. The social bond that arises around the reality of birth, or the transmission of life to new human beings, is in each instance unquestionably generated by an act of free will, although it corresponds in the strictest way possible to the laws of being itself: the laws of being and becoming as they pertain to human beings. Human persons—men and women as spouses and parents—do not make these laws, but they participate in them by an act of will and accept them as an essential part of their earthly existence. Along with this, they choose a certain state of life in society and take upon themselves specific social functions.

Is the family indispensable as a means of social formation, as a basic form of "socialization," i.e., of uniting people for a common end? Is the family as indispensable from the social point of view as it is from the procreative point of view? This question is extremely timely in an age in which, as the Pastoral Constitution says, "people's ties with one another are constantly being multiplied, and, at the same time, *socialization brings new ties, which, however, are not always conducive to the proper maturation of the personality and to truly personal relationships* ('personalization')" (*Gaudium et Spes* 6).

This conciliar statement seems particularly relevant for the problem at hand. It observes that the multiplication of social ties, i.e., "socialization," is a fact. This fact is certainly also a consequence of demographic factors: social ties multiply as the number of people in the world increases. Along with this quantitative factor, however, the cultural factor is also decisive here. New social ties arise always around some center that generates them, e.g., a new industrial endeavor, a new cultural phenomenon, a joint economic or political interest, etc. I intend to discuss all of this at a later time in a separate work dealing specifically with the sociodemographic side of the question. Here, however, I wish to keep the focus on the theological problematic of community as presented in the sources of revelation and the documents of the magisterium, especially the statements of Vatican II. When the Council in the text just cited makes the important distinction between "socialization" and "personalization," it is being faithful to the whole traditional Christian teaching on the human person and community. "Christian revelation," we read in the Pastoral Constitution, "leads us to a deeper understanding of the laws of social life that the Creator has inscribed in the spiritual and moral nature of the human being" (*Gaudium et Spes* 23). One of the main principles that the Council formulates in this regard, in keeping with the whole tradition of Christian teaching, is captured in the following statement: "The social order and its development must always be directed toward the welfare of persons, because the order of things should be subordinated to the order of persons, and not the other way around" (*Gaudium et Spes* 26).

These words express and illuminate in a different and deeper way the opposition between socialization and personalization mentioned earlier. Socialization as such responds to a genuine human need. Vatican II, in keeping with the whole Christian tradition, emphasizes this as strongly as possible. At the same time, however, the Council calls attention to a certain danger that threatens to reverse the proper order in this regard, namely, the danger that the "order of things" will take precedence over the "order of persons," even though the latter is ontologically and axiologically prior and more basic. In such a system, socialization may be diverted from its basic orientation "toward the welfare of persons," which for it is normative and upon which the proper social order depends. In other words, Vatican II perceives in contemporary social processes—those connected with the enormous advance of technological, industrial, and material factors—the *danger of a fundamental alienation of human beings.* People can easily become tools in the process of the system of things, the material system created by their own intelligence, and they can also become objects of different kinds of social manipulation—all of which, as the Council says, is opposed to "personalization."

By *personalization* the Council understands "the proper maturation of the personality" and "truly personal relationships." This brings us back to the concepts of community and *communio* in the sense in which they were presented at the beginning of this essay: "The human being, who is the only creature on earth that God willed for itself, cannot fully find himself or herself except through a disinterested gift of himself or herself" (*Gaudium et Spes* 24).

In the light of all that was said above, it follows that *the family is irreplaceable* not just in its procreative function, but also, and even more deeply so, in its personalistic and communal function. None of the other existing or possible social bonds has such a basic and strong claim as the family in this regard. If other social structures, in many ways far more powerful than the family, must likewise guarantee the fulfillment of their personalistic function (which is, after all, their basic task, for it enters into the very definition of the social order), and if they are to safeguard the people existing socially within those structures from the danger of alienation, then they must be based on the family. In particular, they must ensure the fulfillment not only of the procreative function of the family, but also of the personalistic and communal function that only the family can perform and in which the family is irreplaceable.

If it is true that no other existing or possible social bond has such a basic and strong claim in this area as the family, it is also true that the family as a social group is the smallest and in some ways the weakest society. The *strength of the family bond* has a natural character, as I said before, and the communal system proper to it is unique in kind and has a purpose all its own, which precludes the possibility of its being replaced by any other system that would be its authentic equivalent. This whole inner strength of the institution of the family is capable of surviving a great deal and of overcoming a great deal, but this does not mean that it cannot be weakened or even at least partially destroyed as a result of external conditions. The procreative function is certainly susceptible to this, and the personalistic function of the family, connected with the communal character of this society, is perhaps even more susceptible.

Contemporary theology of the family allows us to view the family in the light of the epochal confrontation of the divine plan, made known in revelation, with past and present human experience. At the same time, this theology, together with the Second Vatican Council, sees a need "to promote the dignity of marriage and the family." Both of these concerns derive from the full truth about the human being and from the integral vocation of this being. Because of this truth and this vocation, the family continues to be, perhaps even increasingly so, though certainly also in new ways, a reality without which it would be impossible for human beings not only to come into the world but also to realize the full dimension of their humanity, the dimension of person and community. And it is precisely in this wholistic sense that the family, both as a factual reality and as a rich and varied ethical imperative, is indispensable and irreplaceable.

22

Pastoral Reflections on the Family

1. PASTORAL MINISTRY AND THE APOSTOLATE

It seems that pastoral theology can be understood and pursued in two ways, in a narrower and in a broader sense. In the narrower sense, it involves a theological investigation of the tasks and activities of ordained ministers, the bishops, priests, and deacons who belong to the hierarchical structure of the Church. Pastoral theology in the traditional sense of the term seems reducible primarily to this. Its full meaning, however, must reflect the integral vision of the Church that was restored to our consciousness by the Second Vatican Council. The Council did not create this image of the Church and pastoral ministry but merely restored it, for it is already wholly contained in revelation, in the sources of the Church's thought and life. Pastoral theology in the broader sense is not limited to a theological investigation of the tasks and activities of ordained ministers alone. Rather, it concentrates primarily on concern for salvation, on concern for the overall temporal and eternal welfare of the human person and community, a concern entrusted to the whole People of God and to its individual members according to their proper vocation and "according to the measure of Christ's gift" (Eph. 4:7).

In this view, pastoral ministry involves more than just the set of tasks and activities of those with the sacrament of orders. The concept of pastoral ministry includes all that the Council referred to by the name "apostolate," and in particular "the apostolate of the laity," which, as we know, has its basis directly in the sacraments of baptism and confirmation. In itself, the apostolate is something different from and no doubt broader

Karol Wojtyla, "Rozwazania pastoralne o rodzinie," *Roczniki Nauk Spolecznych* **3** (1975): 59–76.

than pastoral ministry. The apostolate of the laity also points to a different and likewise broader subject[1] in the Church as the society of the People of God. A very subtle but essential difference of meaning appears here, which should be established right from the start so that what follows in these reflections may be as clear and precise as possible. Since I intend to adopt the broader meaning of pastoral theology, a meaning that arises from the nature and mission of the whole Church as the People of God, I am also prepared to maintain that this meaning corresponds better to the pastoral view of the theology of the family. I might also add that the view of pastoral ministry as something more than just the set of hierarchical tasks and activities of ordained ministers allows us—and even requires us—to take a deeper and more comprehensive look at ordained ministry itself particularly in relation to the family, that is, at what we have already become accustomed to calling *family ministry*.

In a pastoral reflection on the family, it seems very important to begin with a proper coordination of pastoral ministry and the apostolate, especially the apostolate of the laity. In itself, the concept of apostolate is linked to a reality basic to revelation, faith, and the Church, namely, the reality of *mission*. In this regard, the Second Vatican Council presents us with certain basic concepts and classic teachings, which will have to be introduced in the course of these reflections. In the Decree on the Apostolate of the Laity we read: "The Church was founded so that, by spreading the Reign of Christ throughout the earth for the glory of the Father, it might bring all people to share in saving redemption, and so that through them the whole world might truly be directed to Christ. All activity of the Mystical Body that aims at this end is called the apostolate, which the Church carries out through all its members, though in different ways: for the Christian vocation is essentially also a vocation to the apostolate" (*Apostolicam Actuositatem* 2).

This tells us certain basic things about the apostolate. First of all, the subject of the apostolate is described universally: the Church carries out the apostolate "through all its members," and "the Christian vocation is essentially also a vocation to the apostolate." This universal scope of the apostolate corresponds to its objective basis and manifold form. To spread the Reign of Christ for the glory of the Father, to bring all people to share in saving redemption, to direct the whole world to Christ—these are generic descriptions that encompass many species of Christian life and activity, or, to put it another way, many vocations. The conciliar text adopts the Pauline analogy of the Mystical Body in order to express as convincingly as possible two main ideas. First of all, similar to a living organism, each of the members of the Mystical Body takes part in its activity, thanks to which "the whole Body, in keeping with the area of activity proper to each part, causes itself to grow" (Eph. 4:16). The second point is a consequence of the first, but goes even farther: "Members who do not make their proper contribution to the growth of the Body should be regarded as useless both to themselves and to the Church" (*Apostolicam Actuositatem* 2).

One could say that in this view the apostolate is situated within what we sometimes call the *self-realization of the Church*, based on the life-giving foundation of Christ. The apostolate may be defined as human activity—manifoldly diversified human activity—that in various ways contributes to the Church's self-realization. Ministry, on the other hand, seems to denote a particular sphere of the apostolate, or rather to highlight a certain aspect of it. It involves concern for the goods of salvation, as preordained by God and brought about by Christ, and intended above all for human souls. Ministry refers, then, to all activity through which people come to share truly in these goods. Does this activity belong only to members of the hierarchy? Is it connected with having the sacrament of orders? This sacrament certainly gives special access to the goods of salvation and makes those who receive it "stewards of the mysteries of God" (1 Cor. 4:1). But concern for the goods of salvation, along with concern for other goods as well, must in some way lie at the heart of every apostolate, including the apostolate of the laity. The family is here a special terrain. This is a truth we must keep constantly before our eyes in a pastoral reflection on the family.

"In the Church, there is a diversity of service but a unity of mission. To the apostles and their successors, Christ entrusted the office of teaching, sanctifying, and ruling in his name and power. But the laity, too, share in the priestly, prophetic, and royal office of Christ and have their own role to play in the mission of the whole People of God in the Church and in the world... Since the attribute proper to those in the lay state is to live in the midst of the world and temporal concerns, God calls upon them to be animated with a Christian spirit and, by becoming a kind of leaven, to carry out their apostolate in the world" (*Apostolicam Actuositatem* 2).

Vatican II teaches, then, that the whole Church as the People of God espouses the mission of Christ and participates in it. This mission has a threefold character: priestly, prophetic, and royal—first of all, as Christ's own ministry and, secondly, as shared in by the Church as the People of God. In the context of this participation, which is universal (all members of the People of God share in Christ's threefold mission), Christ established in the Church the office of teaching, sanctifying, and ruling "in his name and power" and entrusted this office to his apostles and their successors according to a hierarchical succession. The hierarchy thus became the subject responsible for performing pastoral service in the Church by virtue of office. But this service by virtue of office, pastoral service, remains strictly connected with the fact that the whole society of the People of God, all of its members, particularly all the laity, participate in Christ's mission basically in unison with the hierarchy, those in the Church who are ministers by virtue of office. Consequently, at the very basis of the pastoral order there is a deep organic community, which makes it imperative that hierarchical priestly service be understood and carried out in the context of a basic unity of mission. The laity bring their own special aspect to this basic unity, an aspect that includes married and family life.

All of these theological premises must be kept in mind. They are indispensable if we are to give the theology of the family its full pastoral dimension. It seems that we should begin here by examining the sacrament of matrimony, with a view to bringing to light its many pastoral implications. These implications were rather poorly perceived in the past and must now be more deeply explored, specifically in the context of the theology of the family.

2. THE PASTORAL MEANING OF THE SACRAMENT OF MATRIMONY

In the minds of both clergy and laity alike, the canonical, or legal, aspect of the sacrament of matrimony is strongly accentuated. This is understandable, proper, and necessary and is also genuinely pastoral in its effects. Marriage as the union of a man and a woman must be fully legitimized in the eyes of society, including the Church; it must be socially justified. But this is not its only or even its most essential aspect. The most fundamental aspect of marriage in the Church is its sacramentality. Sacramentality, in turn, signifies inclusion in Christ's own saving activity, carried out continually by the Church. The Church, which according to the words of Vatican II "is a kind of sacrament in Christ," is the diversified society of the People of God, a people whom Christ "made...a royal house and priests of his God and Father" (Rev. 1:6), as the Council also calls to mind. This society "is actualized through sacraments and through virtues" (*Lumen Gentium* 11).

Among the sacraments, matrimony has a special significance. The Dogmatic Constitution on the Church expresses this most succinctly in the context of its teaching on the People of God: "Christian spouses, by virtue of the sacrament of matrimony, through which they express and participate in the mystery of the unity and fruitful love that exists between Christ and the Church (cf. Eph. 5:32), mutually assist one another in their married life and also bear children and teach them the way to holiness. And so the spouses in their state and order of life have their own special gift among the People of God (cf. 1 Cor. 7:7)." I shall be returning to this "special gift" of the married state a number of times, since it is extremely rich in content. The text goes on to say: "For from Christian marriage there comes the family, and in it are born new citizens of human society, who by the grace of the Holy Spirit become children of God through baptism, so that the People of God may continue to exist down through the centuries. In this, so to speak, domestic Church, the parents should by their word and example be the first heralds of the faith to their children and nurture the vocation proper to each of them, with special solicitude in the case of a religious vocation" (*Lumen Gentium* 11).

This conciliar statement on the sacrament of matrimony, which may rightly be regarded as a pivotal statement, is noteworthy for the very distinct emphasis it places upon the pastoral meaning of this sacrament. It also contains in a nutshell the whole theology of the family in its pastoral profile. The rest of this essay will be concerned with properly developing that profile.

The sacrament of matrimony as the basic reality of the theology of the family, understood and practiced in a pastoral way, must be examined in its very essence, that is, from the point of view of its sacramentality. Sacramentality, as I already mentioned, signifies inclusion in Christ's own saving activity, carried out by the Church. And so the sacrament of matrimony should also be viewed as a special activity of Christ in and by the Church. In this visible, ecclesial order, the stewards of this sacrament (for each sacrament in the Church has its proper steward) are the nuptial couple themselves—the two persons, the man and woman, who enter into matrimony. At the same time, stewardship of the sacraments is something priestly; it is an active participation in Christ's own priesthood. The nuptial couple, as stewards of the sacrament through which they become husband and wife in the Church, express by this act (i.e., actualize in a special way) their participation in the priesthood of Christ, which they have and inherit already by virtue of the sacraments of baptism and confirmation.

Canon law deals here chiefly with the aspect of consent, focusing on the content and importance of the mutual agreement that forms the basis of the commitment. The theology of the family, on the other hand, bids us see in the sacrament of matrimony, which is equivalent to the beginning of a new family community, those particular theological aspects that are essentially pastoral in their ultimate meaning. Two people, a man and a woman, who approach the altar as authentic members of the People of God, bring with them, together with their lay character, the whole Christian endowment that they have received from Christ in the Church starting from the time of baptism. This endowment includes both grace and vocation. In the past, theology seems to have examined the sacrament of matrimony (as it did the other sacraments) more from the side of the gift of grace that the spouses receive and less from the side of vocation, which arises from participation in the mission of Christ as Priest, Prophet, and King. This other aspect of the sacrament of matrimony is so very new and still so foreign to us that a great deal of effort will be needed to bring to light and comprehend its full significance.

I do not mean to say that this aspect was completely unknown and, practically speaking, ignored in the pastoral approach to the sacrament of matrimony. The whole past practice in this regard indicates that in the minds of the spouses, especially newlyweds, the sacramentality of marriage was always connected not only with the grace that the sacrament brings, but also with the moral responsibility and commitment incumbent upon the spouses in the area of married life and also of family life, which they begin as well. This awareness in the minds of the spouses finds, as it were, its correlate and confirmation in the conciliar teaching on the spouses' vocation, which arises on the basis of participation in Christ's own mission: "The spouses in their state and order of life have their own special gift among the People of God," as the previously cited text from the Dogmatic Constitution on the Church proclaims. This "special gift" refers to both the grace of the sacrament of matrimony and its accompanying vocation in the full sense that derives from Christ as Priest, Prophet, and King in the community of the Church.

For this reason, too, the conciliar Pastoral Constitution emphasizes that this is the spouses' own special gift "among the People of God." It has always been strongly stressed (at least in catechetical instruction) that marriage is a social sacrament. The mission of Christ as Priest, Prophet, and King, a mission inherited and carried out by the whole People of God in the Church, stands at the basis of the social bond proper to this People; it designates the communal task and function that the individual members of the People of God are to carry out in accord with this description of their obligation and responsibility. All of this is included in the reality of vocation. Hence, we can safely say that participation in the mission of Christ gives an essentially Christian meaning to the vocation of the spouses in the family by virtue of the sacrament of matrimony. In other words, the sacrament of matrimony initiates their special apostolate (for the apostolate is nothing other than the mission of Christ himself and participation in that mission). This is also the sphere in which the pastoral basis of the theology of the family should be sought.

In theology and catechesis on the sacrament of matrimony, what was chiefly (and even almost exclusively) emphasized in the past was grace as a gift of God. This grace primarily confirms and deepens the spouses' supernatural adoption by God (sanctifying grace) and is also a token of divine assistance in the couple's new life and new responsibilities as spouses and parents. An increase in sanctifying grace and sacramental grace—these are the effects that the sacrament of matrimony occasions in the souls of the spouses, as long as they do not place any impediments in the way of its operation (*non ponentibus obicem*). The teaching of Vatican II bids us think of these effects also in categories of the special vocation of the laity, through which they carry out in marriage and the family the ongoing mission of the People of God received from Christ as Priest, Prophet, and King. The realization of this mission obviously begins with the spouses themselves, but it also gives the whole family its properly Christian profile, down to its innermost human depths. This profile may be briefly described as follows: the family as a community, as a special *communio personarum*, in which the parents transmit life to their children, to new persons, conditions by its very essence the fundamental and full realization of the humanity of each of its members by means of education. The spouses as parents should continually initiate this realization in the community. The sacrament of matrimony as their own sacrament is simultaneously the family's sacrament as well. This sacrament has a completely pastoral basis: the spouses as parents are themselves the ones who primarily perform the ministry of salvation with respect to themselves and their children.

Performing the ministry of salvation is in a certain respect identical with "offering a spiritual sacrifice," which the Second Vatican Council in a number of places refers to as the basic expression of universal participation in the priesthood of the mission of Christ. If we analyze the essence of the family as a community of persons (*communio personarum*), we can detect the basis of this community in the very nature of the human person, who, as Vatican II teaches, "cannot fully find himself or herself except through a disinterested gift of himself or herself" (*Gaudium et Spes* 24). There seems to be a kind of existential connection between this gift of self in the marital and familial community and the "offering of a spiritual sacrifice" that is essential for the Christian vocation as an expression of participation in the one priesthood of Christ. The completely devoted love of the spouses and parents, along with the maturing love of the children, as the readiness to make a disinterested gift of themselves, is a realization of the community of the family as a *communio personarum*. It is also a mark of the universal priesthood through which the family realizes its participation in the mission that Christ the Priest has entrusted to the whole People of God. The liturgical expression of this universal priesthood takes the form of participation in the Eucharistic sacrifice, but the place for offering a spiritual sacrifice is life itself—in this case, married and family life. A family that strives in its life to become an authentic community of persons through this diversified "disinterested gift of self" on the part of all its members, especially the parents, develops as that "royal priesthood" of which St. Peter, and following him the Second Vatican Council, taught.

In this light, the content of the ritual by which the sacrament of matrimony is imparted also reveals its full meaning. We know that an essential aspect of this ritual is the mutual pledge of marital love, fidelity, and honesty that the nuptial couple make to each other, calling upon the triune God and all the saints to witness their vows. This pledge precedes the declaration in which the bride and groom, each in turn, affirm that they consciously and freely wish to enter into an indissoluble marriage and start a family ("Will you accept children lovingly from God and bring them up according to the law of Christ and his Church?"). The whole liturgy of the sacrament of matrimony is worthy of serious reflection, since it so clearly accentuates the connection between making a gift of oneself and offering a spiritual sacrifice. The entire perspective of the life of the spouses in the family is thus solidly anchored in the reality of the universal priesthood of the faithful from the very beginning.

The realization of a community of persons (*communio personarum*) in the family, in the sense in which it was presented earlier in the theoretical part of this study, allows us and even requires us to connect the whole reality of married and family life firmly to the royal mission (*munus regale*) of Christ. The whole People of God and each of its members receive this mission from Christ that they might express it in their own lives. This royal mission is expressed in the spiritual attitude of self-governance, which enters so deeply into the ethos of the human person and community. For Christ "has communicated this power to his disciples that they might have a state of royal freedom and that by self-denial and a holy life they might conquer the reign of sin in themselves (cf. Rom. 6:12). Further, he has shared this power so that by serving Christ in their neighbors they might through humility and patience also lead their sisters and brothers to that King whom to serve is to reign" (*Lumen Gentium* 36). Such a spiritual reign, which is marked by "royal freedom" and the constant readiness to serve, is, so to speak, the very quintessence of all ethical demands, without which an authentic *communio personarum* can neither be conceived nor realized.

If the disinterested gift of self that shapes marriage and the family as an interpersonal communal system is not to remain a mere phrase or, at best, an unrealized "ideal," it must fulfill the whole content of Christian morality. In this way, the family expresses its participation in Christ's royal mission. The moral effort and energy that the couple as spouses and parents, along with all the other members of the family society, invest in bringing into reality a community worthy of persons is also the "offering of a spiritual sacrifice." The royal aspect of the People of God and each of its members is, of course, very intimately connected with their priestly aspect. In the words of St. Peter, reiterated by Vatican II, they are to become a "royal priesthood." Even without going into detail at the moment, we are well aware of the measure and form in which a couple as spouses and parents, and all the members of the family society within the orbit of their parental influence, really need this spiritual "priesthood" and ethical maturity. The pastoral aspect of the theology of the family refers precisely to this and also leads to it in practice.

Participation in the prophetic mission of Christ (*munus propheticum*) goes hand in hand with this. When Christ the Prophet "proclaimed the Reign of his Father by the testimony of his life and the power of his words," he made the laity "his witnesses and gave them a sense of faith and the grace of speech (cf. Acts 2:17–18; Rev. 19:10), so that the power of the Gospel might shine forth in their daily family and social life." The Second Vatican Council thus singles out family life as a proper place for realizing the prophetic mission: "The laity become powerful heralds of a faith in things to be hoped for (cf. Heb. 11:1), provided they steadfastly combine their profession of faith with a life of faith... In carrying out this task, the state of life that is sanctified by a special sacrament, namely, married and family life, has exceptional value. Where Christian piety permeates the whole content of life and transforms it day by day, there exists both the practice of the lay apostolate and an excellent school of it. There, too, the spouses find their vocation, which consists in being witnesses to one another and to their children of faith in Christ and love for him. The Christian family loudly proclaims both the present virtues of the Reign of God and the hope of a blessed life to come. In this way, by its example and witness, it brings the world to recognize the sin of the world and enlightens those who seek the truth" (*Lumen Gentium* 35).

The Second Vatican Council, as can be seen, places great importance on this mission of the family, which it also describes as a participation in Christ's own prophetic mission. This mission is realized within the family, in the mutual relationships of the spouses and of the parents and children. It is also realized in the Christian family's relation to the larger society. One could say that the Council sees the family as the primary and basic community of the People of God that heralds and bears witness to the Reign of God by the sheer fact of its Christian reality: by being an authentic communion of persons and by attempting to realize this communion in the mutual relationship, development, and education of all its members.

"Taking advantage of the present time and distinguishing eternal realities from those subject to change, Christians should diligently uphold the values of marriage and the family... Let the spouses themselves, created in the image of the living God and placed in the authentic personal order, be united in equal affection, like mind, and joint holiness, so that following Christ, the principle of life, they might by the joys and sacrifices of their vocation and through their faithful love become witnesses of the mystery of love that the Lord revealed to the world by his death and resurrection" (*Gaudium et Spes* 52).

The pastoral meaning of the sacrament of matrimony for the whole theology of the family consists above all in bringing into relief the Christian aspects—both the apostolic and the strictly ministerial ones—that this sacrament presupposes and reinforces in the spouses and parents, and through them in the whole family community. The sacrament of matrimony presupposes these elements, since they are found in every Christian man and woman who receives this sacrament in the Church. They are implanted in the souls of engaged and newlywed couples as a living deposit from the moment of baptism. Through the sacrament of confirmation, these elements are reaffirmed, strengthened, and oriented toward a Christian vocation in life, which usually takes the form of the vocation of married and family life. Thus the sacrament of matrimony finds these special elements of likeness to Christ, which are linked to his priestly, royal, and prophetic mission, already present in a young Christian woman and man when they enter into this sacramental union. These elements are, so to speak, inscribed in the bride and groom's spiritual profile, in their past formation and attitude. They are also part of the content of the love that leads the woman and man to the altar, to the sacrament, to the matrimonial vows. Every effort should be made to identify this fact and help the couple become aware of it. Naturally, these elements of the Christian vocation will not be present in the couple's awareness in the same state in which we find them defined by the magisterium of the Council. But we do find them there in a more or less clear and transparent state of existential equivalence. And this is what we should focus on most of all.

At the same time, we should note that the sacrament of matrimony reinforces all of these elements of the Christian vocation in the souls of the spouses and future parents and initiates them into a new way of life. This is a special kind of initiation, whose future development, confirmation, and fulfillment will become the lifelong task of marriage and the family. The spouses must rediscover their Christian vocation in the context of their new life—or, better yet, they must keep on discovering it. Both of them must in some way, together with their whole family, watch over and affirm this vocation, for they are charged with becoming "witnesses of the mystery of love that the Lord revealed to the world by his death and resurrection." The sacrament of matrimony provides a strong and sufficient foundation in this regard. The whole life of the family is capable of arising upon this foundation as an authentic testimony to the love that God has revealed to the world. This testimony is also an expression of the pastoral reality that establishes the family and that is also created by the family. We should never lose sight of this.

The family is here, first and foremost, the subject responsible for caring for the goods of salvation and the subject responsible for realizing these goods—not just the object of such care and realization. In this subjectivity, the parents play the primary role (they are, after all, the stewards of the sacrament of matrimony). From a further perspective, however, the children also have a role to play in this rich subjectivity—and not necessarily only once they have become mature and independent. They actually take part in it from the moment of birth, and especially from the moment of baptism. Experience is very telling in this regard. We can observe how much the Christian life of families—especially that of parents themselves—owes to children. We can see the extent to which children are stewards of these manifold goods of salvation, grace, and morality in family life. In going from their wedding toward their family's future,

Christian spouses should include in their vision of this future all that children bring to a couple's marital love, fidelity, and honesty, to carrying out their own vocation. Clearly, the pastoral system here has many dimensions; it corresponds to the deep structure of the *communio personarum* that the family is and that it should continually become.

This system is also primarily immanent. The pastoral reality of the family and all the potentialities for its development reside mainly within the family itself, within the individual persons and their mutual bond. This bond receives its basic form from the sacrament of matrimony, which infuses it with new elements of the economy of salvation. Those who have entered into this sacrament, as well as those who result from it, receive all the gifts needed to enable them in and through their community to realize the whole good of salvation to which they have been called and introduced by the sacrament of matrimony. All family ministry, as a special work of the Church, must know how to stand consistently on this ground. I shall later be making a number of other observations in this regard.

In the tradition of the Catholic Church, the sacrament of matrimony is a sacrament of the laity. To be a lay person means to go out into the world, to have a special relationship to the world. This world is "the theater of the history of the human species, marked by the monuments of human energies, tragedies, and triumphs, a world—as Christians believe—that, called into being and sustained by the Creator's love, fell indeed into the bondage of sin, but was liberated by Christ, who was crucified and rose again to break the power of Evil, so that the world might be transformed according to God's design and reach the Fullness of perfection" (*Gaudium et Spes* 2). The Christian vocation of the laity, and in particular the vocation of marriage and the family, is connected with the world understood in the integral sense given it by the Gospel and Christ. We know that the term "world" can also have other meanings, and that the meaning of human existence and the course of events in temporal life can be formulated in keeping with those other meanings. But the Christian vocation of the laity, whose very name speaks of a certain "going out into the world,"[2] takes its notion of the meaning of existence and the course of events in the world from the evangelical view of the world, from the meaning Christ gave it.

This applies in a special way to family life, which is why it was fitting to link the pastoral aspect of the family intimately to the mission of Christ. One could say that the familial and parental vocation is in a special sense "worldly," for the family shapes the world in a most basic way by continually bringing new people into the reality of the world. One could also say, in keeping with the view contained in revelation, that creation—the earth—is made into a "world" by human beings, by every single human being without exception. In their earthly life, people also share the fate of the world and, like the world, are subject to development and change. Within these limits—between birth and death—people should also shape the world. The family is both the place where this process begins and its basic environment. Family life is also the most frequent vocation of lay people, the first and fundamental terrain of their Christian mission. "They are called there by God so that by carrying out their proper task, guided by an evangelical spirit, they might promote the sanctification of the world like leaven from within, and in this way, by the example of lives radiant with faith, hope, and charity, reveal Christ to others. Their special task, therefore, is to illumine and direct all temporal affairs with which they are engaged in such a way that these affairs may always take place and develop according to the mind of Christ and serve the glory of the Creator and the Redeemer" (*Lumen Gentium* 31).

The idea of the consecration of the world (*consecratio mundi*) finds its primary and basic arena in family life, in those "ordinary circumstances of family life" from which the existence of so many lay Catholics is woven (*Lumen Gentium* 31). This idea, and especially its realization, also defines the pastoral character of the family, for the consecration of the world must begin with human beings, since it is to be brought about by them. The family, which gives the "world" its meaning in the most rudimentary sense—for it continually brings new people into the world—should also be the place where the consecration of the world begins.

3. THE POSSIBILITIES AND CONDITIONS OF FAMILY MINISTRY

Now that we have before us an outline of the pastoral implications of the sacrament of matrimony for the inner nature of the family, we are ready to consider—also in outline—the basic issues surrounding that activity of the Church known as *family ministry*. I do not intend here to go into a detailed discussion of this activity; I wish only to present some basic thoughts about it.

If the sacrament of matrimony indicates that the Church entrusts two people as husband and wife with concern for the goods of salvation in relation to their family life, then this sacrament also indicates that the

Church intends to share this concern with the spouses in a very real and effective way. Here, again, we should reflect upon the canonical aspect of the sacrament of matrimony, not only in its legal but also in its pastoral sense. We know that the marriage ceremony must take place before someone who serves as an official witness on behalf of the Church—an ordained minister authorized to perform this function—and in the presence of other witnesses as well. The latter attest to the fact that the marriage has been "legally entered into before God and approved by the Church." From the canonical point of view, all of this is necessary to establish the legal fact of a marriage in the Church. From the pastoral point of view, however, the participation of witnesses—both the official witness, who is the ordained minister, and the other witnesses present—indicates that the Church wishes to share with the spouses this concern for the goods of salvation in relation to their family life, a concern that at this important moment the Church entrusts primarily to them. This is also why marriage requires the blessing of the Church.

According to a teaching expressed first in Vatican II's Pastoral Constitution, and then later repeated in a more detailed way in the encyclical *Humanae Vitae*, the task of fostering this concern is everyone's responsibility. The welfare of each marriage and each family—by virtue of the fact of the sacrament—becomes to some extent the concern of the whole People of God in the broadest sense of the term: "Christians should diligently uphold the values of marriage and the family, both by the example of their own lives and by harmoniously cooperating with other people of good will... The Christian intuition of the faithful, the upright moral conscience of human beings, and the wisdom and experience of those versed in the sacred sciences will assist greatly in achieving this end" (*Gaudium et Spes* 52). The conciliar document has summed up—as though in a single breath—the constitutive elements of this great and important process in the life of the Church and society that forms the essence of family ministry. This is a process in which the deepest dimensions of Christian ministry—a "sense of faith" and an "upright conscience"—bear fruit, and thus a process that in a way develops of its own accord, but that is also mindful of and consciously guided by the "wisdom and experience of those versed in the sacred sciences." The conciliar text is speaking in a basic and general way. Those versed in the sacred sciences are theologians; but both "wisdom and experience" are needed in the process of family ministry, and the latter may be found in people with no theological training at all, and even in completely simple folk.

Nevertheless, "specialists, especially in the disciplines of biology, medicine, sociology, and psychology, can contribute to the welfare of marriage and the family and to peace of conscience if by pooling their research they ardently labor to explain the various conditions conducive to a proper regulation of human birth" (*Gaudium et Spes* 52). In the light of modern science and the experience of the Church, that which we call family ministry should be viewed as a process made up of many factors. The most important is, of course, the inner factor of a sense of faith and an upright conscience. But the Church is well aware of how great an influence various conditions of a social nature have upon this process. Sound public opinion has an enormous significance in this regard, and so a great responsibility lies with all who shape and create public opinion. Vatican II also fully appreciates the input of the sciences, especially when it comes to the issue of birth and the transmission of life, an issue central and essential to every family.

Against the background of this large and diversified process, priests as ordained ministers have a special role to play in family ministry. In carrying out their ministerial function, they must take into consideration that whole extensive social process; they must somehow find themselves in the middle of this process and render their own proper service to the family. And, as we know from experience, this service has many dimensions. "The task of priests...is to support the spouses in their married and family life by a variety of ministerial means, such as preaching the Word of God, liturgical worship, and other spiritual aids; and also to sustain them sympathetically and patiently in difficulties and strengthen them in love, so that truly resplendent families might be formed" (*Gaudium et Spes* 52).

The ministerial service of priests is a special kind of concern for the goods of salvation brought by Christ. A basic condition for effectively performing this service on behalf of the family is an awareness—a very deep awareness—of the fact that the Church through the sacrament of matrimony entrusts this concern primarily to the spouses as parents, and then gradually also to their children in the family community. The function of the ordained minister, therefore, must conform here to the principle of subsidiarity. This is implied by the sacramental order itself. The priest's task is to prepare each engaged couple for the sacrament of matrimony and to accompany each family in his parish community in such a way that concern for the goods of salvation rests primarily with them. The priest should kindle in them the awareness and energy of the royal priesthood, the responsibility connected with the prophetic mission of the People of God. Each family as an individual Christian community is an organic part of the great community of the Church, the People of God.

It, therefore, shares in the mission of Christ in its own proper way, in keeping with its own "special gift," as the constitution *Lumen Gentium*, recalling the words of St. Paul, teaches.

In this regard, we should bear in mind that the "special gift" connected with the sacrament of matrimony also involves "special graces," the charisms of which St. Paul taught in his day in his Letter to the Corinthians and of which Vatican II reminds us in our own day: "'Each receives the manifestations of the Spirit for the public benefit' (1 Cor. 12:7). And because these charisms, both the most outstanding ones and those that are more common and widely distributed, are exceedingly suitable and useful for the needs of the Church, they should be welcomed with thanksgiving and consolation." These are the special graces through which the Holy Spirit renders the faithful of every state "fit and ready to undertake the various works and functions needed for the renewal and continued beneficial growth of the Church" (*Lumen Gentium* 12).

The priest, guided by a living faith in the Holy Spirit's activity, which by virtue of the sacrament of matrimony pervades the whole sphere of family life, must somehow at the very point of departure of his work in family ministry presuppose not only sacramental grace but also even the possibility of the charisms of family life. These charisms may be the "more common and widely distributed" ones of which the constitution *Lumen Gentium* speaks, but they, too, are of the greatest importance for the "renewal and continued growth of the Church." In any event, there can be no doubt that family life serves as a special foundation for the growth of the whole community of the People of God and of secular society as well. Viewed in this light, it often happens that various seemingly ordinary expressions of family love—the devotion of parents to their children, the at times heroic sacrifice made for a suffering or incurably ill spouse, child, or parent, the often amazing pedagogical talent of otherwise simple and uneducated people—can be manifestations of these special graces or charisms.

The priest must have all of this before his eyes. The fact that he himself, in choosing the sacrament of orders, chooses to remain single, and therefore does not establish a family of his own, should make him even more sensitive to the true values of married and family life. After all, he usually in some way owes his priestly vocation to his own family and its Christian atmosphere. Now that he has decided not to establish a family, now that he has chosen celibacy as a special charism of God's Reign on earth and made it his lifelong duty, he should by virtue of this very charism bear witness in a still more disinterested way to the human and Christian values connected with the family. Scheler observed (and he was probably not the first to do so) that the person who is able to sense and understand these values best is the one who foregoes them for a higher cause. It seems, then, that this inner testimony of the priest, this expression of his belief and attitude, of his spiritual maturity, must lie at the basis of his whole ministry to married couples and families. People living in a family—spouses, parents, children—should easily be able to perceive in him a testimony to the value of their own vocation. The priest achieves this not so much through a human understanding of these values but more through a living faith in the Word of God, a faith that allows him to come in touch with the divine meaning of the values of married and family life and to express and communicate this meaning in the whole of his service.

Thus the issue of family ministry as a special function of ordained ministers reaches deep into priestly formation, into the realm of beliefs and attitudes stemming from faith and incorporated into the life of the priest. This is a difficult and delicate matter, touching upon a whole series of experiences—which are also very personal. It requires the priest constantly to overcome schematic thinking and to be both firm and understanding. In family ministry, the priest also bears witness to his apostolic concern for the whole human being, for all of the person's problems—in imitation of Christ. This pastoral ministry is a test of spiritual maturity and is its constant postulate. The following words of the Second Vatican Council, though said in a broader context, certainly apply here as well: "The laity...have the right to receive in abundance from their pastors the spiritual goods of the Church." Pastors, in turn, "aided by the experience of the laity, can more efficiently and appropriately arrive at decisions regarding both spiritual and temporal matters. In this way, the whole Church, strengthened by each of its members, will more effectively fulfill its mission for the life of the world" (*Lumen Gentium* 37).

The theology of the family must be pastoral throughout because revelation as the source of theology and of the magisterium of the Church, the official and authentic channel through which revelation is transmitted, is pastoral throughout. For this reason and in this sense all theology of the family must be pastoral—both the part having to do with the theological theory of the family and the practical part. Obviously, this is accomplished in different ways. The theological *theory* (vision) of the family is pastoral in one way, and the theological *practice* of it in another. There can be no doubt, however, that the latter has its grounds and roots in the former, just as the Pastoral Constitution on the Church in the Modern World has its grounds and roots in the Dogmatic Constitution on the Church.

The fact that *doctrine* is pastoral is characteristic, first of all, of revelation itself, which in its entirety and in each of its elements is not simply a pure theorem or a mere ideology. One could say that the whole of revelation as God's teaching and activity in relation to human beings is in its deepest essence a *pastoral* work and process—an expression of God's concern for the welfare and salvation of humanity. A predominant image in revelation is that of the Shepherd [Lat. *pastor*]—the Shepherd of Israel in the Old Testament and Christ the Good Shepherd in the Gospel. The family as a human reality, one that corresponds to the deepest nature of the human being, enters into the eternal plan of salvation that was fostered and gradually revealed by God. Thus the family was inscribed in the history of salvation from the very beginning—and forms the vital tissue of this history in each of its stages. Just as the family has its human history (each family individually and each in the historical current of great societies, nations, and peoples), revelation tells us that the family also has a place in the history of salvation. And this is also its place in the Church as well, for the history of salvation is the essential thread of the Church's historical being and unchanging mission.

To disclose the pastoral aspect of the theology of the family is simply to bring to light the family's unique role in the mission of the Church as the People of God, for through this role the family is connected with the history of salvation and constantly assumes its place anew in this history. "Anew," because the family is a reality that continually begins to exist anew; it arises anew when two people, a man and a women, decide to transmit life to a new human being, making this decision and carrying it out with full responsibility for the good of family life, that is, for the manifold system of values that belongs to the divine plan of salvation. At the point of departure of this decision, or, more precisely, at the point of departure of carrying out this decision, lies the sacrament of matrimony.

The family, then, is continually realized "anew," as a result of which each family forms an entirely new, concrete reality with its own unrepeatable history and its own "place" in the history of salvation. This fact, however, in no way prevents us from viewing the reality of the family in a general way or from conceiving the good, the system of values, that corresponds to it in the plan and history of salvation in a general way. That which is historical, far from obscuring that which is essential and basic, tends to disclose and accentuate it even more profoundly.

NOTES

1. The term "subject" here refers to those in whom the task resides to carry out the apostolate, in contrast to the "object" of the apostolate, those who are the intended beneficiaries of apostolic works. Wojtyla uses the term "subject" in this sense in other parts of the article as well. —Trans.

2. The Polish word for "laity," *swiecki,* is derived from the word *swiat,* meaning "world," and so the term "laity" in Polish literally means "those who are of the world." —Trans.

INDEX